Charles Alfred Maxwell

The Battle History of Scotland

Tales of Chivalry and Adventure

Charles Alfred Maxwell

The Battle History of Scotland
Tales of Chivalry and Adventure

ISBN/EAN: 9783337247348

Printed in Europe, USA, Canada, Australia, Japan

Cover: Foto ©ninafisch / pixelio.de

More available books at **www.hansebooks.com**

THE BATTLE HISTORY

OF SCOTLAND.

The Battle History of Scotland.—*Frontispiece.*

THE BATTLE HISTORY

OF

SCOTLAND.

TALES OF CHIVALRY AND ADVENTURE.

BY

CHARLES ALFRED MAXWELL,

AUTHOR OF "THE WARS OF ENGLAND AND SCOTLAND," "THE SEA KINGS OF ORKNEY," ETC.

EDINBURGH:
WILLIAM P. NIMMO,
MDCCCLXX.

THE following Historical Tales have been carefully selected and compiled from the most authentic Histories, Chronicles, Diaries, and Original Manuscripts preserved in the public Libraries of the Kingdom and in private Collections. They have been constructed with a view to combine variety with agreeable and interesting information, but due care has been taken to preserve the historical facts in all their integrity, as in most instances the authorities are laid before the reader in each Narrative.

CONTENTS.

	PAGE
The Feud of Frendraught,	1
The Scotish Troops in the service of Gustavus Adolphus,	12
The Macgregors,	43
The Strifes of Mortlach,	52
The Siege of Bergen-op-Zoom,	56
The Execution of Lady Jane Douglas,	60
The Frolics of James V.,	70
The Demolition of the Monasteries,	79
The Heart of Robert Bruce,	101
The Battle of Prestonpans,	106
The Barns of Ayr,	125
James the Sixth's severity against Pasquil writers,	130
The Battle of Inverury,	135
The Changes and Wars of Moray,	140
The Siege of St. Sebastian,	146
Somerled the Thane of Argyle,	155
The Wails of Yarrow,	160
The Macdougalls,	168
The Highland Regiments in Germany,	173
The Troubles of Carrick,	180
The Battle of Gamrie,	195
The Monks of Melrose,	198
The Scotish Invasion of England under Charles II., in 1651,	207
The Life and Character of James III.,	214
The Scotish Troops at Quatre-Bras and Waterloo,	223
Cardinal Beaton and his Victims,	231
The Murder of Rizzio,	256
The Lords of Galloway,	263

CONTENTS.

	PAGE
The Legend of Kilchurn Castle,	270
The Siege of Redhall and Skirmish of Gogar,	274
The Burning of Towie Castle,	277
The Battle of Sheriffmuir,	280
The Feud between Lords Airlie and Argyle,	294
The Scotish Troops under the King of Denmark,	299
Raising of Charles Edward's Standard,	315
The Battle of Tara,	328
The Conquest of Quebec,	334
The Life and Death of Sir William Wallace,	347
The Early Christians of Britain,	360
The Fights and Forays of Branxholm,	368
The Exploits of Colkitto,	379
The Turmoils of Merse and Teviotdale	390

THE BATTLE HISTORY OF SCOTLAND.

THE FEUD OF FRENDRAUGHT.

In the year 1630, Banffshire and other districts on the south side of the Moray Frith were convulsed by a dispute which occurred between James Crichton of Frendraught, Frendret, or Frennet, and William Gordon of Rothiemay, which ended in tragical consequences. These two gentlemen were near neighbours, and their lands lay adjacent to each other Part of Gordon's lands which marched with those of Crichton, were purchased by the latter; but a dispute having occurred about the right to the salmon fishings belonging to these lands, an irreconcilable difference arose between them, which no interference of friends could reconcile, although the matter in dispute was of little moment. The parties having had recourse to the law to settle their respective claims, Crichton prevailed, and succeeded in getting Gordon denounced rebel. He had previously treated Rothiemay very harshly, who, stung by the severity of his opponent, and by the victory he had obtained over him, would listen to no proposals of peace, nor follow the advice of his best friends. Determined to set the law at defiance, he collected a number of loose and disorderly characters, and annoyed Frendraught, who, in consequence, applied for, and obtained a commission from the privy council for apprehending Rothiemay and his associates. In the execution of this task, he was assisted by Sir George Ogilvy of Banff, George Gordon, brother-german of Sir James Gordon of Lesmoir, and the uncle of Frendraught, James Leslie, second son of Leslie of Pitcaple, John Meldrum of Reidhill, and others.

Accompanied by these gentlemen, Crichton left his house at Frendraught on the first day of January 1630, for the house of Rothiemay, with a resolution either to apprehend Gordon, his antagonist, or to set him at defiance by affronting him. He was incited the more to follow this course, as young Rothiemay, at the head of a party, had come a short time before to the very doors of Frendraught, and had braved him to his face. When Rothiemay heard of the advance of Frendraught, he left his house, accompanied by his eldest son, John Gordon, and about eight men on horseback armed with guns and lances, and a party of men on foot with muskets, and crossing the river Deveron, he went forward to meet Frendraught and his party. A sharp conflict immediately took place, in which Rothiemay's horse was killed under him, who being unprovided with another, fought manfully, for some time, on foot, until the whole of his party, with the exception of his son, were forced to retire. The son, notwithstanding, continued to support his father against fearful odds, but was, at last, obliged to save himself by flight, leaving his father lying on the field covered with wounds, and supposed to be dead. He, however, was found still alive after the conflict was over, and being carried home to his house died within three days thereafter. George Gordon, brother of Gordon of Lesmoir, received a shot in the thigh, and died in consequence, ten days after the skirmish. These were the only deaths which occurred, although several of the combatants, on both sides, were wounded. John Meldrum, who fought on Frendraught's side, was the only person severely wounded.

The Marquis of Huntly was highly displeased at Frendraught, for having, in such a trifling matter, proceeded to extremities against his kinsman, a chief baron of his surname, whose life had been thus sacrificed in a petty quarrel. The displeasure of the Marquis was still farther heightened, when he was informed that Frendraught had joined the Earl of Moray, and had craved his protection and assistance; but the Marquis was obliged to repress his indignation. John Gordon of Rothiemay, eldest son of the deceased laird, resolved to avenge the death of his father, and having collected a party of men, he associated himself with James Grant and other freebooters, for the purpose of laying waste Frendraught's lands, and oppressing him in every possible way. Frendraught who was in the south of Scotland when this combination against him was formed, no sooner heard of it than he posted to England; and, having laid a statement of the case before the king, his majesty remitted the matter to the privy council of Scotland, desiring them to use their best endeavours for settling the peace of the northern parts of the kingdom.

A commission was thereupon granted by the lords of the council to Frendraught and others, for the purpose of apprehending John Gordon and his associates; but, as the commissioners were not able to execute the task imposed upon them, the lords of the council sent Sir Robert Gordon, tutor of Sutherland, who had just returned from England, and Sir William Seaton of Killesmuir, to the north, with a new commission against the rebels; and, as it seemed to be entirely out of the power of the Earl of Moray to quell the disturbances in the north, they gave the two commissioners particular instructions to attempt, with the aid of the Marquis of Huntly, to get matters settled amicably, and the opposing parties reconciled. The lords of the council, at the same time, wrote a letter to the Marquis of Huntly to the same effect. Sir Robert Gordon and Sir William Seaton accord ingly left Edinburgh on their way north, in the beginning of May 1630. The latter stopt at Aberdeen for the purpose of consulting with some gentlemen of that shire, as to the best mode of proceeding against the rebels; and the former went to Strathbogie to advise with the Marquis of Huntly.

On Sir Robert's arrival at Strathbogie, he found that the Marquis had gone to Aberdeen to attend the funeral of the laird of Drum. By a singular coincidence, James Grant and Alexander Grant descended the very day of Sir Robert's arrival at Strathbogie from the mountains, at the head of a party of two hundred Highlanders well armed, with a resolution to burn and lay waste Frendraught's lands. As soon as Sir Robert became aware of this circumstance, he went in great haste to Rothiemay-house, where he found John Gordon and his associates in arms ready to set out to join the Grants. By persuasion and entreaties, Sir Robert, assisted by his nephew, the Earl of Sutherland, and his brother, Sir Alexander Gordon, who were then at Frendraught, on a visit to the lady of that place, who was a sister of the Earl, prevailed not only upon John Gordon and his friends to desist, but also upon James Grant and his companions-in-arms, to disperse.

On the return of the Marquis of Huntly to Strathbogie, Rothiemay and Frendraught were both induced to meet them in presence of the Marquis, Sir Robert Gordon, and Sir William Seaton, who, after much entreaty, prevailed upon them to reconcile their differences, and submit all matters in dispute to their arbitrament. A decree-arbitral was accordingly pronounced, by which the arbiters adjudged that the laird of Rothiemay, and the children of George Gordon, should mutually remit their father's slaughter; and, in satisfaction thereof, they decerned that the laird of Frendraught should pay a certain sum of money to the laird of Rothiemay, for relief of the debts which he had contracted during the disturbances between the two families, and that he should pay some money to the children of George Gordon. Frendraught fulfilled these engagements most willingly, and the parties shook hands together in the orchard of Strathbogie, in token of a hearty and sincere reconciliation.

The laird of Frendraught had scarcely reconciled himself with Rothiemay, when he got into another dispute with the laird of Pitcaple, the occasion of which was as follows :— John Meldrum of Reidhill had assisted Frendraught in his quarrel with old Rothiemay, and had received a wound in the skirmish, in which the latter lost his life, for which injury Frendraught had allowed him some compensation; but, conceiving that his services had not been fairly requited, he began to abuse Frendraught, and threatened to compel him to give him a greater recompense than he had yet received. As Frendraught refused to comply with his demands, Meldrum entered the park of Frendraught privately in the nighttime, and carried away two horses belonging to his pretended debtor. Frendraught, thereupon, prosecuted Meldrum for theft, but he declined to appear in court, and was consequently declared rebel. Frendraught then obtained a commission, from the lords of the privy council, to apprehend Meldrum, who took refuge with John Leslie of Pitcaple, whose sister he had married. Under the commission which he had procured, Frendraught went in quest of Meldrum, on the 27th of September 1630. He proceeded to Pitcaple's lands, on which he knew Meldrum then lived, where he met James Leslie, second son of the laird of Pitcaple, who had been with him at the skirmish of Rothiemay. Leslie then began to expostulate with him in behalf of Meldrum, his brother-in-law, who, on account of the aid he had given him in his dispute with Rothiemay, took Leslie's remonstrances in good part; but Robert Crichton of Couland, a kinsman of Frendraught, grew so warm at Leslie's freedom, that from high words they proceeded to blows. Couland then drawing a pistol from his belt, shot at and wounded Leslie in the arm, who was, thereupon, carried home apparently in a dying state.

This affair was the signal for a confederacy among the Leslies, the greater part of whom took up arms against Frendraught, who, a few days after the occurrence, viz. on the 5th of October, first went to the Marquis of Huntly, and afterwards to the Earl of Moray, to express the regret he felt at what had taken place, and to beg their kindly interference to bring matters to an amicable accommodation. The Earl of Moray, for some reason or other, declined to interfere; but the Marquis undertook to mediate between the parties. Accordingly, he sent for the laird of Pitcaple to come to the Bog of Gight to confer with him; but, before setting out, he mounted and equipped about thirty horsemen, in consequence of information he had received that Frendraught was at the Bog. At the meeting with the Marquis, Pitcaple complained heavily of the injury his son had sustained, and avowed, rather rashly, that he would revenge himself before he returned home, and that, at all events, he would listen to no proposals for a reconciliation till it should be ascertained whether his son would survive the wound he had received. The Marquis insisted that Frendraught had done him no wrong, and endeavoured to dissuade him from putting his threat into execution; but Pitcaple was so displeased at the Marquis for thus expressing himself, that he suddenly mounted his horse and set off, leaving Frendraught behind him. The Marquis, afraid of the consequences, detained Frendraught two days with him in the Bog of Gight, and, hearing that the Leslies had assembled, and lay in wait for Frendraught watching his return home, the Marquis sent his son John, Viscount of Aboyne, and the laird of Rothiemay along with him, to protect and defend him if necessary. They arrived at Frendraught without interruption; and being solicited to remain all night, they yielded, and, after partaking of a hearty supper, went to bed in the apartments provided fo.

them. A beautiful little poem, founded upon some old lyrics, and published among Finlay's Ballads, supposes the party to have in the course of the feud slain the laird of Frendraught, and represents them as wilily and treacherously enticed to Frendraught Castle by his lady with a view to revenge :—

"When Frennet Castle's ivied walls
　　Thro' yellow leaves were seen;
When birds forsook the sapless boughs,
　　And bees the faded green;

Then Lady Frennet, vengeful dame,
　　Did wander frae the ha',
To the wild forests dowie gloom
　　Among the leaves that fa'.

Her page, the swiftest of her train,
　　Had clumb a lofty tree,
Whose branches to the angry blast,
　　Were soughing mournfullie.

He turn'd his e'en towards the path,
　　That near the castle lay,
Where good Lord John, and Rothemay,
　　Were riding down the brae.

Swift darts the eagle from the sky,
　　When prey beneath is seen,
As quickly he forgot his hold,
　　And perch'd upon the green.

'O hie thee, hie thee, lady gay,
　　Frae this dark wood awa,
Some visitors, of gallant mien,
　　Are hasting to the ha','

Then round she row'd her silken plaid,
   Her feet she did na spare,
Until she left the forest skirts,
   A lang bow shot and mair.

'O where, O where, my good Lord John,
   O tell me where you ride;
Within my castle wall this night
   I hope you mean to bide.

Kind nobles, will ye but alight,
   In yonder bower to stay;
Saft ease shall teach you to forget
   The hardness of the way.'

'Forbear entreaty, gentle dame;
   How can we here remain?
Full well you ken your husband dear
   Was by our father slain.

The thoughts of which with fell revenge,
   Your angry bosom swell;
Enrag'd, you've sworn that blood for blood
   Shoul' this black passion quell.'

'O fear not, fear not, good Lord John,
   That I will you betray,
Or sue requital for a debt,
   Which nature cannot pay.

Bear witness, a' ye powers on high,
   Ye lights, that 'gin to shine,
This night shall prove the sacred cord,
   That knits your faith and mine.'

> The lady slee, with honeyed words,
>   Entic'd thir youths to stay;
> But morning sun ne'er shone upon
>   Lord John nor Rothemay."

The sleeping apartment of Lord John was in the tower of Frendraught, leading off from the hall. Immediately below this apartment was a vault, in the bottom of which was a round hole of considerable depth. Robert Gordon, a servant of the Viscount, and his page, English Will, as he was called, also slept in the same chamber. The laird of Rothiemay, with some servants, were put into an upper chamber immediately above that in which the Viscount slept; and in another apartment, directly over the latter, were laid George Chalmer of Noth, Captain Rollock, one of Frendraught's party, and George Gordon, another of the Viscount's servants. About midnight the whole of the tower almost instantaneously took fire; and so suddenly and furiously did the flames consume the edifice, that the Viscount, the laird of Rothiemay, English Will, Colonel Ivat, one of Aboyne's friends, and two other persons, perished in the flames. Robert Gordon, called Sutherland Gordon, from having been born in that country, who lay in the Viscount's chamber, escaped from the flames, as did George Chalmer and Captain Rollock, who were in the third floor; and it is said that Lord Aboyne might have saved himself also, had he not, instead of going out of doors, which he refused to do, ran suddenly up stairs to Rothiemay's chamber for the purpose of awakening him. While so engaged, the stair-case and ceiling of Rothiemay's apartment hastily took fire, and, being prevented from descending by the flames, which filled the stair-case, they ran from window to window of the apartment piteously and unavailingly exclaiming for help. The fragment of an old ballad on the subject says:—

"The reek it rose, and the flame it flew,
  An oh! the fire augmented high,
Until it came to Lord John's chamber window,
  And to the bed where Lord John lay.

' O help me, help me, Lady Frennet,
  I never ettled harm to thee;
And if my father slew thy lord,
  Forget the deed, and rescue me.'

He looked east, he looked west,
  To see if any help was nigh;
At length his little page he saw,
  Who to his lord alone did cry,

' Loup down, loup down, my master dear;
  What tho' the window's dreigh and hie,
I'll catch you in my arms twa,
  And never a foot from you I'll flee.'

' How can I loup, you little page?
  How can I leave this window hie?
Do you not see the blazing low,
  And my twa legs burnt to my knee?'"

The news of this calamitous event spread speedily throughout the kingdom, and the fate of the unfortunate sufferers was deeply deplored. Many conjectures were formed as to the cause of the conflagration. Some persons laid the blame on Frendraught; though he himself was a considerable loser, having lost not only a large quantity of silver plate and coin, but also the title deeds of his property and other necessary papers, which were all consumed. Others ascribed the fire to some accidental cause. But the greater number suspected the Leslies and their adherents, who were then so enraged at

THE FEUD OF FRENDRAUGHT. 11

Frendraught, that they threatened to burn the house of Frendraught, and had even entered into a negotiation to that effect with James Grant the rebel, who was Pitcaple's cousin-german, for his assistance, as was proved before the lords of the privy council against John Meldrum and Alexander Leslie, Pitcaple's brother, by two of James Grant's men, who were apprehended at Inverness and sent to the lords of the council, by Sir Robert Gordon, sheriff of Sutherland.

The Marquis of Huntly, who suspected Frendraught to be the author of the fire, afterwards went to Edinburgh and laid a statement of the case before the privy council, who, thereupon, issued a commission to the Bishops of Aberdeen and Moray, Lord Carnegie, and Crowner Bruce, to investigate the circumstances which led to the catastrophe. The commissioners accordingly went to Frendraught on the 13th of April 1631, where they were met by the Lords Gordon, Ogilvie, and Deskford, and several barons and gentlemen, along with whom they examined the burnt tower and vaults below, with the adjoining premises, to ascertain, if possible, how the fire had originated. After a minute inspection, they came to the deliberate opinion, which they communicated in writing to the council, that the fire could not have been accidental, and that it must either have been occasioned by some engine from without, which was highly improbable, or raised intentionally within the vaults or chambers of the tower. A tradition, embodied in an old but lost song, says that the laird and lady of Frendraught locked the door of the tower, and flung the keys into the draw-well; and this tradition is alleged by another and more modern one to have been corroborated, about two generations or so ago, by the finding of the keys at the clearing out of the well.

THE SCOTISH TROOPS IN THE SERVICE OF GUSTAVUS ADOLPHUS.

In the year 1626, a regiment was levied in the north of Scotland by Mackay, Lord Reay, for the service of the King of Denmark; and in 1629, at the conclusion of the war, after performing many acts and travelling about 900 Dutch miles, throughout two unsuccessful campaigns against the imperialists, it received an honourable discharge. It then enlisted under the banners of Gustavus Adolphus, the royal heir of Sweden; and was soon after incorporated with three other regiments into a national brigade. Great numbers of Scotish and English officers and mercenaries, both before and after this event, were attracted by Gustavus's bounty and fame; and they made a prominent figure in his wars, and contributed largely to many of his most brilliant successes. The brigade which comprised Mackay's regiment, amounted to upwards of 2,000 men; and other brigades of British soldiers of fortune were formed which raised the entire number of British troops under Gustavus to about 10,000. And if we may judge from the officers, the great majority of these were Scots; for while so many as thirty-five colonels and fifty lieutenant-colonels were Scots, only three colonels were English. All were incorporated with Gustavus's ordinary army; and acted as strictly under his own orders, or under those of his marshals, as if they had been Swedish subjects; and they displayed a fidelity, a constancy, and a heroism quite as distinguished as are usually found in armies of patriots fighting for the protection of their own hearths and the liberties of their native land. The original brigade, in particular, was generally one of the most zealous and efficient corps in all the army; it achieved wonders of both endurance and performance in some of the most notable crises of the campaigns; it was elastic under privations and mighty in assaults and stormings; and it bore a large and very efficient part in the great victory of Leipsic which opened to the conquering Swede the whole of Germany, from the Baltic to the Rhine, and from the mouth of the Oder to the sources of the Danube.

When Gustavus invaded Germany, another British force, paid with British money, and kept much more distinct than the other, crossed the German ocean from Britain to his aid. This consisted of 6,000 men; and was secretly furnished by Charles I. of Britain, with the view of procuring the restitution of the palatinate; but, in order that Charles might have the appearance of preserving a neutrality in the war, it was levied, maintained, and put into co-operation with the Swedish army in the name of the Marquis of Hamilton, as if he had been an independent prince. A charge was brought against the Marquis by Lord Ochiltree, his hereditary enemy, that a design was on foot, and had been communicated to Lord Reay on the Continent, to raise the Marquis to the throne of Britain when his army should return from Germany; and this occasioned a delay in the expedition, but ended in the complete exculpation of the Marquis, and in the punishment of Lord Ochiltree for leasing-making. The Marquis's force was disembarked on the banks of the Oder; and a report speedily spread through the neighbouring country that it amounted to 20,000; and this report occasioned the detaching of a powerful body from the imperial army to meet it, and, by the consequent weakening of Tilly's strength, contributed materially to Gustavus's splendid and momentous victory of Leipsic. The Marquis's force afterwards co-operated with the Swedes in the recovery of Magdeburgh, and in other important achievements; but it gradually became much reduced by pestilence and slaughter, and was eventually incorporated with Gustavus's army.

The Marquis of Hamilton now solicited from Gustavus the restoration of the palatinate; but could not obtain h' consent except on terms which would have made the palati nate an hereditary province of Sweden, and reduced the elector to the condition of a vassal. Gustavus seems not to have had a high opinion of the Marquis's importance, or of the value of his services, and paid little deference to his judgment, and thought him too young, too inexperienced, and too fiery to be able to make a good use of any supreme military command. The Marquis, on the other hand, cherished very lofty notions about himself, and was impatient of control, and could not endure the position of a subordinate; and he therefore gave up his connexion with Gustavus in disgust, and set out for Britain a few weeks before Gustavus's death at the great victory of Lutzen.

The Marquis's soldiers, however, continued to adhere to the Swedish standard; and both they and the other British brigades shared in the fortunes of the Swedish generals after Gustavus's death, and were occasionally recruited with fresh adventurers from their native land; and many of them eventually returned to Britain, highly experienced in the military art, warmly attached to the principles of religious liberty, hotly zealous against the political domination or encroachments of Roman Catholicity, and therefore every way qualified and ready to act a conspicuous part in the dissensions and civil wars of this country, from the time of Charles the First's rupture with the English parliament till the epoch of the Revolution; and not a few of their officers held high posts, and exerted powerful influence, in the armies of the Covenanters and the Cromwellians.

Robert Monro, who was at first a lieutenant in Mackay's regiment, and who afterwards rose to the rank of Colonel, published in 1637 a small folio volume of 354 pages, describing the career of that regiment in a long series of services, "first under the magnanimous King of Denmark during his wars against the emperor, afterwards under the invincible King of Sweden during his Majesty's life-time, and since under the Director-General the Rex-Chancellor Oxensterne and his generals." This work is graphic, perspicacious, and fine-spirited far beyond most military and historical works of the 17th century; and besides fully narrating the fortunes of the particular regiment to whom it was devoted, it affords instructive glances at all the British brigades under the Swedish flag, and charmingly illustrates the peculiar character of our countrymen in the capacity of mercenary soldiers, and largely, though incidentally and unwittingly, depicts the training through which many of them passed for afterwards performing high deeds as patriots at home. We once thought of presenting our readers with a digest of the volume,—but we suspect the spirit and manner of Monro will be felt almost as interesting as his matter; and we now prefer to make four extracts, which may be taken as a good specimen of the whole, and which fully describe four events,—the perilous landing of Monro's battalion at Dantzic on its way to join Gustavus's army, the taking of Frankfort-on-the-Oder, the battle of Leipsic, and the battle of Lutzen; and we shall not take much further liberty with them than to correct the punctuation and modernize the spelling.

The Adventures of a Scotish Battalion in Pomerania.

"The twelfth of August, 1630, having received his Excellency's orders the Rex-Chancellor, for to ship my soldiers at Pillau in Prussia, and from thence to transport them unto Dutchland, towards Wolgast in Pomerania, in obedience to the orders, having divided the companies at Pillau, my own company, Captain Hector Monro's, and Captain Bullion's company, were put, with myself, in a a ship of his Majesty's called the Lilly-Nichol; the other three companies, (viz.), Major Senott's, Captain John Monro's and Lermond's were put on another ship of his Majesty called the Hound, our horses and baggage being put on a small skoote or boat, the wind favouring us, we being victualled for a week, we make sail from Pillau towards Pomerania, having calm weather for two days. The third day with a strong wind, and a great tempest from the west, we were severed from the fleet, and our ship striking a leak, we were driven into Bornholm Road in Denmark, where the tempest being past, we go ashore to victual our ship anew. The wind favouring us, we weigh anchor again, and setting sail, we take our course towards Wolgast. Being near the coast, the wind contrary, we were not able to double our course, and our ship being leaky, we durst not adventure far from land; and putting forty-eight soldiers to pump continually by turns, they were not able to keep her dry, and being overcharged with much water, though there blew a great wind after us, we made but a slow course. Our resolution was, being turned back, and before the wind, to make for Dantzic, as our best refuge. But keeping so near the land, under night, we bayed within lands, the wind blowing hard, with a great tempest on the shore, being a shallow sandy coast, all sails being up, by eleven o'clock at night we struck on ground. Our ship, old and weak, breaks in the midst below, but kept fast above. Our soldiers coming all above hatches, they were pitifully drenched and wet with the waves, and being in danger of out-washing they tie themselves with ropes to the ship's sides. Yet two that took a pride in their swimming, (a Dane, and a Scot called Murdoch Piper), thinking by swimming to gain the shore, were both drowned; the mariners setting out one boat after another, were both broken, and they being feeble fellows they lost courage. Thus under the mercy of the raging seas and waves, going higher than the masts over the ship's sides, we patiently attended the Lord's mercy with prayers, till one of the clock the next day; during which time I forced the mariners and soldiers that could best work, having cut the masts and the ends of the cross yards, with deals and the decks of the ship to make a float. Being made, it was tied to the ship within with tows hanging at it which the waves could carry ashore. The float, thus ready, with strength of men was let down by the ship's side; whereon four of the most courageous soldiers did adventure to go. Some boors ashore having got hold of the tows that were bound to the float, with the help of the waves, draw the float ashore; and being drawn back to the ship, we did continue in this manner ferrying out our soldiers, till at last the most part were landed,—who being landed sought along the coast, and finding a boat, did bring it with horses on a waggon, whereof we made use in landing the rest of our soldiers,—whereof I remained the last, till I saw our armies landed. But our ammunition and baggage being lost, we were in a pitiful fear, being near unto our enemies, and above twenty Dutch miles from his Majesty's army. Being without fix arms, and lacking ammunition, we had nothing to defend us but swords and pikes, and some wet muskets.

" Our resolution behoved to be short, where having learned of the boors how near the enemy was unto us, I suffered none to go from us, lest we might be discovered to our enemies. After advisement I sent Captain Bullion with a guide to the Captain of the castle of Rougenvalde, belonging to the Duke of Pomerania, offering, if he would furnish us some fix muskets, with some dry ammunition and bullets, we would cut off the enemy that lay in the town, and defend town and castle from the enemy for his Majesty, till such time as his Majesty might relieve us. The proposition so pleased the Captain, that he gave way to my suit, and withal, he, for fear of such suspicion, goes unto the country, having sent a gentleman with ammunition to me, to convey me a secret way unto the castle, where I should receive fifty muskets, my Captain retiring to me, with the gentleman and ammunition. I marched till I came safe to the castle, and then from the castle falling on the town with commanded musketeers, under the command of Captain Bullion, I stayed myself with the reserve. My folks entering the town, the

B

enemy aloft drew to arms. Thus service began. My party being strongest, some of the enemy shot, the rest got quarters and mercy, our watch duly set, the keys of the town and castle being delivered unto me, my greatest care was then, how to put ourselves in safety against our enemies, being at Colberg within seven miles of us. I begun to learn from those on the castle what passes did lie betwixt us and Colberg. I was told of a little river did lie two miles from us, which was not passable but at one bridge; where I went to recognosce. And finding it was so, I caused them to break off the bridge; where I did appoint a company of boors with arms, and horses by them to watch the pass; and if in case the enemy should pursue them, they had orders from me to defend the pass so long as they could, commanding them also at the first sight of the enemy to advertise me, whereby they might be supplied, and I put on my guard.

"Being retired from the pass, immediately I did send a boor on horseback, in the night, to acquaint his Majesty of Sweden (the army then lying at Stetin, twenty Dutch miles from us) with the manner of our hard landing, and of our happy success after landing; as likewise desiring to know his Majesty's will, how I should behave myself in those quarters, the enemy being strong, and I very weak. His Majesty returned for resolution unto me, that I should do my best to fortify and beset the passes that were betwixt me and the enemy, and to keep good watch and good order over the soldiers, and not to suffer them to wrong the country people, whom I should press to keep for my friends. This order being come, I began with the country boors, first to fortify the passages without me, and next to make sconces and redoubts without the town, as also to repair the fortifications about the castle, and in cleansing of the moat, that it might be deeper of water. The other parts also without me, I brought under contribution to his Majesty, by sending parties of dragoniers athwart the country, in Hinder Pomerania, betwixt me and Dantzic, being twenty Dutch miles in length; which all in short time I did bring under contribution to his Majesty. As also the enemy having had a magazine of corn at Rougenvalde and Stolpe, by our landing here, was made good for his Majesty's use and his army.

"Being thus busied for a few days, another ship of the same fleet, being long beaten with the tempest at sea, at last was forced, for scarcity of victuals, to anchor on the same coast, being four hundred men, of Colonel Fretz Rosse's regiment of Dutch. His Lieutenant-Colonel, called Tisme Howsne, did come ashore, entreating me to supply him with victuals, which I did. In the meantime he asked my advice, if he might land his soldiers there. I told him I had no counsel to give him, seeing there was no necessity of his landing, and which was more, his orders were to land at another part, so that he had to advise whether he should follow his orders, or for second respects if he might neglect his orders; so that on all hazards he landed his people also, which were quartered with me in the town. Shortly after, he would contest with me for command, which bred a coldness betwixt us. Whereupon I again advertised his Majesty of our difference, desiring his Majesty might dispose of the command. His Majesty, offended with the other, did send an absolute warrant unto me to command him and the whole garrison at my pleasure, for the weal of his Majesty's service, during our being there, where we remained nine weeks, fighting and skirmishing with the enemy, till Sir John Hepburne with his regiment was sent by his Excellence the Rex-Chancellor from Prussia to relieve us."

The Taking of Frankfort-on-the-Oder.

"The twenty-fourth of March, 1631, his Majesty having disposed of his army, in putting them in good order of brigades, horse and foot, through the several occasions and accidents happening in war, his Majesty before his march, finding the enemy lay strong in the Silesian and at Lansberg, lest he might fall down unto Pomerania and Mark, to disturb the new forces that were expected to come from Prussia and from Scotland, his Majesty directed Field-marshal Horne, with a part of his horse that crossed the bridge at Swede unto Pomerania, and the Wart, to collect the forces there, to be embodied and led towards the Wart and Lansberg, to give the enemy somewhat to think on, while as his Majesty might march with the rest of the army (consisting then of ten thousand foot and horse) towards Frankfort, where, under the command of the Field-marshal Tuffenback and the Grave Fon-Schonberg Governor of Frankfort-on-the-Oder, there were drawn together of the Imperialists near nine thousand foot and horse. General Tilly, with his main army then lying at Rapin, after his return from Brandenburg with two and twenty thousand foot and horse; his Majesty then not being sure neither of his brother-in-law the Duke of Brandenburg, nor yet of the Duke of Saxony, though the league was ended with the King of France; his Majesty's affairs thus standing doubtful, we marched towards Frankfort, with a resolution to pry into the enemy's designs, more than any ways resolved for a beleaguring, having such strong enemies and armies about us, without assurance of our pretended friends and confederates.

"Yet having continued our march till within a mile of Frankfort, our enemies retiring out of all quarters were come into one body at Frankfort, who having joined, we did hear the enemy was almost as strong within as we were without, and he having of us the advantage of the town behind him for his retreat, we expected no other thing than that the enemy should come out and offer us battle. Wherefore his Majesty himself discharging the duty of a General Major (as became him well) having sought the aid and assistance of Sir John Hepburne, beginneth to put the army, horse, foot, and artillery, in order of battle. The commanded musketeers, as his forlorn hope, advanced before the army. Having placed platoons of them by fifties, to march with his squadrons of horse, all being in even front, the sign given for advancing, trumpets sounding, drums beating, colours displayed, advanced and flying, every commander directed and appointed on his command and station, the magnific and royal King leads on. This royal army marching in battle order for half-a-mile, as comely as one body could do, with one pace and one measure, advancing, stopping, moving, and standing alike, till at last coming near the town, and finding no hostile rencontre made by the enemy, we halt standing a while in the ranks, and then resolved, since the enemy durst not meet us in the fields, we would press on the sudden to be masters of Frankfort, or not at all, knowing of the nearness of our enemies, and of the great strength they had together. And seeing we were not sure of the Princes, we resolved the taking of time was the best for us; and incontinent, his Majesty commanded out the most part of his cavalry, to make a caracole behind us, betwixt us and Berlin, fearing General Tilly with his army might come behind us, while we were engaged with the town; keeping only of all the cavalry the Rhinegrave and his regiment, besides the infantry, in case of out-falling, to second us against the horsemen, that were within the town.

" The cavalry thus directed, his Majesty then perceiving the fear of his enemies, having voluntarily fired their fore-town (took their fear as a presage of his future victory) commanded a part of the commanded musketeers to go in, through the fore-town being on fire, and to lodge themselves, being advanced to the very port, till such time as his Majesty should dispose of the rest of the army, in directing every brigade apart to their several posts. The yellow and the blue brigade were directed to lodge in the vineyards on the side of the town next Castrene, being commanded to advance their guards before them, while as the rest of the brigade should lodge and lie in one body at their arms, to be still in readiness in case of an out-fall; the white brigade, called Damit's brigade, was appointed to lodge in the fore-town, to guard the commanded musketeers that lay betwixt them and the danger, at the port right under the walls. Hepburne's brigade was commanded to lie near unto the other port, and to advance their guards also; the rest of the commanded men to lie near unto the other port, and to advance their guards also. The rest of the commanded musketeers being commanded by Major John Sinclair, were commanded to lie on a height near a church-yard that was direct before the enemy's works, besides which, there was a battery made, and the artillery and ammunition of the army (as commonly was usual) was placed behind our brigade, and the Rhinegrave's horsemen behind us; all things thus ordered and placed, commanded folks out of all brigades were commanded out proportionally for making of cannon baskets, and for casting of trenches.

"Then, according to custom, his Majesty himself and Colonel Tyvell went to recognosce near the wall, where Colonel Tyvell was shot in the left arm, his Majesty then making openly great moan for him, alleging he had no help then but of Hepburne. In the same instant my lieutenant, David Monro, was shot in the leg with a musket bullet, and my Major, John Sinclair, commanding the commanded musketeers near to his Majesty, where the battery was making. The enemy hanging out a goose in derision, they presently fell out above two hundred of them upon our guard, who received them with volleys of musketry; and they being too strong for the guard, his Majesty commanded the Major to send an officer and fifty musketeers more to second the guard. Nevertheless, the enemy still pushing our guard backwards, making them give ground, incontinent his Majesty commanded the Major, with a hundred musketeers more, to fall on, and to resist the enemy in relieving the guard, which the Major suddenly obeyed, making the enemy retire with greater haste than he advanced, where their Lieutenant-Colonel and a Captain were taken prisoners. And after the Major taking in a church-yard, that lay right before the enemy's works, and keeping his guard there, he did keep the enemy under awe; so that we were no more troubled with their out-falling, though divers of our officers and soldiers were hurt by them from their works, the church-yard being no shelter for our guard, that lay just under their works.

"On Sunday, in the morning, being Palm-Sunday, his Majesty with his whole army in their best apparel, served God. His Majesty, after sermon, encouraging our soldiers, wished them to take their evil days they had then in patience, and that he hoped before long to give them better days, in making them drink wine instead of water they were then drinking; and immediately his Majesty gave orders unto General Bannier to command all the brigades to be in readiness with their arms against the next orders. This command given, some of the commanded men that were under Sinclair, suspecting a storm, provided themselves of some ladders. By five of the clock in the afternoon, his Majesty coming towards our brigade, called for a Dutch Captain under Hepburne's regiment, named Guntier, and desired him to put on a light corselet, with his sword drawn in his hand, and to take a sergeant and twelve other good fellows with him, and to wade through the grass, and then to ascend to the top of the wall, and to see if men could be commodiously lodged, betwixt the mud-wall of the town and the stone-wall, and then to retire so suddenly as they might. Which being done, his Majesty getting resolution that there was room betwixt the two walls to lodge men, the brigades being already in array, they fall on at a call, the Captain being retired without hurt. Whereupon his Majesty directed Bannier and Hepburne with our brigade, to pass the grass and to storm, and if they repulsed the enemy from the outward wall, to lodge under the stone wall, betwixt both the walls, and if the enemy fortuned to retire to press in with him. The like orders given to the rest of the brigades, all being in readiness, his Majesty having a number of cannon great and small charged on the batteries, caused to give notice at all posts, that when the cannon had discharged, the first salvo in the midst of the smoke, they should advance to the storm, as they did. Where in passing the grass, we were over the middle in water and mud, and ascending to storm the walls, there were strong palisades, so well fastened and fixed in the wall, that if the enemy had not retired from the walls in great fear, we could not without great hazard have entered.

"The enemy feebly retiring, our commanders and leaders following their orders received from his Majesty, we press to follow in after the enemy, at a great sallying port, that was betwixt both the walls, that opened with two great leaves, where they entered. After their retreat, they planted a flake of small shot, that shot a dozen of shot at once; besides which there were set two pieces of small ordnance, that guarded also the entry, and musketeers besides, which made cruel and pitiful execution on our musketeers and pikemen. The valorous Hepburne leading on the battle of pikes of his own brigade, being advanced within half a pike's length to the door; at the entry he was shot above the knee, that he was lame of before, which dazzling his senses with great pain, forced him to retire, who said to me, ' Bully Monro, I am shot,' whereat I was wondrous sorry. His major, then, a resolute cavalier, advancing to enter, was shot dead before the door, whereupon the pikes falling back and standing still, General Baunier being by, and exhorting all cavaliers to enter, Colonel Lumsdale and I, being both alike on the head of our own colours, he having a partisan in his hand, and I a half pike, with a head-piece, that covered my head, commanding our pikes to advance, we led on shoulder to shoulder, Colonel Lumsdell and I fortunately without hurt, entered the port, where at our entry some I know received their rest; and the enemy forced to retire in confusion, being astonished at our entry, they had neither wit nor courage as to let down the portcullis of the great port behind them, so that we entering the streets at their heels, we made a stand till the body of our pikes were drawn up orderly, and flanked with musketeers, and then we advanced, our pikes charged, and our musketeers giving fire on the flanks, till the enemy was put in disorder. After us entered General Bannier with a fresh body of musketeers, he following the enemy in one street, and Lumsdell and I in another, having rencountered the enemy again, they being well beaten, our officers took nine colours of theirs, which were to be presented to his Majesty. And the most part of the soldiers were cut off, in revenge of their cruelty used at New Brandenburg; but some of their officers got quarters, such as they had given to ours. This regiment defeated, we directed an officer with a strong party to possess the bridge, and that to hinder their escape. Their passage being cut off, they were also cut down themselves, till the streets were full of dead bodies, and that the most part of our soldiers and officers disbanded to make booty, leaving me and a few number of honest soldiers to guard my colours; which disorder, I confess, stood not in my power to remedy. Thus far for Lumsdell's part and mine, which I dare maintain to be truth.

"And as I have spoken truth of our own actions, without ostentation, which no man can control that is a friend to virtue, I will now relate other men's actions, so far as I know to be truth by relation of my honest comrades. Lieutenant-Colonel Musten being appointed to command the musketeers of Lumsdell's regiment and of my Colonel's, then under my command, he seeing us entered did follow after us, and commanded those he led on execution apart, giving no better quarters than we did. The Dutch also, remembering the enemy's cruelty used at Brandenburg, they gave but slight quarters

Major John Sinclair, as I was credibly informed, being accompanied with Lieutenant George Heatly, being both resolute and stout, were the first that came over the walls with ladders, who at their first entry having but a few musketeers with them, they were charged on the streets by the enemy's cuirassiers, or best horsemen, where they were forced to stand close, their backs to the wall where they entered, and to give several salvos of musketry upon the enemy, till they were made to retire. Likewise after we were entered, the yellow and the blue brigades, being esteemed of all the army both resolute and courageous in all their exploits, they were to enter on the Irish quarter, where they were twice with great loss furiously beaten off, and were cruelly spoiled with fire-works thrown by the Irish amongst them. But at last they having entered, notwithstanding the inequality of their strength, the Irish though weak stood to it, and fought with sword and pikes within works a long time, till the most part of the soldiers fell to ground where they stood fighting, so that in the end, Lieutenant-Colonel Walter Butler, who commanded the Irish, being shot in the arm, and pierced with a pike through the thigh, was taken prisoner, so that the next day it was to be seen on the post where the best service was done and truly had all the rest stood so well to it as the Irish did, we had returned with great loss, and without victory.

"The fury past, the whole street being full of coaches and rusty waggons richly furnished with all sorts of riches, as plate, jewels, gold, money, clothes, mules and horses for saddle, coach and waggons, whereof all men that were careless of their duties were too careful in making of booty, that I did never see officers less obeyed and respected than here for a time, till the height of the market was past. And well I know, some regiments had not one man with their colours, till the fury was past, and some colours were lost the whole night, till they were restored the next day, such disorder was amongst us, all occasioned through covetousness, the root of all evil and dishonesty. At last the execution past, his Majesty entered himself, being guarded with the Rhinegrave and his horsemen, who immediately were commanded to cross the bridge, and to follow the enemy at their heels, being on flight towards Glogoe, where the Field-marshal Tuffenback, the Count Schonberg, and Mounte De Cucule had retired with such as escaped. His Majesty having but scarce quartered in the town, the fire beginning to burn the city accidentally, orders were given with stroke of drum with a bank beaten in all streets, that all officers and soldiers, under pain of death, should repair presently to their colours, on the other side of the Oder, in the outer works, where Sir John Hepburne was ordained to command within the works, except such as were appointed to guard the posts of the town, his Majesty's quarter, and the general's lodging on the market-place, where a strong guard was kept to suppress plundering and the insolency of soldiers. Nevertheless these orders proclaimed and published, many disobeyed, remaining in the town for plundering.

"In this conflict, the enemy lost near three thousand men, besides the officers that were killed, viz. four colonels, and above thirty-six other officers. Likewise there were taken prisoners, one colonel and five lieutenant-colonels of Dutch and one Irish cavalier,—that behaved himself both honourably and well; colours also they did lose, as I did see the next day made count of before General Bannier, forty-one, and cornets of horse nine. On our side were lost also at least eight hundred men, whereof the blue and yellow, for their parts, lost five hundred. His Majesty also did get here a great deal of provision for the army, as corn, ammunition, and eighteen pieces of ordnance. The next day his Majesty appointed General Major Leslie as governor over the town, giving him orders to repair the ruinous works and walls, as also orders were given for burying of the dead, which were not buried fully in six days; in the end they were cast by heaps in great ditches, above a hundred in every grave. The next day we were ordained to assemble our regiments, and to bring them together in arms, that they might be provided of what they wanted of arms, having lost many in their disorder."

The Battle of Leipsic.

"The conjunction agreed upon betwixt his Majesty and the Duke of Saxony, all things sealed and subscribed, his Majesty gave orders to break up with the army, and to cross the Elbe, over the bridge at Wittenberg, for to join with the Duke's army. The orders were obeyed with great contentment; and entering into Saxony, we quartered the first night not far from Diben, the place appointed for our rendezvous. The next morning we marched thither, and were drawn up in order on the fields, where in the afternoon the Duke's army arrived, being drawn up in order within cannon shot of us. The whole officers of our army were commanded to be in readiness on horseback, to convey his Majesty for to welcome the Duke and his army, which for pleasing the eye, was the most complete little army, for personages of men, comely statures, well armed, and well arrayed, that ever mine eyes did look on, whose officers did all look as if they were going in their best apparel and arms to be painted, where nothing was defective the eye could behold. This show seen by his Majesty and his officers, his Majesty returning, the Duke with his followers did convey his Majesty to the sight of our army, which being called to their arms, having lain overnight on a parcel of ploughed ground, they were so dusty, they looked out like kitchen-servants with their uncleanly rags, within which were hidden courageous hearts, being old experimented blades, which, for the most part, had overcome by custom the toil of wars. Yet these Saxon gentry, in their bravery, did **judge of us and ours** according to our outsides, thinking but little of us; nevertheless, we thought not the worse of ourselves. The ceremony past, we were all remitted to take rest for that night in our former quarters.

"The next morning, by break of day, we were called up to march, where both our armies were ordained to march on several streets; one rendezvous being appointed for us at night, within a mile and a half of the enemy's army; where being come to our rendezvous by four o'clock in the afternoon, and drawn up in battle, our guards drawn out to watch, were directed to their posts, and then we resting by our arms, as we were in order, we slept lying where we stood, that in case of an alarm, we were not to be found in disorder, being ready to fight where we stood. Immediately after the army was settled in quarters, news was come to his Majesty in post, that the castle of Leipsic was given over by accord to the enemy; as also that General Tilly, with a mighty and strong army, was come a mile from Leipsic, and was preparing for a fight; which news did nowise alter his Majesty's countenance, being resolved before for the like, to have sought him to fight. So that being both willing, and so near, it was easy bringing them together. Our baggage was appointed to go back to Diben; our horse and foot watches were strengthened; and we were in readiness, and refreshing first our bodies with victuals, we slept till the next morning.

"As the lark began to peep, the 7th September 1631, having stood all night in array a mile from Tilly's army, in the morning the trumpets sound to horse, the drums calling to march, being at our arms and in readiness, having before meditated in the night, and resolved with our consciences, we began the morning with offering our souls and bodies as living sacrifices unto God, with confession of our sins. Lifting up our hearts and hands to heaven, we begged for reconciliation in Christ, by our public prayers and secret sighs and groans; recommending ourselves, the success and event of the day, unto God, our Father in Christ. Which done by us all, we marched forwards, in God's name, a little, and then halted again, till the whole army, both the Duke's and ours, were put in good order; our army marching on the right hand, and the Duke's on the left, our commanded musketeers marching in the vanguard, being in one body before the army consisting of three regiments, whereof two of Scots, and one Dutch, all musketeers, led by three Scotch Colonels, men of valour and courage, fit for the command concredited unto them, being made choice of, as men, that could fight exemplarily to others,—viz., Sir James Ramsey, called the Black, Sir John Hamilton, and Robert Monro, baron of Fowles. We marched thus, both the armies in order, horse, foot, and artillery, till about nine of the clock in the morning. We halted half-a-mile distant from the Imperial army that were attending us in order, consisting of forty-four thousand men, horse and foot, our army consisting of thirty thousand men, whereof, to my judgment, his Majesty's army were eight thousand foot and seven thousand horse. The Duke also would be eleven thousand foot and four thousand horse. Having refreshed ourselves with victuals, leaving our coaches behind us, the whole army did get green branches on their heads; and the word was given, 'God with us,' a little short speech made by his Majesty.

"Being in order of battle, we marched towards the enemy, who had taken the advantage of the ground, having placed his army on a place called God's Acre; where their General did make choice of the ground most advantageous for his foot, artillery, and horses. He also did beset the dorps, that environed the ground, which was left for us, with dragoneers and crabbats, to encumber our wings by their evil neighbourhood. Yet, notwithstanding of all the advantages he had of ground, wind, and sun, our magnanimous King and leader, under God, inferior to no general we ever read of, for wisdom, courage, dexterity, and good conduct, was not dejected; but with magnanimity and Christian resolution, having recommended himself, his army, and success to God the director of men and angels, able to give victory with few against many, he ordered his army, and directed every supreme officer in the field, on their particular charge and stations committed unto them for that day. As also he acquainted them severally of the form he was to fight unto, and he appointed platoons of musketeers by fifties, which were commanded by sufficient officers to attend on several regiments of horse; and he instructed the officers how to behave themselves in discharging their duties on service. Likewise he directed the officers belonging to the artillery how to carry themselves, which orderly done, the commanded musketeers were directed to their stand where to fight. His Majesty then led up the four brigades of foot, which were appointed to be the front of the army, with a distance betwixt every brigade, that a regiment of horse might march out in gross betwixt the brigades, all four being in one front, having their ordnance planted before every brigade, being four pieces of great cannon, and eight small; whereof four stood before the colours, that were the front of the brigade, with ammunition and constables to attend them. On the right hand pikes, before the colours were the other four pieces of cannon, with ammunition and constables conform; and on the left wing of pikes and colours were placed the other four pieces of cannon, as we said before. Behind these four brigades were drawn up the three brigades of reserve, with their artillery before them, standing at a proportionable distance behind the other four brigades, with the like distance betwixt them, as was betwixt the brigades of the front. The brigades of horse which had platoons of musketeers to attend them, were placed on the right and left wings of the foot, and some were placed betwixt the front of foot and the reserve, to second the foot as need were; other brigades of horse were drawn up behind the reserve of the foot brigades. The Field-Marshal Horne, General Bannier, and Lieutenant-General Bawtish were commanded to oversee the horsemen; his Majesty the Baron Tyvell, and Grave Neles, were to command the front of foot; Sir James Ramsey, as eldest colonel, had the command of the fore-troops, or commanded musketeers; and Sir John Hepburne, as eldest colonel, commanded the three brigades of reserve.

"Our army thus ordered, the Duke of Saxony and his Field-Marshal Arnhem having ordered their army (whereof I was not particularly inquisitive of the manner,) they were ordained to draw up on our left hand; and being both in one front thus ordered, we marched in order a little, and then halted again, till his Majesty had commanded out some commanded horsemen, on the wings of the army, a large distance from the body, to secur the fields of the crabbats. We marched again in order of battle, with trumpets sounding, and drums beating, and colours advanced and flying, till we came within reach of cannon to our enemy's army; then the magnific and magnanimous Gustavus the invincible, leads up the brigades of horse one after another to their ground, with their platoons of shot to attend them. As also he led up the brigades of foot one after another to their ground, during which time we were drawn up according to our former plot, the enemy was thundering amongst us, with the noise, and roaring whistling and flying of cannon-bullets; where you may imagine the hurt was great. The sound of such music being scarce worth the hearing, though martial I confess, yet, if you can have so much patience, with far less danger to read this story to an end, you shall find the music well paid; but with such coin, that the players would not stay for a world to receive the last of it, being overjoyed in their flying.

"By twelve of the clock on Wednesday the 7th of September, in despite of the fury of the enemy's cannon, and of his advantages taken, they were drawn up in even front with the enemy, and then our cannon began to roar, great and small, paying the enemy with the like coin, which thundering continued alike on both sides for two hours and a-half, during which time, our arrays of horse and foot stood firm like a wall, the cannon now and then making great breaches amongst us, which was diligently looked unto, on all hands, by the diligence of officers in filling up the void parts, and in setting aside of the wounded towards chirurgeons, every officer standing firm, overseeing their commands in their own stations, succeeding one another as occasion offered. By half three, our cannon a little ceasing, the horsemen on both wings charged furiously one another, our horsemen with a resolution, abiding unloosing a pistol, till the enemy had discharged first, and then at a near distance our musketeers meeting them with a salvo. Then our horsemen discharged their pistols, and then charged through them with swords; and at their return, the musketeers were ready again to give the second salvo of musketry amongst them. The enemy thus valiantly resisted by our horsemen, and cruelly plagued by our platoons of musketeers, you may imagine, how soon he would be discouraged after charging twice in this manner, and repulsed.

"Our horsemen of the right wing of Finnes and Haggapells, led by the valorous Field-Marshal Horne, finding the enemy's horsemen out of order, with resolution he charged the enemy's left wing, forcing them to retire disorderly on their lines of foot; which caused disorder among the foot, who were forced then to fall to the right hand. Our horsemen retiring, his Majesty seeing the enemy in disorder, played with ordnance amongst them; during which time, the force of the enemy's lines falls on the Duke of Saxony, charging with horse first in the midst of the lines, and then the foot giving two salvos of musketry amongst them, they were put to the rout, horse and foot, and the enemy following them cried 'Victoria,' as if the day had been won, triumphing before the victory. But our horsemen charging the remnant of their horse and foot, where their general stood, they were made to retire in disorder to the other hand towards Leipsic; our army of foot standing firm, not having loosed one musket. The smoke being great, by the rising of the dust, for a long time we were not able to see about us; but being cleared up, we did see on the left hand of our reserve two great bodies of foot, which we imagined to have been Saxons, that were forced to give ground. Having heard the service, though not seen it, we found they were enemies, being a a great deal nearer than the Saxons were. His Majesty having sent Baron Tyvell to know the certainty, coming before our brigade, I certified him they were enemies, and he, returning towards his Majesty, was shot dead. His Majesty coming by, gave directions to Colonel Hepburne to cause the brigades on his right and left wing to wheel, and then to charge the enemy. The orders given, his Majesty retired, promising to bring succours unto us.

" The enemy's array standing firm, looking on us at a near distance, and seeing the other brigades and ours wheeling about, making front unto them, they were prepared with a firm resolution to receive us with a salvo of cannon and muskets; but our small ordnance being twice discharged amongst them, and before we stirred, we charged them with a salvo of muskets, which was repaid; and incontinent our brigade advancing unto them with push of pike, putting one of their divisions in disorder, fell on the execution, so that they were put to the rout. I having commanded the right wing of our musketeers, being my Lord of Rhees and Lumsdell's, we advanced on the other body of the enemy, which defended their cannon; and beating them from their cannon, we were masters of their cannon, and consequently of the field. But the smoke being great, the dust being raised, we were as in a dark cloud, not seeing the half of our actions, much less discerning either the way of our enemies or yet the rest of our brigades. Whereupon, having a drummer by me, I caused him beat the Scotch march, till it cleared up, which re-collected our friends unto us, and dispersed our enemies, being overcome; so that the brigade coming together, such as were alive missed their dead and hurt comrades. Colonel Lumsdell was hurt at the first, and Lieutenant-Colonel Musten also, with divers other ensigns, were hurt and killed, and sundry colours were missing for that night, which were found the next day. The enemy thus fled, our horsemen were pursuing hard till it was dark; and the blue brigade, and the commanded musketeers were sent by his Majesty to help us. But before their coming, the victory and the credit of the day, as being last engaged, was ascribed to our brigade, being the reserve, were thanked by his Majesty for their service, in public audience; and in view of the whole army, we were promised to be rewarded.

"The battle thus happily won, his Majesty did principally under God ascribe the glory of the victory to the Swedish and Finnish horsemen, who were led by the valorous Fieldmarshal Gustavus Horne. For though the Dutch horsemen did behave themselves valorously divers times that day, yet it was not their fortune to have done the charge, which did put the enemy to flight. And though there were brave brigades of Swedes and Dutch in the field, yet it was the Scotch brigade's fortune to have gotten the praise for the foot service; and not without cause, having behaved themselves well, being led and conducted by an expert cavalier and fortunate, the valiant Hepburne, being followed by Colonel Lumsdell, Lieutenant-Colonel Musten, Major Monypenny, Major Sinclair, and Lieutenant-Colonel John Munro, with divers others cavaliers of valour, experience, and of conduct who thereafter were suddenly advanced unto higher charges. The victory being ours, we encamped over night on the place of battle, the living merry and rejoicing, though without drink at the night-wake of their dead comrades and friends, lying then on the ground in the bed of honour, being glad the Lord had prolonged their days for to discharge the last honourable duty in burying of their comrades. Our bonfires were made of the enemy's ammunition-waggons, and pikes left for want of good fellows to use them; and all this night our brave comrades, the Saxons, were making use of their heels in flying, thinking all was lost, they made booty of our waggons and goods, too good a recompense for cullions that had left their Duke, betrayed their country and the good cause, when strangers were hazarding their lives for their freedom.

"Our loss this day with the Saxons did not exceed three thousand men, which for the most part were killed by the enemy's cannon. Of principal officers we lost a number, and chiefly our horsemen, as Colonel Collenbagh, Colonel Hall, and Addergest; and of the foot colonels, the Baron Tyvell, being all of them brave and valorous gentlemen, we lost also four Lieutenant-Colonels, together with a number of rutmasters, captains, lieutenants, and ensigns. Of the Saxons were lost five colonels, three lieutenant-colonels, with divers rutmasters and captains, and of inferior officers many. To the enemy were lost on the field nearly eight thousand, besides officers of note, such as the Fieldmarshal Fustenberg, the Duke of Holstein, the Count of Schomberg, old General Tilly hurt and almost taken. A number of other officers of the field were killed, and taken prisoners. They lost also thirty-two pieces of cannon, with three score waggons of ammunition; and their general and Papingham were chased towards Halle, and from thence were forced with a small convoy to take their flight for refuge to Hamell on the Weser."

The Battle of Lutzen.

"The King's Majesty of Sweden, knowing that the Duke of Friedland had quit the town and castle of Visenfelts, and had, the fourth of November marched with his army towards Lutzen, two miles from Leipsic, his Majesty, on the fifth of November, with the whole army, two hours before day break up from Nawnburg, setting after the enemy, coming the same day after noon-tide in sight of them. He presented himself with his army in order of battle; so that incontinently the skirmish went on apace by the troops, which were commanded out from both armies; whereupon the Swedes made still good use with their small cannon, till the night did put them asunder, in which skirmish the Swedes had gotten one of the crabbat's standards, whereon was drawn the fortune and the eagle, which on our side was holden for a good beginning.

"The Swedish army this whole night standing in line, his Majesty was of intention to have fallen on the imperial army two hours before day. But by reason of a thick mist which had fallen, it behoved his Majesty to attend the rising and clearing up of the day. But the enemy perceiving the Swedes coming so near unto him, it could not go off without fighting. He did in the meantime see well to his own advantage, giving out orders they should incontinent make the moat or ditch they had before their front deeper than it was first made, and to lodge musketeers within it, which they might have before them, equal to any breastwork or parapet for their better safety. His Majesty then having ended the morning prayers, and that the mist was vanishing away, by the rising of the sun, giving out, by all appearance, the tokens of a clear day, his Majesty then with comfortable exhortation exhorted every man, foot and horse, to fight bravely, especially directing his speech to the Swedes and Finns: 'You true and valiant brethren, see that you do valiantly carry yourselves this day, fighting bravely for God's word and your king; which if you do, so will you have mercy of God, and honour before the world, and I will truly reward you; but if you do not, I swear unto you, that your bones shall never come into Sweden again.' The Dutch also his Majesty exhorted after this manner: 'You true and worthy Dutch brethren, officers and common soldiers, I exhort you all, carry yourselves manfully, and fight truly with me; run not away and I shall hazard my body and blood with you for your best, if you stand with me, so I hope in God to obtain victory, the profit whereof will redound to you and your successors; and if otherwise you do, so are you and your liberties lost.' His Majesty, having ended this speech, saith: 'Now let us to it, and let us cry unto God with one voice, Jesu, Jesu, Jesu help me this day to fight, for the glory of thy name.'

"He advanced then in full array fasting, having neither tasted meat nor drink, right forwards towards the town of Lu... en, where on both sides the Duke of Friedland's horsemen did present themselves, until such time as their General had brought their infantry in order, beside the wind-mill, and then to a side, by the ditch that was before their front. They retired back a little, and set themselves in order, on the right hand of the town of Lutzen, and then putting the town on fire, to the end the Swedes on that quarter could do them no harm. Notwithstanding whereof, with full resolution the Swedish army, in full array, marched by the side of the town on the ditch, where their musketeers were lodged, and presented themselves in good order, against the mighty and strong imperial army. Whereupon the Imperialists' great cannon, that were planted by the wind-mill, began to give fire in the midst of the Swedish army, and were incontinent repaid and answered with the like noise; so that the cannon played two long hours on both sides, the fight going bravely on, betwixt nine and ten of the clock, that his Majesty himself advanced towards the enemy, with the vanguard of his army, even to their grass, where their musketeers were set much to his Majesty's disadvantage, so that sundries of his majesty's forces fell therein. Nevertheless, they chased the enemy a little out of the ditch, and took seven of the Imperialists' cannon that were planted along the moat. After this, the other Swedish brigade or yellow regiment of the guard is come after, and not esteeming of the moat in their way, or of the three squadron, or divisions of the enemy's foot, being four times stronger than they, which they manfully did beat, making them to give ground till they were ruined, and then on **the second** time, scattering them also even until the third **advancing, and being** grown weak and weary with **so many brave** charges, being resisted by **the enemy's third division, which** were seconded well with **two squadrons of horsemen, at last,** with **the blue regiment coming** up to **relieve them, driven back, and almost so** scattered that they were **ruined, and the seven** cannon which formerly they had won, **were taken from** them again. In the meantime the Swedes' **small cannon,** that were planted before the brigades, being righted **on the** enemy's **cannon at** the wind-mill, whereon also Duke Barnard's cannon, **which were before his** brigade, played on the enemy's **cannon towards the wind-mill,** doing great hurt to the enemy, **so that they were forced to** retire their cannon a little behind **the miller's house.** In this meantime, his Majesty, with **some squadrons of horse, charged** the enemy, that was thrice **stronger than they, charging with** their right wing, **his left wing falling on them with such fury, that** their **rear-guard or reserve** were astonished, being so furious that they went through their enemies, putting them to the flight. But especially his Majesty himself having charged too far with four cornets in the midst of the enemy's troops, being deadly wounded, gave up the ghost. Fighting for God and for the defence of the true religion, he departed valiantly and happily for him in Christ our Saviour.

"Nevertheless, **two great bodies of crabbats of the enemy's left wing stood firm, and falling on the right wing of the** Swedish horsemen, **with such a cry and fury, advanced so far** that they were **masters of the Swedes' ammunition waggons,** bringing also some **of the Swedes' horsemen in disorder.** Whereupon incontinent did fall **on three squadrons of the** Swedish horsemen, under whom Lieutenant-Colonel **Relingen** was one, that did second the **rest** bravely, who was **shot in** the army. Nevertheless the crabbats were beaten **back** again with loss, during which time, Duke Barnard of Weimar was not idle, with the left wing of the Swedish horsemen, but with the commanded musketeers being of Leslie's regiment, and with the small cannon, charged the enemy's right wing, making them retire on their cannon by the wind-mill and gallows; and after long fighting, they were made at last to give ground, quitting to the Swedes fourteen pieces of great ordnance. As the Duke of Weimar did charge the enemy, their ammunition-waggons took fire, which did endamage the enemy much; but thereafter, Papenhaim coming from Halle with a fresh supply unlooked for, the service was begun again more sharp and violent than before, which continued for a while very vehement, he having re-collected the scattered troops, the order whereof can scarce be well set down, by reason it was so near night before Papenhaim's coming, yet the service continued hot and cruel so long as he lived, till it was past eight o'clock at night; that in end Papenhaim being killed, the Imperialists losing courage, through the assistance of God, and the manly and valiant courage of Duke Barnard of Weimar, the victory was come on the Swedes' side, the enemy having quit the field, and burnt off his leaguer with his whole baggage, and three pieces of cannon, which he could not get carried away with him. He took his retreat again on Leipsic.

"There were killed of the Imperialists the abbot of Fulda, the grave Fon Papenhaim, Colonel Lane, Colonel Vestrum, Lieutenant-Colonel Lorda, Lieutenant-Colonel Taphim, Lieutenant-Colonel Camerhooffe, Colonel Soves, with many other inferior officers and soldiers. On the Swedish side were lost, with his Majesty, General-Major Isler, Colonel Gerstorfe, General-Major Grave Neeles, a Swede, Colonel Vildesten, and divers more were hurt, and of our nation was hurt with the cannon and musket, twice Captain Henry Lindesay, brother to Bainshow, who for a time did lie almost dead in the field, divers officers of Colonel Lodowicke Leslie's regi ment were also hurt, having behaved themselves well, being, for the most part, old expert officers, and old-beaten blades of soldiers. In this battle, as was thought, were killed nine thousand men, besides those were hurt, whereof many thereafter died of their wounds, such as on the emperor's side Grave Berhertbold, Fon Walestine, Colonel Comargo, Colonel Browner, the old Colonel Viltzleben, and others. On the Swedish side also died of his wounds after the battle, General-Major Grave Neeles.

"After his Majesty's death, there was great and extraordinary grief and sorrow over the whole army. Yet they never suffered the same to be seen outwardly, but prosecuted still the enemy more vehemently, and more cruelly than before. For the Duke of Weimar, and the rest of the cavaliers of the army, understanding the great misfortune of his Majesty's death, resolved all alike, it was better to die on the place with his Majesty than to retire one foot of ground. Which resolution was the cause, that in the end they did crown the lamentable death of the King's Majesty with a stately and heroical victory, so that his Majesty in the highest degree of glory may be imagined before any king or emperor to have died; and his life doth eternize alike both his praise and glory, being victorious before death, in his death, and after death."

Drummond of Hawthornden, apostrophising the dead Gustavus Adolphus, says,

"O could not all the purchased victories
Like to thy fame thy flesh immortalize?
Were not thy virtue, nor thy valour charms
To guard thy body from those outward harms
Which could not reach thy soul? Could not thy spirit
Lend somewhat which thy frailty could inherit,
From thy diviner part that death nor heat
Nor envy's bullets e'er could penetrate?

Could not thy early trophies in stern fight
Turn from the Pole, the Dane, the Muscovite?
Which were thy triumphs, seeds as pledges sown,
That when thy honour's harvest was ripe-grown
With full-plumed wing thou falcon-like could fly,
And cuff the eagle in the German sky,
Forcing his iron beak, and feathers feel
They were not proof 'gainst thy victorious steel.
Could not all these protect thee, or prevail,
To fright that coward Death, who oft grew pale
To look thee and thy battles in the face?
Alas they could not; destiny gives place
To none. Nor is it seen that princes lives
Can saved be by their prerogatives.
No more was thine; who, clos'd in thy cold lead,
Dost from thyself a mournful lecture read
Of man's short dated glory. Learn you kings,
You are like him but penetrable things;
Though you from demi-gods derive your birth,
You are at best but honourable earth.
And howe'er sifted from that coarser bran
Which doth compound and knead the common man,
Nothing immortal, or from earth refined
About you, but your office and your mind.
Hear then, break your false glasses which present
You greater than your Maker ever meant.
Make truth your mirror now, since you find all
That flatter you, confuted by his fall."

THE MACGREGORS.

A TRAVELLER who approaches **Loch Katrine** from Stirling or Callendar, passes through the **narrow defile of the Trosachs**, where Fitz-James's

> "Gallant horse exhausted fell;"

and will mark the "narrow and broken plain" where Sir Walter Scott represents the Scotish troops under the Earls of Mar and Moray to have paused ere they entered

> "The dangerous glen."

Nor will the vivid description of the scene which took place when the archers entered the defile be forgotten. No trace of a foe could at first be seen; but

> "At once there rose so wild a yell
> Within that dark and narrow dell,
> As all the fiends, from heaven that fell,
> Had peal'd the banner-cry of hell!
> Forth from the pass in tumult driven,
> Like chaff before the wind of heaven,
>   The archery appear;
> For life! for life! their flight they ply—
> And shriek, and shout, and battle-cry,
> And plaids and bonnets waving high,
> And broadswords flashing in the sky,
>   Are maddening in the rear.
> Onwards they drive in dreadful race,
>   Pursuers and pursued."

Although this is merely the description of an imaginary fight between the Scotish troops and the men of Clan-Alpine or Clan-Gregor, yet it has become so familiar to every reading mind as almost to be considered the account of a real transaction; and we believe few now pass through the Trosachs without thinking of Roderic Dhu and his Macgregors, and those days when their cliffs oft-echoed to " dying moan and dirge's wail." The first appearance of the lake at this extremity gives little promise of the wide and varied expanse to which it stretches out as the traveller proceeds. Sir Walter has indeed well described it here as

> " A narrow inlet still and deep,
> Affording scarce such breadth of brim,
> As served the wild duck's brood to swim."

In advancing onwards, the lake is lost for a few minutes, but it again opens with increasing grandeur and presents new and picturesque views at almost every step as we advance. Helen's isle, which will immediately arrest attention, was the " islet rock" from which, at the blast of the Knight of Snowden's bugle, started forth the little skiff which brought Helen Douglas to the " beach of pebbles bright as snow;" and on which also was the rustic retreat where Fitz-James spent the night. It was to the same island that the women and children of the Clan-Alpine or Clan-Gregor are represented to have fled for refuge:—

> " Moray pointed with his lance,
>   And cried—' Behold yon isle!—
> See none are left to guard its strand
> But women weak that wring the hand,
> Tis there of yore the robber-band
>   Their booty wont to pile;—
> My purse, with bonnet-pieces store,
> To him will swim a bow-shot o'er
> And loose a shallop from the shore.

The Battle History of Scotland.—*Page* 44.

Lightly we'll tame the war-wolf then,
Lords of his mate, and brood and den!'
Forth from the ranks a spearman sprung,
On earth his casque and corslet rung,
  He plunged into the wave.
    *   *   *   *   *
  He nears the isle—and lo!
His hand is on a shallop's bow.
I marked Duncraggan's widow'd dame,
Behind an oak I saw her stand
A naked dirk gleamed in her hand:
It darkened; but amid the moan
Of waves I heard a dying groan."

In the graphic narrative which we have here quoted from the poem of Sir Walter, we have indeed but the fictions of the poet; yet when we recollect who were the ancient inhabitants of this district, we can feel little doubt that such scenes were formerly not unfrequent during that period,

" When tooming faulds, or sweeping of a glen,
Had still been held the deeds of gallant men."

When the Clan-Gregor, or as they were called, the Clan-Alpine, held this district, there can be no question that on this island their wives and children often sought shelter from the numerous enemies of their name; and it is said that during Cromwell's usurpation, one of his soldiers who had swam to the island, and was about to seize one of the boats, met his doom from the hand of a woman in the manner described in the poem. But, whatever be the truth of the legends connected with it, " the mighty minstrel" has " waved his visioned wand," and they have now obtained an absolute and permanent existence in the imagination.

The upper part or western extremity of Loch Katrine, or

the part which is first approached by a traveller from Inversnaid on Loch Lomond, was eminently the land of the Macgregors,—the central part of their territory,—the district of seclusion and strengths and fastnesses, where they commonly sought refuge from oppression, and to which they usually retired after their unsuccessful conflicts with other clans, or after their predatory incursions into the Lowlands. This tract does not possess the picturesque or romantic interest which so powerfully characterises the scenery toward the eastern end of the lake; yet there is a rude grandeur, a lonely sublimity about it, which at least inspires awe, and fills the mind with pleasing melancholy, though it may fail to realize the images associated with its name in our fancy. When we look upon the utter desolateness which spreads around,—the bluff head-lands which project their weather-beaten fronts into the water,—the noble outline of the lofty mountains,—the bare and rugged rocks with which they are covered,—the deep ravines that form the beds of the innumerable streams which flow down their sides,—the heath-covered muirs that intervene,—and the contrasted stillness and purity of the transparent lake,—we feel that it is altogether highly characteristic Highland scenery. The Macgregors were long the entire masters of this district, and of a wide periphery of glen and mountain and lake and forest on all sides of it; but were from time to time dispossessed by the superior address and craftiness of the neighbouring clans; and they were a sad instance of the fluctuations of prosperity and character, and the violent alternations between comparative good and comparative evil, the sudden and startling mixtures of wrong done and wrong suffered, of crime and victimization, which chracterise an unsettled feudal state of society.

In the early part of the year 1602, a large portion of the west of Scotland was tossed into commotion by the renewal of some old quarrels between Colquhoun of Luss, the chief of that surname, and Alexander Macgregor, chief of the Clan-

Gregor. Aggressions had formerly been committed on both sides; first by Luss and his party against some of the Macgregors, and then by John Macgregor, the brother of Alexander, against the laird of Luss and his dependants and tenants. To put an end to these dissensions, Alexander Macgregor left Rannoch, accompanied by about 200 of his kinsmen and friends, entered Lennox, and took up his quarters on the confines of Luss's territory, where he expected, by the mediation of his friends, to bring matters to an amicable adjustment. As the laird of Luss was suspicious of Macgregor's real intentions, he assembled all his vassals with the Buchanans and others, to the number of 300 horse and 500 foot, with the design, if the result of the meeting should not turn out to his expectations and wishes, to cut off Macgregor and his party. But Macgregor, anticipating his intention, was upon his guard, and, by his precautions, defeated the design upon him. A conference was held for the purpose of terminating all differences; but the meeting broke up without any adjustment; Macgregor then proceeded homewards.

The laird of Luss, in pursuance of his plan, immediately followed Macgregor with great haste through Glenfruin, about 10 miles west of Dumbarton, in the expectation of coming upon him unawares, and defeating him; but Macgregor, who was on the alert, observed, in due time, the approach of his pursuers, and made his dispositions accordingly. He divided his company into two parts, the largest of which he kept under his own command, and placed the other part under the command of John Macgregor, his brother, whom he dispatched by a circuitous route, for the purpose of attacking Luss's party in the rear, when they should least expect to be assailed. This stratagem succeeded, and the result was, that after a keen contest, Luss's party was completely overthrown, with the loss of 200 men, besides several gentlemen and burgesses of the town of Dumbarton. It is remarkable that of the Macgregors, John, the brother of Alexander, and another person alone were killed, though some of the party were wounded.

The laird of Luss and his friends sent early notice of their disaster to the King, and they succeeded so effectually by misrepresenting the whole affair to him, and exhibiting to his majesty eleven score bloody shirts belonging to those of their party who were slain, that the King grew exceedingly incensed at the Clan-Gregor, who had no person about the King to plead their cause, proclaimed them rebels, and interdicted all the lieges from harbouring them or having any communication with them. The Earl of Argyle and the Campbells were afterwards sent against the proscribed clan, and hunted them through the country. About 60 of the clan made a brave stand at Bentoik against a party of 200 chosen men belonging to the Clan-Cameron, Clan-Nab, and Clan-Ronald, under the command of Robert Campbell, son of the laird of Glenorchy, when Duncan Aberigh, one of the chieftains of the Clan-Gregor, and his son Duncan, and seven gentlemen of Campbell's party were killed. But although they made a brave resistance, and killed many of their pursuers, the Macgregors, after many skirmishes and great losses, were at last overcome. Commissions were thereafter sent through the kingdom, for fining those who had harboured any of the clan, and for punishing all persons who had kept up any communication with them; and the fines so levied were given by the King to the Earl of Argyle, who converted the same to his own use as a recompense for his services against the unfortunate Macgregors.

Alexander Macgregor, the chief, after suffering many vicissitudes of fortune, and many privations, at last surrendered himself to the Earl of Argyle, on condition that he should grant him a safe conduct into England to King James, that he might lay before his majesty a true state of the whole affair from the commencement, and crave the royal mercy; and as a security for his return to Scotland, he delivered up to

Argyle thirty of his choicest men, and of the best reputation among the clan as hostages to remain in Argyle in custody, till his return from England. But no sooner had Macgregor arrived in Berwick on his way to London, than he was basely arrested, and brought back by the Earl to Edinburgh, and, by his influence, executed along with the thirty hostages. Argyle hoped, by these means, ultimately to annihilate the whole clan; but in this cruel design he was quite disappointed, for the clan speedily increased, and became almost as powerful as before.

About the year 1708, the well-known Rob Roy captured Graham of Killearn, and confined him during three days on an island near the head of Loch Katrine. The Duke of Montrose had, by the forfeiture of a wadset, obtained a right to dispossess Rob Roy of his property of Inversnaid and Craigrostan. In this it does not appear that there was any harshness on the part of his Grace; but Killearn, his chamberlain, had recourse to a mode of expulsion inconsistent with the rights of humanity, and had grossly insulted Macgregor's wife in her husband's absence. Rob Roy, on his return, being informed of what had occurred, withdrew from the scene of the outrage, and vowed revenge. In order to make up for the loss of his property, he regularly seized a portion of his Grace's rent; but on Killearn he took a personal satisfaction, which certainly shows the mildness of his character when we consider the habits and mode of thinking of the Highlanders of his day. The chamberlain was collecting rents at Cappeleroch, in Stirlingshire, when Rob Roy came upon him with an armed force, and demanded his share of the rents. For this he gave the chamberlain a receipt: and afterwards carried the unwilling gentleman to Loch-Katrine, where he kept him in durance for three days, and then set him at liberty.

Glengyle, a lonely tract of country among the hills at the upper extremity of Loch-Katrine, belonged to a family of

Macgregors, who, during the time when the name was prohibited, changed theirs to Graham. Rob Roy was of this family. He was the second son of Donald Macgregor, brother to the laird of Glengyle, and a lieutenant-colonel in the King's service,—most probably in one of the independent companies raised for the internal defence of the Highlands. The family of Glengyle were descended from a fifth son of the laird of Macgregor about the year 1430. He was named *Dugald Ciar*, or 'Dugald of the mouse colour.' Dugald had two sons, of whom the youngest, Gregor Dhu, or Black Gregor, was the founder of the family of Glengyle. Rob Roy originally possessed no patrimonial estate. His father lived on Glengyle as a tenant, and latterly was tutor to his nephew, Gregor Macgregor of Glengyle, styled in the language of the Highlands, *Gregor-Gluine-dhu*, or 'the Black knee'd Gregor,' from a black spot on his knee. The lands of Craigrostan and Inversnaid were afterwards acquired by Rob Roy; and we find him sometimes styled Robert Macgregor of Craigrostan, and sometimes Baron of Inversnaid. The name of Macgregor being proscribed, Rob Roy assumed that of Campbell, from respect to the Duke of Argyle.

The character and exploits of Rob Roy are so generally known from popular tradition and from many productions of popular literature, especially from Sir Walter Scott's far-famed romance of "Rob Roy," that they need not be mentioned here; but some powerful lines by Mrs Charles Tinsley, on his last words, are much less known, and well deserve to be transcribed. The last words were " Now it is all over—tell the piper to play, *Ha til mi tulidh*"—(We return no more;) and the following are the lines upon them;—

" ' We return no more! we return no more!'
   Said the chief, ere he breathed his last;
For he knew that the reign of the fierce and free,
   And the bold in deed, was past;

He knew that the slogan of Border war—
  All mute as the sleuth hound's breath—
Should never awaken the hills again
  With shouts whose echo was death;—
      'Ha til, ha til mi tulidh!'

Did they crowd around him, the brave of old,
  In the dreams of that solemn hour,
All the mighty chiefs of his royal line,
  In the pride of their early power?—
Macalpine, who reigned o'er a conquered race,
  And those that held rule in Lorn—
Did he think of these as he turned to die?
  And his words—were they words of scorn?
      'Ha til, ha til mi tulidh!'

Did he brood o'er the wrong that 'whelmed his sires,
  Making all their hearthstones bare,
Through the ages that saw them held at bay,
  And hate-hunted everywhere?—
Did he call to mind their scattered haunts,
  In Balquhidder and Glenstrae,
And breathe in his spirit's bitterness,
  One trust ere he passed away?
      'Ha til, ha til mi tulidh!'

O why was the gift of the seer of old
  Withheld in that parting hour?
Why stood not the future before him then
  In the might of its deathless power?
Why did it coldly, tamely, still
  Its truths from the dauntless keep,
Leaving the brave, proud heart to sigh—
  Ere it sank in dreamless sleep—
      'Ha til, ha til mi tulidh!'

For they shall not die! for they shall not die!
   Whilst the hills their fame can keep;
Whilst fancy—bold as the boldest still—
   Can the gulfs of time o'erleap;
Whilst the wild, free spirit of old romance
   Yet haunteth each loch and glen;
Whilst Scotland can say, from her heart of hearts,
   'Thus speak not my mighty men—
              'Ha til, ha til mi tulidh!'

And mighty they were those chieftains bold,
   With their germs of noble thought,
By the rugged nurture of rugged times
   To growths of wild grandeur brought;
With their generous love of freedom, still
   Unchanged through the changes round;
And, oh, not for them 'mid their native hills,
   Should those parting words resound—
              'Ha til, ha til mi tulidh!

In their sometimes lawless bravery,
   They shall yet around us throng,
Where the clinging love of their native soil,
   Was than wrath and death more strong;
They were suited well to their own rude times,
   And ours will not let them go,
Till the last of Scotland's sons shall say—
   'Mid the final wrecks below—
              'Ha til, ha til mi tulidh!'"

THE STRIFES OF MORTLACH.

MORTLACH, a large parish in the Moray district of Banff-shire, is famous as the scene of a signal victory achieved by

Malcolm II., in 1010, over the Danes. He had been beaten by these foemen in the preceding year, and compelled to leave them in possession of the province of Moray. Returning from the south with a reinforced and powerful army, he burned to expel the intruders, and found them in readiness to give him battle. The armies came in sight of each other near the church of Mortlach, and engaged a little to the north. Three of the Scotish generals fell in the first shock of collision; and panic and confusion followed among the Scotish troops. The King was reluctantly borne along with the retreating crowd till he was opposite the church of Mortlach, then a chapel dedicated to St. Molach; and here, while his army were partially pent up in their flight by the contraction of the vale, and the narrowness of the pass, he performed some of the showy rites of saint-worship, and rallied and roused his troops with an animated appeal to their patriotism, and, placing himself at their head, wheeled round upon the foe, threw Enotus, one of the Danish generals, from his horse, and killed him with his own hand. The Scots, now flung back from fear to enthusiasm, made an impetuous onset, carried victory in their van, and thickly strewed the ground with the corpses of their foes. A fuller account of this battle, together with some notice of local vestiges of it, is given in a companion volume of this series. Had the Danes been victors on this occasion, they would in all probability have obtained as broad and firm a footing in Scotland as they did in England; but they were all along indefatigably and most determinedly opposed, and only four years afterwards were completely and almost finally chased out of the country, by the Scotish monarch of the period, he who

> " Thirty years of variegated reign,
> Was King by fate, Malcolm."

THE STRIFES OF MORTLACH.

About the year 1670, a hereditary feud which had long existed between the powerful clans of the Mackintoshes and the Gordons, and which had often been alternately suppressed and revived, broke suddenly out and came to a curious tragical termination. The castle of Auchindune, Auchindoun, or Auchindown, situated on a green conical mount, overlooking the river Fiddish, in the parish of Mortlach, is supposed to have been built by Cochrane, the favourite of James III., and was for some time the property of the Ogilvies, and part of the lordship of Deskford, but passed in 1535 into the possession of the Gordons, and continued till 1670 to be one of their princeliest residences and most imposing fortalices. William Mackintosh, a young man of high spirit, was the heir to the chieftainship of the Clan Chattan or clan of the Mackintoshes; but, in consequence of the feud with the Gordons, and of confusions which it had occasioned, he did not get into possession of his rights without difficulty; and he seems to have promptly and sternly formed a purpose to hurl his newly acquired power at the Gordons by burning their castle of Auchindune. The execution of this purpose is commemorated in the following terse stanzas of an old song:—

> "As I came in by Fiddich-side
>   In a May morning,
> I met Willie Mackintosh
>   An hour before the dawning.
>
> 'Turn again, turn again,
>   Turn again, I bid ye,
> If ye burn Auchindown,
>   Huntly he will head ye.
>
> 'Head me, hang me,
>   That sall never fear me,
> I'll burn Auchindown
>   Before the life leaves me.'

> As I came in by Auchindown
> In a May morning,
> Auchindown was in a bleeze
> An hour before the dawning."

The Marquis of Huntly immediately marched against the aggressor at the head of his retainers; and a fierce struggle ensued. The Mackintoshes were overpowered; and the chief despairing of mercy at the hands of Huntly, appealed to his lady, before whom he presented himself as a suppliant, in the absence of her husband. The marchioness, however, showed herself a fit mate for such a lord. Seeing the enemy of her house suing for mercy upon her hearth, the inexorable virago, insensible alike to compassion and humanity, caused his head to be struck off, and by this bloody act for ever dishonoured her family and name. The death of the chief, however, was productive of no further injury or loss to the clan. The feud seems to have been extinguished in his blood; and as Huntly now found himself opposed by a party of the nobility, all of them more or less intimately connected with Mackintosh, he was obliged to put the son of that ill-fated chief in possession of his paternal inheritance.

Another old fortalice in Mortlach, the house of Edinglassie, though vastly inferior in both architectural grandeur and historical note to Auchindune Castle, possesses considerable interest in connexion with the ensanguined story of Highland feuds, and was the scene of an appalling instance of the miseries of civil war, and of the tyrannical and detestable power which was often wielded by the chieftains and barons of the feudal age. Some of the Highland clans, on their march from Strathspey through Mortlach to Strathbogie, in 1690, the year of the engagement on the haughs of Cromdale, having burnt the house in prosecution of the public dissensions of the period, the laird, whose name was Gordon, seized 18 of them at random, when they were returning a few weeks after, and hanged them all on the trees of his garden.

THE SIEGE OF BERGEN-OP-ZOOM.

The bravery displayed by Lord John Murray's Highlanders at Fontenoy opened the eyes of government to the importance of securing the military services of the clans. It was, therefore, determined to repair, in part, the loss sustained in that well-fought action, by raising a second regiment in the Highlands; and authority to that effect was granted to the Earl of Loudon. By the influence of the noblemen, chiefs, and gentlemen of the country, whose sons and connexions were to be appointed officers, a body of 1,250 men was raised, of whom 750 assembled at Inverness, and the remainder at Perth. The whole were formed into twelve companies, under the colonelcy of the Earl of Loudon, the lieutenant-colonelcy of the Duke of Argyle, and the subordinate officership of gentlemen who were connected with some of the most distinguished families in the Highlands, and who received their commissions under date of 8th June, 1745.

The regiment embarked on the 30th of May 1747 for Flanders; but it did not join the Duke of Cumberland's army till after the battle of Lafeldt, on the 2d of July. Though disappointed of the opportunity which this battle would have given them of distinguishing themselves, another soon offered for the display of their gallantry. Marshal Saxe having determined to attack the strong fortress of Bergen-op-Zoom, with an army of 25,000 men under General Count Lowendahl, all the disposable forces in Brabant, including Loudon's Highlanders, were sent to defend the lines, which were strongly fortified. To relieve the garrison, consisting of six battalions, and to preserve a communication with the

THE SIEGE OF BERGEN-OP-ZOOM.

country, eighteen battalions occupied the lines. The fortress, which was considered impregnable, was defended by 250 pieces of cannon. The siege was carried on unremittingly from the 15th of July till the 17th of September, during which interval many sorties were made. In the Hague Gazette, an account is given of one of these, which took place on the 25th of July, in which it is stated "that the Highlanders, who were posted in Fort Rouro, which covers the lines of Bergen-op-Zoom, made a sally, sword in hand, in which they were so successful as to destroy the enemy's grand battery, and to kill so many of their men, that Count Lowendahl beat a parley, in order to bury the dead. To this it was answered, that had he attacked the place agreeably to the rules of war, his demand would certainly have been granted; but as he had begun the siege, like an incendiary, by setting fire to the city with red-hot balls, a resolution had been taken neither to ask nor grant any suspension of arms."

Having made breaches in a ravelin and two bastions, the besiegers made an unexpected assault on the night of the 16th of September, and throwing themselves into the fosse, mounted the breaches, forced open a sally port, and, entering the place, ranged themselves along the ramparts, almost before the garrison had assembled. Cronstrun, the old governor, and many of his officers were asleep, and so sudden and unexpected was the attack, that several of them flew to ranks in their shirts. Though the possession of the ramparts sealed the fate of the town, the Scotish troops were not disposed to surrender it without a struggle. The French were opposed by two regiments of the Scotish brigade, in the pay of the States-general, who, by their firmness, checked the progress of the enemy, and enabled the governor and garrison to recover from their surprise. The Scots assembled in the market-place, and attacked the French with such vigour that they drove them from street to street, till fresh reinforcements pouring in, they were compelled to retreat in their turn,—disputing every inch as they retired, and fighting till two-thirds of their number fell on the spot, killed or severely wounded,—when the remains brought off the old governor, and joined the troops in the lines.

The troops in the lines, most unaccountably, retreated immediately, and the enemy thus became masters of the whole navigation of the Scheldt. "Two battalions," says an account of the assault published in the Hague Gazette, "of the Scotish brigade have, as usual, done honour to their country, —which is all we have to comfort us for the loss of such brave men, who, from 1,450, are now reduced to 330 men,— and those have valiantly brought their colours with them, which the grenadiers twice recovered from the midst of the French at the point of the bayonet. The Swiss have also suffered, while others took a more speedy way to escape danger." In a history of this memorable siege, the brave conduct of the Scots is also thus noticed: "It appears that more than 300 of the Scotish brigade fought their way through the enemy, and that they have had 19 officers killed and 18 wounded. Lieutenants Francis and Allan Maclean of the brigade were taken prisoners, and carried before General Lowendahl, who thus addressed them, 'Gentlemen, consider yourselves on parole. If all had conducted themselves as you and your brave corps have done, I should not now be master of Bergen-op-Zoom.'"

The loss of a fortress hitherto deemed impregnable was deeply felt by the allies. The eyes of all Europe had been fixed upon this important siege; and when the place fell strong suspicions were entertained of treachery in the garrison. Every thing had been done by the people of the United Provinces to enable the soldiers to hold out: they were allowed additional provisions of the best quality, and cordials were furnished for the sick and dying. Large sums of money were collected to be presented to the soldiers, if they made a brave defence; and £17,000 were collected in one day in Amsterdam, to be applied in the same way, if the soldiers compelled the enemy to raise the siege. Every soldier who carried away a gabion from the enemy was paid a crown, and such was the activity of the Scots, that some of them gained ten crowns a-day in this kind of service. Those who ventured to take the burning fuse out of the bombs of the enemy, (and there were several who did so) received ten or twelve ducats. In this remarkable siege the French sustained an enormous loss, exceeding 22,000 men; that of the garrison did not exceed 4,000.

The following anecdote of faithful attachment is told by Mrs. Grant, in her 'Superstitions of the Highlanders.' Captain Fraser of Culduthel, an officer of the Black Watch, was a volunteer at this celebrated siege, as was likewise his colonel, Lord John Murray. Captain Fraser was accompanied by his servant, who was also his foster-brother. A party from the lines was ordered to attack and destroy a battery raised by the enemy. Captain Fraser accompanied this party, directing his servant to remain in the garrison. "The night was pitch dark, and the party had such difficulty in proceeding that they were forced to halt for a short time. As they moved forward, Captain Fraser felt his path impeded, and putting down his hand to discover the cause, he caught hold of a plaid, and seized the owner, who seemed to grovel on the ground. He held the caitiff with one hand, and drew his dirk with the other, when he heard the imploring voice of his foster-brother. 'What the devil brought you here?' 'Just love of you and care of your person.' 'Why so, when your love can do me no good; and why encumber yourself with a plaid?' 'Alas! how could I ever see my mother had you been killed or wounded, and I not been there to carry you to the surgeon, or to Christian burial? and how could I do either without any plaid to wrap you in?' Upon inquiry it was found that the poor man had crawled out on his knees and hands between the sentinels, then followed the party to some distance, till he thought they were approaching the place of assault, and then again crept in the same manner on the ground, beside his master, that he might be near him unobserved." Captain Fraser was unfortunately killed a few days thereafter, by a random shot, while looking over the ramparts.

After the loss of Bergen-op-Zoom, Loudon's Highlanders joined the Duke of Cumberland's army; and at the peace of 1748, they returned to Scotland, and were reduced at Perth in June of the same year.

THE EXECUTION OF LADY JANE DOUGLAS.

LADY JANE DOUGLAS was the daughter of George, Master of Angus—the grand-daughter of the great Earl of Angus, commonly called Bell-the-Cat,—the niece of Archibald Douglas, the well-known butt of James V.'s enmity,—and the sister of the sixth Earl of Angus, Chancellor of Scotland, who suffered forfeiture under James V., and lived long in exile at the court of England. She married John, sixth Lord Glammis, who died on the 12th of December, 1527,—and bore to him a son, who became the seventh Lord Glammis; and soon after her first husband's death, she married Archibald Campbell, the second son of the second Earl of Argyle.

When her brother, the Earl of Angus, and another brother, and her uncle Archibald Douglas fell under the wrath of James V., and were proclaimed by him as rebels and traitors whom no persons might sanction with their intercourse or assist with food, raiment, or shelter, she braved the King's denunciation, and afforded them all the aid in her power, and in consequence became a sharer in the fiery hatred which he had sworn to cherish toward all the Douglas race. The King and his minions appear to have hunted up several pretexts for prosecuting her, and to have been constantly and keenly on the outlook for some feasible reason to imprison and kill her; but they did not succeed for years, till they became aided by one of the most profligate and atrocious outbursts of private revenge which anywhere disfigure the records of authentic history. In December, 1528, she was summoned along with others to answer before parliament for an alleged assisting of the Earl of Angus in an insurrectionary design against the King's person; but seems not to have been prosecuted, in consequence of a total want of evidence. In July 1531, or perhaps earlier in that year, she suffered a forfeiture of goods for "intercommunying with our souerane lordis rebellis or for ony other crymes." In January 1531–2, she was bound in surety to appear at the next assize of Forfar for the pretended crime of destroying her first husband's life *per intoxicationem*, which probably signified by means of drugs, philtres, charms, or enchanted potions.

"This shifting of the ground, in relation to the charge of crime against her," remarks Mr. Pitcairn, "seems to have proceeded from the repeated refusal of the barons to come forward as assisors or jurors on her trial, and from the fear on the part of the public prosecutor, that the case would break down for want of legal and satisfactory proof of her being guilty of any treason. Such suspicious circumstances naturally lead us to infer that her real crime was the political offence of her being a true-hearted Douglas, and as such a contumacious despiser of the royal tyranny, which would attempt to force her to deny succour to her oppressed brothers and uncle, and other 'rebels.' As Lord Glammis died Dec. 12, 1527, it is highly improbable that all legal proceedings would be allowed by the advisers of the Crown to be totally suspended for nearly four years against one who was, at any rate, obnoxious to the King. There were never awanting enough of officious spies about the Scotish court to ferret out the truth of even the shadow of suspicion of crime against those who were unhappy enough to be under its ban ; and had there been any just ground of accusation, Lady Glammis's career would have at once been cut short."

Various subsequent attempts were made to bring this ill-used lady under the anathema of the law; and failed either from the repugnance of gentlemen to act as jurors against her, or from the glaringly false and malicious nature of the allegations of her accusers. But at length, on the 17th of July, 1537, she was brought to trial and condemned, upon the information and testimony of a seemingly disinterested party, for an alleged crime of a much more heinous nature than the majority which had hitherto been laid to her charge, —including indeed the old offence of treasonably assisting, supplying, resetting, intercommuning, and fortifying the Earl of Angus and his brother, but adding the extraordinary item of imagining and conspiring the destruction of the King by poison. The fabrication of this charge, and the circumstances which gave rise to it, together with the condemnation and execution of the lady on the ground of it, constitute one of the most remarkable chapters in the history of public prosecutions; and they are narrated with much clearness and piquancy in a rare extant Life of James V., which was written not long after the period, and which bears marks of being a careful and impartial compilation from contemporary papers and chronicles.

" The Lady Jane Douglas," says this document, " was the most renowned beauty of Britain, at that time. She was of an ordinary stature, not too fat; her mien was majestic, her eyes full, her face was oval, and her complexion was delicate and extremely fair. Besides all these perfections, she was a lady of a singular chastity. As her body was a finished piece, without the least blemish, so Heaven designed that her mind should want none of those perfections a mortal creature can be capable of. Her modesty was admirable; her courage was above what could be expected from her sex; her judgment solid; her carriage was gaining and affable to her inferiors, as she knew well how to behave herself to her equals. Her second husband, Archibald Campbell, had a good estate, and was of a good family, and commanded the third squadron of King James' army; and this gentleman, who equally admired her beauty and virtue, made his addresses to her with all possible respect, and they were married to both their satisfactions. William Lion, a near relation of her first husband, and one of her former suitors, not being able to stifle his former flame, nor dissemble his rage and discontent for the loss of her, became almost frantic upon this disappointment; and though he was so unhappy as to lose her, yet he did not forbear his addresses. This beautiful lady repulsed him with disdain, and told him, that the reason why she formerly treated him with civility, was more owing to his relation to her last husband, and to her son, than to any regard to himself; but now she hated the sight of him. His last interview with her was spent in complaints, entreaties, reproaches, and threatenings; after which he departed and never visited her more. From that time his feelings were changed into rage and revenge. His thoughts were divided, whether he should kill her himself, or contrive some plot against her life; the first seemed unworthy of his courage, whereas the latter required very nice conduct, and too long a delay, seeing he was enraged to that degree, that he thirsted for present revenge; but at last the latter carried it. So after brooding over his resentment for some months, at last he lighted upon one of the blackest contrivances that hell could suggest, viz. he accused this lady, her son, her husband, and one John Lion, an aged priest, and his own near relation, as guilty of a design to poison the King. This was the most unlikely thing in the world, if we consider the characters and conversation of the persons accused, who lived for the most part in the country at a great distance from court, and seldom had an occasion of seeing the King. However, upon this, those innocent persons were apprehended and imprisoned in the castle of Edinburgh, and their goods were seized, with a strict charge to the judges of the justice-court to proceed to their trials.

"William Lion, the accuser, who had the ear of the jealous King, used all his rhetoric to aggravate the matter, and that he might dispose the King to treat them with all possible cruelty, he represented 'that the family of Douglas had always been dangerous and troublesome to his predecessors, and even to himself and his kingdom; and reminded him of the insolent behaviour of Archibald Douglas, Earl of Angus, the brother of the prisoner, in the time of his Majesty's minority, whose practices were so pernicious, that by a public decree he was banished the kingdom as a disturber of the peace of his native country; that since that time he was become the subject of Henry, King of England, his Majesty's enemy, and was now the incendiary betwixt the two kingdoms, and advised all the inroads that were made from England upon Scotland; and that, seeing he could not be restored to his honours and fortune, without great difficulty revenge incited him to plot all the mischief possible against the King's person; and whom could he employ for compassing such wicked designs more fit than his own sister, who was obliged to secrecy by the ties of blood? That he engaged her in that conspiracy, thinking that her sex, character, and birth, would make her the less suspected; therefore, if his Majesty had any regard either to his interest or safety, it was necessary to exterminate that race which produced nothing but monsters of rebellion, and especially that woman, whom if he spared, he would put it in her power to accomplish her wicked designs.' This discourse found too easy a belief with the King, who was naturally jealous and suspicious, and was wholly ignorant of the hatred which William Lion bore to that lady. Upon which he ordered that they should be put upon their trial in all haste; so that small regard was had either to their characters, birth, or defences they made.

"Before the judges gave sentence, this lady was brought to the bar according to custom, that they might hear what she could say for herself. She knew well enough that her misfortunes proceeded from her near relation to the Earl of Angus. When she had answered to all the questions which the judges asked, with the greatest courage and boldness imaginable, she delivered the following speech:—'Those who hate the merit of my brother are enraged because he is not in their power, that he might fall a sacrifice to their malice; and they now discharge their spite upon me, because of my near relation to him; and to gratify their revenge with my blood, they accuse me of crimes which, if true, deserve the severest death. But seeing it is only the prerogative of God to punish men or women for the faults of others, which belongs to no judge on earth, who are obliged to punish every one according to their personal crimes, you ought not to punish in me the actions of my brother, how blameable soever. Above all, you ought to consider if those things I am accused of have the least appearance of truth imaginable; for what gives the greatest evidence either of the guilt or innocence of an impeached person, is their former life. What fault could any hitherto lay to my charge? Did any ever reproach me with any thing that is scandalous? Examine, I entreat you, my former conversation; vice hath its degrees as well as virtue, and none can attain to a perfection in either, except by long use and practice; and if you can find nothing reprovable in my conduct, how can ye believe that I am arrived all of a sudden to contrive this murder, which is the very height and perfection of impiety? I protest I would not deliberately injure the most despicable wretch alive; could I then make the murder of my sovereign, whom I always reverenced, and who never did me any wrong, the first essay of my wickedness? None are capable of such damnable and unnatural actions, except two sorts of persons, viz. those of desperate fortunes who are weary of their lives, or those who are hurried into them by revenge. My birth and manner of life put me beyond the suspicion of the first kind; and for the latter, seeing I was never injured by the King, how can I be suspected to thirst for any revenge? I am here accused for purposing to kill the King; and to make my pretended crime appear more frightful, it is given out, that the way was to be by poison. With what impudence can any accuse me of such wickedness, who never saw any poison, nor know I any thing about the preparation of it? Can any say they ever saw me have any of it? Let them tell me where I bought it, or who procured it me. And though I had it, how could I use it, seeing I never came near the King's person, his table nor palace? It is well known, that since my last marriage with this unfortunate gentleman, I have lived in the country, at a great distance from the court; what opportunity could I ever have then to poison the King? You may see by those circumstances, which give great light in such matters, that I am entirely innocent of those crimes I am charged with. It is the office of you judges to protect injured innocence; but if the malice and power of my enemies be such, that whether innocent or guilty I must needs be condemned, I shall die cheerfully, having the testimony of a good conscience; and assure yourselves that you shall certainly find it more easy to take away my life, than to blast my reputation, or to fix any real blot upon my memory. This is my last desire of you, that I may be the sole object of your severity, and that those other innocent persons may not share in my misfortunes. Seeing my chief crime is, that I am descended of the family of Douglas, there is no reason that they should be involved in my ruin; for my husband, son, and cousin, are neither of that name nor family. I shall end my life with more comfort if you absolve them, for the more of us that suffer by your unjust sentence, the greater will be your guilt, and the more terrible your condemnation when you shall be tried at the great day by God, who is the impartial Judge of all flesh, who shall then make you suffer for those torments to which we are unjustly condemned.'

"This admirable speech, which was spoken with such boldness and manly courage, astonished the judges extremely; and when they had reasoned upon what she had alleged in her own defence, they determined, before they gave sentence, to send two of their number to the King, and to represent to him, 'that, though the witnesses had proved the articles of impeachment, and that, according to the law of the land, upon this evidence she deserved death, yet, upon a serious consideration of the whole circumstances of the matter, they could not perceive the least probability of her guilt; they were afraid lest the rigour of the law in this case should prove the height of injustice,—therefore they wished rather that equity and mercy should take place, it being more safe to absolve a criminal, than to condemn an innocent person; that time alone could discover the truth of the matter, by making known the character of those witnesses who had sworn against her, whether they were men of honesty, or had been bribed to accuse her; that nothing was so advisable as to delay the whole affair for some days, which could be no danger to the King, seeing those persons were not to have their liberty; but whenever they could perceive any presumptions of their guilt, they should not escape justice. As for themselves, they were tied up to the formalities and letter of the law,—it belonged only to his Majesty to temper and moderate the severity of it by his clemency; upon which account they addressed themselves to him, seeing in such cases wherein the life, honour, and estates of persons of distinction are concerned, all possible caution is necessary.' The King, who was naturally merciful enough, had yielded to this reasonable request, if Lion, who had contrived that hellish plot, and was afraid, if they had escaped, his wickedness would be discovered, had not prevailed with the King to give this answer to the judges, 'that the exercise of justice was a considerable part of the royal dignity, which he had entrusted them with when he made them judges; that it belonged to their office to preserve the innocent, and punish the guilty; that the book called Regiam Majestatem, contained all the forms and rules which ought to determine them in such cases; wherefore he gave them full power to proceed in that business according to justice, and the laws of the land; and said, he knew of nothing that could hinder them from doing their duty like men of honour.' Upon receiving that answer, those that were sent to wait upon the King, returned to the Exchequer, where the Court of Justice then sat, and reported to the rest of the judges, what the King had given them in charge; upon which the judges gave sentence against that lady, which was, that she was to be led out to the place of execution, and there to be burnt alive till she was dead.

" A little time after the sentence, she was delivered into the hands of the executioner, to be led out to suffer. The constancy and courage of this heroine are almost incredible, which astonished all the spectators. She heard the sentence pronounced against her without the least sign of concern; neither did she cry, groan, or shed a tear, though that kind of death is most frightful to human nature. When she was brought out to suffer, the people who looked on could not conceal their grief and compassion; some of them who were acquainted with her, and knew her innocence, designed to rescue her; but the presence of the King and his ministers restrained them. She seemed to be the only unconcerned person there; and her beauty and charms never appeared with greater advantage than when she was led to the flames; and her soul being fortified with support from heaven, and the sense of her own innocence, she outbraved death, and her courage was equal in the fire, to what it was before he, judges. She suffered those torments without the least noise only she prayed devoutly for divine assistance to support her under her sufferings. Thus died this famous lady with a courage not inferior to that of any of the heroes of antiquity.

"The day following, her disconsolate husband, designing to make his escape from the castle of Edinburgh, was let down over the walls by a cord, which happening to be too short, he fell upon the rocks, where he was dashed to pieces. The King was very sad upon hearing of that lamentable accident, and immediately ordered that Lion, the old priest, should have his liberty, because his great age made him incapable of any such design. As for the young Lord Glammis, though his childhood was sufficient proof of his innocency, yet he was kept still in prison, from whence he was not released till after the King's death.

"William Lion, after this virtuous and incomparable lady had fallen a victim to his fury, whenever he began to think coolly upon the wickedness he had done, was so filled with horror, that he was not able to endure the lashes of his awakened conscience. He lamented, when it was too late, that his malice had occasioned the loss both of the lives and fortunes of those who were his near relations; so that having confidence in the King's mercy, he confessed the whole matter secretly to him. The King, abhorring such frightful wickedness, banished him from the court, and designed his punishment should be answerable to his guilt; but affairs of greater concern, which happened immediately after, made the King forget that matter."

Mr. Pitcairn gives a very full account of the case of Lady Jane Douglas, together with an interesting collection of illustrative papers upon it in his Criminal Trials; and he remarks, among other things, respecting it, "There is one circumstance which strikes me as affording a very extraordinary feature in these proceedings. The truly amiable Magdalene Queen of Scotland, who had only arrived from France on May 19, died on July 7, 1537; which plunged the King and the nation into the deepest sorrow. Never did a Queen-consort commence her reign under happier auspices, and with so entire a love of all her subjects. James V. had to all appearance abandoned himself to grief for her loss, and had retired from the pleasures of the Court, and from all his usual sports and employments, when suddenly, 'in the very crisis of domestic and national affliction,' these rigorous proceedings were adopted and perpetrated, with feelings of private revenge and hatred altogether abhorrent to human nature. Had such a course been previously determined upon by the advisers of the Crown, certainly the time was the worst that could possibly have been chosen, for even had this excellent Queen survived, Lady Glammis must either have been put to death by burning at the stake during the midst of the festivities which followed her marriage and public reception, or at the very moment of the celebration of her funeral obsequies! The whole complexion of this shocking tragedy bears such savage traces of a furious and unmanly revenge against a noble and unprotected female, who was the only individual of her family on whom they could lay their hands, that it can hardly be compared with any other event, either in ancient or modern history."

THE FROLICS OF JAMES V.

A BATTERY immediately within the present chief entrance of Stirling Castle, and called the over or upper port battery commands in all its amplitude and gorgeousness the surpassingly brilliant panorama from Benlomond, Benvenue, Benledi, and Benvoirlich, through the Trosachs, the vales of the Forth, the Teith, and the Allan, to the plains of Lennox and the Lothians. The ground immediately overhung by the battery, and overlooking the nearest sweep of the Forth, is not precipitous, but breaks gradually down in the little rocky range of the Gowan hills, stretching away to their termination in Hurly-Haaky near the bridge. On the brow of the nearest eminence are remains of a low rampart, extending in a line parallel to the battery,—the vestige of works constructed against the castle, in 1746, by Prince Charles Edward. Between this rampart and the castle-walls a road or narrow path comes up the acclivitous hill from the village of Raploch, and passes on to a point where formerly there was a large gateway through the exterior wall, conducting to an esplanade on which the magazines are now situated, and, across it, to a low-browed archway, called 'the Laird of Ballangeich's entry,' and alleged to have once been the main entrance to the castle. This wild path, thus anciently terminating at a point of such prime importance, is called the Ballangeich road, from two words which signify 'the windy pass;' and, having furnished James V. with his well known fictitious designation of the Guidman of Ballangeich, figures as to name, at least, in many curious and oft-told anecdotes of that monarch's incognito rovings through his kingdom.

Two comic songs, 'The Gaberlunzie Man,' and 'We'll gang nae mair a roving,' are said to have been founded on the success of the Guidman of Ballangeich's licentious adventures when travelling in the disguise of a beggar. The following anecdotes respecting him are given by Sir Walter Scott:—" Another adventure, which had nearly cost James his life, is said to have taken place at the village of Cramond, near Edinburgh, where he had rendered his addresses acceptable to a pretty girl of the lower rank. Four or five persons —whether relations or lovers of his mistress is uncertain— beset the disguised monarch as he returned from his rendezvous. Naturally gallant, and an admirable master of his weapon, the King took post on the high and narrow bridge over the Almond river, and defended himself bravely with his sword. A peasant, who was thrashing in a neighbouring barn, came out upon the noise, and, whether moved by compassion or by natural gallantry, took the weaker side, and laid about with his flail so effectually as to disperse the assailants, well threshed, even according to the letter. He then conducted the King into his barn, where his guest requested a bason and towel to remove the stains of the broil. This being procured with difficulty, James employed himself in learning what was the summit of his deliverer's earthly wishes, and found that they were bounded by the desire of possessing, in property, the farm of Braehead, upon which he laboured as a bondsman. The lands chanced to belong to the Crown; and James directed him to come to the palace of Holyrood and enquire for the Guidman (*i. e.* farmer) of Ballangeich, a name by which he was known in his excursions, and which, answered to Il Bondocani of Haroun Alraschid. He presented himself accordingly, and found, with due astonishment, that he had saved his monarch's life, and that he was to be gratified with a crown-charter of the lands of Braehead, under the service of presenting an ewer, bason, and towel, for the King to wash his hands, when he shall happen to pass the Bridge of Cramond. In 1822, when George IV. came to Scotland, the descendant of this John Howison of Braehead, who still possesses the estate which was given to his ancestor, appeared at a solemn festival, and offered his Majesty water from a silver ewer.

" Another of James's frolics is thus narrated by Mr. Campbell, from the Statistical Account. 'Being once benighted when out a-hunting, and separated from his attendants, he happened to enter a cottage in the midst of a moor, at the foot of the Ochil hills, near Alloa, where, unknown, he was kindly received. In order to regale their unexpected guest, the gude-man (*i. e.* landlord, farmer) desired the gude-wife to fetch the hen that roosted nearest the cock, which is always the plumpest, for the stranger's supper. The King highly pleased with his night's lodgings and hospitable entertainment, told mine host, at parting, that he should be glad to return his civility, and requested that the first time he came to Stirling he would call at the castle, and enquire for the gude-man of Ballangeich. Donaldson, the landlord, did not fail to call on the gude-man of Ballangeich, when his astonishment at finding that the King had been his guest afforded no small amusement to the merry monarch and his courtiers; and, to carry on the pleasantry, he was thenceforth designated by James with the title of King of the Moors, which name and designation have descended from father to son ever since, and they have continued in possession of the identical spot, the property of Mr. Erskine of Mar, till very lately, when this gentleman, with reluctance, turned out the descendant and representative of the King of the Moors, on account of his Majesty's invincible indolence, and great dislike to reform or innovation of any kind, although, from the spirited example of his neighbour tenants on the same estate, he is convinced similar exertion would promote his advantage.'"

The following anecdote is extracted from the genealogical work of Buchanan of Auchmar, upon Scottish surnames:— " This John Buchanan of Auchmar and Arnpryor was afterwards termed King of Kippen, upon the following account. King James V., a very social debonair prince, residing at Stirling, in Buchanan of Arnpryor's time, carriers were very frequently passing along the common road, being near Arnpryor's house, with necessaries for the use of the King's family, and he having some extraordinary occasion, ordered one of these carriers to leave his load at his house, and he would pay him for it; which the carrier refused to do, telling him he was the King's carrier, and his load for his Majesty's use; to which Arnpryor seemed to have small regard, compelling the carrier, in the end, to leave his load; telling him if King James was King of Scotland, he was King of Kippen, so that it was reasonable he should share with his neighbour King in some of these loads, so frequently carried that road. The carrier representing this usage, and telling the story, as Arnpryor spoke it, to some of the King's servants, it came at length to his Majesty's ears, who, shortly thereafter, with a few attendants, came to visit his neighbour King, who was in the meantime at dinner. King James having sent a servant to demand access, was denied the same by a tall fellow with a battle-axe, who stood porter at the gate, telling there could be no access till dinner was over. This answer not satisfying the King, he sent to demand access a second time; upon which he was desired by the porter to desist, otherwise he would find cause to repent his rudeness. His Majesty finding this method would not do, desired the porter to tell his master that the good-man of Ballangeich desired to speak with the King of Kippen. The porter telling Arnpryor so much, he, in all humble manner, came and received the King, and having entertained him with much sumptuousness and jollity, became so agreeable to King James, that he allowed him to take so much of any provision he found carrying that road as he had occasion for; and, seeing he made the first visit, desired Arnpryor in a few days to return him a second at Stirling, which he performed, and continued in very much favour with the King, always thereafter being termed King of Kippen while he lived." The last King of Kippen, we may add, was hanged in 1746, at Carlisle, for fighting in the rebel army of Prince Charles Edward.

James's matrimonial campaign, though necessarily a very serious affair for both himself and the nation, was conducted with sufficient eccentricity to give it some of the characters of a frolic; and, even when related in the most solemn style of historiography, bears such strong marks of the outré monarch's peculiar spirit as unavoidably to provoke a smile. The following lachrymose account of the active or successful part of it, after James had declined matrimonial offers from the courts of England, Austria, and Denmark, is given in his Life in the Miscellanea Scotica:—" King James resolved at last to match with some of the Royal family of France, from whence he could expect the surest assistance when his affairs wanted it. For this end he sent his ambassadors to France, viz. James, Earl of Murray, his bastard brother, William Stuart, Bishop of Aberdeen, John Erskine, and Robert Reists, to negotiate a marriage betwixt him and the Lady Magdalen of France. The French King received them courteously, but was greatly at a loss what to do in that matter, seeing the design of the marriage was to tie the two kingdoms together by a more close alliance. He was afraid that both their enemies would make use of that match as a handle to disunite them; because King James could not promise himself any children by his daughter, who was a sickly lady, so in the end would rather prove the occasion of indifference betwixt them. Francis therefore proposed to the ambassadors a match betwixt their master and the Lady Mary of Bourbon, the daughter of Charles, Duke of Vendosme. The ambassadors refused to treat about it without instructions from King James; so desired time to acquaint him with the proposal, and to know his pleasure. This account of affairs made the King very melancholy. Sometimes he doubted lest some selfish views in the Earl of Murray, and the Bishop of Aberdeen, might incline them to embarrass that match; at another time, the confidence he had in John Erskine and Robert Reists made him easy, because he was sure they would not betray the trust reposed in them, but would use all possible application towards the accomplishing the desired match. Notwithstanding, to prevent delays, and considering that the great reason why the matches of most princes are so unhappy, is, because they never see their queens before marriage, he determined to go over to France, and to court in person. But the great heats at that time obliged him to defer his voyage till they were a little abated. But, after a while, being uneasy with impatience because his ambassadors were not like to conclude the marriage with that despatch he wished for, notwithstanding the inconveniences of the season, he resolved to sail for France; and having given orders that a fleet should be ready, he went aboard at Leith, together with the great ministers of his court, without owning whither he was bound. Many thought he designed to go into England to visit his uncle, and now repented, that the former year he refused an interview with that King. They were scarcely got out of the haven, when a storm began to arise, and the wind turned contrary: upon this the pilot asked the King which way they should steer their course? He answered, 'Whither you please except to England.' This convinced them all that the King designed for France, which was impracticable at that time, because of the contrary winds; which, when the King understood, he chose rather to sail round the coasts of his kingdom, and try if they could have better passage by St. George's Channel, than to put in again at Leith. Neither did that succeed, for still the storm increased, which made those who attended him bethink that it was safest to return home, and not expose their King's and their own life to visible danger; and that it was fool-hardiness to struggle with the unrelenting winds and waves; that there was no need for such haste; and that they might lie in some harbour till the storm was over, without any prejudice to the King's affairs. So whilst the King was asleep, they tacked about and sailed for the coasts of Scotland. When the King awakened, he was in a great rage, and never pardoned those who advised the sailing back to Scotland. When the bad weather was over the nobility who were with the King, in complaisance to his Majesty, desired him to think of sailing with the first fair wind, which he did; and setting sail from Scotland on the first day of September, ——, he landed at Dieppe ten days after, and went incognito to Vendosme, to see the Lady Mary of Vendosme,—where he was satisfied that she was an excellent and well accomplished princess, and that fame had not been too favourable to her. But seeing he had had the choice of three princesses, all daughters of kings, he thought he could not in honour marry one of a lower degree. So he left Vendosme, and had still the disposing of his own heart, notwithstanding the charms of that fair lady, and went straight for Paris to meet with the French King, whose coming was a surprisal to the court. The King, who knew nothing of it till about two hours before he saw him, immediately went to meet him and welcome him to Paris, being accompanied with all the nobility then at court, and received him with all the grandeur and honour that King James could desire. He had not been long at Paris before the Lady Magdalen owned that she loved him. He desired the King her father to agree to the match, and said, ' He hoped that the change of air, and more years, would confirm her in perfect health, and doubted not but he should have children by her.' The French King consented to the match, and told him, there was nothing that he could deny the King of Scotland. So the marriage was solemnized with all the pomp and ceremony imaginable; and King James and his Queen set out for Scotland, having with them a great number of French ships. When they arrived in Scotland, they were received with the universal joy of their subjects; but as in human life our gladness is still allayed with sorrow, so this joy was short lived, and was interrupted by the great grief occasioned by the death of the young queen, who lived only six months after her landing in Scotland; for the sea air, and the fatigue of the voyage, had occasioned her sickness. There was such an universal and real grief over all the kingdom, upon the news of her death, that to testify the sense the court, and other persons of note, had of the great loss, they went into mourning, which was the first time that ever that custom was used in Scotland. After the funeral ceremonies were over, King James was more desirous than ever of children, and was unwilling to live any time a widower. He cast his eyes upon the Lady Mary of Lorrain, sister to Francis, Duke of Guise, a famed general, and the widow of the Duke of Longueville; for the charming virtues of that lady had made a mighty impression upon his heart during his stay in France."

A poetical frolic, the well-known, old humorous ballad, called 'The Wife of Auchtermuchty,' has been very generally ascribed to James V.; and though certainly not written by him, yet on account of popular opinion regarding it as an index or expression of his taste and genius, two or three stanzas of it may here be quoted:—

> "In Auchtermuchty dwelt a man,
>   An husband, as I heard it tauld,
> Quha weil could tipple out a can,
>   And nowther luvit hungir nor cauld;
> Till anes it fell upon a day,
>   He zokit his plewch upon the plain;
> But schort the storm wald let him stay,
>   Sair blew the day with wind and rain.
>
> He lowsd the plewch at the land's end,
>   And draife his owsen hame at ene;
> Quhen he came in he blinkit ben,
>   And saw his wyfe baith dry and clene,
> Set beikand by a fyre full bauld,
>   Suppand fat sowp, as I heard say:
> The man being weary, wet and cauld,
>   Betwein thir twa it was nae play.
>
> Quod he, 'Quhair is my horses corn?
>   My owsen has nae hay nor strae;
> Dame, ye maun to the plewch the morn,
>   I sall be hussy gif I may.
> This seid-time it proves cauld and bad,
>   And ze sit warm, nae troubles se;
> The morn ze sall gae with the lad,
>   And syne zeil ken what drinkers drie.

'Gudeman,' quod scho, 'content am I,
  To tak the plewch my day about,
Sae ye rule weil the kaves and ky,
  And all the house baith in and out.
And now sen ze haif made the law,
  Then gyde all richt and do not break;
They sicker raid that neir did faw,
  Therefore let naething be neglect.'"

The bargain proved, as might be anticipated, a most unfortunate one for the gudeman, whose successive disasters in 'hussyskep' brought him 'meikle schame,' fairly sickened him of his new employments before night-fall, and forced him upon the sound reflection and wise resolution with which the ballad closes :—

" Quod he, 'When I forsuke my plewch,
  I trow I but forsuke my skill!
Then I will to my plewch again,
  For I and this house will nevir do weil.'"

THE DEMOLITION OF THE MONASTERIES.

John Knox returned to Scotland in the beginning of May, 1559. The whole country was in commotion in consequence of the extensive progress of Reformation principles among the people, and of stern and furious opposition to them by the court. The Protestants were arming in self-defence; and the Queen-Regent, Mary of Guise, was framing vigorous measures for putting down what she called rebellion. The Reformation preachers had greatly multiplied, and went boldly about their work, and were protected by some of the barons and nobles, and had just disobeyed a general citation to appear before the Queen-Regent at Stirling, and on the 10th or May were denounced by her as rebels. Some of the most populous towns had become almost saturated with Protestantism; the greater part of Perthshire, Fifeshire, and Forfarshire were burning with resentment against the Popish priests and the government; and the city of Perth, besides being of itself a warm partisan of the Reformation, had recently been made the rendezvous of a great concourse of the Protestant leaders,—who felt themselves so hotly pursued by both the prelatic and the civil powers that they must now either make an unconditional and ruinous submission to the Queen-Regent, or draw the sword and demand protection and security for their religion, their liberty, and their lives.

On the 11th of May, Knox preached in the old church, or church of St. John, in Perth. " That spacious building, not shorn as now of its fair proportions, nor cut down into separate apartments, but forming one simple and majestic temple, was, long ere the speaker appeared, thronged in every part, save in those divisions of the aisles which were set apart for the altars and shrines of the several saints, to whose service the wealth of not a few substantial burghers and powerful barons had at various times been dedicated. Within the little sanctuaries many a churchman now stood, looking with no benignant eye on the crowds who occupied the steps, or pressed irreverently against the balustrades, which they until now were wont to approach with bended knee. Within the pale of the altar a number of the priests stood in a line in front, clothed in their gorgeous vestments, as if to overawe the multitude by the splendour with which the altar and its attendants were adorned; but they looked in vain for the homage of the once subservient crowd." Though the Protestant preachers had for some time occupied the pulpit when they pleased, they had never yet sought to dispossess the priests or to suppress the symbols and ceremonies of the Roman Catholic worship, but contented themselves with merely preaching a sermon. Knox seemed at first confused and he-

Battle History of Scotland.—*Page* 80.

sitating, and spake in a somewhat feeble tone; but as he moved out of the preliminaries of his subject, and began to descant on the idolatries and oppressions of Popery, he became collected and bold, and rose into animation and vehemence. "With the energy of the preacher, the attention of the assembly awoke; every eye was fixed upon him; every word seemed to find its way to their bosoms, calling up the most marked expressions of enthusiasm and approbation from the great mass of the crowd, and of stern defiance among the priests, whom the fervour of his address brought by degrees out of the lateral recesses, and who were now seen peering from among the protecting balustrades. From contrasting the present with the past state of the church, he proceeded to hurl against her the sublime denunciations of the Old Testament prophets against Babylon, confirming them with the anathemas against her spiritual antitype from the Revelation; and as he quoted the passage in which an angel is represented as casting down a great millstone, and pronouncing, 'Thus with violence shall Babylon be thrown down,' the pulpit seemed to yield with the almost frantic energy by which he was agitated. Had he ceased at that moment, the enthusiastic feelings of the auditory were so wound up, that nothing could have withheld them from executing literally on the monuments around them the predictions of the prophets. But gradually subsiding from this enthusiastic tone, he addressed himself to his hearers, and closed by exhorting them to put away the unclean thing from among them. So rapt were the audience, that Knox withdrew from the church with the attendant noblemen almost unobserved; and for some time afterwards the people stood as if expecting the preacher again to appear amongst them."

While the congregation was still in suspense, undetermined whether to remain awhile or to disperse, the priests commenced preparations to celebrate mass. A magnificent tabernacle was opened up; an ebony crucifix, with an ex-

quisitely carved figure of our Saviour, was disclosed; the
tapers were lit; several priests, in gorgeous canonical vestments, knelt around the altar; the chaunt of the mass-sayers
began, and was responded to by voices in the opposite aisle;
a curtain behind the crucifix slowly rose, and revealed a picture of the martyrdom of St. Bartholomew; and, at the usual
climax in the idolatrous ceremony, the chief officiating priest
elevated the host, or large consecrated wafer, to be worshipped by the people. A young man in the crowd, at that instant, exclaimed to the persons near him, "This is intolerable! Shall we stand by and see that practised which God
in his word has plainly condemned as idolatry?" A priest
heard him, exclaimed, "Blasphemer!" and gave him a severe
blow. The young man took up a stone, and cast it at the
priest, but, missing his mark, hit the tabernacle, and broke
down an image. This served as a signal for a general onset.
The multitude rushed toward the altar, beat the priests, tore
off their vestments, broke down all the paraphernalia of their
worship, smashed the tabernacle, destroyed images, pictures,
and decorations, and converted the whole Romish furniture of
the church into havoc and rubbish. The destruction was so
rapid that not one tenth of the city's population knew of it
till it was finished,—and so complete and sweeping that little
of the church was left except the bare walls.

The news speedily got abroad, and threw the whole city
into violent agitation. Before an hour elapsed a vast concourse assembled to follow up the deeds of the destroyers,—
"not of the gentlemen," says Knox, "neither of them that
were earnest professors, but of the rascal multitude." They
ran from St. John's to the Greyfriars or Franciscan monastery, and thence to the Charterhouse or Carthusian establishment, to the Blackfriars, to the Whitefriars, and to several
nunneries and chapels; and they hurled altars, crucifixes, and
images to ruin, demolished statuary and architectural ornaments, plundered repositories, made enormous spoil of trea

DEMOLITION OF THE MONASTERIES.

sures and provisions, and laid the walls of several of the most ornate and sumptuous structures nearly level with the ground,—yet withal displayed a surprising degree of both zeal against idolatry and regard for the rights of some of its principal abettors. "The first invasion at the Greyfriars," says Knox, "was upon the idolatry; and thereafter the common people began to seek some spoil. And in very deed the Greyfriars was a place so well provided, that unless honest men had seen the same, we would have feared to report what provisions they had; their sheets, blankets, beds, and coverlets were such, that no Earl in Scotland had the better; their napery was fine; they were but eight persons in convent, and yet had eight puncheons of salt beef,—consider the time of the year, the 11th of May,—wine, beer, and ale, besides store of victuals effeiring (corresponding) thereto. The like abundance was not in the Blackfriars; and yet there was more than became men professing poverty. The spoil was permitted to the poor; for so had the preachers before threatened all men, that for covetousness' sake none should put their hand to such a reformation, that no honest man was enriched thereby the value of a groat. Their conscience so moved them, that they suffered these hypocrites to take away what they could of that which was in their places. The prior of Charterhouse was permitted to take with him even so much gold and silver as he was able to carry. So were men's consciences before beaten with the word, that they had no respect to their own particular profit, but only to abolish idolatry, the places and monuments thereof; in which they were so busy and so laborious, that within two days these three great places, monuments of idolatry, to wit, the Black and Grey friars, and the Charterhouse monks, a building of a wondrous cost and greatness, was so destroyed, that the walls only did remain of all these great edifications."

Some inhabitants of Cupar-Fife were among the Perth mob, and performed an active part in their work of destruction; and on their return to their own town, they boastfully narrated their exploits, and infected their fellow-townsmen with their spirit,—insomuch that a multitude speedily assembled, and went right heartily to work in spoiling and demolishing the ecclesiastical edifices of the town, comprising the parish church, a Dominican convent, and a nunnery of St. Catherine of Sienna. The mob plundered the moveable property, carried away the very stones and timber, and left little of the edifices standing except the steeple of the parish church. The Romish parochial clergyman was so horrified and maddened at the occurrence, that he committed suicide.

When the Queen-Regent heard of the tumult at Perth, she foamed with fury, and vowed awful things against the Protestants, and declared that she would utterly destroy Perth, man, woman, and child, and consume the city with fire, and afterwards salt it in sign of a perpetual desolation. She had already her French mercenaries under arms at Stirling, and she made a sudden levy of whatever Scotish forces could be gathered to her standard, and marched at the head of all her available troops toward Perth. She had, by wily and disingenuous promises, induced the Protestant leaders to dismiss their armed followers; and she hoped to surprise the town before any new or effective force could be collected to oppose her. But though her army were 7,000 strong, and led by the experienced French general, D'Oysel, and powerfully aided by her unprincipled tampering with truth and honourable dealing, they found themselves confronted by such a large and lofty-spirited host, whom the bruit of the Queen's proceedings, and zeal for their religion and liberties had poured suddenly down from all quarters upon the town, that they dared not attempt their meditated enterprise, and could only stand embodied as a practical argument for a peaceful negotiation. Both armies having been disbanded by mutual stipulation, Mary peacefully entered the town on the 29th of May; yet she no sooner found herself in quiet possession, and knew the Protestant forces to be broken up and at a distance, than she flung her agreement by treaty to the winds, introduced French troops to the town, dismissed the magistracy, and restored the Popish rites and the priestly domination. When she departed, the inhabitants again became tumultuously insurgent, and invoked the Protestant leaders to send soldiers to their aid. Lords Argyle and Ruthven and others marched in consequence to the town, and prepared regularly to invest it; they were plied, through the mediation of Lords Huntly and Erskine, with proposals from the Queen-Regent designed to divert them from their purpose; but they could no longer believe her word, or regard her terms in any other light than that of faithless artifice; and they stoutly began and conducted the siege, and, against the 26th of June, 1559, compelled the garrison to capitulate.

After the Protestant leaders—or, as they were now called, the Lords of the Congregation—had been deceived by the Queen-Regent, and had lost all hope of seeing the Reformation sanctioned and promoted by either the Crown or the Hierarchy, or about the beginning of June, they resolved to adopt overt measures of their own for abolishing the popish worship, removing all the symbols of its idolatry, and fully setting up the reformed religion in all places where their friends were predominant or over which their influence might be sufficiently powerful. " This step," remarks Dr. M'Crie, " is justified in part by the feudal ideas respecting the jurisdiction of the nobility, which at that time prevailed in Scotland. The urgent and extreme necessity of the case, however, forms its best vindication. A great part of the nation loudly demanded such a reformation; and had not regular measures been adopted for its introduction, the popular indignation would have effected the work in a more exceptionable way." The very zeal of the Protestant leaders, their assumption of extreme power, the comparative impetuosity of their proceedings, and even in fact the part which the mobs acted in driving the external reformation to excess, in knocking down the buildings, and in compelling the priests to flee, were all abundantly provoked by the crying wickedness which the Romish Church in Scotland had long been practising. The Reformers and the monastery-demolishers might well say, as one of their "gude and godly ballates" represents them as doing:—

> " Had not yourself began the weiris,
>   Your stepillis had been standand yit;
>   It was the flattering of your friers
>   That ever gart Sanct Francis flit.
>   Ye grew sa superstitious
>   In wickednesse,
>   It gart us grow malicious
>   Contrair your messe."

The campaign began at the "East Neuk o' Fife." Knox, at the head of a strong body of followers, entered the collegiate church of Crail,—which had attached to it a provost, a sacrist, ten prebendaries, and some singing boys; and, from the pulpit, he delivered such a blazing oration as instantly fired his hearers with a similar fury to that of the mob at Perth. They rose in a mass, and tumultuously smashed to pieces the altars, the images, the decorations, and whatever else pertained to the Romish worship, but were considerate enough not to destroy the building. Next day, the same mob, greatly augmented in numbers and increased in excitement, proceeded to Anstruther, and there made havoc of everything which was or seemed to be popish. The major part of them went next to Pittenweem, and there destroyed a large Augustinian priory belonging to the abbey of St. Andrews;—while a detachment proceeded to St. Monance, and gutted the parish church of that place of every article which it contained. The prior of Pittenweem had made himself infamous by assisting at the trial and condemnation of the Protestant martyrs who had been burnt at St. Andrews; and, aware that little mercy might be expected for his priory, he tried to defend it in fortress-fashion against the assailants; but he found himself unable to resist, and was obliged to abandon it, with all its contents, to their consuming rage.

Knox and his followers now moved toward St. Andrews. Archbishop Hamilton, who was then at Falkland with the Queen-Regent, either learning or suspecting their intention, set out for St. Andrews at the head of one hundred armed men from the royal troops; and sent word thence to Knox that he would order the soldiers to shoot him if he came to the cathedral. But the Archbishop found the citizens much disaffected, and got exaggerated accounts of the numbers who followed Knox; and he speedily went back, dispirited and mortified, to Falkland. When Knox and his company came within view of the city, at a place about two miles distant from it, they raised a loud shout of exultation and defiance; yet they apprehended serious resistance, and were not without fear of bloodshed, and felt a strong necessity to proceed with caution. The leaders consulted as to what should be done; and, as their retinue was slender, and many of the inhabitants of the city were supposed to be inimical to them, and the Queen-Regent lay only twenty miles distant with a considerable army, they agreed that Knox should not at that time attempt to preach in St. Andrews, and earnestly urged him to concur with them in opinion. Knox, however, was of a different mind, and felt instigated to action by the very difficulties which surrounded them, and resolutely said, " As for the fear of danger that may come to me, let no man be solicitous; for my life is in the custody of Him whose glory I seek. I desire the hand nor weapon of no man to defend me. I only crave audience; which, if it be denied here unto me at this time, I must seek where I may have it." This intrepid reply silenced all remonstrance, and induced the most hesitating to proceed.

Knox entered St. Andrews on Sabbath, the 10th of June, and went directly to the cathedral, and preached to a numerous assembly, including many of the clergy, without experiencing the slightest interruption. He discoursed on our Lord's ejecting the profane traffickers from the temple at Jerusalem, and took occasion to expose the enormous corruptions of the Romish Church, and to point out what was incumbent on Christians, in their different spheres, for removing them. On the three following days he preached in the same place; and so mightily did he move his audience that, not only his immediate followers and the common people of the city, but the provost, the bailies, and the respectable inhabitants, rose up zealously and indignantly to tear the cathedral and the monasteries to pieces. "Down with the nests," cried Knox, "and the rooks will fly away!" The magnificent cathedral, the labour of ages, with its stately towers and shining copper roof, fell in one day before the rage of some thousands of assailants, and was completely gutted and destroyed. Tennant, the author of 'Anster Fair,' in a clever though less pleasing and less successful poem, entitled 'Papistry storm'd,' has sung in quaintest dialect, and with all the facetious strength, fluency, and vivacity which he attributes to the vernacular idiom of Scotland:

> "The steir, strabush, and strife,
>   Whan, bickerin' frae the touns o' Fife,
> Great bangs of bodies, thick and rife,
>   Gaed to Sanct Androis town,
> And, wi' John Calvin i' their heads,
> And hammers i' their hands and spades,
> Enraged at idols, mass, and beads,
>   Dang the Cathedral down."

While the main body were destroying the cathedral, other

parties assailed and ruined the noble Augustinian priory, the Dominican monastery, the Franciscan monastery, the parish churches and chapels of the city, and the establishment in the vicinity called the provostry of Kirkheugh. The destroyers everywhere displayed astonishing energy and courage; they prosecuted their hard toil through the whole day, and through a great part of the night; they shrunk not from the danger of vast falling masses of masonry, and of the reeling and tumbling of huge loosened stones; and they sought not a breathing time, nor paused to reflect or rest, till they made the city look almost as ruinous and desolate as if it had been overthrown by an earthquake.

The Queen-Regent, on getting intelligence of the comparative fewness of Knox's followers, hastily summoned her troops at Falkland, and made an attempt to come on the Protestants at St. Andrews by surprise. But many Protestants in Forfarshire so opportunely received notice of the critical situation of their brethren, and came with such celerity and good will to their assistance, that the combined forces were able to face the royal army at Cupar Moor; and there the Queen-Regent, afraid to risk a battle, consented to a truce, and engaged to remove her French troops from Fife. The Protestant leaders now proceeded to Perth; and on their way thither sanctioned or promoted the destruction of the abbey of Lindores, the abbey of Balmerino, and every other edifice, large or small, which seemed a prop of the popish worship.

After they were a few days in possession of Perth, they found that the Queen-Regent still persisted in hostility and perfidiousness, and learned that she intended to fortify the passage of the Forth at Stirling, and to cut off all communication between them and the Protestants in the south; and they then determined to act more vigorously against Romanism than ever, and to make a rapid and resolute march of attack upon Stirling. Meanwhile, a mob, acting without

DEMOLITION OF THE MONASTERIES.

their sanction, and consisting principally of Perth-men and Dundee-men, some of whom had private purposes of pillage or revenge to gratify, went tumultuously to Scone, and sacked, burnt, and totally destroyed its ancient and splendid abbey, amidst a jubilation of shouts and yells. The party who set out for Stirling was led by the Earl of Argyle, and the Prior of St. Andrews, afterwards the famous Earl of Moray, and consisted principally of about 300 citizens of Perth; and so galled had these men been by the combined tyranny of priests and Frenchmen, and so determined were they to succeed in their enterprise or perish in the attempt, that, to indicate their zeal and resolution, they wore ropes about their necks to be hung up with them in ignominious death if they should desert their colours or be vanquished. A picture of their march is still preserved in Perth, and the circumstance of their substituting ropes for neckerchiefs or ribands is the subject of the frequent popular allusion to " St. Johnstone tippets." When they approached Stirling, the garrison evacuated the castle, and the Queen-Regent retired with her forces toward Dunbar; so that, by this bold stroke on the part of a small band of resolute men, the Protestants suddenly became masters of what was then the capital of the kingdom.

The Reformers now in possession of Stirling, and strengthened by great numbers of the towns-people, swept the town of its symbols of idolatry, by destroying the Dominican monastery, and spoiling or gutting the other ecclesiastical edifices; and, in order to economise their time and labour, they arranged themselves into parties or detachments, to scour the adjacent country, and cleanse it from Romish altars and images. One chief party went to Cambuskenneth, and desolated the beautiful and magnificent abbey of that place, whose ruins continue to the present day to form a striking feature in the rich flat landscape of the links of the Forth; and another chief party, headed by the commanders who had led the expedition from Perth, went to Dunblane, and swept away the images of its gorgeous cathedral, then under the episcopate of William Chisholm. "On a beautiful morning towards the end of June, 1559," says Lieutenant-Colonel Murray, "as the people were attending mass in the cathedral, a noise as of armed men was heard within the surrounding court. Presently a band of warriors entered by the western portal, and advanced towards the choir in two lines, the one led by the Earl of Argyle, and the other by the Prior of St. Andrews. The worshippers in the body of the church, rising from their prostrations, retreated into the aisles, while those within the choir, forgetting their devotions, rose up and turned with inquiring eyes towards the intruders, who, halting in their double array, nearly filled the body of the cathedral. Their appearance was every way calculated to excite the curiosity of the spectators. Some of them were completely armed, while the greater part wore the guise of citizens, who seemed to have taken up arms in a moment of excitement or alarm; but whatever diversities in other respects were visible, in one part of their dress, and it was a truly singular one, they were alike—a rope or *halter* was suspended around the neck of each! One of the officials at the altar descending the steps, and advancing towards the balustrade which divided the choir from the main body of the church, said, 'My lord of Argyle, and you my lord Prior, what means this martial array in the house of God, and what the symbols your followers wear? Methinks, if they betoken penance, it were fitter to enter this threshold as suppliants than as conquerors!' 'We come, dean,' replied the Earl, 'to set forward the reformation of religion according to God's word, and to purify this kirk; and, in name of the congregation, warn and charge you, that whatsoever person shall plainly resist these our enterprises, we, by the authority of the Council, will reduce them to their duty.' 'And, moreover,' added the Prior, 'we, with three hundred burgesses of

Perth whom you see here, have banded ourselves together in the kirk of St. John, now purified from idolatry, and bound ourselves by a great oath, that we are willing to part with life, as these symbols around our necks testify, if we turn back from this our holy calling, or desist from this our enterprise until we have purged the land. So, therefore, shall we, with all the force and power which God shall grant unto us, execute just vengeance and punishment upon you; yea, we shall begin that same war which it was commanded the Israelites to execute against the Canaanites, that is, contract of peace shall never be made till ye desist from your open idolatry and cruel persecution of God's children.' 'We are here in the peaceable exercise of our holy religion,' replied the dean; 'if there be persecutors within these walls, they who violate the sanctuary are the men.'—'Peace!' interrupted the Prior, 'we are not here to wrangle, but to see the commands of the Council executed. Say if ye and your brethren are willing to obey, and of your own consent to remove the stumbling-blocks, even these monuments of idolatry?' 'Most reverend father and you, most puissant Earl,' answered the churchman, 'we that are here are but servants or menials, so to speak; whatsoever our will may be, our power reacheth not to the things whereof ye speak. Our beloved bishop is even now with the Queen-Regent, conferring, doubtless, on these weighty matters. To him your request shall be made known, and by his orders we shall abide and act.' The Prior and the Earl conferred a short time together, when the latter again addressed the dean. 'We are even now on an expedition of great weight and moment which brooketh not delay, and but turned aside to warn the lieges of Dumblane of the danger of upholding the errors and enticements of papistry, else we had not departed without leaving this house stripped of these vain trappings. Ye are now in our hands, time passeth, and we cannot trust William Chisholm. He hath bent himself too pliantly to the will of that woman who still teacheth the people of this land to eat things sacrificed unto idols; yet we would not have it said that the people here assembled, and whom ye yet strive to deceive, were not allowed time to repent of their evil ways. This, therefore, will we do:—We will not advance beyond this barrier, nor disturb those who are assembled within it, but with our own hands we will cast down the images and destroy the altars which on every side ye have reared to the gods of your own making; and let the desolation now to be executed be an earnest of that which awaits not only the place where you stand, but every high place and every abominable thing within the land.' The words were scarcely out of the speaker's mouth, when the shrines were entered, the images and pictures displaced, and trampled under foot. 'To the brook with them,' cried the Prior; and the armed multitude, rushing out at the portal by which they had entered, bore the relics to the banks of the Allan, and cast them in. It was the work but of a few moments, and the troops were again marshalled, and on their march to Stirling. The multitude within the choir saw what passed with an air of stupified surprise; and leaving the services of the morning unfinished, gradually withdrew to their respective houses, wondering at the things which they had witnessed."

The Reformers remained three days in Stirling, destroying altars and images all round the adjacent country; and they then proceeded toward Edinburgh, with the intention of making similar havoc in the metropolis. They were everywhere unopposed, and found themselves complete masters of the country; yet they seem generally to have kept free from such excesses as characterised the outbursts in Perth and throughout Fifeshire, and to have acted with similar comparative moderation as at Dunblane, destroying only the symbols of idolatrous worship, and doing little or no injury to the masonry or the carpenters' work of edifices. Linlithgow was the chief place through which they passed; and there they did not attack the palace or its chapel, but contented themselves principally with "purifying" the church of St. Michael.

At Edinburgh, they found that their vocation had been in a main degree anticipated. The magistrates and citizens themselves had swept out all popish paraphernalia from St. Giles' church, Holyrood Abbey, the Greyfriars monastery, the Blackfriars monastery, and various minor convents, oratories, and chapels,—and had expended many of the more costly utensils and decorations first in soberly refitting St. Giles's, and next in replenishing the treasury of the town corporation; and now some mobs who took occasion from the renewed excitement to go more devastatingly to work did not do worse than plunder Holyrood Abbey, and pillage and destroy the houses of the prebendaries of Trinity College Church at the foot of Leith Wynd. Yet Father Alexander Baillie, the author of " True Information of the unhallowed offspring, progress, and impoisoned fruits of our Scottish-Calvinian Gospel and Gospellers," published on the continent in 1628, wrote as follows respecting the Edinburgh demolition, and may be quoted as a fair specimen of the terrific exaggeration and malevolence with which the Romanists of the day spake of the Reformers:—" Truely, among all their deeds and devises, the casting doun of the churches was the most foolish and furious worke, the most shreud and execrable turne that ever Hornok himself culd have done or devised. For out of al doubt that great-grandfather of Calvine, and old enemie of mankind, not only inspired every one of those sacrelegious hellhounds with his flaming spirit of malice and blasphemie, as he did their forefathers Luther and Calvine; bot also was then present as maister of worke, busily beholding his servands and hirelings working his wil and bringing to pass his long desired contentment. They changed the churches (which God himself called his house of prayer) into filthie and abominable houses of sensual men, yea, and of unreasonable beasts: whereas they made stables in Halyrud-hous, sheep-houses of S. Antone, and S. Leonard's chapels, tolbooths of S. Gillis, &c. which this day may be seene, to the great griefe and sorrow of al good Christians, to the shame and confusion of Edinburgh, and to the everlasting damnation of the doers thereof, the sedicious ministers, Knox and his complices."

The zeal of the Reformers against monasteries and the symbols of idolatry spread from Edinburgh into all the Lowlands between the Forth and the Tweed, and from the German Ocean and the Cheviots to the Frith of Clyde and the Mull of Galloway. But a large part of its work, particularly in the rich counties of Berwick and Roxburgh, had been anticipated in the spoliations and burnings of a recent English invasion; and the magnificent abbey structures of Melrose, Kelso, and Jedburgh were already in a similar state to that in which they stand at the present day. In Glasgow, the work of destruction was attempted; though not till nearly twenty years afterward was its cathedral seriously menaced. Some ecclesiastical structures in various parts of Lanarkshire and Renfrewshire, and particularly the greater part of the fine abbey of Paisley, were demolished.

The havoc north of the Tay was very extensive, and in some places mild, in others terribly severe. The following instructions from the Earl of Argyle and Lord James Stewart to the Lairds of Arntilly and Kinraid, respecting the cathedral of Dunkeld, show the style in which they wished the work of "purification" to be conducted: "Traist freindis, after maist harty commendacion, we pray yow faill not to pass incontinent to the kyrk of Dunkeld, and tak doun the haill images thereof, and bring furth to the kyrkzayrd, and burn thaym oppinly. And siclyk cast down the altaris, and purge the kyrk of all kynd of monuments of idolatrye. And this ye faill not to do, as ye will do us singular empleseur; and so committis you to the protection of God.—Faill not, bot ye tak guid heyd that neither the dasks, windocks, nor durris, be ony ways hurt or broken; eyther glassin wark or iron wark." A band of professed Reformers proceeded to Arbroath in Forfarshire, and, aided by a considerable number of the inhabitants of the town and neighbourhood, destroyed its magnificent abbey by fire; and a tradition exists that the leaden roof of the structure, when liquefied by the flames, ran down the streets like a stream of water. The Reformers then marched northward; and, after performing the work of their vocation in various towns and villages on their way, entered Aberdeen, and made an immediate attack on the cathedral. But the magistrates, in anticipation of their visit, had secreted most of its moveable articles of great value; an armed force, under the command of Leslie of Balwhain and the Earl of Huntly, repelled the assailants and protected the edifice; a tumultuous mob afterwards plundered and dilapidated the monasteries of the Carmelites and the Blackfriars; and the magistrates finally agreed, of their own accord, to make a regular demolition of all things in the city connected with Romish idolatry, to sell the valuables of them for the public benefit, and to furnish a quota of forty men for the military service of the Protestant leaders.

Though the great cathedral of Glasgow stood untouched during the whole of the period of demolition, yet Mr. Andrew Melville, the Principal of the College of that city, long importuned the magistrates to allow it to be pulled down, and at last obtained their consent. The reasons urged for its demolition—which read rather curiously at this time of day—were somewhat to the following effect:—That they might build with its materials various little churches in other parts, for the ease of the citizens,—that it was the resort of superstitious people who went there to perform their devotions,—that the church was too large, and the voice of the preacher could with difficulty be heard by the congregation, —and above all, the propriety of removing an idolatrous monument, which was the only one of all the cathedrals in the country left undestroyed, and in a condition to be repaired. A number of quarriers, masons, and other workmen were accordingly engaged by a special day to pull down this beautiful edifice; but while they were assembling, by beat of drum, the craftsmen of Glasgow, who justly regarded the cathedral as the architectural pride of their city, flew to arms, and informed Mr. Melville that if any one dared to pull down a single stone of the building, he should that instant be buried under it. So much incensed were they at the attempt to demolish this ancient building, that if the magistrates had not succeeded in appeasing them, they would have put Melville to death with all his adherents. Upon this a complaint was made by the ministers, and the leaders of the insurrection were cited to appear before King James, who was not yet thirteen years of age; but his Majesty took the craftsmen under his protection, approved of the opposition they had made,—and prohibited the ministers from following the work of demolition farther,—saying, that "too many churches had been already destroyed, and that he would not tolerate more abuses of that kind." And thus was saved the cathedral of Glasgow,—which stands to the present day entire, and constitutes one of the noblest Scotish monuments of the ecclesiastical architecture of the middle ages.

Archbishop Spottiswoode describes the general work of demolition throughout Scotland, in the following terms:— "Thereupon ensued a pitiful vastation of churches and church buildings, throughout all the parts of the realm. For every one made bold to put to their hands, the meaner sort imitating the example of the greater, and those who were in authority. No difference was made, but all the churches either defaced or pulled to the ground. The holy vessels, and whatsoever else men could make gain of, as timber, lead, and bells, were put to sale. The very sepulchres of the dead were not spared; the registers of the church and bibliothecs cast into the fire; in a word, all was ruined; and what had escaped in the time of the first tumult, did now undergo the common calamity. And the preachers animated the people to follow these barbarous proceedings by crying out, that the places where idols had been worshipped ought, by the law of God, to be destroyed, and that the sparing of them was the reserving of things execrable." But this account is manifestly a great exaggeration. Few of the parish churches were destroyed; some of even the monastic churches were not only preserved uninjured, but appropriated to the Protestant worship; much of the spoliation which took place was devoted to the uses of the poor, to the replenishing of corporation funds, to the defraying of the general expenses of the Reformation, or to other valuable and public purposes; and however much actual demolition was recommended or sanctioned by Knox or by other leaders, yet the main part of it all, as well as almost the whole of such spoliation as went to the ends of pillage and of private enrichment, was the work of unprincipled mobs, who took advantage of the commotions of the times, and refused all deference to the rebukes or commands or example of the true reformers. "A great many, not onely of the raskall sorte, but sundry men of name and worldly reputation," said Robert Pont, one of the most respectable and influential preachers of the period, "joyned themselves with the congregation of the reformers, not so much for zeale of religion, as to reape some earthly commoditie, and to be enriched by spoyle of the kirkes and abbey places. And when the preachers told them that such places of idolatrie should be pulled down, they accepted gladly the enterprise; and rudely passing to worke, pulled down all, both idoles and places where they were found: not making difference betweene these places of idolatrie, and many parish kirks, where God's word should have bin preached in many parts where they resorted, as in such tumults and suddainties useth to come to passe,—namelye, among such a nation as we are. Another thing fell out at that time, which may be excused by reason of necessitie; when as the lordes, and some of the nobilitie, principall enterprysers of the Reformation, having to do with the Frenchmen, and many their assisters of our owne nation, enemies to these proceedings, were forced, not onely to ingage their owne landes, and bestowe whatsoever they were able to furnishe of their own patrimonie, for maintenance of men of warre, and other charges, but also to take the lead and belles, with other jewelles and ornaments of kirkes, abbayes, and other places of superstition, to employ the same, and the prises thereof, to resist the enemies, the most parte of the realme beand in their contraire;—this, I say, cannot be altogether blamed."

"It is true," remarks Dr. M'Crie, "that some churches suffered from popular violence during the ferment of the Reformation; and that others were dilapidated, in consequence of their most valuable materials being sold to defray the expenses of the war in which the Protestants were involved. But the former will not be matter of surprise to those who have attended to the conduct of other nations in similar circumstances; and the latter will be censured by such persons only as are incapable of entering into the feelings of a people who were engaged in a struggle for their lives, their liberties, and their religion. Of all the charges thrown out against our reformers the most ridiculous is, that, in their zeal against popery, they waged war against literature, by destroying the valuable books and records which had been deposited in the monasteries. The state of learning among the monks, at the era of the Reformation, was wretched, and their libraries poor; the only persons who patronised or cultivated literature in Scotland were Protestants; and so far from sweeping away any literary monuments which remained, the reformers were disposed to search for them among the rubbish, and to preserve them with the utmost care. In this respect we have no reason to deprecate a comparison between our Reformation and that of England, notwithstanding the flattering accounts which have been given of the orderly and temperate manner in which the latter was conducted under the superintending control of the supreme powers. But, even although the irregularities committed in the progress of that work had been greater than have been represented, I must still reprobate the spirit which disposes persons to dwell with unceasing lamentation upon losses, which, in the view of an enlightened and liberal mind, will sink and disappear in the magnitude of the incalculable good which rose from the wreck of the revolution. What! do we celebrate, with public rejoicings, victories over the enemies of our country, in the gaining of which the lives of thousands of our fellow creatures have been sacrificed? and shall solemn masses and sad dirges, accompanied with direful execrations, be everlastingly sung for the mangled members of statues, torn pictures, and ruined towers? Shall those who, by a display of the horrors of war, would persuade their countrymen to repent of a contest which had been distinguished with uncommon feats of valour, and crowned with the most brilliant success, be accused of a desire to tarnish the national glory? Shall the topics on which they insist, however forcible in themselves, the effusion of human blood, the sacking of cities, the devastation of fertile provinces, the ruin of arts and manufactures, and the intolerable burdens entailed even upon the victors themselves—be represented as mere commonplace topics, employed as a cover to disloyalty? And do not those, who at the distance of nearly three centuries, continue to bewail evils of a far inferior kind which attended the Reformation, justly expose themselves to the suspicion of indifference and disaffection to a cause, in comparison with which all contests between rival kingdoms and sovereigns dwindle into insignificance? I will go farther, and say, that I look upon the destruction of these monuments as a piece of good policy, which contributed materially to the overthrow of the

Roman Catholic religion, and the prevention of its re-establishment. It was chiefly by the magnificence of its temples, and the splendid apparatus of its worship, that the popish church fascinated the senses and imaginations of the people. A more successful method of attacking it, therefore, could not be adopted than the demolition of what contributed so much to uphold and extend its influence. There is more wisdom than many seem to perceive in the maxim which Knox is said to have inculcated, " that the best way to keep the rooks from returning, was to pull down their nests." In demolishing, or rendering uninhabitable, all those buildings which had served for the maintenance of the ancient superstition (except what were requisite for the Protestant worship,) the reformers only acted upon the principles of a prudent general, who dismantles or razes fortifications which he is unable to keep, and which might afterwards be seized and employed against him by the enemy. Had they been allowed to remain in their former splendour, the popish clergy would not have ceased to indulge hopes, and to make efforts to be restored to them; occasions would have been taken to tamper with the credulous, and to inflame the minds of the superstitious; and the reformers might soon have found reason to repent their ill judged forbearance."

THE HEART OF ROBERT BRUCE.

When King Robert Bruce was in his last illness, at Cardross in Dumbartonshire, he requested that, as soon after his death as suitable arrangements could be made, his old and faithful companion in arms, the good Sir James Douglas, should carry his heart to Jerusalem, and humbly deposit it at the Sepulchre of our Lord. One motive for this request may have been state policy, to the effect that Douglas and Randolph, his two chief barons, of nearly equal fame, had hitherto worked well together principally through his own controlling influence, that they might fall out and form conflicting factions after his death, and that the speedy removal of one of them to a great distance for a sufficient length of time to allow the affairs of the next reign to become consolidated, would powerfully promote the public peace; but the predominant motive, perhaps almost the sole one, was the peculiar superstition of the age,—the associating of a pilgrimage to Palestine and a reverencing of the holy places in Jerusalem with the hope of salvation and the honouring of Christ,—enhanced, in Bruce's case, by remorse for the murder of the Red Comyn at Dumfries, by the habit of doing homage to sacred places and saintly relics throughout the vicissitudes and perils of his eventful life, and by a purpose which he had long cherished, but now felt to be for ever disappointed, of completing his military renown and giving evidence of his faith and zeal in the cause of the Catholic religion, by carrying his arms into Syria, and there performing high soldierly service against the Saracens.

The royal heart was put into a precious casket; and, in June 1330, exactly a twelvemonth after Bruce died, Douglas set sail with it, at the head of a numerous and splendid retinue. Froissart says that he had in his train a knight bearing a banner, seven other knights, twenty-six squires, all "comely young men of good family," and many attendants of inferior rank; that he kept open table, with timbrels and trumpets, as if he had been king of Scotland; that he was served on gold and silver plate; and that all persons of condition who visited him on ship-board were well entertained with a variety of wine and condiments. He anchored off Sluys in Flanders—then the great emporium of the Low Countries—expecting to find there adventurers who would take part in his expedition to Jerusalem; and he remained twelve days, receiving many visitors with princely hospita lity, and astonishing them by the magnificence of his retinue and equipments.

At Sluys he learned that Alonzo, the young king of Leon and Castile, was carrying on a war with Osmyn, the Moorish governor of Granada; and he felt a sudden and strong sympathy with him, and resolved to visit Spain, and render him assistance against the Saracens, before proceeding to Palestine. He seems indeed to have cherished some firm general idea in this direction from the very commencement of his preparations to carry away the royal heart; for on the 1st of September, 1326, he obtained from Edward III. of England a passport, " Versus Terram Sanctam in auxilium Christianorum contra Saracenos cum corde Domini Roberti Regis Scotiæ nuper defuncti." And, at all events, he felt stimulated by the spirit of the times, which regarded all warfare against the Saracens as a holy service; and he probably viewed the opportunity of attempting some exploit against them in Spain as a providential occasion for promoting and making illustrious the grand ultimate object of his mission to Jerusalem.

Douglas and his companions were received with great respect and favour by Alonzo, and had an honourable place assigned to them in the Spanish army. Some of Alonzo's chief men were veteran warriors, and brave, and were well able to appreciate the enterprise and heroism which brought the Scotish travellers to their standard. " I am astonished," said one of them, whose face was wholly disfigured with the scars of wounds received in battle,—addressing himself to Douglas,—" I am astonished that you, who are said to have seen much service, should have no marks of wounds on your face." " Thank Heaven," replied Douglas, " I had always an arm to protect my face."

The Spaniards, with their new allies, marched out against the Moors, and came in view of their camp near Theba, on the frontier of Andalusia, toward the kingdom of Granada.

Osmyn the Moor made arrangements that three thousand of his horsemen should make a feigned attack on the Spaniards, while he himself, with the rest of his army, should make a concealed circuitous march, and fall on the rear of the Spanish camp by surprise. But Alonzo got intelligence of his stratagem, and set a sufficient body of troops to oppose the feigned attack, and drew up his main force, including the Scots, in readiness to receive the onset from the rear. When therefore the Moorish army came in sight from their circuitous march, the Spaniards readily repulsed them, and broke up their array, and drove them back in discomfiture and flight; nor did they stop the chase till they reached the Moors' camp, and got possession of their stores and baggage. Douglas and his companions even went farther and became hotter; for while most of the Spaniards drew bridle at the camp, the Scots thought only of hunting down the Saracens, and therefore continued to pursue them till the number of the pursuers became a mere handful compared to the host of the pursued. The Moors soon perceived this, and rallied in strong force, kept their ground, and surrounded the Scots. Douglas endeavoured to cut his way through the enemy, and most probably would have succeeded, had he not turned at a critical point of the contest, to attempt the rescue of Sir William Saint Clair of Roslin, whom he saw to be in imminent danger. In making this attempt, he became inextricably involved with the Moors; and, taking from his neck the casket which contained the heart of Bruce, he cast it before him, and cried aloud, " Onward, brave heart, that never failed, and Douglas will follow thee or die." And, a few moments after, a body of the Spaniards came down like a hurricane, and swept away the Moors. The conflict down to this crisis is graphically described as follows by Mr Aytoun in his " Lays of the Scottish Cavaliers:"—

"The trumpets blew, the cross-bolts flew,
  The arrows flashed like flame,
As spur in side, and spear in rest,
  Against the foe we came,

And many a bearded Saracen
  Went down both horse and man;
For through their ranks we rode like corn,
  So furiously we ran!

But in behind our path they closed,
  Though fain to let us through,
For they were forty thousand men,
  And we were wondrous few.

We might not see a lance's length,
  So dense was their array,
But the long fell sweep of the Scottish blade
  Still held them hard at bay.

'Make in! make in!' Lord Douglas cried,
  'Make in, my brethren dear!
Sir William of Saint Clair is down;
  We may not leave him here!'

But thicker, thicker, grew the swarm,
  And sharper shot the rain,
And the horses reared amid the press,
  But they would not charge again.

Now Jesu help thee,' said Lord James
  'Thou kind and true St. Clair!
And if I may not bring thee off,
  'I'll die beside thee there!'

Then in his stirrups up he stood,
  So lionlike and bold,
And held the precious heart aloft
  All in its case of gold.

He flung it from him, far ahead,
  And never spake he more,
But—'Pass thee first, thou dauntless heart,
  As thou wert wont of yore!'

The roar of fight rose fiercer yet
  And heavier still the stour,
Till the spears of Spain came shivering in
  And swept away the Moor."

But Douglas fell and died amidst the mellee; and three of his knights, and many of his companions, were slain around him. His body and the casket of the royal heart were afterwards found by his surviving friends, and conveyed mournfully to Scotland; and the former was entombed in the Douglas cemetery at Douglas, and the latter in the abbey of Melrose. The Douglasses have ever since borne the armorial device of the Bloody Heart surmounted by the crown; and the descendants of the knight who brought the royal heart and the body of Douglas home from Spain, adopted the name of Lockhart and took for their effigy a heart within a fetterlock.

THE BATTLE OF PRESTONPANS.

On the 16th of September, 1745, while the heralds were proclaiming James at the market-cross of Edinburgh, Sir John Cope was landing his troops at Dunbar. The landing was finished on the 17th; but the disembarkation of the artillery and stores was not completed till the 18th. Desirous of engaging the Highland army before the arrival of their expected reinforcements, Cope left Dunbar on the 19th, in the direction of Edinburgh, and halted on the evening of that day on a field to the west of the town of Haddington. Resuming his march on the morning of the 20th, along the high road to Preston, he halted his army, and formed his troops in order of battle, with his front to the west, on reaching the plain betwixt Seaton and Preston. His right extended towards the sea in the direction of Port-Seaton, and his left towards the village of Preston. These dispositions had scarcely been taken when the whole of the Highland army appeared descending the heights in the direction of Tranent. On approaching Tranent the Highlanders were received by the King's troops with a vehement shout of defiance, which the Highlanders answered in a similar strain. About two o'clock in the afternoon, the Highland army halted on an eminence called Birsley-Brae, about half-a-mile to the west of Tranent, and formed in order of battle about a mile from the royal forces.

In the expectation that the Highlanders were advancing by the usual route through Musselburgh, Cope had taken up the position we have described, with his front to the west; but as soon as he observed the Highlanders on the heights upon his left, he changed his front to the south. This change of position, while it secured Cope better from attack, was not so well calculated for safety as the first position was in the event of a defeat. On his right was the east wall of a park belonging to Erskine of Grange, which extended a considerable way from north to south, and still farther to the right was the village of Preston. The village of Seaton was on his left, and the village of Cockenzie and the sea in his rear. Almost immediately in front was a deep ditch filled with water, and a strong and thick hedge. Farther removed from the front, and between the two armies was a morass, the ends of which had been drained, and were intersected by numerous cuts. And on the more firm ground at the ends were several small enclosures, with hedges, dry stone-walls, and willow trees.

As the Highlanders were in excellent spirits, and eager to close immediately with the enemy, Charles felt very desirous to comply with their wishes; but he soon ascertained, by examining some people of the neighbourhood, that the passage across the morass, from the nature of the ground, would be extremely dangerous if not altogether impracticable. Not wishing, however, in a matter of such importance to trust altogether to the opinion of the country people, Lord George Murray ordered Colonel Ker of Gradon, an officer of some military experience, to examine the ground, and to report. Mounted upon a little white poney he descended alone into the plain below, and with the greatest coolness and deliberation surveyed the morass on all sides. As he went along the morass several shots were fired at him, by some of Cope's men, from the sides of the ditches; but he paid so little regard to these annoyances that on coming to a dry stone wall which stood in his way he dismounted, and making a gap in it led his horse through. After finishing this perilous duty, he returned to the army, and reported to the lieutenant-general that he considered it impracticable to pass the morass and attack the enemy in front, without risking the whole army, and that it was impossible for the men to pass the ditches in a line.

While his lieutenant-general was, in consequence of this information, planning a different mode of attack, the Prince himself was moving with a great part of his army towards Dauphinstone on Cope's right. Halting opposite Preston tower he seemed to threaten that flank of the English general, who, thereupon, returned to his original position with his front to Preston, and his right towards the sea. As Lord George Murray considered that the only practicable mode of attacking Cope was by advancing from the east, he led off part of the army about sunset through the village of Tranent, and sent notice to the Prince to follow him with the remainder as quickly as possible. When passing through the village, Lord George was joined by fifty of the Camerons, who had been posted by O'Sullivan in the churchyard at the foot of Tranent. This party being within half cannon shot of Cope's artillery, had been exposed during the afternoon to a fire from their cannon, and one or two of the Camerons had been wounded. To frighten the Highlanders, who, they imagined, had never seen cannon before, Cope's men huzzaed at every discharge; but the Camerons remained in their position, till, on the representation of Lochiel, who went and viewed the ground, and found his men unnecessarily exposed, they were ordered to retire in the direction of Tranent. O Sullivan, who was in the rear when this order was given, came up on the junction of the party, and asking Lord George the meaning of the movement he was making, was told by him, that as it was not possible to attack the enemy with any chance of success on the west side of the village, he had resolved to assail them from the east, and that he would satisfy the Prince that his plan was quite practicable,—that for this purpose he had ordered the army to march to the east side of the village where there were good dry fields covered with stubble, on which the men could bivouack during the night,—and that with regard to the withdrawal of the party which O'Sullivan had posted in the churchyard, they could be of no service there, and were unnecessarily exposed. On being informed of the movement made by Lord George Murray, Charles proceeded to follow him; but it was dark before the rear had passed the village. To watch Cope's motions on the west, Charles left behind the Athole brigade, consisting of five hundred men, under Lord Nairne, which he posted near Preston above Colonel Gardiner's parks.

After the Highland army had halted on the fields to the east of Tranent, a council of war was held, at which Lord George Murray proposed to attack the enemy at break of day. He assured the members of the council that the plan was not only practicable, but that it would in all probability be attended with success,—that he knew the ground himself, and that he had just seen one or two gentlemen who were also well acquainted with every part of it. He added, that there was indeed a small defile at the east end of the ditches, but if once passed there would be no farther hinderance, and though, from being obliged to march in a column, they would necessarily consume a considerable time on their march, yet when the whole line had passed the defile they would have nothing to do but face to the left, form in a moment, and commence the attack. Charles was highly pleased with the proposal of the lieutenant-general; which having received the unanimous approbation of the council, a few piquets were, by order of Lord George, placed around the bivouack, and the Highlanders, after having supped, wrapped themselves up in their plaids, and lay down upon the ground to repose for the night. Charles, taking a sheaf of pease for a pillow, stretched himself upon the stubble, surrounded by his principal officers, all of whom followed his example. Before the army went to rest, notice was sent to Lord Nairne to leave his post, with the Athole brigade, at two o'clock in the morning, as quietly as possible. To conceal their position from the English general, no fires or lights were allowed, and orders were issued and scrupulously obeyed, that strict silence should be kept, and that no man should stir from his place till directed.

When Cope observed Charles returning towards Tranent, he resumed his former position with his front to the south, having thus, in the course of a few hours, been obliged, by the unrestrained evolutions of the Highlanders, to shift his ground no less than four times. He now began to perceive that his situation was not so favourable as he had imagined, and that while the insurgents could move about at discretion, select their ground, and choose their time and mode of attack, he was cramped in his own movements and could act only on the defensive. The spectators who felt an interest in the fate of his army, and who had calculated upon certain success to Cope's arms during the day, now, that night was at hand, began to forebode the most gloomy results. Instead of a bold and decided movement on the part of Cope to meet the enemy, they observed that he had spent the day in doing absolutely nothing,—that he was in fact hemmed in by the Highlanders, and forced at their pleasure to change his position at every movement they were pleased to make. They dreaded that an army which was obliged to act thus upon the defensive, and which would, therefore, be obliged to pass the ensuing night under arms, could not successfully resist an attack next morning from men, who, sheltered from the cold by their plaids, could enjoy the sweets of repose, and rise fresh and vigorous for battle.

To secure his army from surprise during the night, Cope placed advanced piquets of horse and foot along the side of the morass, extending nearly as far east as the village of Seaton. He, at the same time, sent his baggage and military chest down to Cockenzie under a guard of forty men of the line and all the Highlanders of the army, consisting of four companies, viz. two of newly raised men belonging to London's regiments, and two additional companies of Lord John Murray's regiment, which had been diminished by desertion to fifteen men each. Although the weather had been very fine, and the days were still warm, yet the nights were now getting cold and occasionally frosty. As the night in question, that of Friday the 20th of September, was very cold, Cope ordered fires to be kindled along the front of his line, to keep his men warm. During the night he amused himself by firing off, at random, some cohorns, probably to alarm the Highlanders or disturb their slumbers; but these hardy mountaineers, if perchance they awoke for a time, disregarded these empty bravadoes, and fell back again into the arms of sleep.

In point of numbers the army of Cope was rather inferior to that of Charles; but many of the Highlanders were badly armed, and some of them were without arms. The royal forces amounted altogether to about 2,300 men; but the number in the field was diminished to 2,100 by the separation of the baggage-guard which was sent to Cockenzie. The order of battle formed by Cope along the north side of the morass was as follows:—He drew up his foot in one line, in the centre of which were eight companies of Lascelles's regiment, and two of Guise's. On the right were five companies of Lee's regiment, and on the left the regiment of Murray, with a number of recruits for different regiments at home and abroad. Two squadrons of Gardiner's dragoons formed the right wing, and a similar number of Hamilton's composed the left. The remaining squadron of each regiment was placed in the rear of its companions as a reserve. On the left of the army, near the waggon-road from Tranent to Cockenzie, were placed the artillery, consisting of six or seven pieces of cannon and four cohorns, under the orders of Lieutenant-colonel Whiteford, and guarded by a company of Lee's regiment, commanded by Captain Cochrane. Besides the regular troops there were some volunteers, consisting principally of small parties of the neighbouring tenantry, headed by the irrespective landlords. Some Seceders, actuated by religious zeal, had also placed themselves under the royal standard.

Pursuant to the orders he had received, Lord Nairne left the position he had occupied during the night at the appointed hour, and rejoined the main body about three o'clock in the morning. Instead of continuing the order of march of the preceding night, it had been determined by the council of war to reverse it. The charge of this movement was intrusted to Colonel Ker, who had signalized himself by the calm intrepidity with which he had surveyed the marsh on the preceding day. To carry this plan into effect, Ker went to the head of the column, and passing along the line, desired the men to observe a profound silence, and not to stir a step till he should return to them. On reaching the rear he ordered it to march from the left, and to pass close in front of the column, and returning along the line, he continued to repeat the order till the whole army was in motion. This evolution was accomplished without the least confusion, and before four o'clock in the morning the whole army was in full march.

The Duke of Perth, who was to command the right wing, was at the head of the inverted column. He was attended by Hepburn of Keith, and by Mr. Robert Anderson, son of Anderson of Whitbrough, who, from his intimate knowledge of the morass, was sent forward to lead the way. A little in advance of the van was a select party of sixty men doubly armed, under the command of Macdonald of Glenalladale, major of the regiment of Clanranald, whose appointed duty it was to seize the enemy's baggage. The army proceeded in an easterly direction till near the farm of Ringan-head, when, turning to the left, they marched in a northerly direction through a small valley which intersects the farm. During the march the utmost silence was observed by the men, not even a whisper being heard; and lest the trampling of horses might discover their advance, the few that were in the army were left behind. The ford or path across the morass was so narrow that the column, which marched three men abreast, had scarcely sufficient standing room, and the ground along it was so soft, that many of the men were almost at every step up to the knees in mud. The path in question, which was about two hundred paces to the west of the stone-bridge afterwards built across Seaton mill-dam, led to a small wooden-bridge which had been thrown over the large ditch which ran through the morass from east to west. This bridge, and the continuation of the path on the north of it, were a little to the east of Cope's left. From ignorance of the existence of this bridge,—from oversight, or from a supposition that the marsh was not passable in that quarter,—

Cope had placed no guards in that direction, and the consequence was, that the Highland army, whose march across could have been effectually stopped by a handful of men, passed the bridge and cleared the marsh without interruption.

The army was divided into two columns or lines, with an interval between them. After the first line had got out of the marsh, Lord George Murray sent the Chevalier Johnstone, one of his aides-de-camp, to hasten the march of the second, which was conducted by the Prince in person, and to see that it passed without noise or confusion. At the remote end of the marsh there was a deep ditch, three or four feet broad, over which the men had to leap. In jumping across this ditch, Charles fell upon his knees on the other side, and was immediately raised by the Chevalier Johnstone, who says, that Charles looked as if he considered the accident a bad omen.

As the column cleared the marsh, it continued its course towards the sea; but after the whole army had passed, it was ascertained that the Duke of Perth had inadvertently, (not being able, from the darkness, to see the whole line,) advanced too far with the front, and that a considerable gap had, in consequence, been left in the centre. The Duke being informed of this error, halted his men till joined by the rear. Hitherto the darkness had concealed the march of the Highlanders; but the morning was now about to dawn, and at the time the order to halt was given, some of Cope's piquets, stationed on his left, for the first time, heard the tramp of the Highlanders. The Highlanders then heard distinctly these advanced guards repeatedly call out, " Who is there?" No answer having been returned, the piquets immediately gave the alarm, and the cry of " Cannons, cannons! Get ready the cannons, cannoniers!' resounded on Cope's left wing.

Charles proceeded instantly to give directions for attacking Cope before he should have time to change his position by

THE BATTLE OF PRESTONPANS.

opposing his front to that of the Highland army. It was not in compliance with any rule in military science, that the order of march of the Highland army had been reversed; but in accordance with an established punctilio among the clans, which, for upwards of seven centuries, had assigned the right wing, regarded as the post of honour, to the Macdonalds. As arranged at the council of war on the preceding evening, the army was drawn up in two lines. The first consisted of the regiments of Clanranald, Keppoch, Glengary, and Glencoe, under their respective chiefs. These regiments formed the right wing, which was commanded by the Duke of Perth. The Duke of Perth's men and the Macgregors composed the centre; while the left wing, commanded by Lord George Murray, was formed of the Camerons under Lochiel, their chief, and the Stewarts of Appin commanded by Stewart of Ardshiel. The second line, which was to serve as a reserve, consisted of the Athole-men, the Robertsons of Strowan, and the Maclauchlans. This body was placed under the command of Lord Nairne.

As soon as Cope received intelligence of the advance of the Highlanders, he gave orders to change his front to the east. Some confusion took place in carrying these orders into execution, from the advanced guards belonging to the foot not being able to find out the regiments to which they belonged, and who, in consequence, stationed themselves on the right of Lee's five companies, and thereby prevented the two squadrons of Gardiner's dragoons, which had been posted on the right of the line, from forming properly. For want of room the squadron under Colonel Gardiner drew up behind that commanded by Lieutenant-colonel Whitney. In all other respects the disposition of each regiment was the same; but the artillery, which before the change had been on the left, and close to that wing, was now on the right somewhat farther from the line, and in front of Whitney's squadron.

There was now no longer any impediment to prevent the

armies from coming into collision; and if Cope had had the choice, he could not have selected ground more favourable for the operations of cavalry than that which lay between the two armies. It was a level cultivated field of considerable extent without bush or tree, and had just been cleared of its crop of grain. But unfortunately for the English general, the celerity with which the Highlanders commenced the attack prevented him from availing himself of this local advantage. The beams of the rising sun were just beginning to illuminate the horizon; but the mist which still hovered over the corn-fields prevented the two armies from seeing each other. Every thing being in readiness for advancing, the Highlanders took off their bonnets, and, placing themselves in an attitude of devotion, with upraised eyes uttered a short prayer. As the Highlanders advanced considerably beyond the main ditch, Lord George Murray was apprehensive that Cope might turn the left flank; and to guard against such a contingency, he desired Lochiel, who was on the extreme left, to order his men in advancing to incline to the left. Lord George then ordered the left wing to advance, and sent an aid-de-camp to the Duke of Perth to request him to put the right in motion. The Highlanders moved with such rapidity that their ranks broke; to recover which, they halted once or twice before closing with the enemy. When Cope, at day-break, observed the first line of the Highland army formed in order of battle, at the distance of 200 paces from his position, he mistook it for bushes; but before it had advanced half way, the rays of the rising sun bursting through the retiring mist showed the armies to each other.

> " Day opened in the orient sky
>   With wintry aspect, dull and drear;
> On every leaf, while glitteringly
>   The rimy hoar-frost did appear.
> The ocean was unseen, though near;

> And hazy shadows seem'd to draw,
>   In azure, with their mimic floods,
>   A line above the Seaton woods,
> And round North Berwick Law."

The army of Cope at this time made a formidable appearance; and some of Charles's officers were heard afterwards to declare, that when they first saw it, and compared the gallant appearance of the horse and foot, with their well-polished arms glittering in the sunbeams, with their own line broken into irregular clusters, they expected that the Highland army would be instantly defeated, and swept from the field. The Highlanders continued to advance in profound silence. As the right wing marched straight forward without attending to the oblique movement of the Camerons to the left, a gap took place in the centre of the line. An attempt was made to fill it up with the second line, which was about fifty paces behind the first; but before this could be accomplished, the left wing, being the first to move, had advanced beyond the right of the line, and was now engaged with the enemy. By inclining to the left, the Camerons gained half the ground originally between them and the main ditch; but this movement brought them up directly opposite to Cope's cannon. On approaching the cannon, the Highlanders fired a few shots at the artillery guard, which alarmed an old gunner who had charge of the cannon, and his assistants, to such a degree that they fled, carrying the powder-flasks along with them. To check the advance of the Highlanders, Colonel Whiteford fired off five of the field pieces with his own hand; but though their left seemed to recoil, they instantly resumed the rapid pace they had set out with. The artillery guard next fired a volley with as little effect. Observing the squadron of dragoons under Lieutenant-colonel Whitney advancing to charge them, the Camerons set up a loud shout, rushed past the cannon, and, after discharging a few shots at the dragoons, which killed several men, and wounded the lieutenant-colonel, flew upon them sword in hand. When assailed, the squadron was reeling to and fro from the fire; and the Highlanders, following an order they had received to strike at the noses of the horses without minding their riders, completed the disorder. In a moment the dragoons wheeled about, rode over the artillery guard, and fled followed by the guard. The Highlanders continuing to push forward without stopping to take prisoners, Colonel Gardiner was ordered to advance with his squadron, and charge the enemy. He accordingly went forward, encouraging his men to stand firm; but this squadron, before it had advanced many paces, experienced a similar reception with its companion, and followed the example which the other had just set.

After the flight of the dragoons, the Highlanders advanced upon the infantry, who opened a fire from right to left, which went down the line as far as Murray's regiment. They received this volley with a loud huzza, and throwing away their muskets, drew their swords and rushed upon the foot before they had time to reload their pieces. Confounded by the flight of the dragoons, and the furious onset of the Highlanders, the astonished infantry threw down their arms and took to their heels. Hamilton's dragoons, who were stationed on Cope's left, displayed even greater pusillanimity than their companions; for no sooner did they observe the squadrons on the right give way, than they turned their backs and fled without firing a single shot or drawing a sword. Murray's regiment being thus left alone on the field, fired upon the Macdonalds, who were advancing, and also fled. Thus, within a very few minutes after the action had commenced, the whole army of Cope was put to flight. With the exception of their fire, not the slightest resistance was made by horse or foot, and not a single bayonet was stained with blood. Such were the impetuosity and rapidity with which the first line of the Highlanders broke through Cope's ranks, that they left numbers of his men in their rear, who attempted to rally behind them; but on seeing the second line coming up, they endeavoured to make their escape. Though the second line was not more than 50 paces behind the first, and was always running as fast as it could to overtake the first line, and near enough never to lose sight of it, yet such was the rapidity with which the battle was gained, that, according to the Chevalier Johnstone, who stood by the side of the Prince in the second line, he could see no other enemy on the field of battle than those who were lying on the ground killed and wounded.

Unfortunately for the royal infantry, the walls of the enclosures about the village of Preston, which, from the position they took up on the preceding evening, formed their great security on their right, now that these park-walls were in their rear, operated as a barrier to their flight. Having disencumbered themselves of their arms to facilitate their escape, they had deprived themselves of their only means of defence, and driven as they were upon the walls of the enclosures, they would have all perished under the swords of the Highlanders, had not Charles and his officers strenuously exerted themselves to preserve the lives of their discomfited foes. The impetuosity of the attack, however, and the sudden flight of the royal army, allowed little leisure for the exercise of humanity; and before the carnage ceased several hundreds had fallen under the claymores of the Highlanders, and the ruthless scythes of the Macgregors. Armed with these deadly weapons, which were sharpened and fixed to poles from seven to eight feet long, to supply the place of other arms, this party mowed down the affrighted enemy, cut off the legs of the horses, and severed, it is said, the bodies of their riders in twain.

Of the infantry of the royal army, about 170 only escaped. From a report made by their own sergeants and corporals, by order of Lord George Murray, between 1,600 and 1,700 prisoners, foot and cavalry, fell into the hands of the Highlanders, including about 70 officers. In this number were comprehended the baggage-guard stationed at Cockenzie, which amounted to 300 men, who, on learning the fate of the main body and the loss of their cannon, surrendered to the Camerons. The cannon and all the baggage of the royal army, together with the military chest, containing £4,000, fell into the hands of the victors. The greater part of the dragoons escaped by the two roads at the extremities of the park-wall, one of which passed by Colonel Gardiner's house in the rear of their right, and the other on their left, to the north of Preston-house. In retiring towards these outlets, the dragoons, at the entreaties of their officers, halted once or twice, and faced about to meet the enemy; but as soon as the Highlanders came up and fired at them, they wheeled about and fled. Cope, who was by no means deficient in personal courage, assisted by the Earls of Home and Loudon, collected about 450 of the panic-struck dragoons on the west side of the village of Preston, and attempted to lead them back to the charge; but no entreaties could induce these cowards to advance, and the whistling of a few bullets discharged by some Highlanders near the village, so alarmed them that they instantly scampered off in a southerly direction, screening their heads behind their horses' necks to avoid the bullets of the Highlanders. The general had no alternative but to gallop off with his men. He reached Coldstream, a town about 40 miles from the field of battle, that night; and entered Berwick next day.

Among six of Cope's officers who were killed was Colonel Gardiner, a veteran soldier who had served under the Duke of Marlborough, and whose character combined a strong religious feeling with the most undaunted courage. He had been decidedly opposed to the defensive system of Cope on the preceding evening, and had counselled the general not to lose a moment in attacking the Highlanders; but his advice was disregarded. Anticipating the fate which awaited him, he spent the greater part of the night in devotion, and resolved at all hazards to perform his duty. He was wounded at the first onset at the head of his dragoons; but disdaining to follow them in their retreat, he joined a small body of foot, which attempted to rally near the wall of his own garden, and while fighting at their head was cut down by the murderous Lochaber axe of a Macgregor, within a few yards of his own house. He was carried to the manse of Tranent in almost a lifeless state, where he expired within a few hours, and was interred in the north-west corner of the church of Tranent. The church has been rebuilt; and the grave of Colonel Gardiner is now without the walls of the edifice. An American tourist—who, with an enthusiasm unknown to Scotsmen, recently made a pilgrimage to the grave of Gardiner—exclaims: "Most true it is, that no monument, not even a stone, marks the ground where sleeps this extraordinary man,—a man whom Caledonia may well be proud to have enrolled among her best and bravest sons!"—Captain Brymer of Lee's regiment, who appears to have participated in Gardiner's opinion as to attacking the Highlanders, met a similar fate. Having been at the battle of Sheriffmuir, he was satisfied of the capability of the Highlanders to contend with regular troops, and dreaded the result of an encounter if assailed by the Highlanders. When encamped at Haddington his brother-officers were in high spirits, and making light of the enemy; but Brymer viewed matters in a very different light. While reading one night in his tent, he was accosted by Mr. Congalton of Congalton, his brother-in-law, who, observing him look pensive and grave, when all the other officers appeared so cheerful, inquired the reason. Brymer answered that the Highlanders were not to be despised, and that he was afraid his brother-officers would soon find that they had mistaken the character of the Highlanders, who would, to a certainty, attack the royal army with a boldness which those only who had witnessed their prowess could have any idea of. These gloomy forebodings were not the result of an innate cowardice—for this officer was, as he showed, a brave man—but from a well-founded conviction that Cope's men could not stand the onset of such a body of Highlanders as Charles had assembled. Brymer was killed, with his face to the enemy, disdaining to turn his back when that part of the line where he was stationed was broke in upon by the Highlanders.

The loss on the side of the Highlanders was trifling. Four officers, and between 30 and 40 privates, were killed; and 5 or 6 officers, and between 70 or 80 privates wounded. After the termination of the fight, the field of battle presented an appalling spectacle, rarely exhibited in the most bloody conflicts. As almost all the slain were cut down by the broadsword and the scythe, the ground was strewed with legs, arms, hands, noses, and mutilated bodies, while, from the deep gashes inflicted by these dreadful weapons, the field was literally soaked with gore.

> " Alas! that British might should wield
>   Destruction o'er a British plain,
> That hands, ordain'd to bear the shield,
>   Should bring the poison'd lance, to drain
>   The life-blood from a brother's vein,
> And steep paternal fields in gore !—
>   Yet, Preston, such thy fray began;
>   Thy marsh-collected waters ran
> Empurpled to the shore."

The Highlanders, happily, had no revengeful feeling to gratify after achieving their victory, and therefore, when they found themselves completely victorious, were easily induced to listen to the dictates of humanity; and when the action was over, they displayed a sympathy for the wounded rarely equalled and never surpassed. Charles himself, too, not only issued orders for taking care of the wounded, but also remained on the field of battle till mid-day to see that his orders were fulfilled. Finding the few surgeons he had carried along with him inadequate to meet the demands of the wounded, he dispatched one of his officers to Edinburgh to bring out all the surgeons, who accordingly instantly repaired to the field of battle. As the Highlanders felt an aversion to bury the dead, and as the country people could not be prevailed upon to assist in the care of the wounded, Charles experienced great obstacles in carrying through his humane intentions. Writing to his father, on the evening of the battle, he thus alludes to them: "'Tis hard my victory should put me under new difficulties which I did not feel before, and yet this is the case. I am charged both with the care of my friends and enemies. Those who should bury the dead are run away, as if it were no business of theirs. My Highlanders think it beneath them to do it, and the country people are fled away. However, I am determined to try if I can get people for money to undertake it, for I cannot bear the thought of suffering Englishmen to rot above the ground. I am in great difficulties how I shall dispose of my wounded prisoners. If I make a hospital of the church, it will be looked upon as a great profanation, and of having violated my manifesto, in which I promised to violate no man's property. If the magistrates would act, they would help me out of this difficulty. Come what will, I am resolved not to let the poor wounded men lye in the streets; and if I can do no better, I will make a hospital of the palace and leave it to them."

All the wounded privates of both armies were carried to the different villages adjoining the field of battle. Those of Cope's officers who were dangerously wounded were lodged in Colonel Gardiner's house, where surgeons attended them. In the evening, the remainder, (who had given their parole,) accompanied by Lord George Murray, went to Musselburgh, where a house had been provided for their reception. Some of them walked, but others, who were unable to do so, had horses provided for them by his lordship. The house into which they were put was newly finished, and had neither table, bed, chair, nor grate in it. Lord George caused some new thrashed straw to be purchased for beds, and the officers on their arrival partook of a tolerable meal of cold provisions and some liquor which his lordship had carried along with him. When about to retire, the officers entreated him not to leave them, as being without a guard, they were afraid that some of the Highlanders, who were in liquor, might come in and insult or plunder them. Lord George consented, and lay on a floor by them all night. Some of the officers, who were valetudinary, slept that night in the house of the minister. Next day, after the departure of the Prince for Edinburgh, the officers had quarters provided for them in Pinkie-house. The other prisoners, privates, were quartered in Musselburgh and the gardens of Pinkie for two nights, and were afterwards removed, along with the officers, to Edinburgh. The latter were confined for a few days in Queensberry-house, when they were released on parole, and allowed to reside in the city, on condition that they should hold no communication with the castle. The privates were confined in the church and jail of the Canongate. Such of the wounded as could be removed were put into the Royal Infirmary, where great care was taken of them. One of the officers having broke his parole by going into the castle, the others were sent to Perth. The privates were removed to Logierate in Athole; and the wounded were dismissed as they recovered, on taking an oath that they should not carry arms against the Prince before the 1st of January, 1747.

When congratulating themselves on the victory they had obtained, the Highlanders related to each other what they had done or seen. Instances were given of individual prowess which might appear incredible, were it not well-known that when fear seizes an army all confidence in themselves or their numbers is completely destroyed. On this occasion "the panic-terror of the English surpassed all imagination. They threw down their arms that they might run with more speed, thus depriving themselves by their fears of the only means of arresting the vengeance of the Highlanders. Of so many, in a condition from their numbers to preserve order in their retreat, not one thought of defending himself. Terror had taken entire possession of their minds." Of the cases mentioned, one was that of a young Highlander about fourteen years of age, scarcely formed, who was presented to the Prince as a prodigy, having, it was said, killed fourteen of the enemy. Charles asking him if this was true, he replied, "I do not know if I killed them, but I brought fourteen soldiers to the ground with my sword." Another instance was that of a Highlander, who brought ten soldiers, whom he had made prisoners, to the Prince, driving them before him like a flock of sheep. With unexampled rashness, he had pursued a party of Cope's men to some distance from the field of battle, along a road between two enclosures, and striking down the hindermost man of the party with a blow of his sword, called aloud at the same time, "Down with your arms." The soldiers, terror-struck, complied with the order without looking behind them; and the Highlander, with a pistol in one hand and a sword in the other, made them do as he pleased. Yet as the Chevalier Johnstone observes, these were "the same English soldiers who had distinguished themselves at Dettingen and Fontenoy, and who might justly be ranked amongst the bravest troops of Europe."

THE BARNS OF AYR.

NEAR the end of the 13th century, during the usurped and military possession of Scotland by Edward I. of England, an encampment or temporary barrack of a portion of his forces, on the south-east side of the town of Ayr, became the scene of a very famous and very appalling exploit of Sir William Wallace. The country around Ayr had been the focus of an insurrection against the English tyranny; and was viewed by the creatures and officers of Edward with wakeful suspicion and malicious dislike. The well-affected and the ill-disposed were regarded with nearly the same feelings,—or rather, the former were either carelessly or sullenly confounded with the latter; and all persons of the upper classes, whatever might be their partisanship, their discretion, or their general character, were viewed indiscriminately as fit subjects to be victimized to the usurper's policy and bloody despotism. Under pretence of holding a Justice-Aire, all near the town were summoned to attend; and a number who appeared, including Sir Reginald Crawford, Sir Bryce Blair, and Sir Hugh Montgomerie, were treacherously made prisoners and put to death without even the formality of a trial. Wallace at the time was not far off, at the head of one of those small, fleet, flying brigades which so often surprised and confounded his enemies; and when he heard of the infamous occurrence, he determined to make a severe retaliation. Selecting fifty of his choicest men, and strengthened by a number of the retainers of the murdered gentlemen, he hastened to the temporary barracks of the English, or barns of Ayr, approached them stealthily, and surrounded them at dead of night, while their inmates were fast asleep in fancied security and after a deep carousal. He placed a cordon of men around them to prevent the possibility of escape, procured combustibles, and set fire so promptly and furiously to the pitch-covered thatch of the roofs that the whole erections were speedily in a blaze. The roused sleepers within rose and rushed outward screaming and horrified, but were everywhere confronted with the Scotish swords, and were either killed in the act of flight or driven back to die in the flames. No fewer than about five hundred perished. Wallace, it is said, went away before the tragedy was completed; and when at an elevated spot about two miles distant, where vestiges of an old ecclesiastical ruin popularly called Burn-weel kirk still exist, he looked back to the blazing scene of his vengeance, and exclaimed to his followers, "The barns of Ayr burn weel!"

Miss Baillie has made good use of this story in her 'Metrical Legend;' and many of the romancing histories of Scotland treat it as one of the most remarkable minor incidents in the story of the war of independence; and the local traditions of Ayrshire proudly point to it as high evidence of the eminent connexion of their county with the life and achievements of Scotland's greatest hero. And though Sir David Dalrymple, Lord Hailes, the most generally accurate of all our historians, has expressed strong scepticism respecting it, he is dealt with, on the subject, in the following effective terms, by the learned Dr. Jamieson:—"The story of the destruction of the barns of Ayr, and of the immediate reason of it, is supported by the universal tradition of the country to this day; and local tradition is often entitled to more regard than is given to it by the fastidiousness of the learned. Whatever allowances it may be necessary to make for subsequent exaggeration, it is not easily conceivable, that an event should be connected with a particular spot, during a succession of ages, without some foundation. Sir D. Dalrymple deems this story 'inconsistent with probability.' He objects to it, because it is said, 'that Wallace, accompanied by Sir John Graham, Sir John Menteith, and Alexander Scrymgeour, constable of Dundee, went into the west of Scotland, to chastise the men of Galloway, who had espoused the part of the Comyns, and of the English;' and that, 'on the 28th August, 1298, they set fire to some granaries in the neighbourhood of Ayr, and burned the English cantoned in them.'— Annals I. 255, N. Here he refers to the relations of Arnold Blair and to Major, and produces three objections to the narrative. One of these is, that 'Comyn, the younger of Badenoch, was the only man of the name of Comyn who had any interest in Galloway; and he was at that time of Wallace's party.' The other two are; that 'Sir John Graham could have no share in the enterprise, for he was killed at Falkirk, 22d July, 1298;' and that 'it is not probable that Wallace would have undertaken such an enterprise immediately after the discomfiture at Falkirk.' Although it had been said by mistake, that Graham and Comyn were present, this could not invalidate the whole relation, for we often find that leading facts are faithfully narrated in a history, when there are considerable mistakes as to the persons said to have been engaged. But although our annalist refers both to Major and Blair, it is the latter only who mentions either the design of the visit paid to the west of Scotland, or the persons who are said to have been associates in it. The whole of Sir David's reasoning rests on the correctness of a date, and of one given only in the meagre remains ascribed to Arnold Blair. If his date be accurate, the transaction at Ayr, whatever it was, must have taken place thirty-seven days afterwards. Had the learned writer exercised his usual acumen here—had he not been resolved to throw discredit on this part of the history of Wallace—it would have been most natural for him to have supposed, that this event was postdated by Blair. It seems, indeed, to have been long before the battle of Falkirk. Blind Harry narrates the former in his Seventh, the latter in his Eleventh Book. Sir David himself, after pushing the argument from the date given by Blair as far as possible, virtually gives it up, and makes the acknowledgment which he ought to have made before. 'I believe,' he says, 'that this story took its rise from the pillaging of the English quarters, about the time of the treaty of Irvine, in 1297, which, as being an incident of little consequence, I omitted in the course of this history.' Here he refers to Hemingford, T. I. p. 123. Hemingford says, that 'many of the Scots and men of Galloway had, in a hostile manner, made prey of their stores, having slain more than five hundred men, with women and children.' Whether he means to say that this took place at Ayr, or at Irvine, seems doubtful. But here, I think, we have the nucleus of the story. The barns, according to the diction of Blind Harry, seem to have been merely 'the English quarters,' erected by order of Edward for the accommodation of his troops. Although denominated barns by the Minstrel, and horreas by Arnold Blair, both writers seem to have used these terms with great latitude, as equivalent to what are now called barracks. It is rather surprising, that our learned annalist should view the loss of upwards of five hundred men, besides women and children, with that of their property, 'as an incident of little consequence,' in a great national struggle. Major gives nearly the same account as Blair. Speaking of Wallace, he says, 'Anglorum insignes viros apud horrea Aerie residentes de nocte incendit, et qui a voraci flamma evaserunt ejus mucrone occubuerunt.'—Fol. lxx. There is also far more unquestionable evidence as to the cause of this severe retaliation, than is generally supposed. Lord Hailes has still quoted Barbour as an historian of undoubted veracity. Speaking of Crystal of Seton, he says—

> It wes gret sorow sekyrly,
> That so worthy persoune as he
> Suld on sic maner hangyt be.
> Thusgate endyt his worthynes.
> And off Crauford als Schyr Ranald wes,
> And Schyr Bryce als the Blar,
> Hangyt in till a berne in Ar.'
> *The Bruce*, III. 260 v. &c.

This tallies very well with the account given by the Minstrel.

> ' Four thousand haill that nycht was in till Ayr.
> In gret bernyss, biggyt with out the toun,
> The justice lay, with mony bald barroun.
> *Wallace*, vii. 334."

JAMES THE SIXTH'S SEVERITY AGAINST PASQUIL WRITERS.

James VI. could not endure any slight upon his kingly dignity, or any taunt against his personal character, or any dishonouring reflection upon places or events with which he imagined his good name to be in any degree identified; and he frequently inflicted most severe chastisement, and even the most terrible public punishments upon well-behaved individuals who, in some hour of unguardedness or of prurient wit, had uttered a speech, lampoon, or hard word against his kingly or personal or relative dignity. In August, 1596, John Dickson, an Englishman, was condemned to be hanged at the market cross of Edinburgh, for saying, in a fit of drunkenness, that James was a bastard king and not worthy to be obeyed. In October, 1600, Francis Tennent, a merchant burgess of Edinburgh, was condemned to suffer forfeiture of all his moveable goods and to be publicly strangled to death, for applying to the King the popular soubriquet of " the Son of Senior Davie," and writing some squibs against him which are described as " slanderous, calumnious, and reproachful," and which probably contained matter relative to the recent conspiracy of the Earl of Gowrie. In April, 1601, Archibald Cornwall, one of the town officers of Edinburgh, was condemned to suffer forfeiture of goods, lands, and life, and to be hanged with a paper declaring his crime on his forehead, for exhibiting a portrait of the King on the upright beams of the public gibbet in the course of a public auction,—an offence, not only exceedingly trivial, but probably originating in pure accident or inadvertency or at worst in an unreflecting and foolish jest. And in May, 1615, John Fleming, an elder in Cockburnspath, was condemned to suffer forfeiture of all his moveable goods and to be hanged at the market-cross of Edinburgh, for "uttering treasonable, blasphemous, and damnable speeches against the King," the chief of which seems to have been a hasty petulant remark to his own parish minister, that " he cared not though the King should be dead before to-morrow, and should die of the falling sickness." All these cases are unquestionably authentic, and are detailed in Pitcairn's Criminal Trials; and a number of other cases of similar complexion might be quoted,—showing that James VI. was one of the most crushing and murdering tyrants, in matters connected with his own fame and dignity, who ever wielded power over the property and lives of a community. But the most remarkable case of all was the condemning of Thomas Ross to death, in 1618, for framing a pasquil against the Scotish nation.

Thomas Ross belonged to the ancient, influential, and highly respectable family of Ross of Craigie near Perth, who were probably a branch of the same sept as the ancient Earls of Ross. He was well educated, and became minister of Cargill, in the Presbyterian Church; but he seems to have embraced episcopacy, and to have gone to Oxford with the view of working his way into the clerical office in England; and he there sank into abject poverty, and contrived the extraordinary expedient of writing a pasquil against his native country as a means of pushing himself into notice, and procuring applause and ecclesiastical preferment. The very thought of such an expedient was crazy and wild,—and the prosecution of it pretty distinctly indicated a distempered state of mind ; and no doubt existed among disinterested contemporaries who inquired into the circumstances, that he was really insane. Yet the thing might readily enough be suggested to him, and was even in some slight degree made feasible, by the peculiar international condition of Scotish and English society. James VI. had not long before ascended the English throne; crowds of needy Scotsmen flocked into England, in hopes of promotion and aggrandizement through the influence of the King and of the Scotish courtiers; hot and angry jealousies existed on the part of the English people against the influx and the successes of the adventurers; the risks of feud and bloodshed, arising out of these jealousies, were so rife and fiery that a special enactment had been made by the legislature to curb and repress them; so that even a wise man, in a moment of need and irritation,—and much more an insane one—might, without any great extravagance, conceive the idea of trying to do something for himself in England by pasquinading the Scots.

Thomas Ross drew up his pasquil in the form of a thesis, and affixed it to the church-door of St. Mary's in Oxford. This was at that time the ordinary manner of procedure at all the great universities of Europe, on all sorts of subjects, and for all sorts of purposes; and, as practised by Ross, it simply constituted a challenge to a public disputation on the points which he specified. His pasquil, therefore, would be understood by all who might see it, as merely the squib of a wrangler or the flourish of a rhetorician, and not at all as a diatribe or an invective or an effusion of any kind of spleen. But it was not printed or disseminated; it was not even read throughout by any person but the Vice-Chancellor of Oxford, to whom it was brought by a student; and it was taken down by that student immediately after it had been put up by Ross, and when the student had read only so much of it as to perceive its nature and tendency. Yet for this ridiculously mimic offence, committed by a starving madman, and devoid of all power to do the slightest harm to a single creature, the unhappy perpetrator was condemned to death by the "British Solomon," James VI.! And what adds immensely to the monstrousness of the affair is that, at the very time when it happened, James was struggling to force episcopacy upon the Presbyterians of Scotland as the established religion of their country, while poor Ross had resigned his ministerial office in the Scotish Kirk, and become a zealous convert to the forms and tenets of the Church of England.

Ross was made prisoner in England, and sent in a ship to Scotland, to be put on his trial at Edinburgh; and on the 20th of August, he was formally convicted of " the devilish and detestable faining, blasphemous uttering, and publicly exposing of a villanous, infamous, and devilish pasquil or thesis, to the effect that all Scotsmen ought to be ejected from the Court of England, excepting his gracious Majesty, his son, and a very few others, and that Englishmen are mightily blinded, befooled, and deceived in suffering such an unprofitable and pernicious multitude and filthy offscourings of people to rage and domineer within their bounds." The justice who presided at the trial ordained him to be taken back to ward, and to be there kept in irons till the King should be informed of his conviction, and should intimate the punishment to be executed upon him; and on the 10th of September, in terms of a communication from the King to the Secretary of State, the sentence was pronounced, that Ross should be taken to a scaffold at the market-cross of Edinburgh, that there first his right hand and next his head should be struck from his body, that thereafter his hand should be fixed upon the West Port and his head upon the Netherbow-Port, and that all his moveable goods and gear, if he had any, should be escheated to his Majesty's use; and two days after, this most atrocious and inexpressibly infamous sentence was carried into execution.

"A very extraordinary instance of the same insane rage on the part of King James VI." says Mr. Pitcairn, "we learn from a rare poem entitled, a 'Counter-buffe to Lysimachus, Junior, calling himself a Jesuite;' quarto, 1640, pp. 16; where the fate of STERCOVIUS, *a Pole*, is alluded to. That stranger had unhappily appeared in Scotland in the dress of his native country, which attracted the attention of the idle, and brought down upon him the derision and abuse of the populace.

> ' Hither he came, clade all in antique sort,
> Where seen in streets the subject of a sport,
> He soone became to childish gazers, who
> With shriecks and clamours hiss him to and fro,
> Till forced he was with shame and speed to pack him,
> And to his feet and loathsome cabin take him!'

"Nettled at such rude and inhospitable treatment, he published 'a Legend of Reproaches' against the Scotish Nation, shortly after his return home; which, having reached the ears of his 'most sacred Majesty,' he procured the *arrest and execution* of the hapless STERCOVIUS! This out-herods Herod, with a vengeance! The death of this Pole was accomplished at an expense to the King of no less a sum than *six hundred pounds sterling*—an immense sum in those days. The instrument whom James employed was one *Mr. Patrik Gordon* a subject of Scotland, then resident in Poland. With a dexterity for which the sapient James was celebrated, he attempted to extort the price of this innocent man's blood from the *Royal Burghs of Scotland!* It is believed, however, that he was foiled in that attempt, by the Privy Council declaring themselves incompetent judges of the matter.

"In a very curious Collection, privately printed at Edinburgh, 1828, 'A Third Book of Scottish Pasquils,' the cases of *Ross* and *Stercovius* are particularly noticed; and a copious extract from the 'Counterbuffe' is there given. That singular Poem introduces *Ross's* story thus—which is enough for our present purpose.

> . . . . 'A *Scot* of ancient race,
> A scholler, too, as thou art, lived a space

In England's Court; and for some private hate,
A Pasquil did against his country wreat,
As thou hast done in fouler sort; more full
Of vild aspersions from thy phrantick skull!
Well, then, King *James* of lasting memorie, who
Could not brook that any calumnie
Should be asperst upon his native land—
After some tryall there, he gave command
The Lybeller should home go, and sustaine
Of doom impartiall laws th' unpitied paine.
And here being tryed, judged, and adjudged, they fand
That he should lose his head and faultie hand;
Which straight was done, in public view—and so
I thinke the matter with thyself will go!"

THE BATTLE OF INVERURY.

In 1307—the year of the death of England's Edward I., of the inglorious retreat of the young Edward II. from Cumnock, and of the commencement of general disheartening among the Scotish partisans of the English usurpers—Robert Bruce crossed the Grampians, overran a large portion of the north of Scotland, and endeavoured to win the northern chiefs by patriotism or policy or terror. But he had a very small army, and had sustained a disastrous defeat in the preceding year at Methven, and was suffering excessive privation of food and clothing and shelter; and never, in the whole course of his thousands of adventures, did he need to rely more than now upon the vigour of his body, the heroism of his mind, the nobleness of his cause, and the celerity and skill and energy of his movements. He achieved his incursion without any material hindrance; but on his way back, he encountered and routed a tumultuary mob of troops brought against him by the Earl of Buchan; and at

Inverury, he fell sick and lost all appetite and became so enfeebled that his friends around him ceased to cherish hopes of his recovery; and having been placed in a litter, he was carried to the Sliach, a fortification of some strength in the parish of Drumblade.

In winter, while Bruce was ill, and when the ground was covered with snow, the Earl of Buchan, with Sir John Mowbray and Sir David Brechin, eager to wipe away the recent disgrace, and anticipating slight resistance and an easy victory, raised a comparatively numerous army, and marched against Bruce. The Earl inspirited his men with music and parade and the conferring of military honours, and approached the Sliach "trumping and making meikle fare;" but he found Bruce's party all alert, and ready to give him a hot reception—determined, indeed, not to offer battle or to leave their fortifications, on account of their master's illness,—yet resolved nevertheless to hold the Earl at arm's length, and to pay him back with interest any favours he might send them; and he felt obliged to sit down at a fair distance, and to content himself with a series of skirmishings in archery. And, says Barbour, who possibly was a witness of the affair—

> "And when the Earl's company
> Saw that they wrought so wisely
> That they their strength shuip to defend
> Their archers forth to them they send
> To bicker them, as men of main;
> And they sent archers them again
> That bickered them so sturdily
> Till they of the Earl's party
> Into their battle driven were.
> Three days on this wise lay they there
> And bickered them everilk day;
> But their bowmen the war had ay."

The forces of Bruce, however, were at last compelled by famine to quit their defences; and, placing the King on a litter, and arming themselves to the teeth, they sallied out with a bold bearing, anxious only to make their way unscathed, yet prepared to repel promptly and fiercely any assault which might be offered them. The Earl was awed by their bravery, and allowed them quietly to pass; and then dismissed his army, or perhaps could not for the present hold it any longer together. And Bruce's forces marched to Strathbogie, and remained there till their master began to be convalescent, and then went to Inverury.

The Earl and Mowbray and Sir David Brechin, in the meanwhile, assembled another army, and encamped at Old Meldrum. This army was upwards of a thousand strong; and after they had been in camp only one night, a small party of them, headed by Sir David Brechin, rode to Inverury, and made a sudden onslaught at the west end of the town, killing several of the King's troops, and driving all the rest to their quarters. Bruce was lying at the east of the burgh, still an invalid and excessively feeble; and, on getting tidings of the onslaught, he started up like a strong man in wrath, and called for his horse, and bade his followers turn out for pursuit and battle.

> " Then said some of his privy men
>   ' What think you, Sir, this gate to fare,
> To fight and not recovered are?'
>   ' Yes,' said the King, ' withouten weer
> This boast has made me haill and feer,
> For should no medicine so soon,
> Have cured me, as they have done;
> Therefore so God himself me see
> I shall have them, or else they me.'
> And when his men had heard the King
> Set him so whole for the fighting,

Of his recov'ring all blythe were
And made them for the battle yare."

The royal force, in number about seven hundred, marched right to Old Meldrum, and almost caught the Earl by surprise. They arrived in furious spirit, with banners flying, and keen for the conflict; and as soon as they got sight of the foe, they rushed down upon him like a whirlwind. The Earl's men had barely time to arm and form; and, when the shock came, they wavered, gave way, and ran,—and in a few minutes, some were captured, some cut down, and all the rest in headlong flight, the fleetest horsed the foremost. The battle was ruin to the defeated; and Bruce, after the barbarous fashion of the period, made awful reprisals on his foes, and so terribly desolated the district of Buchan with fire and sword that it continued to be a theme of lamentation for fifty years. The Earl and Mowbray fled to England, and died there; and Sir David Brechin soon after espoused the cause of Bruce.

Many popular traditions of the battle are still afloat among the peasantry of the district around Inverury and Old Meldrum; and the chief of these, together with their legendary exaggerations, we are told in the New Statistical account of the parish of Bourtie, may be incorporated as follows:—
" On a time lang syne, when the English wished to tak awa our liberties, the fause Comyn cam up frae Buchan wi' a' his falluwers and a fouth o' English forbye, to win the crown to the English tirran Edward. In ae nicht, they biggit a' that camp o' the Hill heed, for the country was mensely agen them. But they thocht themselves that they had the ba' fairly at their fit noo, for Bruce was lyin at death's door at Inraurie; and frae the time that he took ill, his folk, thinkin' a' was o'er wi' them, had turnit few in number. But fan the nicht's mirkest, its nearest the crawin' o' the cock. Fan he heard o' their bein' at's very door as 'twar

up he sprang frae his bed, like a fey man, and cryin' for's
sword said, ' I'se make a spoen or spoil a horn. These loons
are physick to me.' So out he gaed amang's folk, and fan
they were dwindled awa till a handfu' amaist; and sair he
seem't dishertent, but only said, ' Fat we wint o' folk, we
wan men' wi' can.' So he order't them a' to be ready by 12
at nicht, wi' a' the nowt and horse they could gather. A well
aff they set, but nae by the stracht road, but ower the tap o'
Lawel Side, which they cam till jist afor' the sky; and for
as bare as it is noo, it was then, as I'm tauld, a braw forest
coveret wi' bonny trees. Bruce noo tied lichts to the horns
o' the nowt, and reed cloth and white napkins to the horse
necks, and dreve them here and there through the wood,
orderin's folk to mak a' the din they could. The heart o'
the Comyns lap to their mou', for they thocht the haill o'
Scotlan' was risen agen them. Jist at this time when a stir
began amo' them, Sir William Wallace, as was agree't on wi'
the Bruce, up's wi' a stane like a house-side, and wi' the
strenth o' ten Galiahs, bungs't frae the tap o' Benachie; and
that they micht ken fa the compliment cam' frae, he first
prented the initials o' his name (W. W.) i' the side o't.
Fung it gaed thro' the air, and lichtin' i' the middle o' the
camp kill't not a few, and gart the yird stot to the very
clouds. The hurly wus noo compleet, and oot they ran oot
o'er ither's heeds like as many sheep oot o' the fauld. In
this confeesion, the Bruce and his folk cam upo' them; and
tho' they foght hard, they war' sae sair defait that they could
never haud up their heeds ahint it. The King's spirits waur
noo high, as ye may believe; but he wus doom't to get a sair
heart-brak afor' nicht. His bosom comarade, the brave Englishman, Sir Thomas de Longueville, was mortally wounded
i' the battle; but he continuet to feght while it lasted. He
raid off the field 'till he cam' to the Dykes o' Fala, but there
fell frae his horse. Callin' to the King ' Noo, Robin,' he
said till him, ' my een will soon be clos't, and I've ae request

to mak. Ye maun jist lay my banes wharever this arra fa's. So drawin's bow, he sent the arra wi' a' his micht through the air, and it fell i' the kirk yard o' Bourtie here, twa mile awa."

THE CHANGES AND WARS OF MORAY.

The ancient province of Moray comprised all the territory of modern Elginshire, all Nairnshire, a considerable part of Banffshire, and nearly one half of the continental portion of Inverness-shire. The eastern part of it is aggregately much more lowland than the western; the mountains which everywhere occupy the south, coming down with increasing approach to the north, till, for some distance on the west, they render the whole country characteristically highland. The northern district as a whole is champaign, and may be described as a band of country prolonged for 60 miles from east to west, with a breadth of from 2 to 12 miles, and a superficial area of about 240 square miles. This long belt of lowlands is greatly diversified with ridgy swells, and terraced or low hilly ranges disposed parallel to the frith; and is intersected by the rivers Ness, Nairn, Findhorn, Lossie, and Spey, running across it to the sea. The grounds behind the lowlands appear, as seen from the coast, to be only a narrow ridge of bold or alpine heights, rising like a rampart to guard the orchards and the woods and the rich expanse of waving fields below from all invasion; but, when approached, they disclose themselves in file behind file of long and broad mountain masses receding, in all the wildness and intricacy of Highland arrangement, to a distant summit-line. Much the larger portion may be viewed as simply the screens of the vast glen,—the long and grand mountain-strath of the Spey, and of the numerous tributaries which cut their way to it along lateral glens; another and considerable portion, partly identical with the former, are the vastly fissured masses of the Monadleah mountains, flanking the Findhorn and its head-waters; and a third, though much smaller section, consists of the heights which tower up from the sides of the east end of the great glen of Scotland, admitting, amidst a little wilderness of alps, broad clefts and long narrow vales of picture and romance.

The lowlands of Moray comprise the main matters of its economical interest, and often appropriate all the historical associations of its name; and they have long been known to fame for fertility of soil, and for mildness and luxuriousness of climate. A certain dryness of their atmosphere, in particular, has been repeatedly celebrated by historians and poets. But this property, so delightful in itself, seems to have intimate connexion with the equally though lugubriously celebrated phenomenon of "the Moray floods." The high broad range of mountains on the southwest shelter the lowlands from the prevailing winds of the country, and exhaust many light vapours and thinly charged clouds which might otherwise produce such drizzlings and frequent gentle rains as distinguish the climate of most other lowland districts of Scotland; but, for just the same reason, they powerfully attract whatever long broad streams of heavy clouds are sailing in any direction athwart the sky, and, among the gullies and the upland glens, amass their discharged contents with amazing rapidity and in singular largeness of volume. The rivers of the country are, in consequence, peculiarly liable to sudden freshets and disastrous floods. One general and tremendous outbreak, in 1829, in which they desolated glen and plain, tore up woods and bridges and houses, and powdered and carpeted scores of square miles with the wreck of regions above them, afforded an awful exhibition of the peculiarities of the climate, and will long be remembered, in connexion with the boasted luxuriousness of Moray, as an illustration of how chastisement and comfort are blended in a state of things which is benignly adjusted for the moral discipline of man, and the correction of moral evil.

Moray, at the epoch of record, or about the close of the first century, was possessed by the British tribe of Vacomagi; one of those communities who, after and even sometime before the period of the Roman abdication, figured predominantly in the history of North Britain under the name of Picts. Their towns, while a separate tribe, were Tarnea, in Braemar, immediately beyond the south-eastern limits of Moray; Banatia, on the east side of the Ness, about 600 yards below its efflux from Loch Ness; Ptoroton, on the promontory of Burgh Head; and Tuessis, on the east bank of the Spey, a little below the parish church of Bellie. In the early Pictish periods, the Vacomagi seem to have held a predominant or at least a distinguished place among the confederated tribes; and, at all events, appear to have had within their territory the earliest seat of the Pictavian monarchy.

When the Scots, bursting beyond the limits of Dalriada, and pushing their stealthy but sure conquests northward among the western Highlands, arrived at the uplands which form the mountain-rampart of Moray, they drove the Picts into the plains, and maintained entire possession of the alpine fastnesses and intervening glens. The distinction between the boundaries of the Picts and those of the Scots was long preserved by Moray, and can be traced in the topographical nomenclature throughout the province. Among the charters of Dunbar of Grange, one granted in 1221 by Alexander II. to the abbacy of Kinloss, and referring to the lands of Burgy names as a boundary *Rune Pictorum*, 'the Picts' cairn;' another charter from Richard, Bishop of Moray, granted after the year 1187 to the same abbacy, mentions *Scoticum molendinum;* and a road among the hills to the east of Dollas from the highland to the lowland districts of the province, is, to this day, or, at least, was forty years ago, called the Scots road.

THE CHANGES AND WARS OF MORAY. 143

After the Pictish and the Scotish dominions became consolidated into one monarchy, the Scandinavian vikingr made frequent descents on the plain of Moray, and even enthralled it for long consecutive periods. Thorstein the Red, Sigurd, and Thorfin ruled over it, either independently or with slender acknowledgment of the superiority of the Scotish kings, from the commencement of the 10th till the middle of the 11th century.

The Scandinavian settlers intermarrying with the Scotish and the Pictish Celts, a mixed race arose who seem to have been a necessitous, unsettled, turbulent people. Their chiefs or maormors soon began to assume the name of Earls; and, having some connexion with the reigning family, they advanced pretensions to the throne, and convulsed the country by rebellions against the sovereign, and by deeds of regicide. They killed Malcolm I., in 959, at Ulern, supposed by Shaw to be Aldearn; they killed King Duffus at Forres, in 966, when he came to punish them for their crimes; and, about the year 1160, in consequence of an attempt, on the part of the government, to intrude the Anglo-Norman jurisdiction upon their Celtic customs, they raised a grand rebellion against Malcolm IV.

The insurgents, in this rebellion, laid waste the neighbouring counties, and were so regardless of the royal authority as actually to hang the heralds who were sent to summon them to lay down their arms. Malcolm despatched the gallant Earl Gilchrist with an army to subdue them; but he was defeated, and forced to recross the Grampians. This defeat aroused Malcolm, who was naturally of an indolent disposition; and he marched north with a powerful army, and found the enemy on the muir of Urquhart, near the Spey, ready to give him battle. After passing the Spey, the noblemen in the King's army reconnoitered the enemy; but they found them so well prepared for action, and so flushed with their late success, that they considered the issue of a battle rather doubtful. On this **account, the** commanders advised the King to enter into a negotiation with the rebels, and to promise, that in the event of a submission their lives would be spared. The offer was accepted, and the King kept his word; but as the Moray men were, as Buchanan says, " Homines inquieto semper ingenio," men of a factious disposition, his Majesty, by the advice of his nobles, ordained that every family in Moray which had been engaged in the rebellion should, within a limited time, remove out of Moray to other parts of the kingdom, where lands would be assigned to them, and that their places should be supplied with people from other parts of the kingdom. For the performance of this order, they gave hostages, and at the time appointed transplanted themselves, some into the northern, but the greater number into the southern counties. Chalmers considers this removal of the Moray men as an "egregious probability," because " the dispossessing of a whole people is so difficult an operation, that the recital of it cannot be believed without strong evidence;" but it is not said that the *whole* people were removed, and it is very probable that only the ringleaders and their families were transported. The older historians say that the Moray men were (*pene internecionem*) almost totally cut off in an obstinate battle, and strangers brought into their place; but this statement is at variance with the register of Paisley, and the fact, that while there are very few *persons* of the name of Murray in Moray, they are numerous in the counties on the English borders, and are to be found in the more northern counties, where some of them have taken the name of Sutherland, favours the account which that writing gives of the transportation of the Moray men.

Both Malcolm IV., after expatriating the rebels, and his successor William the Lion, appear to have frequently resided in the province; for, from Inverness, Elgin, and various others of its localities, they dated several of their charters.

Among the new families who were brought in to replace the expatriated, the chief are supposed to have been **the powerful Earls of Fife and Strathern, and the once potent Comyns and Byset Ostiarii**; among the original families who remained were **the Inneses, the Calders,** and others; and among those who speedily appeared in the possession of extensive property and great local influence, the chief was the family of De Moravia, whose founder, or at least whose earliest figurant, was Freskinus, **Lord of Duffus.**

The mixed and altered race who henceforth were sons of the soil, lived for many centuries apart from their Celtic neighbours; and—as still appears by the resemblance of the vocalic sounds of the provincial idiom to those of the languages spoken north of France—they retained in speech, and probably in customs, many of the characteristics of their semi-Scandinavian predecessors. They appear also to have become, if not effeminate, at least greatly more peaceable, less hardy, and less acquainted with the use of arms than the stern mountaineers of the upland districts of Badenoch and Lochaber.

Either from the superior richness of the country, or from the comparatively easy and peaceful character of the inhabitants, the Highland caterans regarded the plain of Moray as open and ever-available spoliage-ground, where every marauder might, at his convenience, seek his prey. So late, in fact, as the time of Charles I., the Highlanders continually made forays on the country, and seem to have encountered marvellously little resistance. The Moray men, it has been remarked, appear to have resembled the quiet saturnine Dutch settlers of North America, who, when plundered by the red Indians, were too fat either to resist or to pursue, and considered only how they might repair their losses; and Pennant supposes that, in consequence of their being so mixed a race, Picts, Danes, and Saxons, and altogether aliens to the pure Celtic communities of the mountains, the Highlanders

K

thought them quite 'fair game,' and never exactly comprehended how there could be any crime in robbing 'the Moray men.' So late as 1565, as appears from the rental of the church-lands in that year, the inhabitants of the province remained entirely a distinct people from the Highlanders, and all bore such names of purely Lowland origin as are still common around Elgin; and not till a comparatively recent period did declining feuds and the prejudices of clanship permit social intercourse and intermarriages with the neighbouring Gordons, Grants, and Macphersons. Moray, in consequence of the attachment of its people to the cause of the Solemn League and Covenant, and of the Marquis of Montrose and his ally, Lord Lewis Gordon, having adopted it as one of their principal scenes of action, suffered more disasters than perhaps any other district of Scotland from the civil wars under the last of the Stuarts. So severe and memorable were the inflictions upon it by Lord Lewis Gordon, that an old rhymer classes his name with the Scottish designations of two of the worst plagues of an agricultural country:

"The gule, the Gordon, and the hoodie craw,
  Are the three warst things that Moray ever saw."

Montrose, after his victory of Inverlochy, in 1645, made a desolating descent upon the province, destroying the houses of all persons who would not join his standard, and inflicting upon the towns of Elgin, Cullen, and Banff the disasters of an indiscriminate pillage.

THE SIEGE OF ST. SEBASTIAN.

Scott has beautifully said respecting the diversities of British troops who fought throughout the eventful wars of the Spanish peninsula:—

A various host they came,—whose ranks display
Each mode in which the warrior meets the fight.
The deep battalion locks its firm array,
And meditates his aim the marksman light;
Far glance the lines of sabres flashing bright,
Where mounted squadrons shake the echoing mead;
Lacks not artillery breathing flame and night,
Nor the fleet ordnance whirl'd by rapid steed,
That rivals lightning's flash, in ruin and in speed.

A various host—from kindred realms they came,
Brethren in arms, but rivals in renown—
For yon fair bands shall merry England claim,
And with their deeds of valour deck her crown.
Hers their bold port, and hers their martial frown,
And hers their scorn of death in Freedom's cause,
Their eyes of azure, and their locks of brown,
And the blunt speech that bursts without a pause,
And freeborn thoughts, which league the soldier with the laws.

And, oh! loved warriors of the Minstrel's land!
Yonder your bonnets nod, your tartans wave!
The rugged form may mark the mountain band,
And harsher features, and a mien more grave;
But ne'er in battle-field throbbed heart so brave
As that which beats beneath the Scotish plaid;
And when the pibroch bids the battle rave,
And level for the charge your arms are laid,
Where lives the desperate foe that for such onset staid."

Three Highland regiments, the 42nd, the 79th, and the 92nd, were specially conspicuous in the peninsular campaigns. The 42nd was the earliest Highland regiment ever raised, and has always moved foremost in the march of fame; the 79th is the regiment of Cameron Highlanders, first raised in the year 1793, among the glens of the central Grampians; and the 92nd is the regiment of Gordon Highlanders, first raised in the year 1794, principally on the estates of the Duke of Gordon, and afterwards always recruited mainly from the counties of Aberdeen and Banff. These regiments fought so bravely in the skirmishes and battles of the Peninsula, and performed so many of the feats which led to victory, and were so often foremost in desperate onset and hindmost in lingering retreat, that the exciting history of the whole peninsular war derives from their achievements much of the colouring and interest of a Scotish narrative. Corunna, Salamanca, Burgos, Vittoria, and most other far-famed names in that eventful history, might all be made appropriate headings of chapters in the grand story of Scotish military exploits; and, since all were so dazzling, we can scarcely go amiss for a specimen, and may select one at random; and in selecting the siege of St. Sebastian, we do less than average justice to the Highlanders, for only the 92nd were present in its feats.

In the summer of 1813, when the French had been driven from all the strengths of the north of Spain excepting Pampluna and St. Sebastian, General Graham was assigned the arduous task of attempting the reduction of the latter,—then esteemed the most important fort within all the Spanish territory excepting Gibraltar. On the 14th of July, the arrangements for the siege were complete, and the batteries began to play on the convent of St. Bartolomeo; and on the 17th, this stronghold, though fortified with a protecting work, and a steep hill on its left flank, was so completely destroyed, that General Graham ordered both to be stormed. The division of General Oswald carried these posts, though bravely defended by a strong body of men. Having made two breaches which were considered practicable, a party of two thousand men made an assault on the 25th; but after an obstinate contest, they were recalled, after sustaining a very

THE SIEGE OF ST. SEBASTIAN.

severe loss. The attention of the commander-in-chief being now directed to the movements of Marshal Soult, who was advancing with a large army, the siege of St. Sebastian was suspended for a time.

At this juncture the allied army occupied a range of mountain passes between the valley of Roncesvalles, celebrated as the field of Charlemagne's defeat, and St. Sebastian; but as the distance between these stations was 60 miles, it was found impossible so to guard all these passes as to prevent the entrance of an army. The passes occupied by the allies were defended by the following troops:—Major-general Byng's brigade and a division of Spanish infantry held the valley of Roncesvalles, to support which General Cole's division was posted at Piscarret, with General Picton's in reserve at Olaque; the valley of Bastan and the pass of Maya was occupied by Sir Rowland Hill, with Lieutenant-general William Stewart's and Silviera's Portuguese divisions, and the Spanish corps under the Condé de Amaran; the Portuguese brigade of Brigadier-General Archibald Campbell was detached to Los Alduidos; the heights of St. Barbara, the town of Pera, and the Puerto de Echelar, were protected by Lord Dalhousie and Baron Alten's light division, Brigadier-general Pack's being in reserve at Estevan. The communication between Lord Dalhousie and General Graham was kept up by General Longa's Spanish division; and the Condé de Abisbal blockaded Pampluna.

Such were the positions of the allied army when Marshal Soult, who had been lately appointed to the command of a numerous French army, recently collected, having formed a plan of operations for a general attack on the allied army advanced on the 25th of July at the head of a division of 36,000 men against Roncesvalles, whilst General Count d'Erlon, with another division of 13,000 men, moved towards the pass of Maya. Pressed by this overwhelming force, General Byng was obliged, though supported by part of Sir Lowry Cole's division, to descend from the heights that commanded the pass, in order to preserve his communication, in which situation he was attacked by Soult and driven back to the top of the mountain, whilst the troops on the ridge of Arola, part of Cole's division, were forced to retire with considerable loss, and to take up a position in the rear. General Cole was again obliged to retire, and fell back on Lizoain. Next day General Picton moved forward to support General Cole; but both were obliged to retire in consequence of Soult's advance.

Meanwhile Count d'Erlon forced the battalions occupying the narrow ridges near the pass of Maya to give way; but these being quickly supported by Brigadier-general Barnes's brigade, a series of spirited actions ensued, and the advance of the enemy was arrested. In the main combat of Maya, the right wing of the 92nd regiment, drawn up in line, met the advancing French column; and after sustaining a most destructive fire, part of it retired, and the other part, consisting more of the wounded and the dying than the dead, lay still like a long and continuous rampart. The French column advanced up to this human rampart, and halted behind it; and the left wing of the 92nd then opened their fire on the column, and inevitably made awful slaughter upon their own fallen comrades. "So dreadful was the slaughter," says Napier, "that it is said the advancing enemy was actually stopped by the heaped masses of dead and dying; and then the left wing of that noble regiment, coming down from the higher ground, smote wounded friends and exulting foes alike, as mingled together they stood or crawled before its fire. . . Maransin, no longer seeking to turn the position, suddenly thrust the head of his division across the front of the British line, throwing as he passed a destructive fire into the wasted remnant of the 92nd, which even then sullenly gave way, for the men fell until two-thirds of the whole had gone to the ground. Still the survivors fought. . The stern valour of the 92nd would have graced Thermopylæ."

THE SIEGE OF ST. SEBASTIAN.

General Hill, hearing of the retrograde movement from Roncesvalles, retired behind the Irurita, and took up a strong position. On the 27th, Sir Thomas Picton resumed his retreat. The troops were greatly dejected at this temporary reverse; but the arrival of Lord Wellington, who had been with the army before St. Sebastian, revived their drooping spirits. Immediately on his arrival he directed the troops in reserve to move forward to support the division opposed to the enemy. He formed General Picton's division on a ridge on the left bank of the Argua, and General Cole's on the high grounds between that river and the Lanz. To support the positions in front, General Hill was posted behind the Lizasso; but, on the arrival of General Pakenham on the 28th, he took post on the left of General Cole, facing the village of Sourarem; but before the British divisions had fully occupied the ground, they were vigorously attacked by the enemy from the village. The enemy were, however, driven back with great loss, after a short but severe contest.

Soult next brought forward a strong column, and advancing up the hill against the centre of the allies, on the left of General Cole's line, obtained possession of that post; but he was almost immediately driven back at the point of the bayonet by the Fusileers. The French renewed the attack, but were again quickly repulsed. About the same time, another attack was made on the right of the centre, where a Spanish brigade, supported by the 40th, was posted. The Spaniards gave way, but the 40th not only kept their ground, but drove the enemy down the hill with great loss.

The enemy pushing forward in separate bodies with great vigour, the battle now became general along the whole front of the heights occupied by the fourth division; but they were repulsed at all points, except one occupied by a Portuguese battalion, which was overpowered and obliged to give way. The occupation of this post by the enemy exposed the flank of Major-General Ross's brigade, immediately on the right, to a destructive fire, which forced him to retire. The enemy were, however, soon dispossessed of this post by Colonel John Maclean, who, advancing with the 27th and 48th regiments, charged and drove them from it, and immediately afterwards attacked and charged another body of the enemy who were advancing from the left. The enemy persevered in his attacks several times, but was as often repulsed, principally by the bayonet. Several regiments charged four different times.

The division of Lord Dalhousie, from the left, having reinforced the centre the following day, Soult withdrew a part of his troops from his strong position in front of the allies, with the intention of turning the left of their position. Though the position occupied by Soult in front appeared almost impregnable, yet Lord Wellington resolved, after this reduction of Soult's force, to attempt it. Accordingly, on the morning of the 30th, Lord Dalhousie made a well-conducted attack on the heights on the right, which was performed with great bravery by Brigadier-general Inglis's brigade. Sir Thomas Picton, during this operation, turned their left, whilst General Pakenham, at the same time, drove them from the village of Ostiz. These successful attacks were followed up by one made in front by General Cole's division, upon which the enemy, to use the words of Lord Wellington, "abandoned a position which is one of the strongest and most difficult of access that I have yet seen occupied by troops." The enemy were now pursued beyond Olaque, in the vicinity of which General Hill, who had been engaged the whole day, had repulsed all the attacks of Count d'Erlon; and though they endeavoured to rally in their retreat, they were driven from one position to another till the 2nd of August, when the allies had regained all the posts they had occupied on the 25th of July, when Soult made his first attack.

After this second expulsion of the French beyond the Pyrenees, the siege of St. Sebastian was resumed with re

THE SIEGE OF ST. SEBASTIAN.

doubled energy. A continued fire was kept up from eighty pieces of cannon, which the enemy withstood with surprising courage and perseverance. At length a practicable breach was made, and on the morning of the 31st of August the troops advanced to the assault. The breach was extensive, but there was only one point where it was possible to enter, and this could only be done by single files. All the inside of the wall to the height of the curtain formed a perpendicular scarp of twenty feet. The troops made the most persevering exertions to force the breach, and everything that bravery could attempt was repeatedly tried by the men who were brought forward in succession from the trenches; but each time, on attaining the summit, all who attempted to remain were destroyed by a heavy fire from the entrenched ruins within, so that "no man outlived the attempt to gain the ridge."

"Sir Thomas Graham, standing on the nearest of the Chofre batteries," says Napier, " beheld the frightful destruction with a stern resolution to win at any cost; and he was a man to have put himself at the head of the last company and died sword in hand upon the breach rather than sustain a second defeat; but neither his confidence nor his resources were yet exhausted. He directed an attempt to be made on the horn work, and turned all the Chofre batteries, and one on the Isthmus, that is to say the concentrated fire of fifty heavy pieces upon the high curtain. The shot ranged over the heads of the troops, who now were gathered at the foot of the breach, and the stream of missiles thus poured along the upper surface of the high curtain broke down the traverses, and in its fearful course shattering all things, strewed the rampart with the mangled limbs of the defenders. When this flight of bullets first swept over the heads of the soldiers, a cry arose from some inexperienced people,' to retire because the batteries were firing on the stormers.' But the veterans of the light division under Hunt, being at that point, were not to be so disturbed; and in the very heat and fury of the cannonade, effected a solid lodgment in some ruins of houses actually within the rampart on the right of the great breach." Hughes in his poem called " Iberia Won " describes this singular passage of military history in the following terms:—

> " Upon the Chofre stood the dauntless Graham,
> And marked the slaughter with determined eye
> Sad, yet unshrinking—poured then forth of flame
> A torrent, hissing red athwart the sky;
> Close o'er the stormers' heads the missiles fly;
> The stone-ribbed curtain into fragments hurled—
> Full fifty cannon streaming death on high.
> Unmoved they stand—no flag of fear unfurled—
> A scene unmatched before since dawning of the world
>
> Even as at Niagara's thundering,
> Where leaps the torrent with gigantic stride;
> Beneath the watery volume, Cyclop wall,
> Of rocks, huge piled, spans the river wide,
> Where dares the venturous voyager abide;
> And while his ears terrific clamour stuns,
> Flies free o'erhead the cataract's foaming tide,
> And scarce crystalline globule o'er him runs:
> Thus stand 'neath Death o'erarched, Britannia's dauntless sons!
>
> 'Retire!' was first the cry, 'A traitorous foe!
> Our batteries' fire is 'gainst the stormers turned;'
> And struck a straggling shot the ranks below;
> But Niall and his men the counsel spurned—
> To win, whate'er the cost, their bosoms burned,
> And mid the fiercest of the cannonade,
> While San Sebastian for his bulwarks mourned,
> Within the rampart solid ground they made—
> First step in victory's march whose laurels ne'er will fade."

The fire of the batteries upon the high curtain was directed with admirable precision; and the troops advanced with perfect confidence. They struggled unremittingly for two hours to force the breach, and, taking advantage of some confusion occasioned by an explosion of ammunition within the ramparts, they redoubled their efforts, and by assisting each other got over the walls and ruins. After struggling about an hour among their works, the French retreated with great loss to the castle, leaving the town, which was now reduced to a heap of ruins, in the possession of the assailants. This success was dearly purchased,—the loss of the allies, in killed and wounded, being upwards of two thousand men. Soult made an attempt to raise the siege, by crossing the Bidassoa on the very day the assault was made with a force of nearly 40,000 men; but he was obliged, after repeated attacks, to repass the river.

SOMERLED THE THANE OF ARGYLE.

SOMERLED is well known in tradition and history and song as the founder of the great family of Macdonald, Lords of the Isles. His grandfather held considerable possessions in the Western Highlands, but was expelled from them by the Norsemen, and took refuge in Ireland; and though he persuaded the Macquarries and the MacMahons of that country to espouse his cause, and made an expedition with their assistance against his enemies, he had no success and was obliged to sit down in permanent poverty. Somerled's father and Somerled himself long remained in the poverty bequeathed to them; but sought an obscure retreat within the limits of their patrimonial territory, and lived in a cave, which is till pointed out as theirs, on the shores of Loch Linnhe. Somerled lived in great retirement, musing on the ruined fortunes of his house, and seemingly more inclined to indulge in melancholy than to watch an opportunity for enterprise or adventure; but, in the course of time, he was roused by an incitement from without, and suddenly proved himself to be a master of expedients and of intrigues and stratagems.

The clan MacInnes were at this time—the early part of the twelth century—occupants of a large portion of Morvern and had suffered great disasters in withstanding repeated invasions of the marauding Norsemen, and were menaced with another attack, and felt at their wit's end for competent skill and resources to repel the foe. They held an assembly, and resolved to fight as one man, and to invite Somerled to organise them and lead them to battle. Their messengers found him angling in the Gear-Abhain. He heard them in silence; and remained silent and thoughtful for some time after they had ceased to speak; and at last observed that he was in pursuit of a sportive salmon, and that if he could succeed in landing him, he would consider it a good omen. He hooked the fish, and, after following it through some bold plunges and struggles, brought it safely to the bank. But he angled not for mere amusement; and before going to the MacInneses, he proceeded to his father's cave, there to present the food which he had obtained for his sustenance, and to make a due discharge of other filial home duties. Yet on parting with the messengers, he gave directions respecting a suitable place of muster, and commanded that a great number of fires—a number so great as to appear to the clansmen wonderful and mysterious—should be lighted round their encampment during the following night, and added that, by the time of the completion of the arrangements, he should be amongst them to assume the generalship, and render them the best efforts of his skill.

Somerled surveyed from a distance the host of invaders, and, concluding them to be vastly superior to the greatest force which he could oppose to them, he invented a stratagem for deceiving them respecting his own numbers. A herd

SOMERLED THE THANE OF ARGYLE   157

of cattle lay depasturing in the neighbouring valley; and all these he ordered to be killed and skinned. He occupied a position which commanded a full view of the enemy's movements; and as soon as he saw them commence their march, he caused his small force to descend the eminence into a small glen at its base which opened toward the shore,—to make a circuit thence round the further side of the hill, over its summit, and back again to the glen,—and to repeat this movement several times continuously, so as to produce the appearance to the enemy of a numerous battalion. And then, ordering every man to wrap himself in an ox's hide, with the smooth side outward, he made the force repeat the same deceptive march, so as to produce the appearance of a second numerous battalion; and afterwards ordering them to reverse the hides, turning the hairy side outward, he made them once more repeat the movement, so as to produce the appearance of a third and very savage-looking battalion. The stratagem succeeded. The Norsemen, supposing that a large and formidable army was descending upon them, fell into disorder, hesitated to stand, and gave way to panic; and Somerled and his associates rushed suddenly against them, and cut down their advanced body with great slaughter. Two of the Norse leaders, Borradill and Lundy, were slain in corries which still bear their name; and a third, Stangadill, was so hotly pursued and so dreadfully terror-struck, that, in order to escape the sword, he leaped into a boiling linn, which is still called Eass Stangadill.

Somerled followed up his first exploit with others of similar daring and success; and, after struggling long with the Norsemen, he expelled them from a great extent of the Western Highlands, and made himself master of all Morvern, Lochaber, and northern Argyle; and not long afterwards, added to his other possessions the southern districts of that country. In the year 1035, when David I. expelled the Norwegians from Man, Arran, and Bute, Somerled appears to have obtained a grant of those islands from the King. But finding himself still unable to contend with the Norwegians of the Isles, whose power remained unbroken, he resolved to recover by policy, what he despaired of acquiring by force of arms; and, with this view, he succeeded in obtaining by stratagem, the hand of the daughter of Olave, surnamed the Red, who was then the Norwegian King of the Isles. The lady thus fraudulently seized and forcibly married, brought him three sons, namely, Dugall, Reginald, and Angus; and, by a previous marriage, he had one named Gillecallum.

The prosperous fortunes of Somerled at length inflamed his ambition. He had already attained great power in the Highlands; and success inspired him with the desire of extending it. His grandsons having formerly claimed the earldom of Moray, their pretensions were now renewed; and this was followed by an attempt to put them in actual possession of their alleged inheritance. This attempt brought the Thane of Argyle into open rebellion against the King, and appears to have excited great alarm amongst the inhabitants of Scotland; but Somerled encountering a more vigorous opposition than he had anticipated, found it necessary to return to the west, where the tyrannical conduct of his brother-in law, Godred, who then wore the Norwegian crown of the Isles, had irritated his vassals and thrown every thing into confusion. Somerled's presence gave confidence to the party opposed to the tyrant; and Thorfinn, one of the most powerful of the Norwegian nobles, resolved to depose Godred, and place another prince on the throne of the Isles. Somerled readily entered into the views of Thorfinn; and it was arranged that Dugall, the eldest son of the former, should occupy the throne from which his maternal uncle was to be displaced. But the result of the projected deposition did not answer the expectations of either party. Dugall was committed to the care of Thorfinn, who undertook to con duct him through the Isles, and compel the chiefs not only to acknowledge him as their sovereign, but also to give hostages for their fidelity and allegiance. The Lord of Skye, however, refused to comply with this demand, and, having fled to the Isle of Man, apprized Godred of the intended revolution. Somerled followed with a fleet of galleys; and Godred having commanded his ships to be got ready, a bloody but indecisive battle ensued. It was fought on the night of the Epiphany; and as neither party prevailed, the rival chiefs next morning entered into a sort of compromise or convention, by which the sovereignty of the Isles was divided, and two distinct principalities established. By this treaty Somerled acquired all the islands lying to the southward of the promontory of Ardnamurchan, whilst those to the northward remained in the possession of Godred.

But no sooner had he made this acquisition than he became involved in hostilities with the government. Having joined the powerful party in Scotland, which had resolved to depose Malcolm IV., and to place the boy of Egremont on the throne, he began to infest various parts of the coast, and for some time carried on a vexatious predatory warfare. The project, however, failed; and Malcolm, convinced that the existence of an independent chief was incompatible with the interests of his government and the maintenance of public tranquillity, required of Somerled to resign his lands into the hands of the sovereign, and to hold them in future as a vassal of the crown. Somerled, however, was little disposed to comply with this demand, although the King was now preparing to enforce it by means of a powerful army. Emboldened by his previous successes, he resolved to anticipate the attack; and having appeared in the Clyde with a considerable force, he landed at Renfrew, where being met by the royal army under the command of the High Steward of Scotland, a battle ensued which ended in his defeat and death.

This celebrated chief has been traditionally described, as

"a well-tempered man, in body shapely, of a fair piercing eye, of middle stature, and of quick discernment." He appears, indeed, to have been equally brave and sagacious, tempering courage with prudence, and, excepting in the last act of his life, distinguished for the happy talent, rare at any period, of profiting by circumstances, and making the most of success. In the battle of Renfrew his son Gillecallum perished by his side, leaving a son, Somerled, who succeeded to his grandfather's possessions.

THE WAILS OF YARROW.

The Yarrow is a river of Selkirkshire, more celebrated in song than any other stream in Scotland. An idea of lugubrious sadness is associated with much of its scenery, and with its early and chief historical reminiscence. What that reminiscence precisely is cannot be ascertained beyond the general tradition of a deadly feud, which terminated in the death of two antagonist lords or leaders, and in the rude inhumation of the bodies of their slain followers in a marshy pool called the Dead-lake. Yet some have identified it with a duel fought between John Scott of Tushielaw and his brother-in-law Walter Scott of Thirlestane,—a duel which was fatal to the latter, but is ascertained to have been fought on Deuchar-swire, at a considerable distance; others suppose it to have been a fray at a hunting-match in Ettrick-forest, which issued in the slaughter of a son of Scott of Harden, residing at Kirkhope, by his kinsman Scott of Gilmanscleuch; and a few, including two or three of eminent celebrity, refer it to the murder of some distinguished gentleman or other by a person of the name of Annan. "In a spot called Annan's Treat," says Sir Thomas Dick Lauder, "a huge monumental stone, with an eligible inscription, was discovered, which is supposed to record the event of a combat, in which the male ancestor of the present Lord Napier was slain. And then two tall unhewn stones are erected on Annan's Treat, about eighty yards distant from each other, which the smallest child tending a cow will tell you, mark the spot where lie the twa lords, who were slain in single fight. Scott tells us, that " Tradition affirms, that be the victim whom he may, he was murdered by the brother, either of his wife, or betrothed bride. The alleged cause of malice was the lady's father having proposed to endow her with the half of his property, upon her marriage with a warrior of such renown. The name of the murderer is said to have been Annan, and the place of the combat is still called Annan's Treat."

But whatever was the precise event which first or chiefly rendered the glen of the Yarrow famous ground, the tradition of the country around it, and above all a well-known ancient ballad entitled " The Dowie Dens of Yarrow," have imparted to it a high tragic interest, and made it sacred in the eyes of all antiquaries and poets. The following is the song:—

" Late at e'en, drinking the wine,
 And e'er they paid the lawing,
They set a combat them between,
 To fight it in the dawing.

' Oh stay at hame, my noble lord,
 Oh stay at hame, my marrow!
My cruel brother will you betray,
 On the dowie houms of Yarrow.'

' Oh fare ye weel, my ladye gaye!
 Oh fare ye weel, my Sarah!
For I maun gae, though I ne'er return
 Frae the dowie banks of Yarrow.'

THE WAILS OF YARROW.

She kissed his cheek, she kaimed his hair,
   As oft she had done before, O;
She belted him with his noble brand,
   And he's away to Yarrow.

As he gaed up the Tinnis bank,
   I wot he gaed wi' sorrow,
Till down in a den, he spied nine armed men,
   On the dowie houms of Yarrow.

'Oh come ye here to part your land,
   The bonny forest thorough?
Or come ye here to wield your brand,
   On the dowie houms of Yarrow?'

'I come not here to part my land
   And neither to beg nor borrow;
I come to wield my noble brand,
   On the bonny banks of Yarrow.

If I see all, ye're nine to ane;
   And that's an unequal marrow;
Yet will I fight while lasts my brand
   On the bonny banks of Yarrow.'

Four has he hurt, and five has slain,
   On the bloody braes of Yarrow,
Till that stubborn knight came him behind,
   And run his body thorough.

'Gae hame, gae hame, good-brother John
   And tell your sister, Sarah,
To come and lift her leafu' lord;
   He's sleeping sound on Yarrow.'

THE WAILS OF YARROW.

' Yestreen, I dreamed a doleful dream,
    I fear there will be sorrow;
I dreamed I pou'd the heather green,
    Wi' my true love on Yarrow.

' O gentle wind, that bloweth south,
    From where my love repaireth,
Convey a kiss from his dear mouth,
    And tell me how he fareth!

' But in the glen strive armed men;
    They've wrought me dole and sorrow;
They've slain—the comliest knight they've slain—
    He bleeding lies on Yarrow.'

As she sped down yon high, high hill,
    She gaed wi' dole and sorrow,
And in the den, spied ten slain men,
    On the dowie banks of Yarrow.

She kissed his cheek, she kaimed his hair,
    She searched his wounds all thorough;
She kissed them till her lips grew red,
    On the dowie houms of Yarrow.

' Now, haud your tongue, my daughter dear!
    For a' this breeds but sorrow;
I'll wed you to a better lord
    Than him ye lost on Yarrow.'

' O haud your tongue, my father dear!
    Ye mind me but of sorrow;
A fairer rose did never bloom,
    Than now lies cropped on Yarrow.'"

THE WAILS OF YARROW.

A modern song by Mr. Hamilton of Bangour, beginning

"Busk ye, busk ye, my bonnie bonnie bride!
Busk ye, busk ye, my winsome marrow!"

was suggested by the same event, and has rivalled the ancient song in influence. The dejected loneliness of the Yarrow's vale, so well and so succinctly depicted in the phrase of 'Dowie Dens,' sadly harmonizes with the wailing tones of the ballads and the traditions, and powerfully appeals to the lachrymose sympathies of poets. The sound of the stream has not one note of the joyousness which would seem naturally to belong to the rate of its current; the aspect of the green hills which come down upon its margin possesses not one indication of the vocal and the vegetable animation which might be expected from their softness and their seeming fertility; and the whole landscape, in spite of objects which, in other circumstances, might arouse and gladden, looks to be in a condition of appalling repose, of unearthly stillness, of strength and beauty in the inertion of death. Hence, of the numerous poems which describe the stream or allude to it, the majority are deeply pathetic. An old fragment, "Willie's drowned in Yarrow," is entirely plaintive. Logan's piece, "Thy braes were bonnie, Yarrow stream," is also plaintive. And the "Douglas Tragedie," the "Sang of the Outlaw Murray," and the oldest verses of the "Yellow-hair'd Laddie," are proved by their allusions to have borrowed both their scenery and much of their sadness from the Yarrow.

Among numerous pieces either descriptive of the stream or chiefly devoted to it, the principal are "the Braes of Yarrow," by Allan Ramsay, and "Yarrow Vale," by Mr. M'Donald. Two songs in praise of the distinguished female beauty so well-known as "the Flower of Yarrow," bear the titles of "Mary Scott" and "the Rose in Yarrow," and have been not a little popular. But the most distinguished verses

The Battle History of Scotland.—*Page* 163.

which have been written upon the stream, or those, at least, which have written it most into notice, are three pieces by Wordsworth, entitled respectively "Yarrow Unvisited," "Yarrow Visited," and "Yarrow Revisited." The first was composed eleven years before, and the latter immediately after the poet saw the vale; and though they entirely refer to the poetical charm thrown over the stream by the various ballads in its praise, they themselves produce an interest fully equal to the aggregate of all that had been previously accumulated. "And is this Yarrow?" exclaims the poet in the " Yarrow Visited,"—

> " And is this Yarrow?—This the stream
>   Of which my fancy cherished
> So faithfully a waking dream?
>   An image that hath perished!
> O that some minstrel's harp were near
>   To utter tones of gladness,
> And chase this silence from the air
>   That fills my heart with sadness!
> Yet why? A silvery current flows
>   With uncontrolled meanderings;
> Nor have these eyes, by greener hills,
>   Been soothed in all my wanderings."

The fortified residence described in the famous old "Song of the Outlaw Murray"—"the fair castelle, biggit wi' lyme and stane," pleasantly situated, grandly decorated, and the frequent scene of crowds and carousals—was the romantic castle of Hangingshaw, on the left declivity of the lower and more picturesque part of the glen of the Yarrow, belonging for ages to the Murrays of Philiphaugh, and long a place ol great strength and magnificence, but now the property of Johnstone of Alva, and reduced to a few low ruins and fragments. Here, says the ballad,

> "Here an outlaw keepis five hundred men,
>   He keepis a royale cumpanie!
> His merryemen are a' in ae liverye clad
>   O' the Lincone grene sae gae to see;
> He and his ladye in purple clad,
>   O! gin they lived not royallie!"

The outlaw was a bold and brave knight, and ruled over a tract of country in the style of a petty sovereign, and probably made raids and over-ran neighbouring territories in the marauding fashion of his age, and believed himself to be as truly king within his own mimic realm as James V. was king over the greater part of Scotland; but he does not appear to have acted tyrannically in his jurisdiction or to have entertained any designs against the Scotish crown or dynasty or government, and therefore was not, in any direct or truculent sense, an outlaw. Yet he was setting a perilous example to the fiery barons of Scotland, and perhaps did more mischief to the monarchy than if he had really defied its power. At any rate, James V. felt nettled to hear of the independent and princely life which Murray was leading, and got up an army to attack him, and bring him into subjugation.

> "The King was coming through Cadon Ford
>   And full five thousand men was he;
> They saw the derke foreste them before,
>   They thought it awsome for so see."

And either from prudent apprehension of ambuscades and stratagems within the "awsome foreste," or from humane reluctance to drive so gallant and noble a knight to extremities, the King halted, made overtures for a treaty, entered into a long negotiation, and eventually conceded such pleasant terms as drew from "the outlaw" a promise to become a faithful vassal of the crown. And while Murray was making terms for himself, he honourably made good ones also for his allies; and the King sweetened all with a spirit of conciliatoriness and generosity; so that the military demonstration which seemed inevitably to lead to a most sanguinary conflict, produced only a pacification, and a fast, useful, public friendship. Murray's chief stipulation and James's reply to it were the following:—

> " I'll give the keys of my castell,
>   Wi' the blessing o' my gay ladye,
> Gin thou'lt make me sheriffe of this foreste,
>   And a' my offspring after me."

> " Wilt thou give me the keys of thy castell,
>   Wi' the blessing of thy gay ladye?
> I'll make thee sheriffe of Ettricke Foreste,
>   Surely while upward grows the tree;
> If you do not traitour to the King
>   Forfaulted sall thou nivir be."

Part of the property concerned in the negociation—a part which the tradition of the neighbourhood regards as more important than Hangingshaw itself, and even asserts to have been "the outlaw's" residence—is Newark Castle, still standing, on a peninsula of the lower part of the Yarrow, amid a fantastically wild scene of grandeur and beauty within the parish of Selkirk. This was the home of Anne, Duchess of Buccleuch and Monmouth, whose husband James, Duke of Monmouth, was beheaded for insurrection in the reign of James VII.; and is the well-known scene in which 'the Last Minstrel' is made to sing his 'lay' to the sad-hearted Duchess:—

> " He passed where Newark's stately tower
>   Looks out from Yarrow's birchen bower:

"The minstrel gazed with wistful eye,
No humbler resting-place was nigh.
With hesitating step at last,
The embattled portal-arch he passed,
Whose ponderous grate and massy bar
Had oft rolled back the tide of war;
But never closed the iron door
Against the desolate and poor.
The Duchess marked his weary pace,
His timid mien and reverend face,
And bade her page the menials tell,
That they should tend the old man well;
For she had known adversity,
Though born in such a high degree;
In pride of power, in beauty's bloom,
Had wept o'er Monmouth's bloody tomb."

THE MACDOUGALLS.

The MacDougalls, as well as the MacDonalds, are descendants of the great Somerled, the Thane of Argyle; and they were long represented by their chief family the Lords of Lorn, just as the MacDonalds were represented by the Lords of the Isles. But they do not come prominently into notice till the time of Robert Bruce; and then the Lord of Lorn and his son John, stimulated by considerations of relationship by marriage to the Red Comyn whom Bruce slew at Dumfries, signalized themselves by hot and fiery efforts on the side of England and the Comyns.

In the summer of 1306, Bruce made his first grand martial thrust for the crown, in an expedition against the city of Perth but was discomfited and very nearly destroyed at Methven. He narrowly escaped personal captivity and death, and suffered severe loss and dispersion of his troops, and retired with only a small and dispirited remnant into the fastnesses of Athole. He lurked some time among the profound solitudes of the central Grampians, enduring excessive privation and fatigue; and then passed for a little into the low country of Aberdeenshire; and then, at the approach of some English forces, retreated back to the Grampians, and crept cautiously along the alpine glens of Perthshire, into the district of Breadalbane.

Here, in the vicinity of a little village which now bears the name of Clifton, he was sought out and confronted by the Lord of Lorn. His force, though very small, was lionhearted, and stood firmly up to the fight. Lorn's army amounted to upwards of a thousand, and had among them the barons of Argyle, and were fresh and full of hope. The clash and fury of the conflict were terrible. Both sides fought with steel, and thrust and tugged in the closest encounter; and, says Barbour,—

> " The King's folk full well them bare
> And slew and fell'd and wounded sare;
> But the folk of the other party
> Fought with axes most fellily."

Two of Bruce's chief knights were soon wounded; and the whole of his small band, though holding doggedly to the conflict, felt speedily compelled to yield some ground. Bruce rode hardily into the thickest of the fray, and not only inspirited his own men, but made havoc among the foe, and " ferl of them there gart he fall." But he promptly saw the necessity for prudence; and, sounding a retreat, he employed dexterous skill and heroic valour in holding his little force together, and defeating the onsets of their pursuers.

> " Then he withdrew them haillily,
> But that was not full cowardly,

> For fast into a sop hold they
> And the King him abandon'd ay
> Behind, for to defend his menzie;
> And through his worship so wrought he,
> That he rescued all the fleers,
> And stinted straggat all the chasers,
> That none durst out of battle chase,
> For always at their hand he was,
> So well defended he his men
> That whosoe'er had seen him then,
> Prove so worthy in vassalage,
> And turn so oft-time his visage,
> He should say, he ought well to be
> A king of a great royalty."

The Lord of Lorn was grievously mortified at the orderliness of Bruce's retreat,—" right angry in his heart," and sorely vexed, at being hindered from reaping some fair fruit of victory; and he made strenuous attempts to hang disastrously on Bruce's rear, but was destined only to experience further mortification. And a story is told by Barbour—perhaps with some embellishment of circumstances—that three of his men " the hardiest of hand in all the country," resolved to slay Bruce in the retreat, or perish,—that they made a simultaneous attack upon him at a choking part of a gorge, where he had scarcely room to turn his horse,—and that he struck off the arm of one, clove another " on the head to the harns," and slew outright and single-handedly all the three, so as to strike awe and respect into all their comrades who were coming on behind.

Some additional notices of this conflict, together with notices of disagreeable consequences of it to Bruce, are contained in the article entitled " The Battle of Dalree," on pp. 56–70 of the Second Volume of these Tales. Nor was this the only instance in which Bruce's life was put in jeo pardy by the unrelenting hostility of the MacDougalls. On another occasion, when he had been obliged to conceal himself from the pursuit of his enemies, he was tracked by John of Lorn and a party of his followers, who were led on by a blood-hound; and he only escaped falling into their hands by an incredible effort of courage and activity. In his day of adversity, they were the most persevering and dangerous of all King Robert's enemies.

But the time for retribution at length arrived. When Robert Bruce had firmly established himself on the throne of Scotland, one of the first objects to which he directed his attention, was to crush his old enemies the MacDougalls, and to revenge the many injuries he had suffered at their hands. With this view, he marched into Argyleshire, determined to lay waste the country, and take possession of Lorn. His adversaries, however, were not unprepared to meet him, and to dispute his progress. On advancing, he found John of Lorn and his followers posted in a formidable defile between Ben Cruachan and Loch Awe, which it seemed impossible to force, and almost hopeless to turn. But the military eye of the King soon discovered that the natural difficulties which this position presented might be overcome by a combined attack; and, accordingly, having sent a party to ascend the mountain, gain the heights, and threaten the enemy's rear, he immediately attacked them in front, with the utmost fury. For a time the MacDougalls sustained the onset bravely; but, at length, perceiving themselves in danger of being assailed in the rear, as well as the front, and thus completely isolated in the defile, they betook themselves to flight; and the difficulties of the pass, which had been of advantage to them in the first instance, now that they were broken and thrown into disorder, proved the cause of their ruin. Unable to escape from the mountain gorge, they were slaughtered without mercy; and by this reverse, their power was completely broken. Bruce then laid waste Argyleshire, besieged and took the castle of Dunstaffnage, and received the submission of Alister of Lorn, the father of John, who now fled to England. Alister was allowed to retain the district of Lorn; but the rest of his possessions were forfeited, and given to Angus of Islay, who had all along remained faithful to the King's interests.

When John of Lorn arrived as a fugitive in England, King Edward was making preparations for that expedition, which terminated so gloriously for Scotland in the ever-memorable battle of Bannockburn. John was received with open arms, appointed to the command of the English fleet, and ordered to sail for Scotland, in order to co operate with the land forces. But the total defeat and dispersion of the latter soon afterwards confirmed Bruce in possession of the throne; and being relieved from the apprehension of any further aggression on the part of the English King, he resolved to lose no time in driving the lord of Lorn from the Isles, where he had made his appearance with the fleet under his command. Accordingly, on his return from Ireland whither he had accompanied his brother Edward, he directed his course towards the Isles, and having arrived at Tarbet, is said to have caused his galleys to be dragged over the isthmus which connects Kintyre and Knapdale. This bold proceeding was crowned with success. The English fleet was surprised and dispersed; and its commander having been made prisoner, was sent to Dumbarton, and afterwards to Lochleven, where he was detained in confinement during the remainder of King Robert's reign.

On the death of Bruce, however, John recovered his liberty, and by a politic alliance with the royal family, regained the possessions which had been forfeited in consequence of his connexion with the Red Comyn. In the early part of the reign of David II., he married a grand-daughter of Robert Bruce, and through her not only recovered the ancient possessions of his family, but even obtained a grant of the property of Glenlyon. These extensive territories, however, were not destined to remain long in the family. Ewen, the last lord of Lorn, died without male issue; and his two daughters having married, the one John Stewart of Innermeath, and the other his brother Robert Stewart, an arrangement was entered into between these parties, in virtue of which the descendants of John Stewart acquired the whole of the Lorn possessions, with the exception of the castle of Dunolly and its dependencies, which remained to the other branch of the family; and thus terminated the power of this branch of the descendants of Somerled. The chieftainship of the clan now descended to the family of Dunolly, which continued to enjoy the small portion which remained to them of their ancient possessions until the year 1715, when the representative of the family incurred the penalty of forfeiture for his accession to the insurrection of that period; thus, by a singular contrast of circumstances, " losing the remains of his inheritance to replace upon the throne the descendants of those princes, whose accession his ancestors had opposed at the expense of their feudal grandeur.'' The estate, however, was restored to the family in 1745, as a reward for their not having taken any part in the more formidable rebellion of that year.

THE HIGHLAND REGIMENTS IN GERMANY.

The 87th regiment, commonly called Keith's Highlanders, was raised in the year 1759, and consisted of three companies of 105 men each, and was placed under the command of Major Robert Murray Keith, who had served in the Scotish Brigade in Holland, and was a relation of the celebrated Field-Marshal Keith. Toward the end of 1759, the regiment joined the allied army in Germany under Prince Frederick of Brunswick; and soon after it entered the camp, it was brought into action.

On the 3d of January, 1760, the Marquis de Vogue attacked and carried the town of Herborn, and made a small detachment of the allies who were posted there prisoners. At the same time the Marquis Dauvet made himself master of Dillemberg, the garrison of the allied troops retiring into the castle, where they were closely besieged. Prince Ferdinand no sooner understood their situation than he began his march with a strong detachment for their relief on the 7th of January, when he attacked and defeated the besiegers. On the same day "the Highlanders, under Major Keith, supported by the hussars of Luckner, who commanded the whole detachment, attacked the village of Eybach, where Beau Fremonte's regiment of dragoons was posted, and routed them with great slaughter. The greater part of the regiment was killed, and many prisoners were taken, together with 200 horses and all their baggage. The Highlanders distinguished themselves on this occasion by their intrepidity, which was the more remarkable, as they were no other than raw recruits, just arrived from their own country, and altogether unacquainted with discipline." The Highlanders on this occasion had four men killed and seven wounded.

Prince Ferdinand was so well satisfied with the conduct of this body, that he recommended to the governor not only to increase it to 800 men, but to raise another regiment of equal strength, to be placed under His Serene Highness. This recommendation was instantly attended to; and, in a few weeks, the requisite number of men was raised in the counties of Argyle, Perth, Inverness, Ross, and Sutherland. The command of the new regiment, the 88th, was conferred on John Campbell of Dunoon; but power was reserved to the Earls of Sutherland and Breadalbane, the lairds of Macleod and Innes, and other gentlemen in the north, to appoint captains and subalterns to companies raised on their respective estates. Major Macnab, son of the laird of Macnab; Captain Archibald Campbell, brother of Achallader; John Campbell of Auch and other officers, were recommended by Lord Breadalbane; and Macleod, who raised a company in Skye, appointed his nephew, Captain Fothringham of Powrie, to it. Sir James Innes, chief of that name, who succeeded to the estates and dukedom of Roxburgh in the year 1810, was also appointed to a company. Keith's regiment was embodied at Perth and Campbell's at Stirling; and, being embodied at the same time and ordered on the same service, an interchange of officers took place. Embarking for Germany they joined the allied army, under Prince Ferdinand, in 1760, and were distinguished by being placed in the grenadier brigade. The allied army moved from Kalle on the 30th of July, in consequence of the advance of the French, who took up a position on the river Dymel. The hereditary Prince of Brunswick, who had passed that river the preceding day, was directed by Prince Ferdinand to turn the left of the enemy, who were posted between Warburg and Ochsendorff, whilst he himself advanced in front with the main body of the army. The French were attacked almost at the same moment both in flank and rear, and defeated with considerable loss. In an account of the battle written by Prince Ferdinand to George II., he says, "that the loss of the allies, which was moderate, fell chiefly upon Maxwell's brave battalion of English grenadiers and the two regiments of Scots Highlanders, which did wonders. Colonel Beckwith, who commanded the whole brigade formed of English grenadiers and Scotch Highlanders, distinguished himself greatly." None of the Highlanders were killed; but Lieutenant Walter Ogilvie, and two privates were wounded.

Another affair soon occurred in which the Highlanders also distinguished themselves. Prince Ferdinand, having determined to beat up the quarters of a large French detachment stationed at Zeirenberg, pitched upon five battalions, with a detachment of the Highlanders and eight regiments of dragoons, for this service. This body began their march on the night of the 5th of August; and when within two miles of the town, the corps proceeded by three different roads, Maxwell's brigade of grenadiers, the regiment of Kingsby, and the Highlanders keeping together. They marched in profound silence; and though their tramp was at last heard by the French, the surprise was too sudden for effectual resistance. "The Scots Highlanders mounted the breaches sword in hand, supported by the Chasseurs. The column of English grenadiers advanced in good order and with the greatest silence. In short, the service was complete, and the troops displayed equal courage, soldier-like conduct, and activity." The loss of the Highlanders in this affair was three privates killed and six wounded.

The hereditary Prince being hard pressed by Marshal de Castries, was reinforced from the camp at Warburg. The Highlanders joined him on the 14th of October, shortly after he had been attacked by the Marshal, who had compelled him to retire. The Prince now attacked the French commander in his turn, but was unsuccessful, being obliged again to retire after a warm contest, which lasted from five till nine in the morning. The Highlanders, who "were in the first column of attack, were the last to retreat, and kept their ground in the face of every disadvantage, even after the troops on their right and left had retired. The Highlanders were so exasperated with the loss they sustained, that it was with difficulty they could be withdrawn, when Colonel Campbell received orders from an aide-de-camp sent by the Prince, desiring him to retreat, as to persist in maintaining his position longer would be an useless waste of human life." In this action, 5 of their officers and 10 men were wounded, and 2 officers and 41 men killed; and about this time, the corps was reinforced by 400 men from Johnstone's Highlanders, —and soon after, by 200 from Maclean's

On the night preceding the Prince of Brunswick's unsuccessful attack on the French, an attempt was made by Major Pollock, with 100 grenadiers and the same number of Keith's Highlanders, to surprise the convent of Closter Camp, where a detachment of the enemy was posted, and where, it was supposed, the French commander and some of his officers were to pass the night; but this attempt miscarried. On reaching the sentinel of the main-guard, Major Pollock rushed upon him and ran him through the body with his sword. The wounded man, before falling, turned round upon his antagonist and shot him with a pistol, upon which they both fell dead.

The next affair in which the Highlanders were engaged was the battle of Fellinghausen, in July 1761. The commander-in-chief, in a general order, thus expressed his approbation of the conduct of the corps in this action: " His Serene Highness, Duke Ferdinand of Brunswick, has been graciously pleased to order Colonel Beckwith to signify to the brigade he has the honour to command his entire approbation of their conduct on the 15th and 16th of July. The soldier-like perseverance of the Highland regiments in resisting and repulsing the repeated attacks *of the chosen troops of France*, has deservedly gained them the highest honour. The ardour and activity with which the grenadiers pushed and pursued the enemy, and the trophies they have taken, justly entitle them to the highest encomiums. The intrepidity of the little band of Highlanders merits the greatest praise." Colonel Beckwith, in making this communication, added, that " the humanity and generosity with which the soldiers treated the great flock of prisoners they took, did them as much honour as their subduing the enemy." In this action, 5 officers, and 72 men were wounded, and 3 officers and 31 men were killed.

No further enterprise of any moment was attempted till the 28th of June, 1762, when Prince Ferdinand attacked the

French army at Graibenstein, and defeated them. The French lost upwards of 4,000 men in killed, wounded, and prisoners, including 200 officers, whilst the loss sustained by the allies did not exceed 700 men. The British troops, who were under the command of the Marquis of Granby, "behaved with a bravery not to be paralleled, especially our grenadiers and Highlanders."

The Highlanders, from the distinction they had earned in these different rencounters, now began to attract the especial notice of the Germans. When an entire ignorance prevailed among the people of England respecting the Highlanders, it is not to be wondered at that the Germans should have formed the most extraordinary notions of these mountaineers. In common with the English, they looked upon the Highlanders as savages; but their ignorance went farther, for the people of Germany actually believed that the Highlanders were still strangers to Christianity. "The Scotch Highlanders," says an article which appeared in the Vienna Gazette of 1762, "are a people totally different in their dress, manners, and temper from the other inhabitants of Britain. *They are caught in the mountains when young,* and still run with a surprising degree of swiftness. As they are strangers to fear, they make very good soldiers when disciplined. The men are of low stature, and the most of them old or very young. They discover an extraordinary submission and love for their officers, who are all young and handsome. From the goodness of their dispositions in every thing—for the boors are much better treated by these savages than by the polished French and English—from the goodness of their disposition, which, by the by, shows the rectitude of human nature before it is vitiated by example or prejudice, it is to be hoped that their King's laudable, though late, endeavours to civilize and instruct them in the principles of Christianity will meet with success!" The article adds, that the " French held them at first in great contempt, but they have met with them so often of late, and seen them in the front of so many battles, that they firmly believe that there are twelve battalions of them in the army instead of two. Broglio himself has lately said that he once wished that he was a man of six feet high, but that now he is reconciled to his size since he has seen the wonders performed by the little mountaineers." An acquaintance with the Highlanders soon dissipated the illusions under which the Germans laboured.

The Highlanders were not engaged in the battle of Johannisberg, in which the allies were worsted; but on the 21st of September, in the subsequent action at Brucher Mühl, they took a part. The French occupied a mill on one side of the road, and the allies a redoubt on the other, and the great object of both parties was to obtain possession of a small post which defended the bridge at Brucher Mühl. At first a slight cannonade was opened from a few guns, but these were speedily augmented to 25 heavy pieces on each side. In the post occupied by the allies there were only at first 100 men; but during the action, which lasted without intermission for 15 hours, no less than 17 regiments were successively brought forward, replacing one another after they had spent their ammunition. Both sides remained in their respective positions; and although the contest was long and severe, the allies lost only 600 men in killed and wounded.

On the conclusion of hostilities in November 1762, the Highlanders were ordered home. In the three campaigns in which they had served, they had established a well-earned reputation for bravery; and so great was the estimation in which they were held by the Dutch, that, on their march through Holland, they were welcomed with acclamations, particularly by the women, who presented them with laurel leaves;—a feeling which, it is said, was in some measure owing to the friendly intercourse which had previously existed between the inhabitants and the Scotch brigade. After landing at Tilbury Fort, the regiments marched for Scotland, and were received every where on their route with the most marked attention, particularly at Derby, the inhabitants of which town presented the men with gratuities in money. Among various reasons assigned for the remarkable predilection shown by the people of Derby, the most probable is, a feeling of gratitude for the respect shown by the Highlanders to the persons and properties of the inhabitants when visited by them in the year 1745.

THE TROUBLES OF CARRICK.

CARRICK is the southern one of three districts of Ayrshire, and takes its name from the brokenness and boldness of a large portion of its surface, the word *carraig* in Gaelic signifying 'a rock.' It abounds in strong natural fastnesses, and has both a bold coast and a very diversified interior, and may easily be supposed to have witnessed many a rude conflict in early times. The old fabulists people it with a King and warriors in very remote times; and Boece assigns to it an ancient city of large size and great magnificence; and some scanty monuments and obscure traditions identify some of its localities with disasters and battles which are unknown to record; and the strongest presumptions, resting on a comparison of its situation and topography with well-ascertained facts in the history of Galloway and the Hebrides and the British territories in general, permit small room to doubt that it had a large share in the troubles of the Roman possession, the Norse invasions, and the wars of the Dalriads.

The castle of Turnberry, on the coast, 6 miles north of Girvan, was early a strength of great importance; and probably stands on or near the site of Boece's ancient city, if ever there were such a place; it seems to have been used as a fortress by the old Gaelic lords of Galloway, during centuries prior to the wars of the succession; and it is mentioned, in the following terms, by Blind Harry, as the scene of an event in the life of Sir William Wallace, when on his way northward, at the head of a party, after some exploits in Galloway:—

" In Carrick syne they bowned them to ride,
Hasted them not, but soberly could fare
To Turnberry, that Captain was of Ayre
With Lord Piercie, to take his counsel haill.
Wallace purpos'd that place for to assail;
A woman told, when the Captain was gone
Good men of fence into that stead were none.
They filled the dyke with earth and timber haill,
Syne fir'd the yate, no succour might avail.
A priest there was, and gentlewomen within,
Which for the fire made hideous noise and din.
' Mercy,' they cryed, ' for Him that died on tree.'
Wallace gart slake the fire, and let them be."

This castle, together with the earldom of Carrick, was the patrimonial inheritance of the Bruce; and contests the honours of his pristine fame and domestic position with the castle of Lochmaben and the lordship of Annandale;—and it probably was the scene of many worse affairs than this of Wallace,—and may have witnessed many alarms and shocks which have become lost to history. During several years after Bruce commenced his warfare for the crown, it was held by an English garrison under Percy. But in the course of the war, Bruce stormed it, drove out the garrison, and compelled them to retire to Ayr; and it received such damage in the storming as to be virtually destroyed; and it does not appear to have ever afterwards been inhabited. Bruce's first approach to it while it was in possession of the English, occurred, in a romantic manner, from his retreat in the Island of Arran; and is narrated as follows by the new statist of the parish of Kilmorie:—" Alone and disguised as a minstrel, he crossed over to Turnberry. Should he find matters favourable to his cause, he was to make a signal to his friends whom he left behind, by lighting a fire on an eminence above the castle, on seeing which they were to follow him. Instead, however, of finding them favourable, he found them quite the reverse. The garrison was strong and vigilant; his partisans, few, feeble, and dispirited; and even his own hereditary vassals indifferent, if not hostile.

> ' Long harassed by oppressor's hand,
> Courage and faith had fled the land,
> And over Carrick, dark and deep,
> Had sunk dejection's iron sleep.'

The minstrel monarch was therefore on the eve of returning, when Providence achieved for him what his own prudence would not have permitted him to attempt. A fire was raised for some other purpose on the very spot where the preconcerted signal was to have been lighted. Aware of the consequence, Bruce spent the night on the beach, that he might apprise his friends of the mistake, before their arrival could be discovered by the enemy. They reached the shore before dawn, but when told of the circumstance, and though assured that any attempt to surprise or carry the castle, or to raise the country, was desperate, and though dissuaded, it is said, by their royal leader, and urged to return in silence to their former retreat, they resolutely refused to quit the land of their fathers, till they had either freed it, or fallen in its rescue.

> " Answered fierce Edward, ' Hap what may,
> In Carrick, Carrick's lord shall stay;
> I would not minstrel told the tale,
> Wildfire or meteor made us quail,

I will not credit that this land,
So famed for **warlike** heart and hand,
The nurse of Wallace and of Bruce,
Will long with tyrants hold a truce,
Prove we our fate, the brunt we'll bide.'
So Boyd—so Haye—so Lennox cried,
So said, so vowed the leaders all.
So Bruce resolved—' And in my hall,
Since the bold Southern make their home,
The hour of judgment soon shall come,
When with a rough and rugged host,
Clifford may reckon to his cost.'"

The earldom of Carrick was given by Robert Bruce to his fiery brother Edward; and it afterwards reverted to the Crown, and became a transferable title among the princes of the blood, and was borne among others by the Duke of Albany's royal victim who was starved to death at Falkland, and is now one of the hereditary titles of the eldest son of the British monarch; so that, if we were to follow the name Carrick through all its historical associations, to say nothing of tracing out all the scenes of conflict and murder and tragedy within the territory itself, we might find thousands of wails and dools to relate under the designation of the Troubles of Carrick. But we shall restrict ourselves, in the sequel, to brief notices of two or three chief things in the history of the Kennedys,—the most powerful of all the Carrick septs, and the ancestors of the present Marquis of Ailsa; and must refer any of our readers who have a curious or antiquarian thirst for acquaintance with smaller events or minuter details, to the Statistical Accounts of the parishes of Carrick, to Pitcairn's Criminal Trials, and especially to a remarkable old work recently printed in a manner uniform with the publications of the Ballantyne and Maitland clubs, under the title of the " Historie of the Kennedyis."

The principal branch of the family were created first Lord Kennedy and afterward Earl of Cassilis; and either directly, or through the medium of collateral and subordinate branches of their sept, they long wielded such power over the district that they were called both popularly and by historiographers "Kings of Carrick;" and they made the castle of Maybole their chief residence, and used it as the metropolitan palace of their "kingdom." This pile still stands in good preservation, near the middle of the town; and is a high, well-built, imposing structure, one of the strongest and finest unfallen buildings of its age and class. It was the scene of some sad events; and the town's people assume looks of solemn mystery when turning a stranger's attention to it, and tell strange traditions respecting things which took place within its walls. The whole town indeed was long the focus of feudal oppression over a large tract of surrounding country, and anciently wielded enormously more influence than is due to any modern provincial metropolis. It possessed the winter residences of a large proportion of the Carrick barons, amounting to no fewer than twenty-eight stately, turreted, strong, baronial mansions; it borrowed great consequence from the ecclesiastics of its own collegiate church, and especially from those of the neighbouring huge abbey of Crossraguel, who, in a dark age, had more power and wealth than most of the nobility; and it was also the place where all the Carrick law cases of any importance in a roistering and litigious age were tried, and therefore the home of many lawyers, and the resort of crowds of litigants, bullies, and retainers. Its very nature was a vortex of troubles.

The Countess of the sixth Earl of Cassilis is famous in balladry and tradition for a very singular and sad elopement. She was the daughter of the first Earl of Haddington, and was born in the year 1607. It is said that she was married to the Earl of Cassilis against her inclination,—that her affection had been previously engaged to a certain Sir John Faa

of Dunbar—and that, soon after her marriage, when she was
residing at Cassilis Castle on the banks of the Doon, and
while her husband was absent on some public mission to the
parliament of England, Sir John Faa, at the head of a body of
followers, all disguised as gypsies, went to her residence, and
contrived to get an interview with her, and persuaded her to
elope with him to England. But an old well-known ballad,
supported by a general tradition and by the verdict of many
matrons, "spinsters and knitters in the sun," asserts that the
abductors were actual gypsies, yet allows that they used
"glamourie," or succeeded with the aid of charms and phil
tres.

> "The gypsies they cam to my Lord Cassilis' yett,
>   And O! but they sang bonnie;
> They sang sae sweet, and sae complete,
>   That doun cam our fair lady.
>
> She cam tripping doun the stairs,
>   Wi' a' her maids before her;
> As soon as they saw her weel-far'd face,
>   They coost their glamourie owre her."

But whether real gypsies or disguised gentlemen, they precipitated both the lady and themselves into dire disaster. The
Earl returned home before they had proceeded far on their
journey; and he pursued and overtook them, and slew all
except one in instant conflict, and brought back the runaway
Countess, and shut her up for life in a dungeon or prison-
chamber of the castle of Maybole. It is alleged that she
lived long enough to work a piece of tapestry, still preserved
at Colzean House, in which she represented her unhappy
flight, but with circumstances unsuited to the details of the
ballad, and as if the deceits of "glamourie" had still bewilder-
ed her memory, for she figures there in gorgeous attire on a

superb white courser, surrounded by a group of persons who bear no resemblance to a gang of gypsies; but some critics have suspected that this tapestry is only some old fragment, with a totally different subject, which the house-keepers of Colzean have ignorantly or craftily identified with the tradition.

Gilbert, the fourth Earl of Cassilis, lived in the unsettled period succeeding the commencement of the Reformation, and made extraordinary efforts of rapacity and crime to obtain a lion's share of the spoils of the Romish Church. He pushed his power into Galloway, and, by means of murder and forgery, seized the large possessions of the abbey of Glenluce. The office of abbot of Crossraguel was, for some time, held by his uncle, but eventually passed to Allan Stewart, who enjoyed the protection of the Laird of Bargany; and the Earl then longed to lay an appropriating hand upon all its revenues and temporal rights. His brother, Thomas Kennedy, having at his instigation enticed Stewart to become his guest, the unprincipled Earl conveyed the ensnared abbot to Dunure Castle, the original residence of the Cassilis family, and there, by subjecting him to such torments as have rarely occurred except among the most ferocious savages, or in the dungeons of the Inquisition, forced him to resign by legal instruments the possessions of the abbacy. The narration of this affair in the original " historie," though very horrible, is worth being quoted; and we shall give it with the simple alteration of modernizing the spelling:—

" And so, as King of the country, the Earl apprehended the said Mr. Allan and carried him to the house of Dunure, where for a season he was honourably entertained (if a prisoner can think any entertainment pleasing). But after that certain days were spent, and that the Earl could not obtain the feus of Crossraguel according to his own appetite, he determined to prove if a collation could work that which neither dinner nor supper could do of a long time. And

so, the said Mr. Allan was carried to a secret chamber; with
him passed the honourable Earl, his worshipful brother, and
such as were appointed to be servants at that banquet. In the
chamber there was a great iron chimney, under it a fire; other
great provision was not seen. The first course was, ' My
Lord Abbot,' said the Earl, ' it will please you confess here,
that with your own consent you remain in my company, because you dare not commit yourself to the hands of others.'
The abbot answered, ' Would you, my Lord, that I should
make a manifest lie, for your pleasure? The truth is, my
Lord, it is against my will that I am here; neither yet have
I any pleasure in your company.'—' But you shall remain
with me at this time,' said the Earl.—' I am not able to resist your will and pleasure,' said the abbot, ' in this place.'—
' You must then obey me!' said the Earl. And with that
were presented unto him certain letters to subscribe, amongst
which there was a five year tack and a nineteen year tack,
and a charter of feu of all lands of Crossraguel. . . After
that the Earl espied repugnance, and that he could not come
to his purpose by fair means, he commanded his cooks to
prepare the banquet. And so first, they flayed the sheep,
that is, they took off the abbot's clothes, even to his skin;
and next, they bound him to the chimney, his legs to the one
end and his arms to the other; and so they began to beat the
fire, sometimes to his buttocks, sometimes to his legs, sometimes to his shoulders and arms. And that the roast should
not burn, but that it might roast in soup, they spared not
' flambing' with oil. (Lord look thou to such cruelty.)
And that the crying of the miserable man should not be
heard, they closed his mouth, that the voice might be stopped. In that torment they held the poor man, while that
ofttimes he cried, ' For God's sake to despatch him; for he
had as much gold in his own purse, as would buy powder
enough to shorten his pain.' The famous King of Carrick,
and his cooks, perceiving the roast to be enough, commanded

it to be taken from the fire, and the Earl himself began the grace in this manner: 'Benedicite Jesus, Maria! You are the most obstinate man that ever I saw! If I had known that you had been so stubborn, I would not for a thousand crowns handled you so! I never did so to man before you! And yet, he returned to the same practice, within two days, and ceased not till that he obtained his foremost purpose; that is, that he had gotten all his pieces subscribed, as well as a half-roasted hand could do it!"

A series of feuds had long raged between the Earls of Cassilis and the Lairds of Bargany, with such fury and frequency that scarcely could one sink into quietness before another arose from some new act of violence and treachery; and the tormenting and plundering of the abbot of Crossraguel, in defiance of the Laird of Bargany's protection, were too terrible an outrage not to be followed by further wrongs and a fierce conflict. Accordingly, fresh wrath was kindled between the Earl and the Laird, and soon set the district in a blaze.

One day in December 1601, the Laird of Bargany had occasion to ride with only a few followers from the town of Ayr to his mansion on Girvan-water; and the Earl of Cassilis rode out from Maybole Castle, at the head of 200 armed men, in order to waylay and attack him. The Earl's party drew up at the Lady Corse, about half a mile north of Maybole; and the Laird of Bargany, with his small retinue soon appeared on the opposite side of the valley; and, seeing the Earl and not wishing to come in his way, passed onward by Bogside, and made no attempt to cross the rivulet and its marshy bed. The Earl's party, however, moved down alongside of him; and, on coming to some earthen walls which offered a good support to the arms of his followers, he ordered them to halt and take a position and fire. Bargany now saw that he could not avoid a rencounter; and determining to make the most of his desperate circumstances, he boldly sprang across the burn, and made a show of fiery courage. But on getting across, he observed that none of his followers had accompanied him except the Laird of Auchendrane, the Laird of Cloncaird, and two others; and he said to them, " Gude sirs, we are ower few!" Yet the five heroes stood firmly to it against the two hundred assailants, and defended themselves with wolfish resolution, and inflicted many wounds and several deaths. But they were soon overwhelmed with numbers. One was slain, another was unhorsed, Auchendrane was shot through the thigh and brought to the ground; and only Bargany himself and Cloncaird remained to bear the whole fury of the fray. Yet in the face of at least thirty mounted antagonists, all struggling to be at him and to hew him down, he continued unyielding and undaunted, and was only raised to red heat by desperation, and dashed wildly in amongst them, calling out for Lord Cassilis in person, and challenging him to stand manfully up to a single combat. But he got no consideration for his bravery,—no attention to his calls of honour; but was overwhelmed by a general pressure upon him, and basely struck down from behind, with a weapon which mortally cut him " through the craig and through the thropill." He was conveyed to Maybole, when Lord Cassilis, in the capacity of " Judge Ordinar" of the country, resolved to kill him if he should show any symptoms of recovery; and he was removed thence to Ayr, and died in a few hours. He was only about 25 years of age; yet seems to have been a person of rare promise and great local celebrity; and he is described by the old historian as " the brawest man that could be found in any land, of high stature and well-made, the bravest horseman and the best at all pastimes, fierce and fiery and wonderful nimble."

This murderous deed is narrated by some writers more favourably for Lord Cassilis than we have done, and possibly comprised some palliative circumstances which we have not mentioned. Yet viewed in any light, it was appallingly truculent, and affords a melancholy illustration of the shattered condition of society at the period when it occurred. The age was one of lawlessness and oppression, of the reckless rioting of the strong over the weak,—of the shadow and framework of kingly government without much of the reality. The murder of Bargany was too flagrant an outrage, and too slenderly propped by all possible apologies and pretences of provocation, to pass wholly without question; and accordingly it reached the ears of the higher authorities, and seemed for a moment to demand investigation and punishment; but it was hushed up by means of court influence and bribery, and came even to be pronounced by a formal act of the council a piece of "good service to the King!"

The absence of public justice, and especially the keen and festering sense of private wrong, unrestrained by right principle and irritated by habits of vice and malice, now led to the concoction of a horrible revenge. Mure of Auchendrane had an old grudge against the Cassilis' family,—and particularly against Sir Thomas Kennedy of Colzean, on account of having been turned out of an office of high trust and respectability, that of the bailiary of Carrick, by the Earl of Cassilis' art and through Sir Thomas Kennedy's influence; and he passed on from mere grudge to deadly hatred, on account of his sympathy and alliance with Bargany, of the attack upon them at the Lady Corse, of his own severe wound and Bargany's mortal injuries there, and of the whole affair being declared good service to the King. He therefore thirsted for the blood of a Kennedy; and he was not long in finding an opportunity to obtain it,—and that too in the quarter which he most wished. He learned that Sir Thomas Kennedy was about to pass his vicinity on a journey to Edinburgh; and he employed a party of his retainers to waylay him at a place appointed for a repast, and there to overwhelm and murder him. Sir Walter Scott, in his Ayrshire Tragedy, makes Mure himself narrate in graphic terms the circumstances of the assassination, but with the poetic substitution of the Earl of Cassilis for Sir Thomas:—

" Midst this, our good Lord Gilbert, Earl of Cassilis
Takes purpose he would journey forth to Edinburgh;
The King was doling gifts of abbey lands,
Good things that thrifty house was wont to fish for.
Our mighty Earl forsakes his sea-washed castle,
Passes our borders some four miles from hence;
And, holding it unwholesome to be fasters
Long after sunrise, lo! the Earl and train
Dismount to rest their nags and eat their breakfast.
The morning rose, the small birds caroll'd sweetly—
The corks are drawn, the pasty brooks incision—
His lordship jests, his train are choked with laughter;
When,—wondrous change of cheer, and most unlook'd for,
Strange epilogue to bottle and to baked meat!—
Flash'd from the greenwood half a score of carabines,
And the good Earl of Cassilis, in his breakfast,
Had nooning, dinner, supper all at once,
Even in the morning, that he closed his journey;
And the grim sexton, for his chamberlain
Made him the bed which rests the head for ever."

So trusty to their master were the assassins, and so wilily and warily had Auchendrane selected and instructed them, that no evidence was ever likely to transpire of his connexion with the murder, except that only of a poor student of the name of Dalrymple who had given him intelligence of the place of repast. He was strongly suspected, indeed, and even openly accused of having instigated the crime; but he indignantly asserted his innocence, and stoutly denied all knowledge of Sir Thomas's intended journey, and went so far as to beard and defy the chiefs of the Kennedys and some of the public authorities who hinted their suspicion of his guilt.

And Sir Walter Scott makes him and a companion say, as in terlocutors in the Tragedy,—

> " Ay, 'tis an old belief in Carrick here,
> Where natives do not always die in bed,
> That if a Kennedy shall not attain
> Methuselah's last span, a Mure has slain him.
> Such is the general creed of all their clan.
> Thank Heaven, that they're bound to prove the charge
> They are so prompt in making. They have clamoured
> Enough of this before, to shew their malice.
> But what said these coward pickthanks when I came
> Before the King, before the Justicers,
> Rebutting all their calumnies and daring them
> To shew that I knew aught of Cassilis' journey—
> Which way he meant to travel—where to halt—
> Without which knowledge I possess'd no means
> To dress an ambush for him? Did I not
> Defy the assembled clan of Kennedys
> To show, by proof direct or inferential,
> Wherefore they slandered me with this foul charge?
> My gauntlet rung before them in the court,
> And I did dare the best of them to lift it
> And prove such charge a true one—Did I not?"
> " I saw your gauntlet lie before the Kennedys,
> Who look'd on it as men do on an adder,
> Longing to crush, and yet afraid to grasp it.
> Not an eye sparkled—not a foot advanced—
> No arm was stretch'd to lift the fatal symbol."

But notwithstanding all this bravado, Mure was tortured with apprehension, and saw the sword of public justice dangling over him suspended by a hair. He was particularly afraid of the poor lad Dalrymple, and put him long out of the way, in several lurking places about Auchendrane and in the Isle of

Man, and even got him to serve five or six years as a soldier in Buccleuch's regiment in Holland. Nor when Dalrymple returned home, after that long period, did Auchendrane feel any abatement of terror, but rather an increase of it; and he therefore resolved, with the help of his son, who now shared his mortal resentments, his guilty horrors, and his tormenting fears, to put an end to the lad's life. The Mures accordingly got a vassal, called James Bannatyne, to entice Dalrymple to his house, situated at Chapel-Donan, a lonely place on the coast; and there, at midnight, they murdered him, and buried his body in the sand. The corpse was speedily unearthed by the tide, and was carried out by the assassins to the sea at a time when a strong wind blew from the shore, but was very soon brought back by the waves, and lodged on the very scene of the murder. The Mures fell under general suspicion; they had been observed to tamper with Dalrymple; they failed any longer to deceive their neighbours and hold the authorities at bay by bravadoing and bullying; they felt the responsibilities of their guilt closing rapidly and sullenly around them; and they resolved, by way of sweeping off the worst evidence which could come against them, to murder Bannatyne also, the accomplice and the witness of their previous murder. But Bannatyne was on his guard, and likewise felt wrung with remorse, and he delivered himself up to the civil authorities, and made full confession of the tragic horrors of Chapel-Donan; and the Mures—who had already been thrown into prison on the strength of the strong presumptive evidence, and the general cry of indignation against them—were brought up to a long and most solemn trial, and were found guilty, and afterwards publicly beheaded at the market-cross of Edinburgh, amid general execration. An affecting circumstance is that, at the time of his execution, the elder Mure must have been nearly eighty years of age.

The trial is published in full from original documents in Pitcairn's Criminal Trials; and is characterised by the editor as " one of the most remarkable in the whole range of the criminal annals of this or perhaps of any other country." " In it," he remarks, " are unfolded the Mures' most hidden transactions, and the secret springs of their most private and craftily contrived plots, all of them leading to the perpetration of crimes so singular in atrocity, and of so deep a dye, that one can hardly expect to meet with their parallel, even in the pages of romantic fiction. By the clew, now afforded, may be traced almost the secret thoughts of two of the most accomplished and finished adepts in crime—individuals who murdered by rule, and who carried forward their deadly schemes of ambition, by means of a regularly connected chain of plots and stratagems, so artfully contrived, as to afford them every reasonable prospect of success—and even in the event of the entire failure of their plans, almost to ensure their escape from suspicion; at the least, in their estimation, to warrant their security against ultimate detection, and consequently exempt them from the penalty of capital punishment. Ambition and the lust of power appear to have been the immediate procuring causes of all the crimes in which these infatuated men were involved. Theirs was not the sudden burst of ungoverned passions, which might have hurried them on to the commission of a solitary deed of frightful but unpremeditated violence—nor were their crimes the consequence of ancient feuds, inherited from their restless and vindictive ancestors—nor yet had they the too common apology that they originated in impetuous assaults made upon them, and that their hasty quarrels sprung from a fiery and unbridled temper, which had unfortunately terminated in fatal results. On the contrary, the whole of their numerous attempts and crimes may be characterised as cool, calculating, and deliberate acts, anxiously studied, and by slow and patient, but sure degrees, matured and prosecuted, for a long series of years, until at length ' the measure of their iniquities overflowed,'—and the unlooked-for concurrence of an

extraordinary train of circumstances, the most unlikely to
have happened, eventually led to a triumphant discovery of
their enormous crimes."

THE BATTLE OF GAMRIE.

The coast of the parish of Gamrie in Banffshire, as also that
of part of the adjacent parish of Aberdour in Aberdeenshire,
is one of the grandest and most picturesque stretches of sea-
board in Scotland. A rocky rampart, in some places perpendicular and in all precipitous, rises sternly up from the
sea, to the height of about 600 feet; and presents everywhere such features of strength and terror as make it a fit
monument of the tremendous convulsions which in old times
shook the world. Parts of it are inaccessible to the foot of
man; and other parts bend just enough from the perpendicular to admit a carpeting of sward, and are here and there
traversed by a winding footpath like a stair-case, which few
strangers have sufficient daring of heart or steadiness of head
and limb to ascend. The summits of the rampart are a few
furlongs broad, and variously ascend or decline to the south,
and then terminate in sudden declivities into glens and dells,
which run parallel with the shore; and they command a sublime view of the ever-changeful ocean to the north, and of a
far-spreading expanse of plains and woods, of tumulated surfaces and mountain tops to the south and west. Several great
chasms cleave the rampart from top to bottom, and look like
stupendous rents made by a stupendous earthquake; they
yawn widely at the sea, and take the form of dells toward the
interior; and they have zigzag projections, with protuber-
ances on one face corresponding to depressions or hollows on
the other. All these ravines are beautifully romantic; and
the largest of them, called the Den of Afforsk, is both a gem
of scenery, and a haunt of historical tradition. Here stands

the old church of Gamrie, alleged to have been built on occasion of a fierce fight with the invading Danes in the year 1004; and the following account of the place, and of the tradition respecting it, is from the pen of the parochial schoolmaster, Mr. Alexander Whyte, and appeared first in the Aberdeen Magazine in 1832, and afterwards in the New Statistical Account of Scotland.

"It is not alone by the natural beauties of the place that this scenery becomes a field peculiarly adapted for the fancy to sport in. These green hillocks, grotesque knolls, rugged rocks, and deep gulleys—these vales which have rested for centuries in peace, were once the scene of deadly conflict; for it was here that our far-off ancestors had to stem the torrent of invading Danes; and this brook, now meandering peacefully over the smooth pebbles, once flowed red with the blood of the slain. That green conical mound that tops the east bank of the den, is the castle hill of Finden. It was garrisoned with a part of the Scotish army stationed here to watch the landing of the Danes; a party of whom effected a lodgement on the opposite bank, in the place where the Old Church now stands. The alarm was immediately given, and communicated by means of fires on the mounds, (several of which mounds yet remain on the highest eminences of this and the neighbouring parishes,) which communicated the intelligence rapidly through the kingdom, and quickly brought up reinforcements. Still the Scotish chief, the Thane of Buchan, considered the issue of an attack rather dubious, and, in order to add the enthusiasm of religion to that of patriotism among his followers, made a solemn vow to St. John, in presence of the whole army, to build a church to him on the spot where the invaders were encamped on condition that the saint would lend his assistance in dislodging them. The superstitious soldiers, thinking this too good an offer for any saint to reject, made themselves sure of St. John's co-operation, and entered with alacrity into the plans of their leader; who being now sufficiently reinforced, sent a detachment round by the head of the den,—and these, fetching a compass by the south-west, succeeded in gaining possession of the top of the hill, directly over the Danish main camp, and by rolling down large stones upon the invaders, obliged them to abandon it, and to make their escape by the north-east brow of the hill which overhangs the sea, where many were killed in the flight; whence the place obtained the name of Ghaemrie, or the running battle.

" After being dislodged from the east, the Danes formed a new camp, (where the entrenchments are still to be seen,) which still preserved their communication with the sea, and also with an extensive barren plain on the top of the hill. Meantime the whole Scotish army, in fulfilment of their leader's vow, set to work and built the church on the spot where the Danes first settled, while both parties were waiting additional reinforcements. The Danes having been joined by a party of their countrymen who had landed at Old Haven of Cullen, about four miles westward, made a successful attack on the Scots, and drove them back to the castle-hill; and, in spite to St. John for assisting their enemies, they polluted his sanctuary by making it a stable for their horses. By this time, however, the alarm had spread far and wide, and the Scots, pouring in from all quarters, not only forced back the Danes to their old position on the brow of the hill, but, getting possession of the whole heights, and enclosing them on all sides except that overhanging the sea, they again commenced their murderous work of rolling down stones, while the helpless Danes could neither oppose nor escape, and then rushing down upon them, sword in hand, the Scots cut them to pieces to a man. The Bleedy pots (Bloody pits) is still the name of the place, which, being incapable of cultivation from its steepness and exposure to the north blast, remains to this day in *statu quo*. Besides the round, the crescent, and variously angled figures in the ground, the graves of the Danes are yet to be seen, sunk and hollow, among the rank brown heather, green at the bottom, and surrounded at the borders with harebells and whortles berries, with fragments of rock and large detached stone lying around, and covered with moss.

"Three of the sacrilegious chiefs were discovered amongst the slain, by whose orders the church had been polluted; and I have seen their skulls, grinning horrid and hollow, in the wall where they had been fixed, inside the church, directly east of the pulpit, and where they have remained in their prison-house 800 years! After the church became a neglected ruin, about twelve years ago, these relics of antiquity (skulls) were pilfered bit by bit, by some of the numerous visitors to the place, (one was subsequently recovered and placed, for greater security, in the Museum of Lit. Inst. Banff, where it is still to be seen,) and nothing of them now remains but the holes in the wall in which they were imbedded."

THE MONKS OF MELROSE.

MELROSE ABBEY, situated at the north base of the Eildon Hills, in the valley of the Tweed, 35 miles south of Edinburgh, was founded for Cistertian monks, by King David I., in 1136. The original edifice is said to have been completed in ten years, but was either wholly or partially destroyed by fire in 1322, and must have been greatly inferior in magnificence to its successor. What now remains of the re-edificed structure exhibits a style of architecture ascertained to belong to a later age than that of David, and gives distinct indications of having been in an unfinished state at the Reformation,—appearances of rough temporary closings-up of design, with a view to subsequent resumption and completion. While the nucleus of the building was constructed at one effort, under the reign and patronage of Robert Bruce, aided perhaps by some preserved and renovated portion of the original erection of David I., the entire edifice, in the extension of its parts, and in the immense profusion of its architectural decorations, seems to have been the progressive work of upwards of two centuries, extending from 1326 till the Reformation. The Cistertians were noted for their industrious habits, and their patronage and practice of such departments of the fine arts and practical science as were known in the Middle ages; and, in common with all the monastic tribes, they regarded the embellishing of ecclesiastical edifices up to a degree as high as their scientific and financial resources could produce, as pre-eminently and even meritoriously a work of piety. The vast magnificence of the Abbey, with its innumerable architectural adjuncts and sculptured adornings, seems thus to have been the result of a constant, untiring, and ambitious effort of the resident monks, powerful in their skill, their numbers, their leisure, and their enthusiasm, and both instigated and aided by the munificent benefactions which made continual additions to their originally princely revenues, and testified the applause of a dark but pompous age for the sumptuousness of the dress thrown around the fane of religious pageants.

The architecture is the richest Gothic, combining the best features of its gracefulness and elaboration, and everywhere showing a delicacy of touch, and a boldness of execution, which evince the perfection of the style. The material, while soft enough to admit great nicety of chiselling, possesses such power of resistance to the weather that even the most minute ornaments retain nearly as much sharpness of edge or integrity of feature as when they were fresh from the chisel. The Abbey, though inferior in proportions to many works of its class, and only about half the dimensions of York Minster, is the most beautiful of all the ecclesiastical structures which seem ever to have been reared in Scotland; and has seldom, in aggregate architectural excellence, been surpassed, or even equalled, by the edifices of any land. What remains is only the principal part of the church, with some trivial fragments of connexion with the cloister. From observable indications on the north side of the standing ruin, the cloister appears to have been a square 150 feet deep, surrounded with a spacious arcade or piazza, and lined along the east, west, and north walls with the habitations of the monks.

Though the Abbey was regularly noticed in topographical works, and figured boldly in history, and lifted up its alluringly attractive form before the eye of every traveller along the Tweed, it excited so little attention, previous to the present century, as to be coolly abandoned to the rough dilapidations of persons who estimated its sculptured stones at the vulgar quarry-price of building material! Much care has, in recent times, been used, at the expense of the proprietor to strengthen its walls, slate the remaining part of the roof, and furnish various other means of conservation; and it has its reward in a promise that the pile will yet long stand to give practical lessons in majestic architectural beauty. The place incidentally owes nearly all its modern fame to "the mighty minstrel," whose princely earthly domicile at Abbotsford on the west, and his low last resting-place in Dryburgh on the east, compete with it in challenging the notice of the tourist. Sir Walter's adoption of it and the town, as the St. Mary's and the Kennaquhair of his tales of " The Monastery" and " The Abbot," brought it boldly before the gaze of the myriad admirers of the national novels of Scotland; and his well-known personal enthusiasm in making it his chief and favourite retreat from study, and in passing successive hours in scanning over, for the five hundredth time, its labyrinth of graces, drew towards it the wondering eye of the judiciously imitative crowds who looked to him as a master of taste. But what first roused attention to it, and kept up the vibration in every subsequent thrill of interest in its attractions, was the masterly description of it which coruscated upon the world in the publication of "the Lay of the Last Minstrel." Two extracts, though already familiar to many a reader, may be acceptable as vivid pictures of the most remarkable parts of the pile, and fine specimens of the enchanting power of the painter. The one describes the beautifully fretted and sculptured stone-roof of the east end of the chancel:

" The darkened roof rose high aloof
    On pillars lofty and light and small;
The keystone that locked each ribbed aisle
Was a fleur-de-lys or a quatre-feuille;
The corbells were carved grotesque and grim;
And the pillars, with cluster'd shafts so trim,
With base and with capital flourish'd around,
Seem'd bundles of lances which garlands had bound."

The other passage describes the surpassingly elegant and beautiful eastern window:—

' The moon, on the east oriel shone,
    Through slender shafts of shapely stone
      By foliaged tracery combined:
Thou would'st have thought some fairy's hand
'Twixt poplars straight the osier wand
    In many a freakish knot had twin'd;
Then framed a spell, when the work was done,
And changed the willow-wreaths to stone."

The monks whom David I. placed in the original abbey were Cistertians from Rievalle, the first of their order who obtained footing in Scotland; and, according to general Cistertian usage, they dedicated the establishment to their patron-saint, the Virgin Mary. David, that "sair saunt for the croon o' Scotland," made them the chief of their class, or the mother-establishment of the kingdom, and bestowed o.. them the church of the parish, extensive lands, and numerous privileges. Their original gift from him consisted of the lands of Melrose, Eildon, and Dernock, the lands and wood of Gattonside, the fishings of the Tweed along the whole extent of these lands, and the rights of pasturage, of pannage, and of cutting wood for fuel and building, in the forests of Selkirk and Traquair, and in that lying between the Gala and the Leader. Other possessions in the form of lands, churches, and privileges, were afterwards so rapidly heaped on them by David, and by his successors and subjects, that, against the close of the 13th century, they had vast property and various immunities in the counties of Roxburgh Berwick, Selkirk, Peebles, Dumfries, Ayr, Haddington, and Edinburgh. In 1192, Hassendean, in its church, tithes, lands, and other emoluments, was given by Jocelin, bishop of Glasgow, to the monks, on condition of their establishing at it a house of hospitality, "ad susceptionem pauperum et peregrinorum ad domum de Melros venientum;" and it now became the seat of a cell, where several of their number resided, to execute the trust of relieving the poor, and entertaining the pilgrim. In some year between 1181 and 1185, a bull of Pope Lucius exempted the monks from paying tithes for any of their possessions.

The monks were now large proprietors, with numerous tenants; great husbandmen, with many granges and numerous herds; lordly churchmen, with uncommon privileges, high powers, and extensive influence. But a pertinacious controversy had long existed between them and the men of Stow, or the vale of Gala-water—then called Wedale—respecting two objects of great importance in that age,—pannage and pasturage, under the several proprietors; and, in 1184, a formal settlement of the controversy, emphatically known in history as "the peace of Wedale," was made by William the Lion, assisted by his bishops and barons Yet during such times, disputes among cattle-drivers and swineherds could hardly be prevented, and, when adopted by their superiors, were sometimes carried up to tumult and homicide. In 1269, John of Edenham, the abbot, and many of his conventual brethren, for the crimes of violating the peace of Wedale, attacking some houses of the bishop of St. Andrew's, and slaying one ecclesiastic, and wounding many others, were excommunicated by a provincial council which sat in Perth.

As Melrose stood near the hostile border, it was usually involved in the rancorous events of Border feud and international war. In 1285, the Yorkshire barons, who had confederated against King John, swore fealty to Alexander II. in Melrose chapter-house. In 1295, Edward I. granted the monks a protection; and in August of next year, while he rested at Berwick after the general submission of Scotland to his usurping and dominating interference, he issued a writ commanding a restitution to the monks of all the property which they had lost in the preceding melée. In 1322, at the burning and desolating of the Abbey by Edward II., William de Peebles the abbot and several of the monks were slain. In 1326, Robert Bruce made a most munificent grant for the re-edification of the abbey, amounting to £2,000 sterling—a vast sum at that period—from his revenue of wards, reliefs, marriages, escheats and fines within Roxburghshire; and he seems to have afterwards made other grants, and to have been followed in his money-giving patronage by David II. In 1328, writs were issued to the abbot by Edward III. for the restitution of pensions and lands which they had held in England, and which had been taken from them, during the war, by the King's father. In 1334, the same monarch granted a protection to Melrose, in common with the other abbeys of the Scotish border; in 1341, he came from Newcastle to keep his Christmas festival in Melrose abbey; and in 1348, he issued a writ " de terris liberandis abbati de Meaurose," to deliver to the abbot his lands

Richard II., in 1378, followed the example of Edward in giving a protection to the monks; yet in 1385, when he made his expedition into Scotland, he set fire to the abbey, in common with other religious houses on the Border. But, four years afterwards, the monks were indemnified for the damage he did them, by the grant of two shillings on each of 2,000 sacks of Scotish wool, and of a portion of the King's customs on hides and woolfels, exported at Berwick; and, in 1390, they received from Richard a formal renewal of protection.

During the period of rude waste and rancorous warfare which intervened between the rebuilding of the edifice under Robert Bruce, and the commencement or precurrent events of the Reformation, the abbey must have sustained many more shocks than are recorded; yet it seems to have rebounded from each blow with undiminished or even increased vigour, and, in spite of temporary demolitions, made steady progress in financial greatness and architectural grandeur. But during the reigns of Henry VIII., Edward VI., and Elizabeth, it suffered collisions and dilapidations, chiefly from the English and partly from the Scotch, too severe and in too troublous times to issue otherwise than in its ruin. In 1544, the English penetrated to Melrose, and destroyed great part of the abbey; in 1545, led by Lords Evers and Latoun, they again pillaged it, and were pursued and beaten on Ancrum-moor; and, in the same year, they recrossed the Border under the Earl of Hertford, and a third time laid the abbey waste. "The English commanders," says George Chalmers, whom, with a collateral reference to other authorities, we are chiefly following, "were studious to leave details of the destruction that they committed, which only perpetuates their own disgrace." At length, in 1569, the nobility of Scotland and their military retainers, under the sacred name of the Reformation, and with an unjust reflection of the odium they incurred on John Knox and his fellow-reformers, completed by pillage, defacement, and dilapidation, what the English had left to be done in order to the conversion of the pile into an unroofed, gutted, partially overthrown and altogether yawning ruin.

Though the monks of Melrose were exempted by charters and custom from rendering military service to the Crown; yet they fought under James the Steward of Scotland, during the war of the succession; and again they fought under Walter the Steward, in strenuous support of the infant-prince, David Bruce. Declarations were afterwards made by both stewards, and subsequently confirmed by the Duke of Albany, on the day of the feast of James the Apostle, in 1403, that the military service of the monks having been rendered by the special grace of the abbot and convent, and not in terms of any duty they owed to the Crown, should not be regarded as any precedent for their future conduct. Owing to mutual benefits, a very intimate connexion seems to have existed, from the days of Bruce, or from the foundation of the monastery, between the abbots of Melrose and the Stewarts of Scotland. In 1541, James V., by a sacrifice of his public policy to his private feelings, solicited and obtained from the Pope, the abbey of Melrose, in addition to that of Kelso, to be held, in commendam, by his natural son James.

At the Reformation, when the lands, rights, and privileges of religious houses were annexed to the Crown, those belonging to Melrose abbey were granted by Queen Mary to James, Earl of Bothwell. Becoming lost to him by forfeiture in 1568, they were next, through the influence of the well-known Earl of Morton, bestowed on James Douglas, the second son of William Douglas of Lochleven. Some years later, they again sought an owner, and, with some exceptions, were erected into a temporal lordship in favour of Sir John Ramsay, who had protected James VI. from the rapier of Gowry, who was created Viscount of Haddington, and Earl of Holderness in 1606, and who, in 1625, died without issue, leaving the estates to fall back to the Crown. Sir Thomas Hamilton, who, from his eminence as a lawyer, rose to high rank and great opulence, who was created Earl of Melrose in 1619, and who afterwards exchanged this title for the vacant one of Earl of Haddington, eventually obtained the abbey and the greater part of its domains; and, in more recent times, he has been succeeded in the splendid heritage, by the family of Buccleuch.

"From Ala's banks to fair Melrose's fane,
How bright the sabre flash'd o'er hills of slain—
I see the combat through the mist of years—
When Scott and Douglas led the Border spears!
The mountain streams were bridged with English dead;
Dark Ancrum's heath was dyed with deeper red;
The ravaged abbey rung the funeral knell,
When fierce Latoun and savage Evers fell;
Fair bloomed the laurel-wreath, by Douglas placed
Above the sacred tombs, by war defaced.

Farewell, ye moss-clad spires! ye turrets grey,
Where science first effused her orient ray!
Ye mossy sculptures, on the roof embossed,
Like wreathing icicles congealed by frost!
Each branching window, and each fretted shrine,
Which peasants still to fairy hands assign!
May no rude hand your solemn grandeur mar,
Nor waste the structure, long revered by war!"

Leyden's Scenes of Infancy

THE SCOTISH INVASION OF ENGLAND UNDER CHARLES II., IN 1651.

In the spring of 1651, immediately after the crowning of Charles II. at Scone, and several months after the overrunning of the country south of the Forth by Cromwell, the Scotish army, in expectation of another visit from the Cromwellian forces, and in order to protect the central and northern parts of Scotland from invasion, raised strong fortifications along the fords of the Forth, and entrenched themselves at the Torwood, between Falkirk and Stirling. Here Cromwell found them when he advanced into Scotland in July. As he considered it dangerous to attempt to carry such a strong position in the face of an army of about twenty thousand men, (for such it is said was the number of the Scots,) he endeavoured, by marches and countermarches, to draw them out; but although they followed his motions, they took care not to commit themselves, by going too far from their lines of defence. Seeing no chance of bringing them to a general engagement, Cromwell adopted the bold plan of crossing the Frith of Forth at Queensferry, and of throwing himself into the rear of the Scotish army. While, therefore, he continued, by his motions along the Scotish lines, to draw off the attention of the Scotish commanders from his plan, he, on the 20th of July, sent over Lambert, with a large division of his army in a number of boats which had been provided for the occasion. He landed without opposition, and proceeded immediately to fortify himself on the hill between the North Ferry and Inverkeithing. General Holburn was immediately despatched with a large force to keep Lambert in check. The parties encountered each other on the 20th of July; and the Scots, though they fought with great bravery, were defeated. A body of Highlanders particularly distinguished themselves. The loss of the Scots was considerable; and among the slain were the young chief of Maclean and about a hundred of his friends and followers. This victory opened a free passage to Cromwell to the north of Scotland. He immediately, therefore, crossed the Forth with the remainder of his army, and proceeded to Perth, of which he took possession on the 2nd of August.

While the Scotish leaders were puzzled how to extricate themselves from the dilemma into which they had been thrown by the singular change which had taken place in the relative position of the two armies, the King alone seemed free from embarrassment, and at once proposed to his generals, that, instead of following Cromwell, or waiting till he should attack them, they should immediately invade England, where he expected to be joined by numerous royalists, who only required his presence among them at the head of such an army, to declare themselves. Under existing circumstances, the plan, though at once bold and decisive, was certainly judicious; and, therefore, it is not surprising that it should have received the approbation of the chiefs of the army. Having obtained their concurrence, the King immediately issued a proclamation on the 30th of July, to the army, announcing his intention of marching for England the following day, accompanied by such of his subjects as were willing to give proofs of their loyalty by sharing his fortunes. This appeal was not made in vain; and Charles found himself next morning in full march on the road to Carlisle, at the head of 11,000, or, as some accounts state, of 14,000 men.

Although Cromwell was within almost a day's march of the Scotish army, yet, so sudden and unexpected had been its departure, and so secretly had the whole affair been managed, that it was not until the 4th of August that he received the extraordinary intelligence of its departure for England. Cromwell was now as much embarrassed as the Scotish commanders had lately been, for he had not the most distant idea, when he threw himself so abruptly into their rear, that they would adopt the bold resolution of marching into England. As soon, however, as he had recovered from the surprise into which such an alarming event had thrown him, he despatched letters to the parliament, assuring them of his intention to follow the Scotish army without delay, and exhorting them not to be discouraged, but to rely on his activity. He also sent Lambert with a force of 3,000 cavalry to harass the rear of the Scotish army, and forwarded orders to Harrison, who was then at Newcastle, to press upon their flank with a similar number; and, in a few days, he himself crossed the Forth with an army of 10,000 men, and proceeded along the eastern coast, in the direction of York, leaving Monk behind him with a force of 5,000 horse and foot to complete the reduction of Scotland.

The Scotish army made a rapid march, and arrived in the neighbourhood of Warrington on the 16th of August. Here Lambert and Harrison, who had just met at Warrington, and whose united forces amounted to 9,000 men, resolved to dispute the passage of the Mersey; but the Scotish army had passed the bridge before their arrival. A few charges ensued, and Lambert and Harrison, in expectation of a general engagement drew up their forces on Knutsford-heath; but the King declined battle, and continued his march towards Worcester, which he entered on the 22nd. A number of the country gentlemen who were confined in that city on account of their loyalty, welcomed the King with the warmest congratulations, and he was immediately proclaimed by the Mayor with great solemnity, amidst the rejoicings of the royalists.

The approach of the Scotish army filled the minds of the English parliamentary leaders with dismay, and they at first imagined that a private arrangement had been made between Cromwell and the King; but their apprehensions were soon relieved, by the receipt of Cromwell's despatches, and by a proclamation which the King had issued on entering England, promising pardon to all his subjects, with the exception of Cromwell, Bradshaw, and Cook. As soon as the alarm had subsided, measures, the most active and strong, were adopted by Cromwell's council, to meet the pressing emergency. They proclaimed the King and his supporters guilty of high treason; and the declaration of the King was burned in London, by the hands of the hangman. All persons suspected of loyalty were either confined or narrowly watched; and death was declared to be the penalty of those who should enter into any correspondence with the King. Bodies of militia were instantly raised in several counties, and marched off to the aid of the regular forces. Had these exertions been met by similar efforts on the part of the English royalists, the cause of the King might have triumphed; but so sudden and unexpected had been the arrival of the King, that they were quite unprepared to receive him, and the measures of the leaders at Westminster were so prompt and energetic, that they had not sufficient time to collect their scattered strength, or to concert any combined plan of operations. Yet notwithstanding these difficulties, a pretty considerable force might have been drawn together, but for the fanaticism of the Scots, who would not, contrary to the order of the King, allow any auxiliaries to join them, who had not taken the covenant.

When Charles, therefore, arrived at Worcester, he found that he had obtained no accession of force on his march, and he even found that his little army had been reduced by desertion. To increase the army he issued a proclamation, calling upon all his male subjects, between the ages of sixteen and sixty, to join his standard at a general muster to be held on the 26th of August; but little attention was paid to the order, and when the day of muster arrived, he found that his army amounted to about 12,000 men only, including about 2,000 Englishmen. To attack this force, large bodies of troops were concentrating near Worcester; and on the

28th of August, when Cromwell arrived to take the command, the army of the republic amounted to upwards of 30,000 men, who hailed the presence of their commander with rapture.

The Lord General now perceived that the time had arrived for striking a decisive blow; but as the anniversary of the battle of Dunbar was near at hand, he resolved to defer his grand attack till that day, so fortunate for his arms, and, in the meantime, employed himself in a series of operations for hemming in the royal army, in the course of which several brilliant affairs took place with alternate success. At last, on the morning of the 3rd of September, 1651, just twelve months after the defeat of the Scots at Dunbar, Cromwell, after reminding his troops of the victory they had achieved on that auspicious day, put his army in motion. The first movement was made by Fleetwood, who having advanced from Upton to Powick, proceeded towards the Team, the passage of which he was ordered to force; and to keep up a communication with him, Cromwell threw a bridge of boats across the Severn at Buns hill, near the confluence of the two rivers. A discharge of musketry in the direction of Powick about one in the afternoon, when the King and his staff were observing the position of the enemy from the tower of the cathedral, was the first intimation they received of Cromwell's attack. The party immediately descended, and the King at the head of a party of horse and foot under the command of Montgomery, flew forward to oppose the advance of Fleetwood's brigade across the Team. A furious contest took place, but the steadiness and perseverance of Fleetwood's men overcame all opposition; yet although they effected the passage of the river, and were afterwards aided by four regiments which Cromwell sent to their assistance, the Scots disputed every inch of ground, and repeatedly charged the enemy with the pike.

While this sanguinary struggle was going on, Cromwell

after securing the communication across the Severn by the bridge of boats which he threw over it, advanced to Perrywood and Red-hill, and directed a fire to be opened from a battery of heavy guns upon a fortification named Fort Royal, which had been recently raised to cover the Sidbury gate of the city. This movement, which isolated the divisions of Fleetwood and Cromwell from each other by the interposition of the Severn, seemed to the King a favourable opportunity for attacking that of Cromwell with success, whilst the other was kept in check on the opposite bank. He, therefore, immediately drew together the remainder of his infantry, with which and the Duke of Hamilton's troop of horse, and the English volunteers, he attacked the division under Cromwell. The King himself at the head of the Highlanders, whom he commanded in person, fought with great bravery: his example animated his troops, who drove back the enemy's vanguard, consisting of some regiments of militia, and captured their cannon. Had Leslie come up with his cavalry as was expected, the defeat of Cromwell would have been inevitable; but that officer from some cause or other, never explained, unfortunately remained in the city and did not make his appearance till Cromwell, who brought up a large body of veteran troops which he had placed in reserve, had repulsed the royalists, who, unable to rally, were fleeing in confusion towards Fort Royal, to seek for protection under its guns. The fugitives entered the city in great disorder, and the King succeeded in rallying them in Friar Street; but although he tried every means which circumstances could admit of, to raise their drooping spirits, he could not prevail upon them to stand firm, and many threw away their arms and fled. In a fit of despair he exclaimed, "Then shoot me dead rather than let me live to see the sad consequences of this day."

In the meantime Fleetwood, after dispersing the division opposed to him, took St Johns; and Cromwell afterwards carried Fort Royal by storm, and put its defenders to the sword. The utmost confusion now prevailed in the city, which was still farther increased by the entrance of Cromwell's troops, who poured into it by the quay, the castle hill, and the Sidbury gate. The situation of the King became critical in the extreme, and his friends advised him to provide immediately for his own safety, as no time was to be lost; he, therefore, instantly threw himself among the Scotish cavalry, and whilst thus surrounded, he was effecting his escape by the gate of St Martin's to the north, the Earl of Cleveland, Sir James Hamilton, Colonel Careless, and a few other devoted adherents at the head of some determined troopers, charged the enemy in their advance in the contrary direction up Sidbury Street, and checked them effectually till the King was out of danger.

This battle, which Cromwell admits " was as stiff a contest for four or five hours as ever he had seen," was very disastrous to the royalists, three thousand of whom were killed on the spot, and a considerably larger number taken prisoners, and even the greater part of the cavalry, who escaped from the city, were afterwards taken by detachments of the enemy. The Duke of Hamilton was mortally wounded in the field of battle, and the Earls of Derby, Lauderdale, Rothes, Cleveland, and Kelly, the Lords Sinclair, Kenmure and Grandison, and the Generals Leslie, Middleton, Massey and Montgomery, were successively made prisoners after the battle. When the King considered himself free from immediate danger, he separated, during the darkness of the night, from the body of cavalry which surrounded him, and with a party of sixty horse proceeded to Whiteladies, a house belonging to one Giffard a recusant and royalist, at which he arrived at an early hour in the morning, after a ride of 25 miles. Here commenced, on the same day, the first of those extraordinary adventures which befel the King, accompanied by a series of the most singular hairbreadth escapes, as related by the historians of the period, between the 3rd of September and the 17th of

October, the day on which he landed in safety at Fecamp in Normandy.

THE LIFE AND CHARACTER OF JAMES III.

JAMES III. succeeded to the throne of Scotland in 1460, when only eight years of age; and was then crowned with great pomp and ceremony in Kelso Abbey. His mother had for some time the main or entire moulding of his mind and managing of his education; and either she, or more probably Bishop Kennedy of St. Andrew's, conducted the chief affairs of the regency. Kennedy was a man of much experience, judgment, firmness, and probity, well able to guide the state amid the difficulties which surrounded it; and up to the period of his death in 1466, he maintained matters in a tolerably healthy state for both the prince and the country. But about the middle of his six years of power, he permitted another person to rise into prominence, who slowly but steadily drugged King and kingdom with disaster. This was Robert, Lord Boyd, who assumed consequential airs on account of the creditable figure his ancestors had made in the reign of Bruce, and who took advantage of the momentary absence of any great leaders around the throne to push himself into power, and succeeded by means of audacity and craftiness in winning the good graces of Bishop Kennedy, and in obtaining a peerage and a high place at court. This man associated some of his nearest and deftest relations with himself in his newly found power; and proceeded silently and cunningly to form around him a strong state faction, with no less lofty an object in view than the exclusive possession of the King's person and the entire usurpation of the government.

Sir Alexander Boyd, the brother of Lord Boyd, and celebrated in the popular histories of the period as a model of all knightly and chivalrous accomplishments, was selected, by the Queen-mother and Bishop Kennedy so early as 1464, as the tutor of the young King in martial exercises; and from that time till near the complete formation of James's character, the Boyds appear to have had the complete control of his education. And they managed it all for their own selfish purposes, and without due reference, or scarcely any reference at all, to the King's true welfare as either a man or a prince. "It was the interest of this family," says Tytler, "the more easily to overrule every thing according to their own wishes, to give their youthful charge a distaste for public business, to indulge him to an unlimited extent in his pleasures and amusements, to humour every little foible in his character, to keep him ignorant of the state of the country, and to avoid the slightest approach to that wholesome severity and early discipline of the heart and understanding, without which nothing that is excellent or useful in after-life can be expected. The effects of this base system pursued by his governors, were apparent in the future misfortunes of the King, whose natural disposition was good, and whose tastes and endowments were in some respects superior to his age."

In 1466, after the death of Bishop Kennedy, while the King was residing in the palace of Linlithgow, the Boyds, at the head of a small body of the chiefs of their faction, suddenly entered the palace, forcibly carried off the King, placed him on horseback, and rode away with him to Edinburgh. They had already acquired a decided ascendancy in the state, and at the same time held the highest place of favour in the royal boy's own estimation; and they took the seemingly perilous step of forcibly abducting him, less as a means of securing their rise than as a measure to prevent their fall,—less for the purpose of attaching him firmly to themselves, than for the purpose of placing him beyond the influence and access of their rivals. Yet though safe at present, they felt that, in some future turn of affairs, they might be accused of treason, and prosecuted for it; and therefore, during the sitting of a parliament which was soon after held in Edinburgh, they obtained first an oral declaration of the King, in the parliament's presence, that he had accompanied them from Linlithgow of his own free will, and next a formal instrument under the great seal, pardoning them for any thing in their conduct which could be construed as offensive to the Crown.

But in 1469, the King married Margaret of Denmark, new counsellors came around his throne, fresh aspirants for his favour formed coalitions and rose to power, and the Boyds were all at once pitched down from their lofty pinnacle and dashed to destruction. Lord Boyd himself made a hasty gathering of his friends and retainers, and marched in military array to Edinburgh, in the hope of overawing parliament, and attracting the support of his old admirers and sycophants; but he speedily found himself weak and forsaken,—and saw cause to retreat precipitately at the first display of the royal banner; and he fled with all speed into Northumberland, and there sickened and died. His son, who had been created Earl of Arran, saved himself by a timeous flight to the continent. But the latter's uncle, Sir Alexander Boyd, the quondam instructor of the King in knightly accomplishments, was formally brought to trial on a charge of treason, found guilty, and executed on the Castle-Hill of Edinburgh.

A tissue of prosperity ran through the public affairs of the kingdom during the whole of James' minority; and it also presented a surface appearance of continuing to run through them till 1477, when he was twenty-five years of age; but it really was frittering away, during many years, under the joint influence of adverse circumstances abroad and adverse circumstances in the court,—and in 1477, it gave complete place to the first of a long series of disasters. Revolutions and usurpations had become common throughout Europe; communication between Scotland and the great theatres of political intrigue and commotion had become frequent; the Scotish nobles of the period were illiterate, rude, haughty, and turbulent, and looked contemptuously on every thing which did not favour warfare or the chase; the King's two brothers, the Duke of Albany and the Earl of Mar, were bold and stirring men,—fierce and unprincipled, rough, wild, and pompous,—well fitted in every way to please or dazzle the nobility; and the King himself possessed only, or at least chiefly, such qualities as made him seem to them a contemptible ninny, a conceited simpleton, or a slobbering fool. He really had considerable mental excellence, and might, in a better age, have been a valuable patron and promoter of public improvement; but he had no tastes in common with his kinsmen and his barons, and knew nothing of the arts of government, and practised such continual mistakes and blunders and absurdities as converted his very strength into weakness, and rendered his superior knowledge worse than ignorance. He had a passion for mathematics and judicial astrology,—but showed it chiefly in promoting an astrologer of the name of Schevez to the highest ecclesiastical dignities, and in employing him to read the stars upon all occasions of importance; he had a fondness for architecture, for music, and for rhetoric, but showed it chiefly in promoting to the greatest honours about the court, and taking into familiar companionship, an architect of the name of Cochrane, a musician of the name of Rogers, and a literateur of the name of Ireland; and, in a word, he had a penchant for all sorts of arts and sciences, except those of governing and fighting,— a penchant for all kinds of thought and action which bore on peace and pleasure and improvement,—and he showed it chiefly in neglecting all his proper kingly duties, and in keeping frequent company with tailors, smiths, fencing-masters, and other persons of lowly station. His brothers and barons, therefore, despised him, and became rapidly ripe for any amount of disaffection or rebellion to which circumstances might tempt them.

The Duke of Albany had inherited the earldom of March, with the castle of Dunbar, and had long held the governorship of Berwick and the wardenship of the eastern marches; and he had used his power wantonly and riotously, and now began, in a great degree, to throw off all the restraints and observances which were proper to him as a subject. He was therefore seized and thrown into prison. But he soon escaped, and took post in his stronghold of Dunbar, and speedily gathered around him a body of Border desperadoes, and set about establishing political connexions for embroiling the whole kingdom, and altogether hurled an absolute and most fierce defiance at the Crown. He saw cause, however, to alter his purposes before going into any actual hostility; and he fled to France with the view of soliciting the French King's support,—but was there unsuccessful, and had to content himself with sitting down, for a time, in the capacity of a self-banished exile.

The Earl of Mar made himself still more obnoxious. He was accused of using magical arts for the purpose of causing the King's death; and, though he may have been neither daring enough to contrive direct assassination nor weak enough to rely wholly on the pretended diablery of witches and warlocks, he certainly appears to have cherished mortal malice against his royal brother, and to have retained in his service a number of very vile professors of "the black art." He was seized, tried, and declared guilty of treason; and some authorities say that he was bled to death, in a warm bath by the King's command, while others say that he took ill and became delirious before any sentence was pronounced against him, that he was carefully attended in his illness by the King's physicians, and that he died from his disease while in a bath which had been prescribed for his advantage.

The dismal sequel of James III.'s history, extending from

the death of the Earl of Mar in 1478 till the King's own death in 1488, narrates, among many concomitant and subordinate matters, how the Duke of Albany passed into England, and ingratiated himself at the English court,—how a powerful army for invading Scotland was led northward by the Duke of Gloucester, afterwards the notorious Richard III., accompanied by Albany,—how a still more numerous army was mustered on the Boroughmuir of Edinburgh to repel the invasion,—how James had carried his low favouritisms to such excess as to raise one of his minions, Cochrane, to the utmost magnificence, and create him Earl of Mar,—how his nobles, when on the march against the invading army, conspired against him, hanged Cochrane and his other chief favourites on Lauder bridge, put himself under arrest, and dispersed the whole camp,—how Albany was reconciled to the King, and made lieutenant general of the kingdom,—how he turned traitor, and was turned out of his office,—how he colleagued with Douglas, and got together a small English army of invasion,—how he afterwards intrigued among the nobles, and drew them into open rebellion, and managed to get possession of the heir-apparent to the Crown,—how a temporary pacification took place, and was followed by a fresh insurrection,—how Shaw of Sauchie, in whom the King primely confided, betrayed his high trust, and shut the castle of Stirling against him in his extremity,—and how the King came to a final encounter with his enemies in the vicinity of that place, and could not obtain assistance from his fleet, under Admiral Wood, though only a few miles down the Forth,—and was overwhelmed in battle, and forced to fly precipitately and alone, and thrown from his horse not far from the field of defeat, and carried into an obscure cottage, and there assassinated by some unknown person, perhaps of the family of Hume, who got access to him under the guise of a priest. Most of these events are fully narrated in the two pieces called 'The Raid of Lauder' and

'The Battle of Sauchieburn,' in the first volume of these Tales; and the conclusion of the tragedy, together with an alleged dying reminiscence of some of the chief facts in the stricken monarch's life, is well told in the following lines of Tait's "Macduff:"—

" It was a low and lonely house, hard by old Milton Moss,
Where Scotia's conquering standard floats o'er Bruce's battle
    cross ;
And Bannockburn, its classic ground spreads to the wander-
    ing eye,
Mid circling hills, mute witnesses of blood and victory.

A King upon a frantic steed rushed on from Torwood green,
His pallid hue and headlong speed were desperate, I ween ;
Across the stream, with sudden bound, the clattering hoofs
    have sped—
Down drops that corse-like thing, and in that lowly house
    is laid.

Can this be he! the son of him who wore the fiery face.
Who died at Rox'bro's thundering siege—a lion of his race—
The while his bold and dauntless queen aveng'd her hus-
    band's fall,
Batter'd and took, and to the earth razed down that castle
    tall!

That steed a monarch might bestride, where fleetness slays
    or saves—
But not a timid king like this—the dupe of fools and knaves—
Of stalwart breed, of matchless speed, well worthy of its
    sires—
The gift of Scotland's bravest knight—Lord Lindsay of the
    Byres!

Scarce from a rising ground had James seen border battle spread—
First in the van his youthful son, and lion-ensign red—
When doom prophetic smote his heart, and conscious guilt his soul—
Dashing his spurs to rowel-head, he fled without controul!

Forth went a dame to Bannock-well, as thus the monarch sped,
But midway left her water-pail, and, fleet with terror fled:—
Shying, the grey steed leapt the stream—'Heard ye the armour ring?'
 Now who art thou, poor, shatter'd man?'—'This morn I was your King.'

Ah! where be they, the flattering herd, that sway'd the monarch's mind
Mid dulcet strains so musical, with sciences refined,
And gorgeous plans for Gothic shrines, and feats of magic skill,
And daring eyes that, in the stars, read destiny at will?

And where may be his glittering hoard of golden treasures, wrung
From subjects murmuring sullenly, with scarce restrained tongue?
But hush! He stirs! The quivering lips are parted by a sigh;
And opens, with a frigid stare, his vacant, cold, grey eye!

Back to the scenes of boyhood's years his wandering thoughts have fled;
Grave Kennedy's him tutoring, whilst gay Boyds round him played:—

My mother dear!' thus murmured James. 'What is it that
    thee ails!
Sin not! nor shame us more with that dark Hepburn of
    Hailes!

And thou, my youngest brother Marre! thy blood is on my
    head!
From thee it was I fled the field! Ah! would thou wert not
    dead!
And, Albany! I feared thee, too, thou gay and gallant
    lance,
Yet rather would I thou wert here, than slain in tilting
    France?

Go, Schevez! scan 'the house of Death,' and tell what danger now
From brethren dead and perished, assails this kingly brow?
Let Cochrane's bones, on Lauder Bridge, bleach in the twilight dew—
No fane he ever planned could shield him from yon rebel
    crew!

Let Rogers' silver cord be snapt! I need its strains no more;
Let Andro Wood's tall A'mirals be tost, as wrecks, ashore;
They've ta'en my castles! one and all! Both gold and safety
    gone!
My nearest kin—my very son—conspires against my throne!

E'en Shaw of Sauchie—he whose faith was yet my latest
    hope—
Holds mine own Stirling for the foes with whom I dare not
    cope!
On! burst my breaking heart to hear Edina's heavy news!
Both hold and gold surrender'd there!—O! 'tis too much to
    lose!

Thus hopes are 'whelmed, like sinking ships, with one last
 sudden lurch—
One consolation lingers yet—I ever loved the Church!'—
'Nay!' cried a stern, harsh voice behind—'James! I'm—no
 matter whom—
I'll tell thee, then, with this death-blow! I'm of the house
 of Home!

How likest thou a border shrift?' 'God! what a death to
 die!'
Gasp'd Scotland's James, with sinking voice and ghastly
 glazing eye.
And there, in that poor mill-house, was the King of Scotland sped,
Nor traced they e'er the secret spot wherein his bones were
 laid!"

THE SCOTISH TROOPS AT QUATRE-BRAS AND WATERLOO.

BESIDES the Scots Greys, and the multitudes of diffused Scotish soldiers, both horse and foot, who shared in the final triumph of the British arms over Buonaparte, three regiments emphatically Scotish because entirely Highland, the 42nd or Original Highlanders, the 79th or Cameron Highlanders, and the 92nd or Gordon Highlanders, were early summoned to the muster in Flanders, on the arrival of the news of Buonaparte's escape from Elba. They had, in common with other Highland regiments, acquired great fame in previous wars; and they were treated by the Belgians with high favour and consideration, and speedily got into such friendly terms with the families in Brussels in whose houses they were quartered as to reciprocate with them the warmest civilities and closest confidences of life, even to the extent of taking charge of their children and of keeping their shops. The intelligence of the approach of the French army arrived suddenly on the evening of the 15th of June, 1815; and was followed by prompt orders on the part of Lord Wellington and prompt movements on the part of the troops.

"And there was mounting in hot haste: the steed,
The mustering squadron, and the clattering car,
Went pouring forward with impetuous speed,
And swiftly forming in the ranks of war;
And the deep thunder peal on peal afar;
And near, the beat of the alarming drum
Roused up the soldier ere the morning star;
While thronged the citizens with terror dumb,
Or whispering, with white lips—'The foe! they come, they come!'

And wild and high the 'Cameron's gathering' rose!
The war-note of Lochiel, which Albyn's hills
Have heard—and heard, too, have her Saxon foes;
How in the noon of night that pibroch thrills,
Savage and shrill! But with the breath which fills
Their mountain pipe, so fill the mountaineers
With the fierce native daring, which instils
The stirring memory of a thousand years;
And Evan's, Donald's fame, rings in each clansman's ears!"

Early on the 16th of July, a strong force took up a position at Quatre-Bras. The 92nd regiment was in brigade with the 28th, the 32nd, and the 95th, under Major-General Kempt; and the 42nd and the 92nd were in brigade with the 44th, under Major-General Pack; and these two brigades, along with a brigade of Hanoverians, the Brunswick cavalry and infantry, and a corps of Belgians, were ordered by Lord Wellington to maintain this important position. A very powerful body of the French, under Marshal Ney, confronted them in nearly a parallel line. An expanse of plain ground lay between the two armies, part of it under growing corn and clear of wood, and part occupied by a piece of dense forest called Bois de Boissu. General Kempt's brigade formed into separate columns of regiments, extended on the plain to the left, and was first attacked by the enemy in great force. These were firmly met by the battalions, who successfully resisted repeated attempts of cavalry and infantry to break them. As the enemy continued to push forward fresh troops, the 42nd and 44th were ordered out on the plain to support General Kempt's brigade. A desperate conflict now ensued, each battalion of the British having to sustain, in several instances separately and independently, the whole weight of the French masses which bore down upon them.

In this arduous struggle the Cameron Highlanders supported the reputation they had acquired in the Peninsular war; for, not satisfied with repelling the enemy, they advanced upon them and drove them off the ground, still preserving, however, a regularity of formation which enabled them to meet every fresh attack. They received the attacks of the enemy sometimes in position, and at other times they advanced to meet the charge of the French infantry, who uniformly declined the onset. The charges of the cavalry were received in squares and always repulsed.

The Duke of Brunswick at the head of the Brunswick Hussars, pushed forward to check a column of French cavalry considerably in advance of the main body. But he was unfortunately killed; and the enemy taking advantage of the confusion into which the loss of their brave commander threw the Brunswickers, charged with great energy, and forced them to retire precipitately in the direction of the ditch along which the Gordon Highlanders were drawn up unperceived by the enemy. As soon as the cavalry came within reach, the Highlanders opened a well directed and destructive fire upon them from behind the ditch. This unexpected attack completely disconcerted the enemy, who, thrown into irretrievable disorder by repeated volleys of musketry, fled in the utmost confusion, after sustaining a severe loss in killed and wounded.

The 42nd was drawn up in a field of barley nearly breast-high. At some distance they observed a corps of cavalry, which they supposed, from their uniform, to be Prussians or Belgians. They were in fact a body of French lancers; but the mistake was not discovered in time to receive the squadrons of the enemy in proper formation. The Highlanders endeavoured to throw themselves into a kind of square, which movement being observed by the enemy, they galloped up and charged the Highlanders with great impetuosity before they had nearly completed their formation. The enemy, however, were repulsed, and forced back at every point. The regiment now formed itself into a compact square, and in that situation gallantly withstood the repeated attacks of the lancers, who were unable to make any impression. At the end of every charge, the enemy, turning their backs, scampered off to a short distance, amid the jeers and laughter of the Highlanders, who kept firing at them both on their approach and retreat. Finding all their attempts against the Highland phalanx fruitless, the enemy desisted from the attack.

During three hours the allies had to contend against the most fearful odds, and had to sustain sometimes together, and sometimes in separate battalions, a series of desperate charges made by an enemy confident of victory. But at six o'clock in the evening, the arrival of a reinforcement from Brussels lessened the great disparity of force, and put the parties upon a more equal footing. A brigade of Guards, part of this reinforcement, was stationed on the right of Quatre Bras, and the other brigades on the left. The enemy now commenced a general discharge from a numerous artillery, which was so stationed as to cover the whole of the British line

They continued the cannonade for an hour, when they advanced in two columns, the one by the high road, the other through a hollow along the skirts of the thick wood Bois de Boissu. Unperceived by the allies, the enemy had already taken possession of a house on the Charleroi road, some hundred yards from the village; and had also occupied a garden and several thickset hedges near to the house. The Gordon Highlanders were no sooner informed of this than they instantly resolved to dispossess the enemy; and whilst one party, headed by Colonel Cameron, rapidly moved forward on the road, another party pushed round by their right. The enemy were so well covered by the garden and hedges that it required great exertions to dislodge them; but the Highlanders at last succeeded, not, however, till they had lost their brave commander, Colonel Cameron, and other valuable lives. After driving the enemy, who were greatly more numerous than their assailants, from this post, the Highlanders pursued them more than a quarter of a mile, until checked by the advance of a large body of French cavalry and infantry, preceded by artillery. Unable to resist this formidable force, the Highlanders retired along the edge of the wood of Boissu to their original position. Marshal Ney having failed in every attempt to force the allies from their position, and despairing of success, finally desisted from the attack at nine o'clock in the evening, leaving the allies in possession of the ground they had occupied at three o'clock, when the battle commenced.

On the morning of the 17th, Lord Wellington had collected the whole of his army in the position of Waterloo, and was combining his measures to attack the enemy; but having received information that Marshal Blucher had been obliged, after the battle of Ligny, to abandon his position at Sombref and to fall back upon Wavre, his lordship found it necessary to make a corresponding movement. He accordingly retired upon Genappe, and thence upon Waterloo,

Although the march took place in the middle of the day, the enemy made no attempt to molest the rear, except by following with a large body of cavalry, brought from his right, the cavalry under the Earl of Uxbridge. On the former debouching from the village of Genappe, the Earl made a gallant charge with the Life Guards and repulsed the enemy's cavalry.

Lord Wellington took up a position in front of Waterloo. The rain fell in torrents during the night; and the morning of the 18th was ushered in by a dreadful thunder-storm,—a prelude which superstition might have regarded as ominous of the events of that memorable and decisive day. The allied army was drawn up across the high roads from Charleroi and Nivelles, with its right thrown back to a ravine near Merke Braine, which was occupied, and its left extended to a height above the hamlet Ter-la-Haye, which was also occupied. In front of the right centre, and near the Nivelles road, they occupied the house and farm of Hougoumont; and in front of the left centre, they possessed the farm of La Haye Sainte. Buonaparte drew up his army on a range of heights in front of the allies; and about ten o'clock in the morning, he commenced the battle by a furious attack upon the post at Hougoumont, and by a very heavy cannonade upon the whole line of the allies.

Major-General Kempt's brigade, with the 28th and 32nd regiments, formed the centre of Lieutenant-general Picton's division. A corps of Belgians and part of the Rifle brigade occupied a hedge, in the rear of which, at the distance of one hundred and fifty yards, the 32nd and 79th were stationed. About two hours after the commencement of the battle three heavy columns of the enemy, preceded by artillery and sharpshooters, advanced towards the hedge. The Belgians fired a volley and retired in great disorder. The enemy then began to deploy into line, but before they could complete this operation the 32nd, 79th, and Rifle corps pushed forward and, forming upon the hedge, fired a volley, charged the enemy, and threw them into confusion. In an attempt to get towards their right the enemy were received by the 28th, which warmly attacked their right as they advanced. The 32nd and 79th followed up their advantage, each attacking the column opposed to them, till at length the enemy gave way in the greatest confusion. At this moment General Picton was killed and General Kempt severely wounded; but although unable, from the severity of the wound, to sit on horseback, the latter would not allow himself to be carried off the field. The enemy rallied, and renewed their attempts to gain possession of the hedge, but without success.

The Gordon Highlanders were in the ninth brigade with the Royal Scots, the Royal Highlanders, and the 44th regiment. This brigade was stationed on the left wing upon the crest of a small eminence, forming one side of the hollow, or low valley, which divided the two hostile armies. A hedge ran along this crest for nearly two-thirds its whole length. A brigade of Belgians, another of Hanoverians, and General Ponsonby's brigade of the 1st or Royal Dragoons, Scotch Greys, and Inniskillings, were posted in front of this hedge. It was not till about two o'clock that these were attacked. At that time the enemy, covered by a heavy fire of artillery, advanced in a solid column of 3,000 infantry of the guard, with drums beating, and all the accompaniments of military array, towards the position of the Belgians. The enemy received a temporary check from the fire of the Belgians and from some artillery; but the troops of Nassau gave way, and, retiring behind the crest of the eminence, left a large space open to the enemy. To prevent the enemy from entering by this gap, the third battalion of the Royal Scots, and the second battalion of the 44th. were ordered up to occupy the ground so abandoned; and here a warm conflict of some duration took place, in which the two regiments lost many men and expended their ammunition. The enemy's columns continuing to press forward, General Pack ordered up the Highlanders, calling out, "Ninety-second, now is your time; charge." This order being repeated by Major Macdonald, the soldiers answered it by a shout. Though then reduced to less than 250 men, the regiment instantly formed two men deep, and rushed to the front, against a column ten or twelve men deep, and equal in length to their whole line. The enemy, as if appalled by the advance of the Highlanders, stood motionless; and upon a nearer approach they became panic-struck, and, wheeling to the rear, fled in the most disorderly manner, throwing away their arms and every thing that incumbered them. So rapid was their flight, that the Highlanders, notwithstanding their nimbleness of foot, were unable to overtake them; but General Ponsonby pursued them with the cavalry at full speed, and cutting into the centre of the column, killed numbers and took nearly eighteen hundred prisoners. The animating sentiment, "Scotland for ever!" received a mutual cheer as the Greys galloped past the Highlanders, and the former felt the effect of the appeal so powerfully, that, not content with the destruction or surrender of the flying column, they passed it, and charged up to the line of the French position. " Les braves Ecossais; qu'ils sont terribles ces Chevaux Gris!' exclaimed Napoleon, when, in succession, he saw the small body of Highlanders forcing one of his chosen columns to fly, and the Greys charging almost into his very line.

During the remainder of the day, the 92nd regiment remained at the post assigned them; but no opportunity afterwards occurred of giving another proof of their prowess. The important service they rendered at a critical moment, by charging and routing the élite of the French infantry, entitle them to share largely in the honours of the victory. " A column of such strength," says Stewart, " composed of veteran troops, filled with the usual confidence of the soldiers of France, thus giving way to so inferior a force, and by their retreat exposing themselves to certain destruction from the charges of cavalry ready to pour in and overwhelm them, can only be accounted for by the manner in which the attack was made, and is one of the numerous advantages of that mode of attack I have had so often occasion to notice. Had the Highlanders, with their inferior numbers, hesitated and remained at a distance, exposed to the fire of the enemy, half an hour would have been sufficient to annihilate them, whereas in their bold and rapid advance they *lost only four men*. The two regiments, which for some time resisted the attacks of the same column, were unable to force them back. They remained stationary to receive the enemy, who were thus allowed time and opportunity to take a cool and steady aim; encouraged by a prospect of success, the latter doubled their efforts; indeed, so confident were they, that when they reached the plain upon the summit of the ascent, they ordered their arms, as if to rest after the victory. But the handful of Highlanders soon proved on which side the victory lay. Their bold and rapid charge struck their confident opponents with terror, paralyzed their sight and aim, and deprived both of point and object. The consequence was, as it will always be in nine cases out of ten in similar circumstances, that the loss of the 92nd regiment was, as I have just stated, only four men, whilst the other corps in their stationary position lost eight times that number."

CARDINAL BEATON AND HIS VICTIMS.

[The following Sketch is an abridgment, with some slight modifications, of a series of short historical papers from the pen of Mr. James Turnbull, published in 1838 and 1839, in a Periodical which is now extinct.]

KING JAMES V. of Scotland died on the 18th of December, 1542, leaving an only child, a daughter, born ten days previously, and afterwards well known to every age as Mary Queen of Scots. The state of Scotland at the time was most perilous. Many of the nobility had fallen in battle; some were in exile, and others in captivity; while they who remained in Scotland were alienated from one another by differences regarding religion. The people also were divided and without confidence in their rulers; and, in addition to all other evils, they were involved in war with England. This was a state of things suited to the ambitious views of the churchmen,—who attempted to take advantage of its peculiarities for their own exaltation. They seem to have imagined that, could they acquire, they would easily retain, the supreme dominion, since the crown had devolved upon an infant female, and her mother was entirely devoted to the interests and views of their chief, Cardinal David Beaton, archbishop of St. Andrews. This man had been destined to the priesthood from his boyhood, and had studied the arts of priestcraft and the mysteries of popery in France, and had succeeded his uncle in the primacy of the Scotish church in 1539; and he possessed a vigorous intellect, cultivated by education, and matured by experience, and transcended all his predecessors in crime.

At the death of James V., no fears or scruples hindered the Cardinal from attempting to secure for himself and his party the chief honours of the state. When the King was on his death-bed, and his mind was agitated and wavering, the Cardinal plied him with arguments and motives—not regarding Christ, repentance, or immortality; no, his heart yearned not then, as it should have done, over the soul of one who had been an ardent worshipper at the altars of sensuality, and whom the grossest debasements had distinguished —but to appoint for his daughter a certain form of regency in which he (the Cardinal) should be supreme. He desired four, himself the chief of these, to be appointed to that dignity; and the persons whom he wished to be appointed were such as would have sympathized with him in all his designs. He desired this, knowing that his associates, though having only the name of office, would be a shelter to him from the consequences of any measures he might adopt for the aggrandizement of his party, and the rendering of the superstitions of his church perpetual; that they, in short, would have the danger and the odium of whatever was unpopular. We are ignorant whether the King gave or could give any assent; but even though his mind, enfeebled and agitated, may have yielded, Beaton trusted not thereto, knowing that it was too fragile a thread upon which to suspend his claims to the possession of the high dignity of the realm, at a period when the clouds of political and religious animosity were accumulating in the horizon. By his direction, as is now well known, a will was forged by one Balfour, a priest, professing to have been written in the presence, and according to the instructions, of the King, in which it was appointed, according to the proposition which Beaton had made, that there should be a council of regency, and he its head. There are insinuations made by writers of these times, of a hand, which had once stretched the sword and swayed the sceptre, having been employed, after it was stiffened in death, in affixing a signature to this document. Let us hope that this mockery of the dead was spared, for without it, the transaction was sufficiently base. By whatever means it was obtained, a will, purporting to be that of the King, signed and attested according to form, was produced,—in conformity with the provisions of which, Beaton immediately assumed the high office of chief regent and governor, with Huntly, Murray, and Argyle as subordinates.

He was exalted only to be cast down. Henry of England, with much dignity and generosity of feeling, released the nobles he had in captivity, and, at the same time, suspended the war, though in it his success had been almost uninterrupted. He would not—as a less noble foe would have done—

take advantage of the condition of the kingdom, however much he had been provoked by injury and insult. The effect was immediate. The nobles refused to submit to the haughty prelate. The deed upon which his claims rested was disputed, denied—the fraud being detected. Hamilton, Earl of Arran, and heir-presumptive to the crown, was raised, by the acclamation of all, except Beaton and his party, to be Governor of the kingdom. This was wormwood to the Cardinal. It was not only that he himself was driven from the dignity he had dishonourably attained; but Hamilton was the object of his peculiar aversion, from his being generally regarded as most favourable to the doctrines of the Reformation, and because he was distinguished by his honesty,—a principle which, at that time, was not in very great repute among the clergy. But Beaton required to yield; and events soon transpired which seemed to justify the fondest expectations which the reformers entertained of the government of Arran.

Two persons, William and Rough, (the former a black friar,) who were distinguished by their faithfulness in preaching the gospel, were, in compliance with very general and earnest applications, appointed by the Governor to the public declaration of the truth. It was in vain that the priests vented their indignation against this and similar measures. Beaton himself, so far from wielding the despotism of which he was formerly possessed, was, in consequence of his opposition to this appointment, subjected for a short time to a species of confinement, which, though slight, sufficiently demonstrated that his power and glory had departed for a season. But an enactment of the legislature raised the hopes of the reformers to the highest degree. It had been forbidden by law to any one to read any portion of the scriptures in their own or in the English tongue, or any tract, or explanation of any part of scripture. This prohibition was abolished; and it was now declared lawful for all to peruse, in their own or in the English tongue, the Bible, or any religious treatise containing wholesome doctrine. This was received as a blessing of the greatest magnitude by those who, though thirsting after a knowledge of the gospel, dared not, without the danger of being punished as heretics, read even the Lord's Prayer in their own language. It was received as an inestimable boon, though clogged by particulars in which the parliament and the church were declared to be possessed of authority to regulate what was proper to be read by the people. The effect was instantaneous and powerful. Everywhere the New Testament became read; men, in consequence, assumed a bolder tone; while many whom timidity had formerly restrained avowed their rejection of the superstition of popery.

The change of affairs in Scotland was most acceptable to England, newly emancipated from the slavery of Rome. Henry, who had anxiously sought to maintain peace with Scotland, but whose desires and efforts had been frustrated by the priesthood, now used all means to unite the kingdoms in close and inseparable alliance. He sought the hand of the infant Queen of Scotland for his son Edward, then a boy. Though strenuously opposed by the whole power of the churchmen, his wishes were cordially responded to by the Governor and nobility; and the contract of marriage was solemnly sworn to, and sealed, in the chapel of Holyrood. Mary having become, by the most sacred engagements, the betrothed of the heir of the throne of England, men rejoiced over the event as the dawn of a day of unbroken happiness. How vain are human hopes, and how wise the exhortation, 'Rejoice with trembling!' The event which caused so much joy was only the little spot of beauty which, for a moment, relieves the dark bosom of the storm.

Unable openly to accomplish their designs, the Cardinal, with the Queen and the French party, sought success by stratagem. The Governor was weak while honest. Taking advantage of his weakness, they accomplished his destruction, and involved his adherents and the nation in calamities, under the sweep of which all for a time was desolate. The wise and faithful were gradually removed from his counsels, and their places supplied by the crafty abettors of former evils. The preachers whom he had appointed required to seek safety in flight; and those who were his former friends and the promoters of reformation became banished from court. They knew that he was most sensitive regarding every thing which infringed, however slightly, upon his claims as heir-presumptive to the crown. He had gazed upon the lustre of the diadem till his perceptions were dimmed. His strongest affections were wound around the honours and the exalted happiness which he believed it contained within its—to him—magic circle. Each of its gems had the longings to obtain it of his whole heart.

This ruling passion was known and cherished by his new and unprincipled associates, until they had prepared him to sacrifice all consistency and honour for its gratification. They taught him, and he believed, that if union were preserved with England, and the Reformation existed and made progress, the crown must be torn from his reach,—that it must be torn from him unless he joined his interests to those of France, and, by crushing heresy, obtained the friendship of the pope. By what means did they persuade him of this, when he had been exalted to the highest dignity in opposition to the combined power of the church, and when, in union with England, he might have courted the hatred and braved the power of Europe? His father was twice married; and his second marriage was, according to Rome, unlawful, he having divorced his first wife. The Governor was of the second marriage: and he was made to believe that, his father's second marriage having been illegal, he was illegitimate, and therefore could not, in the event of the death of Mary, succeed to the throne, but that the pope could, by his dispensing power, render the marriage valid, and his claim indisputable. He believed; and, rather than forfeit his claim, he forfeited a good conscience, and, for a broken reed, cast away the support of popular influence upon which he was secure. Religion was again a sacrifice at the altar of ambition.

The Governor did not fully, at least openly, yield, until the Cardinal and bishops, with the few of the nobles who adhered to their faction and idolatries, with the Queen mother and her daughter who had assembled at Stirling, threatened to deprive him of his office of governor for disobedience to their 'holy mother the kirk.' Abandoned by the wise, and left to the influence of his own fears and ambition, he resolved on the ignoble course of unlimited submission to the will of his enemies; he humbled himself before Beaton, confessing whatever was dictated to him as offences,—abjuring the doctrines of the Reformation, and pledging himself to the annulling of the contract made with England; and having done this, he received absolution and unqualified assurance of the affectionate support of the church. Beaton would have cast him off, now that his conduct had rendered him powerless, now that he had rendered himself an object, not of pity, but of loathing; but he retained him to bask in his deceitful smiles, so that he might use him as a willing or unconscious agent in promoting the schemes by which he was about to minister to his own ambition and the cupidity and revenge of the church.

He had now another object to be gained, the regaining for the church a supremacy in the general mind. For this purpose, he and the Governor—whom he took with him either to prevent the influence of his former friends, or to show his power as did the conquerors of old when captive kings were dragged at their chariot wheels, or to involve him so deeply in his purposes and actions that an impassable gulf would be dug between him and his former associates—

passed through several places in the north, and at last came to Perth, where, by reddening their hands in the blood of the saints, they sought to give power to the polluted and merciless system faithfully and graphically described as " the mother of the abominations of the earth."

The clergy of Perth sympathizing in their views and purposes, had a number of persons suspected of heresy brought before them. Among these were six persons, five men and a woman, whom they accounted worthy of death. One of them had interrupted a friar while impressing upon the mind of another that he could not be saved without praying to saints; three of them were charged with having spoken disrespectfully of an image, and with having eaten a goose on Friday; the fifth with having adorned his house in mockery, as was supposed, of the " three-crowned diadem of St. Peter ;" and the woman with having refused, when in distress, to invoke the aid of the Virgin Mary. These were the charges against them. Examples were wanted of the power of the church; and the priests had long been deprived of banquetting on the sufferings of the righteous. The accused were brought before them, only to be condemned. Four of them were sentenced to be hanged, one to be burned, and the woman to be bound in a sack and drowned in the Tay. Their history has not been preserved. We are acquainted with only their names, the accusations against them, and their execution. Their names, which shall not perish, were: James Hunter, Robert or William Lamb, William Anderson James Finlayson, James Rennalt, or Rawleson, and Helen Stark. On one day the four men condemned to be hanged, and the woman, met their doom; and on the following day the sixth victim embraced the stake. However great the interest connected with all of these persons, the chief interest arose from the circumstances and fate of the poor woman who was the first female martyr in Scotland, and whose murder fixed the deepest stain on the bloated memory of Beaton.

Her husband was one of the four who died upon the gibbet. They were fondly attached to each other. They had long rejoiced in mutual affection, and been the light of each other's mind. Children had strengthened every tender tie. She sought no respite, though they had little ones—though a babe was being suckled at her breast. She had many, and these very strong, inducements to desire to live; but she sought only this—it was not mercy—though to her it would have been happiness—she sought that she might be permitted *to die with her husband*. The poor petition was spurned. Again she pleaded—but her prayer was presented to the savage—she pleaded that she might be put to death before her husband, that she might be spared the agony of beholding his dying struggles; but this also was rejected, and scornfully. She sought refuge in God. She cast her burden on him, and he sustained her. She was no more the weeping trembling woman, but the Christian heroine. She soothed the troubled bosom of her husband. The influence of her love mingled with that of Christ's, over his mind, as he passed from the scene of the triumph of guilt over innocence and godliness, to—may we not believe?—the fellowship of the souls that were beneath the altar for the testimony of God, and whose voice, as he died, must have thus pleaded:—' How long, O Lord, holy and true, dost thou not judge and avenge our blood on them that dwell upon the earth?'

Having witnessed, (and with what feeling must it have been?) the sufferings of her husband, she took her babe from her bosom, where it was fondly nestling, and bathed its smiling happy countenance with her tears. Warm were her caresses as she pressed it for the last time to her throbbing breast, and prayed that the great Shepherd would carry in his bosom this lamb of his flock. Kindness and sympathy had gathered a few of her neighbours around her, who had known her virtues, and who now, bold by outraged feeling, dared to soothe her with their words, and who, overcome by tender emotions, mingled with hers their tears. To them she gave her infant, and then, having done with earth—the last fond tie being broken—she prepared herself in faith and confidence to meet death. She was bound, as had been decreed, and cast into the river. Its waters closed over her, and then flowed on peaceful as before. How unlike the conscience of her murderers! This was in 1543.

Having thus renewed the sufferings of the godly, and apparently imagining that the sword of persecution would be of sufficient edge and temper to destroy all existing and future heresies, the Cardinal seems to have imagined that, to establish his own power, and the authority and splendour of the church, he required only to prevent the importation from England of the doctrines of the Reformation. In peace this was impossible, and therefore war was courted and obtained. The Governor and others, unfaithful to their sacred engagements, and seeking war by a variety of injuries which could not be submitted to, war again raged between two nations whom every motive should have retained in close affection. Doubtless the prelate imagined that the tide of war would roll, in irresistible majesty, over the power and the doctrines of his enemies. Their doctrines, however, had a foundation which could not be shaken,—one to which God had given strength; and though the Cardinal persecuted, the doctrines extended.

We pass over a number of minor efforts which were made by him for their suppression, and advert to the martyrdom of one whose dying groan was the funeral knell of the tyrant's power and glory,—one by whose death the scattered elements were so united and brought into operation, that the friends of the reformation confronted their foes, and were victorious. It would have been enough to have rendered the death of this saint imperishable, that it was the means of bringing into the field of moral action that man to whom, under God, Scotland owes most,—whose arm, in the future, was to be the first in the strife,—and around whom our fathers gathered, with brave hearts, and planted, amidst the ruins of the spiritual despotism by which they had been debased and made miserable that broad and glorious banner of civil and religious freedom, which still floats over us in the breeze of victory.

The name of George Wishart is indelibly engraven on the heart of every one who has even slightly investigated the annals of our country. It is a name which has never been dimmed, by a breathing of scorn, even from enemies; to the Christian, it is the name of one who walked in brightness amidst the gloom of our troubled land. He was of the family of Pittarrow, in Mearns,—a family, several of the members of which were subsequently imitators of his spiritual heroism. He completed his education at Cambridge, where, in addition to scientific and classical information, he acquired just views of the salvation that is in Christ; and he returned to Scotland, in the year 1544, with the commissioners who had been sent by Henry to treat for the continuance of peace. He commenced his labours as a preacher of the gospel in Montrose; but, persecution gathering around him, he went to Dundee; and there he lectured publicly on the epistle to the Romans, to the admiration of all, and the conviction of many. Private insinuation and public denunciation of the doctrines of the New Testament which he taught, and which some of the clergy affirmed was a heretical book written by one Martin Luther, whom the devil had sent into the world for the destruction of the souls of men, having proved equally unavailing, he was publicly, and by authority, commanded to depart from Dundee. He knew the vanity of attempting to resist, single-handed, the power that was arrayed against him; and he went into Ayrshire,—then a sanctuary to the persecuted; and he there preached in many parish churches, and often in the fields, and was always attended by many hearers, and made a great impression throughout the country. "The word of the Lord was precious in those days;" and "the Spirit of the Lord was present to heal"

Wishart's labours in Ayrshire were interrupted by the information that the plague—formerly a frequent visitant of Scotland—was in Dundee. He was deeply interested, for the people of that place were near his heart; and he hastened to Dundee, as if its destinies had depended on his presence. The day following his arrival there—while powerfully impressed by the scenes of misery around, in which the dying were blended with the dead, and the wailings of the bereaved mingled with the cries of the suffering and the fearful—having felt in his own mind the power of the gospel to sustain and comfort, he assembled the people at the east port of the town, and, placing the healthy within and the diseased without the gate, preached to them the safety and consolation which are in Christ. In application to their state he selected as his text, "He sent forth his word and healed them;" and their circumstances produced intensity of feeling and earnestness of attention. His instructions had power. The awakening was general, and the effects abundant,—all of which, however, shall not be known till that day when, from the book of God's remembrance, there shall be recounted the influence of every sermon which has been addressed to the perishing. The same place was his pulpit daily. There he held forth the word of life; while he also, from house to house, visited and taught the dying and the diseased. How like to his Master while thus occupied!

Could it have been imagined that, while Wishart was thus superior to all personal considerations, and anxious only that sinners might be turned unto the Lord, his enemies would have chosen such a time to circumvent his life? The spirit that betrayed Christ must have been in them. They felt themselves condemned by his labours; their malignity was aroused, and they sought to obtain his assassination. Beaton hired a person—a priest too—to accomplish their purpose who sought to carry it into execution on the very spot where Wishart preached. The latter's warfare, however, was not completed; and God averted the danger. But the discovery tended to entwine Wishart more in the affections of the people; and it also stimulated him to renewed zeal in his labours, leading him to think that his time would be short,—that he would one day fall by the hands of his enemy; and his intercourse with God became, in consequence, still more frequent, and his pleading with him still more fervent and enlarged.

When the plague was removed, or at least its power was broken, Wishart went to Montrose. There his time was occupied in preaching and private meditation. Beaton sought again for his destruction. Having failed to induce the Governor publicly to arrest his progress, for the Governor—whether withheld by friends, or deterred by remorseful recollections of former events, or whether the slavery of the Cardinal was beginning to become galling to him—would not be persuaded. Beaton's rage was measureless. He could not with safety give public expression to his malignity; but again he endeavoured to insnare Wishart. By false letters purporting to be from Wishart's friends, requiring his assistance, he sought to bring him within his power. When almost successful, the deceit was discovered, and Wishart was spared for a season; but the circumstance threw over his mind a deep foreshadowing of his approaching martyrdom.

According to his own phraseology, "when God had put an end to one battle, he found himself called to another." His friends in Ayrshire, earnestly requested him to meet them in Edinburgh, "for they would require disputation of the bishops, and he should be publicly heard." He assented and, at the time fixed, he left Montrose, in opposition to the tearful entreaties of the faithful. He was like Paul, when that apostle had set his face to go up to Jerusalem, and would not be hindered, though knowing the dangers that were around him. During his journey, he was deeply exercised in spirit, and felt much the necessity of prayer. "I am assured," said he, "that my travail is near an end; therefore call to God with me that now I shrink not when the battle waxes most hot."

With a few friends he arrived at Leith, where, not finding those whom he had expected, and having no intelligence of them, he remained for a time in secret. This became irksome to him. "What differ I," he would say, "from a dead man, but that I eat and drink?" On the Sabbath he, at last, preached in Leith; but apprehensive of the consequences, from the known hostility and the power of the clergy of Edinburgh, and from a daily expectation that the Cardinal would be there, he was taken by a few gentlemen of the Lothians, who had come to him, and who remained with him as his guides and protectors, to Long-Niddry, Ormiston, and Brownston, residing for only short periods in one place, that his refuge might not be discovered. But his crown was almost gained.

He preached, as we learn, in Inveresk church, subsequently in Tranent, where, while urging his hearers to diligence, he publicly declared his belief that his remaining course would be short. His preaching in these places was with power. About Christmas he went to Haddington, where a very great concourse of people was expected; but by the power of Bothwell, who was instigated by the Cardinal, the people were prevented from assembling. On the first occasion, few attended; and on the second, the number was still smaller. His mind was much troubled, so that he said to John Knox, who had attended him during the time he was in the Lothians, and had derived much benefit from his ministry, "I am wearied of the world,"—assigning as the cause, that "men appeared to be wearied of God." He dealt faithfully in his discourse—his last sermon—with the people. While he directed them to 'the hope set before them' in the gospel, he boldly reproved their sins, and unfolded to them, in their magnificence, the terrors of the Lord. He affectionately, but solemnly, bade farewell to the few loved ones, the faithful in Christ, who gathered round him at the close of this his concluding testimony to the truth.

Wishart went on the same evening to Ormiston. John Knox would have gone with him, and entreated to be permitted; but Wishart forbade, saying, " No, no; one is enough for a sacrifice." There were with him the lairds of Ormiston, Brownston, and Calder. The evening was spent in religious exercises, after which, and some discourse, approaching to the cheerful, he sought his pillow and found repose. His time, however, had come. About midnight, and without warning, the house was surrounded by a party of soldiers, conducted by Bothwell. Resistance, obstruction, or an attempt to escape, would have been equally vain, even though Beaton had not been, as he was, at Elphinstone, with a superior force. So soon as Wishart was aware of the circumstances in which his friends and he were placed, he bade them open the gates, saying, with cheerful resignation, " The blessed will of my God be done." The Earl of Bothwell and a few gentlemen were admitted, who gave solemn assurances that Wishart should be in perfect safety. Bothwell, especially, promised either to preserve him from all injury, or, if he should perceive that the doing of this would be impossible, to restore him to the place where he found him, notwithstanding any opposition which might be made by the Cardinal or his party. These assurances were implicitly relied on; and, therefore, Wishart's friends, with lessened sorrow gave him up to Bothwell. He was carried immediately to the Cardinal at Elphinstone; who, having obtained possession of his much desired victim, immediately sent the party who had apprehended him to secure also the lairds of Ormiston, Brownston, and Calder, who had been with him. Brownston alone escaped. The others were sent to Edinburgh, and lodged in the castle. Ormiston effected his deliverance; but **Calder** was not released for a considerable time, and then only upon submission **to Beaton.**

Wishart was conducted to Edinburgh; but Bothwell, perceiving danger from having him there, and seemingly feeling some sense of obligation from his promise, carried him from Edinburgh to his mansion at Hailes. He would perhaps have been faithful to his engagements; but the condemnation of Wishart being reckoned necessary for the security of religion, and of the party then in power, and the weaknesses or rather sinful propensities of Bothwell being known, the Cardinal and the Queen Mother, by ministering to his covetousness and sensuality, induced him to deliver up his prisoner unconditionally. Wishart was now placed within the **grasp** of Rome's vengeance; and its Cardinal must have exulted at the anticipation now before him of trampling on another spirit that had detected and **exposed** her superstitions, and **defied her unholy power. The Governor** also, weak and wavering—who was everything by fits and nothing long at a time—yielded; **and then** the lamb was irrecoverably in the **paw of the** lion.

About the end of January, 1546, Wishart was removed to St. Andrews, whither the Cardinal had summoned the bishops and all of eminence in the church. He wished to give dignity and importance to his purpose, and, by example, to influence the priesthood generally to vigorous efforts; or, perhaps, by involving them in the condemnation of Wishart, he sought to isolate them from the sympathies of the reformed, so that they might act against them as personal ene**mies.** The summons was obeyed. The clergy assembled in all the pageantry with which antichrist arrays and surrounds the priests **of** his idolatry, and were attended by the military in the trappings of **war.** All this was in order to the laying **of an unresisting sacrifice on** the altar of spiritual despotism, **—to make the death of God's** servant a means of perpetuating the alienation **from God** of the human mind; and it was devised by men who professed themselves ministers of righteousness and messengers of peace. Ought we to wonder that the infidel has so often mocked?

They met in the abbey church. After a sermon, bold yet cautious, had been preached by Dean Winram, who was suspected of favouring the opinions of the reformed, and who most probably was appointed to that duty with the design of obliging him either to lay open his supposed opinions, or so to retract them by advocating the power and doctrines of the church, that he should be for ever separated from all association with the reformers. Wishart was then placed in the pulpit, that he might be the more exposed while he listened to his accusation, and gave, if permitted his defence. His accusation was read, with great violence and bitterness, by one Lauder, a priest, who, in the true spirit of the master he was serving, spat, at the conclusion of it, in Wishart's face, saying, " What answerest thou to these sayings, thou renegade, traitor, thief?" a phraseology which was repeated at the beginning of the several charges, and fully demonstrated that justice was not among the proud and powerful on the judgment-seat. It is not necessary to record the several articles upon which Wishart was condemned. To call the proceedings against him a trial would be a mockery of the word. Suffice it to note that his accusation seems to have been framed in order to produce a sensation among the multitude, and to make them recoil from Wishart as if he had been an incarnation of every thing worthless, and account his baptism of fire a punishment too brief and slight for his atrocities. Among the charges against him, were his denying the authority of the church and of the pope, his opposing the seven sacraments, auricular confession, extreme unction, and transubstantiation, and his teaching that purgatory had no existence, that no sin was committed by eating flesh on Friday, and that to pray to saints or angels was sinful.

Wishart's defence was calm, firm, and unanswerable. His pleading was so powerful that the prelates themselves said " If we give him license to preach, he is so crafty, and in holy scripture so exercised, that he will persuade the people to his own opinion, and raise them against us." The testimony was an invaluable, though an unintentional one, both to his ability and his knowledge. But though it undoubtedly expressed their genuine sentiments, they showed that no conviction in his favour could change their stern and unholy resolution. He was, in all forms which a malignant ingenuity could suggest, sought to be insnared; but the grace of God was sufficient for him. . He witnessed a good confession ; his eloquence was fringed with heaven's lightning; yet die he must; no voice said, spare; no heart dictated mercy; even pity was not allowed to modify the formula of his martyrdom. The flames were his doom.

The Cardinal pronounced his sentence, and remanded him to his prison till the fire should be prepared. He was unmoved; he breathed a prayer to God that he would pardon the guilty tribunal, and was led away. By sending two friars to him to receive his confession, his persecutors seem to have been unwilling that he should have the enjoyment of the few moments of life that remained to him; for they knew he would not receive such messengers. He rejected their services, and requested that Winram, who had that day preached, might be sent to him. Winram immediately joined him. Their conversation, or spiritual exercises, of whatever kind, were brief. All was ready for Wishart's sufferings and victory. He was brought to the place of execution with a rope about his neck and a chain around his body, and was bound with them to the stake. The guilty mind of the Cardinal, or his knowledge of the number and power of the reformers, made him take all possible precaution to prevent a rescue. Among other means for this, the guns of his castle were pointed down upon the spot where Wishart suffered while the soldiery were prepared to resist any attack. Such a measure as this was unnecessary. There was no banding together of the righteous to deliver, deterred as they must have been by the impossibility of working advantage to the sufferer, while they would only increase the enmity of their persecutors, and endanger their own safety.

When bound to the stake, Wishart's courage did not forsake him, nor was his joy in God dimmed by even a passing cloud. He exhorted the assembled multitude to faith, repentance, and purity, defended himself from the calumnies of his enemies, and spoke of the blessedness and glory of better times, when the ark of God would float triumphant upon the waters. He prayed humbly and fervently, not for himself only and the persecuted of God's people, but for his persecutors, for their penitence, their pardon, and illumination. The multitude were powerfully impressed by his resignation, his heroism, and his agonies. They could not refrain their expressions of sorrow; they mourned aloud; and their mourning subsequently ripened into detestation of his murderers, and a purpose of revenging his death. To hinder his influencing them farther, the rope around his neck was tightened until he was almost strangled. The fire blazed around him, and he continued suffering yet rejoicing till his soul entered into the joy of his Lord; and, very soon, all that remained of his body was a few smouldering ashes.

From a regard to our common nature, we would, if possible, conceal the conduct of the Cardinal on this occasion, which nothing but intense malignity could have caused. It might have been supposed that his knowledge that the murder was being perpetrated, that the blazing pile was shooting up embers upon his very walls, would have satisfied his thirst for vengeance, or that, if he must farther be gratified by a sight of his victim, a stolen glance through his casement would have sufficed. Was conscience dead that he desired more? He chose for himself the window directly opposite the place of execution, which was on the western side of his castle; and from this thrown open and cushioned, he looked out, attired in all the pomp of official array, upon the agonies of the saint. Emotion burned upon his countenance as the sufferer seemed to writhe amidst his tortures; and joy sparkled in his eyes, and the smile gathered upon his lips, as the body wasted away until its form became undistinguishable from the burning mass which his decree had kindled. Nor was he alone gloating over the tragic scene. The archbishop of Glasgow, with passions equally debased, and feelings equally excited, gazed, in the same pomp, from another window upon the martyr; and, wherever a full view could be obtained, their coadjutors also were seen gazing with satisfaction. They seemed as if all sympathy had perished from their minds.

There have been many unsupported statements made regarding the last hours of Wishart. It has been affirmed by some that when, at his request, Dean Winram came to him, he desired that the Lord's Supper might be administered to him according to his own views of the ordinance,—that, in other words, he wished to partake of both bread and wine. Winram is represented as having consulted with the bishops, who are said to have indignantly forbidden him, at the same time charging Winram with being a supporter of the opinions for which Wishart was condemned. Disappointed in his expectations, we are informed that, being with the captain of the castle, and a few friends, Wishart, after religious discourse, after having spoken of the love and death of Jesus, took bread and wine, and administered to them the sacrament himself, partaking along with them, and closing the service by prayer immediately before the entrance of the executioners to prepare him for the stake. It is also affirmed that when Wishart was amidst the flames, the captain of the castle, who was strongly attached to him, approached so near, while comforting him, as to suffer injury, and that while the captain was entreating him to be of good courage, Wishart said, "This fire torments my body, but noway abates my spirit," and then, looking towards the Cardinal, added, "He who, in such state from that place, feedeth his eyes with my torments, within few days shall be hanged out of the same window to be seen with as much ignominy as he now leaneth there in pride." These words have been often quoted as an evidence that some measure of the inspiration of the Spirit rested on the persecuted in Scotland. Apart altogether from the theological objections to the idea, which, when calmly investigated, will be found insuperable, and the fact that an examination of most of the sayings which have been received as prophetic, would prove them to have been only the anticipations of minds accustomed to observation, from the character of the times, or the complexion of some particular event,—there is no evidence that these words were spoken by Wishart. The passage is undoubtedly an interpolation. George Wishart was judged, sentenced, and burned on the first day of March, 1546.

Not long after Wishart's death, reports reached the Cardinal that there were persons who had determined to revenge the martyr's death. We have, however, reason to believe that the murder of Wishart was only one of a series of actions of pride, oppression, and despotism, by which Beaton had sought to elevate himself to a place of supremacy over every natural right and legal institution, and by which he had goaded on his enemies to vengeance. Apart from religion, his actions had created against him the greatest enmity, and seemingly would have brought him to a tragical end. Though reports of designs against him reached his ear, he not only felt secure, but was boastful of how he would defeat them. He vaunted that he had laid snares, that he had "limed a bush" for those who threatened him, and that they could not possibly escape. Much of his confidence resulted from the connexions he had formed with the nobility, and the power which he possessed over them. He also relied on the Queen-Mother whom he ruled, and the aid of France, which he had purchased at the expense of war with England. When urged to consult his safety by those who were dependent on his continuance in power for the promotion of their own purposes and hopes, he was wont, in his own coarse style, to reply " A fig for the feud, and a button for the heretics! Is not my Lord Governor mine? Is not his eldest son my pledge? Have I not the Queen, the Pope, and the King of France? Is not my daughter the wife of the eldest son of the Earl of Crawford?"

Among the persons who had determined on his destruction, John Leslie, brother of the Earl of Rothes, was the chief. Other causes than those connected with religion had made him his foe. There was joined with him Norman Leslie, son of the Earl of Rothes, and Sheriff of Fife, who had formerly been the faithful and zealous abettor of the Cardinal in all his schemes, but who, in consequence of some disputes, willingly allied himself with his enemies. He, with five other persons, came to St. Andrew's on Friday the 28th May, 1546, where, according to agreement, they found other ten persons, among whom were John Leslie, and William Kirkaldy of Grange. The united parties consulted on the means of putting Beaton to death. He had called a meeting of the gentlemen of Fife; who were to have assembled at Falkland on the Monday following, for the purpose, as afterwards appeared from his papers, of crushing the friends of the Reformation, and also of securing those persons who, from other than religious causes, were the objects of his fear or hatred. The appointing of this meeting was the occasion of hastening on his death. The Leslies, and those associated with them, fearing that they would have directed against them the whole strength of his vengeance, resolved to anticipate him. Having, on that evening, arranged their plans, they separated to meet and execute them in the morning. When we consider their purpose, let 't be remembered that, apart from religion, there were causes sufficiently powerful to have incited them to it, and that several of those by whom it was accomplished acted on the principle of personal revenge. It is necessary to remember this; as Beaton's death has sometimes been attributed exclusively to religious feeling, and employed as an argument of reproach against those who were the leaders in the spiritual emancipation of our country.

On the morning of Saturday, the 29th May, Beaton was hurriedly and violently put to death. The scene was awfully tragical, but does not need to be described here, as it has already been very fully detailed on pp. 322—325 of the second volume of these Tales. When we allow our minds to rest on the Cardinal's cruelties and aggravated crimes, we are ready, under the impulse of our feelings, to justify the manner of his death. When, however, we permit ourselves to think calmly upon the event, our minds recoil from the men who circumvented his death as murderers, however strongly they professed—and in the case of some of them we believe sincerely—that they were acting under the impulse of religious principles. That he deserved to die, we grant, but not by the assassin; for we cannot sustain the plea that, when there were no constitutional means for bringing him to account for his atrocities, when the fountains of justice were sealed up, when every court was impressed with the image of the injustice and cruelty of his mind, persons acting in a private capacity were warranted to punish him. That some of them acted under the belief that they did God service, tends only to show the defectiveness of the knowledge of the reformers, and how much, upon some points, there was affinity between their faith and that of their persecutors, and also between their feelings and desires.

The servants of the Cardinal, who had been ejected by the assailants, aroused his friends in the city. The castle was soon surrounded by a multitude, clamorous about the safety of Beaton. It was in vain that they were entreated to depart since they could not in any form be of advantage to the dead. The provost of the city, with other officials, the abettors of the Cardinal in many crimes, cried out: "What have you done with my Lord Cardinal!" Finding that the multitude would not disperse without seeing Beaton, (for they seem never to have imagined the possibility of his death, but to have thought that the sacredness of his character would have been a defence against any spear,) his body was carried to a window —the window, it is said, from which he had looked on the martyrdom of Wishart—and shown lifeless to the multitude. The spectacle seems to have appalled them; and it was well fitted to do so. How strongly it contrasted with what they had seen of the proud man, of his pomp and glory, when the might of a nation was in his arm, when its destiny was seemingly pendent upon his will, and when the ignorant and admiring, though oppressed, thousands that surrounded him, supposed that, equally as on earth, he had power in the kingdom of God! The dishonoured corpse, as exhibited from the window of that palace, on the construction of which he had lavished thousands, gave a lesson the most impressive, that human ambition is vain, and that every fabric of cruelty and crime is based upon the sand. It produced an instantaneous and deep impression of fear upon the assembled multitude. They fled to their homes lest they should be implicated in the consequences of the action, which they must have regarded as one not only of blood but of sacrilege. Yet great though the departed had been, no voice chaunted his requiem, no voice breathed the wonted supplication that the disembodied spirit might have glory. His body lay surrounded by enemies, in whose hearts each one of his wounds created feelings of exultation; and the joys of revenge blended with the charms of hope. They looked on the body; and, as they did so, they thought as do the oppressed when they have burst their chain, and, nerved by a remembrance of their wrongs, have torn the despot from his blood-stained throne, and trampled his diadem in the dust; or as when the image of idolatry, before which the lovely and the pure has often been presented as an offering, and to satisfy whose thirst for blood, the blood of childhood has streamed plentifully, is dashed from its pedestal, and is prostrate and broken, as Dagon before the ark of God. They gazed, imagining they had done well; for whether they were under religious or under earthly feelings and principles, they all believed that they had secured their personal liberty by the death of him who was planning their destruction. Their first care was how to dispose of his body. They had no means of interring it; and, the weather being hot, they required to conceal the dead for the safety of the living. They accordingly wrapped it in a copse of lead—"giving him," according to the phraseology of Knox, "salt enough"—and put it at the bottom of the sea-tower in the palace. Could anything have warmed into a consciousness of sin the silent dead, it would have been this place chosen as the depository of his body. It was a place which had been constructed by him for the imprisonment of heretics, and in which the victims of his tyranny had suffered all the accumulated anguish which can be heaped upon the prisoner. Its walls had often echoed to their groans and the utterance of their grief, as there came back fresh upon their minds the memory of other years,— and also of their hope, while, though fettered and condemned, they anticipated the joy and sublimity of their rest with God, after the fires of their persecutors had consumed all that was mortal of them.

The death of Beaton produced results which bore assimilation to the views previously entertained of him. The court was agitated. It felt itself helpless. The Queen and her favourites, whom he had mingled in hostilities with England, now dreaded the vengeance of that country, and looked to France as their only refuge from the impending storm.

The ambitious, in the path of whose hopes he had been a hinderance, rejoiced, anticipating that henceforth there would be no obstruction to the gratifying of their desires,—though professedly they were enraged at his death. Various opinions existed among the reformed respecting the manner of his death; but they all had this happiness that, by whatever means, their deadliest foe was removed,—a happiness, however, which was fringed by apprehensions of the consequences, knowing that they would all be implicated, and that the combined power of the court of France, of the Pope, and of the Queen, would be brought to act against them.

In the meantime the number of those who occupied the castle was increased by many of the most influential of the reformers joining themselves to them; and events soon occurred by which popery, with civil tyranny, perished, and our country acquired a liberty and a purity of ecclesiastical institutions by which, though her limits were confined and her soil sterile, she became the most distinguished among the nations,—national glory depending not on numbers, wealth, or power, but on freedom and religion. The morning of a day bright and blessed had dawned on Scotland. Men were startled from their dreams, and, devising in godliness and acting in zeal, left the image of their character on the destiny of their country.

THE MURDER OF RIZZIO.

THE murder of David Rizzio or Riccio, the secretary and favourite of Mary Queen of Scots, occurred on the evening of the 3d of March, 1565. The motives which led to it, the political considerations mixed up with them, and some of the precurrent and concomitant circumstances, are obscure and have been the subjects of much controversy; but the fact itself,

The Battle History of Scotland.—*Page* 257.

in all its main incidents, is one of the clearest and best known in Scotish history.

"It was an eve of raw and surly mood,
And in a turret-chamber high of ancient Holyrood
Sat Mary, listening to the rain, and sighing with the winds,
That seem'd to suit the stormy state of men's uncertain minds.
The touch of care had blanch'd her cheek—her smile was sadder now,
The weight of royalty had press'd too heavy on her brow;
And traitors to her councils came, and rebels to the field;
The Stuart sceptre well she sway'd, but the sword she could not wield.
She thought of all her blighted hopes—the dreams of youth's brief day,
And summoned Rizzio with his lute, and bade the minstrel play
The songs she loved in early years—the songs of gay Navarre,
The songs perchance that erst were sung by gallant Chatelar:
They half beguiled her of her cares, they soothed her into smiles,
They won her thoughts from bigot zeal, and fierce domestic broils:—
But hark! the tramp of armed men! the Douglas' battle cry,
They come—they come—and lo! the scowl of Ruthven's hollow eye!
And swords are drawn, and daggers gleam, and tears and words are vain,
The ruffian's steel is in his heart—the faithful Rizzio's slain!
Then Mary Stuart brushed aside the tears that trickling fell;
'Now for my father's arms!' she said; 'my woman's heart farewell!'"

So many narratives of this horrible murder have been written that small apology exists for adding to their number; and we have undertaken to handle the subject mainly for the sake of introducing some extracts from the original " Relation of Lord Ruthven himself,—in many respects the most interesting of all the narratives, either contemporary or modern —especially for the awful calmness of its tone and iron effrontery of its manner,—one of the most singular auto-historiettes of the shedding of human blood which ever was penned. Ruthven was one of the principal actors in the tragedy; and not only did he think that he was doing perfectly right, serving both God and man, amidst the excitement and fanaticism of the actual occurrence, but, at a subsequent period, when he might have had time to reflect, and when powerful odium had extensively arisen among the public against the perpetrators of this deed, he continued to regard it as a commendable affair, worthy of honourable mention, substantially a piece of useful public service,—and he fully engrossed that opinion of it in his narrative.

About seven o'clock, or as soon as the twilight had ceased, the Earls of Morton and Lindsay, with 150 armed men bearing torches, took possession of the courtyard of Holyrood, seized the gates of the palace, and appointed guards to keep out all persons except their own friends. The Queen, at that moment was supping in a closet off her bed-chamber, attended by Rizzio, the Countess of Argyle, and two or three persons of the royal household; and she was then in the seventh month of pregnancy. Darnley, the Queen's husband, ascended from his own chamber below by a secret turnpike, to the Queen's closet, threw up the arras which concealed the entrance so that Ruthven and the other conspirators might see where to follow, and seated himself beside the Queen, putting his arm round her in the manner of fondness. About a minute after, Ruthven abruptly entered, clad in complete armour, and wearing a cadaverous and dismal appearance from the effects of a recent illness; and immediately behind him came others with torches and weapons and clamour. Some words passed between Ruthven and the Queen; Rizzio, on finding himself

denounced, clung to Mary, and cried out, in his broken
language, " Giustizia, giustizia, suave ma vie, Madame, sauve
ma vie ;" the conspirators attempted to tear him away, and
stabbed at him even where he clung; the table was overturned, the lights were knocked over, and everything tossed
into uproar; and the conspirators at last dragged their victim
away to the outer chamber, and there stabbed him so hotly
and ferociously as to wound one another in their haste, and
to inflict upon him no fewer than fifty-six wounds, and to draw
from him a little pool of blood, which the exhibitors of Holyrood palace down to the present day pretend to have left
an indelible stain upon the floor; and, by way of suitable finish,
some one of the assassins had got possession of Darnley's
dagger, and left it sticking in Rizzio's body, as a significant
and emphatic notification of the prominent part which Darnley's jealousy had acted in the conspiracy.

" The said Lord Ruthven," narrates the principal stabber
respecting his own share in the transaction, "passed in through
the King's chamber, and up through the privy way to the
Queen's chamber, as the King had learned him; and he found
the Queen's Majesty sitting at her supper at the middes of a
little table, the Lady Argyle sitting at one end, and Davie
at the head of the table with his cap on his head. The said
Lord Ruthven, at his coming in said to the Queen's Majesty,
—'It would please your Majesty to let yonder man Davie
come forth of your presence, for he hath been overlong here.'
Her Majesty answered,—' What offence hath he made?'
The said lord replied again, that he had made great offence
to her Majestie's honour, the King her husband, the nobility,
and commonweal of the realm. ' And how?' said she. ' It
will please your Majesty,' said the said lord, ' he hath offended
your Majestie's honour, which I dare not be so bold to speak
of.'" And then, according to the continuation of his narrative, he proceeded to lecture her in a style of coarseness and
indelicacy which the politeness of the present age would think

too rude from the lips of a policeman to an outcast from society.

After the murder had been completed in the chamber, Ruthven went back to the closet, whether with his dagger sheathed or still reeking in his hand is not stated, and enacted a scene of cool effrontery which has few parallels in the history of assassination. "The said lord being so feebled with his sickness and weary of his travel," that is, the trouble of assisting to murder Rizzio, "that he desired her Majesty's pardon to sit down upon a coffer, and called for a drink for God's sake. So a Frenchman brought him a cup of wine; and after that he had drunken, the Queen's Majesty began to rail against the said lord. 'Is this your sickness, Lord Ruthven?' The said lord answered, 'God forbid that your Majesty had such a sickness; for I had rather give all the moveable goods that I have.' Then said her Majesty, if she died, or her bairn or commonweal perished, she should leave the revenge thereof to her friends, to revenge the same upon the said Lord Ruthven and his posterity; for she had the King of Spain her great friend, the Emperor likewise, and the King of France her good brother, the Cardinal of Lorrain, and her uncles in France, besides the Pope's Holiness, with many other princes in Italy. The said Lord answered, that these noble princes were over great to meddle with such a poor man as he was, being her Majesty's own subject. And when her Majesty said, that if either she, her bairn, or the commonweal perished, the said Lord Ruthven should have the weight thereof, the said lord answered, that if either of the three perished, her Majesty's self, or her particular counsel, should have the weight thereof, and should be accused as well before God as the world." Some curious exchanges of courtesy now took place:—"And because there was some enmity unreconciled betwixt the Earls of Huntly and Bothwell, and the Earls of Argyle and Murray, and their colleagues, the said lords promised in their names, that it should be mended at the sight of two or three of the nobility; they doing such like to them; whereupon the said Earls of Huntly and Bothwell gave the Lord Ruthven their hands, and received his for the other part; and after they had drunken, the said Lord Ruthven took his leave of them."

These scenes and others of a similar kind occurred while the body of the murdered man continued to lie on the spot where it had fallen. Lord Ruthven's account of its removal is one of the most graphic passages in his narrative, and shows him to have been far from destitute of literary polish. "The gates being locked," says he, "and the Queen's Majesty walking in her chamber, the said Lord Ruthven took air upon the lower gate and at the privy passages. And at the King's command, in the meantime, Davie was hurled down the steps of the stairs from the place where he was slain, and brought to the porter's lodge; where the porter's servant taking off his clothes, said, 'This hath been his destiny; for upon this chest was his first bed since he entered this place, and now here he lieth again, a very ingrate and misknowing knave!' The King's whiniard was found sticking in Davie's side, after he was dead; but always the Queen enquired of the King where his whiniard was; who answered that he wit not with, Well,' said she, 'it will be known afterwards.'"

The conspirators kept the Queen a prisoner in her apartment, and adopted measures to prevent all communication between her and the city. But four of her friends within the palace contrived to escape, and gave intelligence of her condition to the city magistrates; and the result was afterwards stated by herself, in the following terms, in a letter to the Archbishop of Glasgow:—"The provost and town of Edinburgh having understood this tumult in our palace, caused ring their common bell, came to us in great number, and desired to have seen our presence, intercommuned with us, and to have known our welfare; to whom we was not permitted to give answer, being extremely boasted by their lords, who in our place declared, if we desired to have spoken them, they would cut us in collops, and cast us over the walls." Darnley addressed the citizens from the window in her stead, and assured them that she was in safety, and commanded them on their allegiance to go home; so that they instantly withdrew, and all hope of rescue from the power of the conspirators seemed extinct.

Mary, however, effected a private reconciliation with Darnley, talked him off from his alliance with the other conspirators, and affected to believe that he had taken no part in the plot for murdering Rizzio and enthralling her; and they two escaped through a wine-cellar, mounted fleet horses, and, accompanied only by Arthur Erskine, fled to Dunbar. The news of their flight spread like wild-fire, and was followed promptly and terribly by the spontaneous muster of an army to support them. The conspirators were now in an awkward plight; and a royal proclamation was speedily issued, requiring their attendance, "under pain of rebellion, and putting them to the horn, and eschetting and inbringing of all their moveable goods." Ruthven's wrath was kindled against this document, and he says regarding it, "The whilk like order is not used in no realm christened; nor is it the law of Scotland of old, but new cropen in, and invented by them that understood no law nor yet good practice." And he remarks that such severity for the slaying of a person like Rizzio " would pity a godly heart;" and pathetically declares his innocence of any act or intention offensive to the Queen beyond the mere killing of the Italian menial. "And," he adds, "where her Majesty allegeth that night that Davie was slain, some held pistolets to her Majesty's breast, some stroke whiniards so near her craig that she felt the coldness of the iron, with many other such like sayings, which we take God to record was never meant nor done; for the said Davie received never a stroke in her Majesty's presence, nor was not stricken till he was at the farthest door of her Majesty's utter chamber."

The upshot of the whole affair, as is well known, was that, for a time, Mary got promptly and completely the upper hand,—that she advanced at the head of a considerable army to the capital, and struck such terror into her antagonists that all the principal ones precipitately fled,—and that she soon and dreadfully let fall the chief weight of her vengeance on Darnley.

THE LORDS OF GALLOWAY.

Galloway is an extensive district, forming the south-west corner of Scotland. Originally and for a considerable period, it included parts of Ayrshire and Dumfries-shire; but, during many ages past, it has been identified simply and strictly with the shire of Wigton and the stewartry of Kirkcudbright. The name, though thoroughly interwoven with history, and incurably familiar to literary and oral usage, designates no political jurisdiction, and is unsanctioned by the strict or civil nomenclature of the country. The present geographical distribution of the district comprises three parts,—Upper Galloway, which includes the northern or mountainous sections of Wigtonshire and Kirkcudbrightshire,—Lower Galloway, which includes the southern or more champaign sections of both civil divisions, east of Lucebay,—and the Rinns of Galloway, consisting of the peninsula south-west of Lucebay and Loch Ryan.

During the 5th century, the tract of country which afterwards got the name of Galloway was inhabited by the immediate posterity of the British tribes, the Selgovæ, the Novantes, and the Damnii, a feeble and a divided people. The Anglo-Saxons rather overran than colonized the territory yet, during the 6th and 7th centuries, they sufficiently mixed

with the British tribes to maintain a rude ascendancy. When
the Northumbrian dynasty became extinct at the close of the
8th century, the Saxon settlers, while they retained their
possessions, were denuded of their power. Colonists from
the Irish coast could, in such circumstances, make an easy
descent upon the country, and effectually overawe its inhabitants. Whatever may have been the defeats of earlier adventurers, the Irish Cruithne, at the end of the 8th century,
made a successful settlement within the Rinns. Fresh
swarms followed from the Irish hive, during the 9th and
10th centuries; and were strengthened by settlements of the
kindred Scots of Kintire, who passed the frith of Clyde in
their curraghs to the Rinns and Carrick and Kyle; while the
Scandinavian Sea-kings domineered over the seas and shores
of the neighbouring regions. These Gaelic settlers, in their
progress of colonization and promptitude of contest, acquired,
in the low Latinity of the times, the appellation of Galli,
which was thought to be a fair representative of their proper
name Gael. Hence, as we may learn from Malmsbury,
" Galli veteribus Gallwaliæ, non Franci dicti." As Scotland
and England took their names respectively from the Scots
and the Angles, so the territory of the Gael or Galli, came
speedily to be called, by chroniclers, Gallwalia, Gallawidia,
Gallawgaia, Gallwadia, Gallwegia, Gallway, Galloway. In
the effluxion of three centuries, the name came to be applied
loosely to the entire peninsula between the Solway and the
Clyde, including Annandale in the south-east, and most of
Ayrshire in the north-west. The Gael, or Galli, or Irish
settlers, in the meanwhile, completely occupied the ample
extent of the country; mingling everywhere with the enfeebled Britons, whose speech they understood, and amalga-
mating with the still fewer and feebler Saxons, whose language, as it was unknown to them, they constantly rejected;
and they hence imposed upon the district a topographical
nomenclature which corresponds much more closely with

that of Ireland, than with that of other districts of Scotland.
Notwithstanding the naval enterprises of the northmen, the
incursions of the Northumbrian Danes, and not a few internal distractions among conflicting tribes, the settlers retained,
in their new possessions, the various rights of a distinct people, and preserved the agreeable independence of their own
customs and laws.

During the earlier parts of the obscure history of the district, we hear seldom, and in uncertain terms, of the rulers or
'lords of Galloway," who claimed and exercised power within the invidious limits of a contested jurisdiction. But, in
973, Jacob, lord of Galloway, was one of the eight reguli who
met Edgar at Chester. Fergus, another lord of Galloway,
and the most potent feudatory subject of the Scotish crown
in the 12th century, was a frequent witness to the charters
of David I., and, supposing Malcolm IV. to be a pusillanimous character, denied his authority and appropriated his
revenues. Malcolm, enraged by Fergus' infidelity and daring, marched into his territory, and, though twice repulsed
and discomfited by him, eventually, in 1160, overpowered
him, obliging him to resign his lordship and possessions to
his sons, and to retire to the abbey of Holyrood, far gone in
the disease of corroding humiliation and a broken heart.
Fergus was son-in-law to Henry I., and, dying next year,
left behind him a family who afterwards ranked high among
the nobles of Scotland and of England.

His two sons, Uchtred and Gilbert, who, like the lords of
other Gaelic districts, owed obedience to the Scotish kings,
followed William the Lion, in 1174, into England; but they
no sooner saw him taken captive, than, at the head of their
naked, nimble, impatient, and rapacious clans, they returned
to their native wilds, broke out into insurrection, attacked
and demolished the royal castles, and murdered the Anglo-Normans who had settled among their mountains. No sooner
had they established their independence of the Scotish go-

vernment, than they began to dispute about pre-eminence and possessions. Gilbert, on the 22d of September, 1174, attacked Uchtred, while residing in his father's house in Loch-Fergus; and, having overpowered him, ordered the infliction upon him of a barbarous death. William the Lion, having, in 1175, made submission to the English king, and regained his liberty, invaded Galloway, subdued Gilbert, and purchased his subsequent peacefulness of conduct by giving him full possession of Carrick in Ayrshire. From this Gilbert sprang, in the third generation, Marjory, Countess of Carrick, in her own right, the wife, in 1271, of Robert de Bruce, and the mother, in 1274, of the royal Bruce, the restorer of the Scotish monarchy. Gilbert dying the 1st of January, 1184–5, Roland, the son of the murdered Uchtred, seized the favourable moment of his uncle's death, to attack and disperse his faction, and to claim possession of all Galloway as his own inheritance; and he, at the same time, overcame Gilcolm, a potent freebooter who had settled in the district, and carried his depredations into Lothian. Making successful resistance to Henry II. of England, who claimed to be superior of Scotland, he was at last, on the condition of surrendering Carrick to his nephew Duncan, the son of Gilbert, confirmed in the lordship of all Galloway. On the restoration of the national independence, Roland obtained the office of constable of Scotland, and was witness of many royal charters. In December, 1200, Alan, his eldest son, succeeded him in his lordship, and afterwards excelled him in power and fame; but, in 1234, he died without a legitimate male heir, and left his prerogatives and possessions to become objects of division and feud.

Alexander II. wishing to invest Elena, the eldest daughter of Alan, with the lordship, the Gallowegians tumultuously demanded it to be conferred on Thomas, his illegitimate son; but, though they writhed under the chains imposed on them, and twice became insurgent, they were compelled to receive as their superior, Roger de Quincey, the husband of Elena. Alexander II.'s enforcing the rights of Alan's daughters, and, at the head of an army, breaking down the spirit of insurrection, was the introduction to the epoch of granting charters for the holding of lands, and of landholders giving leases to tenants, and of the security of property and the cultivation of the arts of husbandry. In 1254, Alexander Comyn, Earl of Buchan, in right of his wife, succeeded De Quincey, and laid the foundation of his family's extensive connexion with Galloway, till they were overthrown and expatriated by Bruce, and of their introducing to the district the important office of justiciary, which in some measure changed the very nature of its jurisprudence.

The Gallowegians, during the wars of the succession, naturally sided with the Comyns and the Baliols, and speedily shared in their disasters. When John Baliol was obliged to resign his dependent crown, Edward I. considered Galloway as his own; and he immediately appointed over it a governor and a justiciary, disposed of its ecclesiastical benefices, and obliged the sheriffs and bailiffs to account for the rents and profits of their bailiwicks in his exchequer at Berwick. In 1298, Wallace is said to have marched into the west " to chastise the men of Galloway, who had espoused the party of the Comyns, and supported the pretensions of the English;" and a field in the farm of Borland, above the village of Minigaff, still bears the name of Wallace's camp. During his campaign of 1300, Edward I. marched from Carlisle through Dumfries-shire into Galloway; and though opposed first by the remonstrances, and next by the warlike demonstrations of the people, he overran the whole of the low country from the Nith to the Cree, pushed forward a detachment to Wigton, and compelled the inhabitants to submit to his yoke. In 1306, Sir Christopher Seton, the brother-in-law of Bruce, being captured in the castle of

Loch Urr, was carried to Dumfries, and put to death on the gallows-hill of the town. In 1307, Robert I. marched into Galloway, and wasted the country, the people having refused to repair to his standard; but he was obliged speedily to retire. In the following year, Edward Bruce, the King's brother, invaded the district, defeated the chiefs in a pitched battle near the Dee, overpowered the English commander, reduced the several fortlets, and at length subdued the entire territory. Galloway was immediately conferred on him by the King, as a reward of his gallantry; and when he was slain in the battle of Dundalk, in 1318, it reverted to the Crown.

When Edward Baliol entered Scotland to renew the pretensions of his father, Galloway became again the wretched theatre of domestic war. In 1334, assisted and accompanied by Edward III., he made his way through this district into the territories north of it, and laid them waste as far as to Glasgow. In 1346, in consequence of the defeat and capture of David II. at the battle of Durham, he regained possession of his patrimonial estates, and resided in Buittle castle, the ancient seat of his family. In 1347, heading a levy of Gallowegians, and aided by an English force, he invaded Lanarkshire and Lothian, and made Scotland feel that the power which had become enthroned in Galloway was a scourge and a curse, rather than an instrument of protection. In 1353, Sir William Douglas overran Baliol's territories, and compelled M'Dowal, the hereditary enemy of the Bruces, to change sides in politics.

After the restoration of David II. and the expulsion of Baliol, Archibald Douglas, the Grim, obtained, in 1369, Eastern and Middle Galloway, or Kirkcudbrightshire, in a grant from the Crown, and, less than two years after, Western Galloway, or Wigtonshire, by negociation from Thomas Fleming, Earl of Wigton. This illegitimate but most ambitious son of the celebrated Sir James Douglas obtained, at

the death of his father, in 1388, on the field of Otterburn,
the high honours and the original estates of the house of
Douglas; and now, while holding in addition the superiority
of all Galloway, became the most powerful as well as the
most oppressive subject of Scotland. On an islet in the Dee,
surmounting the site of an ancient fortlet, the residence of
former lords of Galloway, rose at his bidding a castle called
the Thrieve, whence the radiations of his own and his successors' tyranny shot, with a blighting and a withering influence,
athwart the surface of the whole country. His usurpation
seems to have struck with indignation all who contemplated
its magnitude and effects.

The power of the Douglases was so enormous, and so exor-
bitantly plied, as to grind into powder the resistance and the
influence of the subordinate chiefs. About the middle of
the 15th century, William, one of the line of Earls, upon
some occasion of pique with Sir Patrick M'Lellan of Bom-
bie, the sheriff of Galloway, besieged and captured him in
his stronghold of Raeberry, carried him off to Thrieve castle,
and there ignominiously hanged him as though he had been
a common felon. The Douglases experienced some reverses,
and were more than once sharply chastised in their own persons, yet seemed unable to learn, no matter how thoroughly
inculcated, a single lesson of moderation; and they continued
to oppress the Gallowegians, to disturb the whole country,
and even to overawe and defy the Crown, till their turbulence
and treasons ended in their forfeiture. James the ninth and
last Earl, and all his numerous relations, ran, in 1453, into
rebellion; and, two years afterwards, were adjudged by parliament, and stripped of their immense possessions.

Galloway now awoke from the haggard dreams of a night-
mare which had been thrown from its breast, and found itself in a state of annexation to the Crown. James II. immediately marched into the district, and was everywhere
received with acclamations of welcome; and he garrisoned

the castle of Thrieve with his own troops, and, from a seat of insufferable oppression, converted it into a source of energizing influence upon the law.

THE LEGEND OF KILCHURN CASTLE.

KILCHURN CASTLE is a noble relic of the feudal ages, situated near the head of Loch-Awe, under the impending gloom of the majestic Bencruachan, which rises in rocky masses abruptly from the opposite shore of the lake. Amid the grandeur and variety which that fine lake derives from its great expanse, and the lofty mountains with which it is surrounded, it cannot be denied that Kilchurn castle forms its leading and most picturesque object,—

> " Is paramount, and rules
> Over the pomp and beauty of a scene
> Where mountains, torrents, lakes, and woods unite
> To pay it homage."

No other ancient castle in the Western Highlands can compete with this in point of magnitude; and none, even throughout Scotland at large, can be compared with it for the picturesque arrangement of its buildings, the beauty and fine effect of its varied and broken outline, or its happy appropriateness to its situation. It stands upon a projecting rocky elevation at the head of the lake, where the water of Orchy flows into it, and which is occasionally converted into an island when the river and loch are flooded by rains; and though now connected with the shore by an extended plain, obviously of alluvial origin, and consequently forming a peninsula, it must have been at one time an island, and has been gradually connected with the mainland partly by the alluvial depositions of the river and partly by the lowering of the

The Battle History of Scotland.—*Page* 271.

waters of the lake. The castle must anciently have been a place of great strength; and it affords abundant indication, by its magnitude, its magnificence, and its strong position, of the feudal splendour of its ancient owners. The great tower of it was five stories high, and had its second story entirely occupied with the baronial hall, and is said to have been built at vast cost and with great labour by the lady of Sir Colin Campbell of Glenorchy, Knight-Templar, crusader in Palestine, and ancestor of the Ducal family of Argyle. That necessary appendage of a feudal castle, the dungeon, is on the ground-floor, and appears to have been sufficiently dark, damp, and wretched to render utterly miserable the unfortunate beings who, from time to time, were forced to tenant it. The remaining portions of the castle, which form a square enclosing the court yard, though of considerable antiquity, are certainly not so ancient as the tower, and doubtless have been added at some more recent period. The second Sir Colin of Glenorchy, surnamed *Dubh*, or Black, son of the Knight-Templar, was proprietor of seven different castles,—a sufficient evidence of the great wealth which must have been possessed, even at that early period, by the ancestors of the now powerful family of Breadalbane. So late as 1745, Kilchurn-castle was garrisoned by the king's troops, and at a much more recent period it was fit to be inhabited; but this fine monument of baronial dignity is now a ruin,—" wild yet stately,—not dismantled of turrets, nor the walls broken down, though obviously a ruin," and hastening to decay.

There is a legend connected with this castle, which has its counterpart in more than one legend of feudal times, as well as in the pages of Homer. During a long absence of Sir Colin, the Knight Templar, on a crusade to the south-east of Europe and to Palestine—an absence which extended to upwards of seven years—he is said to have visited Rome, where he had a very singular dream. He applied to a monk for his advice, who recommended his instant return home, as a very serious domestic calamity, which could only be averted by his presence, was portended by his dream. Sir Colin immediately took his departure for Scotland, and, after much difficulty and danger, reached a place called Succoth, the residence of an old woman who had been his nurse. In the disguise of a mendicant, he craved food and shelter for the night; and was admitted to the poor woman's fireside. From a scar on his arm she recognised him as the laird; and instantly informed him of what was about to happen at the castle.

It appeared that for a long period, no information had been received with regard to Sir Colin, nor had any communication from him reached his lady. On the contrary, it had been industriously circulated that he had fallen in battle in the Holy Land. Sir Colin perceived treachery on the part of some one; for he had repeatedly despatched clansmen with intelligence to his lady, and surely all of them could not have perished before reaching Scotland. His suspicions were well-founded. Baron MacCorquadale, a neighbouring laird, who had been the most busy in propagating the report of Sir Colin's death, had intercepted and murdered all the messengers. He had thus succeeded in convincing the lady of the death of her husband; and had finally won her affections, and the next day had been fixed for the marriage.

Incensed at what he had just heard from the faithful nurse, Sir Colin set out early next morning for his castle at Kilchurn, where he was told his lady then resided; and, as he followed the romantic windings of the Orchy, the sound of the bagpipe, and the acclamations of his clansmen, who had assembled to join the approaching festivity, were wafted to his ears. He crossed the drawbridge, and entered the gates of the castle—at this happy season open to all—undiscovered and unregarded. While he stood silently gazing on the scene of riot which now met his view, he was asked what he wanted. "To have my hunger satisfied, and my thirst

THE LEGEND OF KILCHURN CASTLE.

quenched," said he. Food and liquor were plentifully put before him; he eat, but refused to drink, except from the hands of the lady herself. Informed of the strange request of the apparent mendicant, the lady, always charitable and benevolent, came at once and handed him a cup. Sir Colin drank to her health, and dropping a ring into the empty cup returned it to her. The lady, observant of the action, retired and examined the ring. It was her own gift to her husband when he departed on his distant expedition; it had been his talisman in the field, and had been kept sacred by him. "My husband! My husband!" she exclaimed, and rushing in, threw herself into his arms. A shout of joy from the clansmen rent the air; and the pipers made the courtyard resound with the pibroch of the Campbells. The Baron MacCorqudale was allowed to depart in safety; but Sir Colin Dubh, the son and successor of the Templar, after his father's death, attacked the Baron, and overcoming him in battle, took possession of his castle and his lands.

Wordsworth has addressed some fine lines to Kilchurncastle, concluding thus:—

> "Shade of departed power,
> Skeleton of unfleshed humanity,
> The chronicle were welcome that should call
> Into the compass of distinct regard
> The toils and struggles of thy infancy!
> Yon foaming flood seems motionless as ice;
> Its dizzy turbulence eludes the eye,
> Frozen by distance; so, majestic pile,
> To the perception of this Age appear
> Thy fierce beginnings, softened and subdued,
> And quieted in character—the strife,
> The pride, the fury uncontrollable
> Lost on the aerial heights of the Crusades!"

THE SIEGE OF REDHALL AND SKIRMISH OF GOGAR.

In the year 1650, while the army of Oliver Cromwell and that of General Leslie confronted and watched each other, in encampments about three miles southwest and west of Edinburgh, the former eagerly waiting for some opportunity of decided action, and the latter resolutely determined not to afford it, two hot little affairs occurred to try the mettle of the belligerents,—the one in the parish of Colinton and the other in the contiguous parish of Corstorphine.

On the barony of Redhall, in the parish of Colinton, not far from the site of the present mansion of Redhall, once stood a castle or baronial fortalice, which made some figure in the frequent warlike commotions of former times. In 1572, in particular, it was, with other strengths in the vicinity of Edinburgh, garrisoned by the Regent Mar against his antagonists; and in 1650, it sustained a regular siege from the army of Cromwell. A short account of this siege is given by Nicol in his Diary, so interesting that we shall transcribe it verbatim, with the simple alteration of modernizing the spelling:—" Cromwell pushed from Berwick to Colinton without opposition, until he came to the house of Redhall within three miles by west of Edinburgh. In the which house of Redhall the Laird of Redhall with threescore soldiers, lay with provisions, and kept and defended the house against the English, and galled his soldiers, and put them back several times, with loss of sundry soldiers. The English general taking this very grievously, that such a weak house should hold out against him and be an impediment in his way, he and his army lying so near unto it, therefore he caused draw his cannon to the house, and there, from four hours in the morning till ten in the forenoon that day, he caused the cannon to play on this house, encamped a great number of his soldiers about it with pike and musket, but all to little purpose; for the Laird and the people in the house defended it valiantly even till their powder failed; and after it failed, they did not give over, ever looking for help from our own army, which was then lying at Corstorphine, within three quarters of a mile to the house,—of whose help they were disappointed. General Cromwell perceiving their powder to be gone, and that no assistance was given them, he caused petards to be brought to the house, wherewith he blew up the doors, entered the doors and windows, and after slaughter on both sides, (but much more to the English than to the Scots,) took all that were in the house prisoners, turned them naked, seized on all the money and goods that were therein, which was much, by reason that sundry gentlemen about had put their goods there for safety. So this house and people therein were taken in the sight and face of our army, who thought it dangerous to hazard themselves in such an expedition, the enemy having the advantage of the ground and hills about him for his defence." " After the enemy had taken the Laird of Redhall prisoner, he thereafter put him to liberty, commending much his valour and activity for holding out so stoutly against him that house of Redhall."

Cromwell's army lay at the base and among the spurs of the Pentlands, and could not without great disadvantage be attacked from the plain; and Leslie's army lay on the expanse of low ground south-east of Corstorphine, now a firm and beautiful series of meadows and corn fields traversed by the Edinburgh and Glasgow railway, but then a wild, intricate, watery wilderness of bogs and swamps and quagmires; and the latter army was therefore as strongly posted and as defiant of an enemy as Cromwell's, though in a different way; so that the two armies could only look at each other, or else practice some stratagem, or forego the advantages of ground. Cromwell at length marched down toward the west side of Leslie's position, with the view of cutting off his communication with Linlithgow and Stirling, and drawing him out to an engagement on the plain. But Leslie anticipated the movement, and manœuvred his army westward about two miles, and entrenched them in a position at Gogar of similar character to his original one, and quite as strong; and there he stood, amid bogs and quagmires, holding Cromwell at bay. The two armies were now pretty close to each other; yet Cromwell tried in vain to force them into collision, either by wading across the swamps himself or by dislodging Leslie; and he was compelled to rest satisfied with opening a brisk fire of artillery, and provoking a contest at long shot. Leslie returned his cannonade with spirit; and, on this occasion, brought into play for the first time several kinds of field-pieces which had recently been invented by his General of Artillery, Colonel Wemyss. The place of conflict is now occupied by the villas of Hanley and Gogar-Burn; and is still known among the old inhabitants of the district by the name of the Flashes; and is said to have got that name in memory of the superior power and range of these new cannons. The conflict lasted about three hours; and though it does not seem to have caused on both sides more than about 100 deaths, it operated as such a severe check on Cromwell's designs, that he retreated immediately to Musselburgh, and four days after toward England.

The sequel was disastrous. Leslie followed in Cromwell's rear, and harassed his march till he reached Dunbar; and then occurred the smashing battle which was lost to the Scots through their impetuosity and want of discipline, and which enabled Cromwell to return to Edinburgh as a victor

THE BURNING OF TOWIE CASTLE.

In the upper part of the valley of the Don, in the Highland district of Aberdeenshire, stands a ruinous quadrangular tower, the remains of an ancient castle, which was the scene of an awful catastrophe, during the political and warlike struggles between the party who contended for the imprisoned Queen Mary and the party who endeavoured to maintain the government in the name of her infant son James VI. Sir Adam Gordon of Auchindoir, the brother of the Marquis of Huntly, then acted as the Marquis's deputy, in his capacity of Lieutenant of the North of Scotland for the Queen; and he committed many acts of oppression on families who were known or suspected to be adverse to the Queen's party; and was particularly incensed against families of the clan of Forbes, and, on one occasion, slew Arthur, the brother of Lord Forbes. Towie Castle, the seat of Alexander Forbes, a very prominent gentleman of the clan, became specially obnoxious to him, and, in November 1751, he sent Captain Ker, with a small body of troops, to summon it in the Queen's name. Its owner was at the time absent; and his lady, whose maiden name was Margaret Campbell, and who was pregnant, and confided too much in her sex and condition, and at the same time had a strong mixture of the virago and the Amazon in her character, not only refused to surrender, but poured on him a torrent of abusive language, and took a deliberate aim at him from the battlement with a musket or other similar weapon, and fired at him. Her shot wounded his knee, and perhaps her words still more wounded his mind; and, in a transport of rage, he ordered his men to set fire to the castle; and so fatal was the result that the lady and her children and all the inmates, amounting altogether to thirty-seven persons perished in the flames. Sir Adam Gordon never took Ker to task for this horrible atrocity, and was therefore held in public opinion to be personally accountable for it; and a ballad which was soon after composed upon it, and became very popular, and has still a place in all our good collections of old balladry, treats himself, and not Ker, as the acting hero of the whole base tragedy.

This document gives a minute account of the affair; and, though obviously not authentic in every particular, is well worth attention as an aggregately correct picture of the barbarous spirit of the times. The assailing party were roaming through the country amid the cold and shrill blasts of winter; and approached Towie-Castle, not on account of more enmity against it than against other residences of the Queen's antagonists, but because it was the most convenient for themselves at the moment, as they needed to "draw to a hauld." The lady had just "buskit hersell" and sat down to supper when they surrounded the place; and she ran with all speed to the battlement, to try the effect of speaking them fair, and of operating on them with her tongue. But the leader was not to be so won or repelled; and

> ' As sune as he saw the ladye fair
> And her yetts all lockit fast,
> He fell into a rage of wrath
> And his heart was all aghast."

He requested her to come down, and made infamous proposals to her. But she replied to him resolutely and disdainfully, and belaboured him with such names as "fause Gordon" and "traitor;" and she, at the same time, jeered and abused one of his chief followers, who had largely shared her bounty, and was a renegade from her service. When the conflagration commenced and the smoke began to be troublesome, her youngest son, who sat on the nurse's knee, entreated her to surrender; but she continued resolute, and told the little sufferer that "come weel, come wae," he must make up his mind to share with her whatever should happen within the castle. Her daughter, who was "baith jimp and sma," with cherry cheeks and pretty mouth and golden hair and snowy complexion and altogether a beauty, then entreated to be wrapped in a pair of sheets, and "towed ower the wa'," in order that she might attempt some deliverance; and over she was "towed" accordingly,—but was received on the point of the ruffian's spear, and mortally wounded; and then followed compunctions and moralizings and relentings, strong and melting, but all too late. And just as the murdering crew were recovering from these, and getting back into a Satanic complacency with their work, the lord of the castle came in sight in the distant landscape, spurring along in fury, at the head of a body of followers; to whom he cried,

"'Put on, put on, my michtie men,
  As fast as ye can drie;
For he that's hindmost o' my men,
  Sall ne'er get gude o' me.'

And some they rade, and some they ran,
  Fu' fast out ower the plain;
But lang, lang, ere he could get up,
  They a' were deid and slain.

But mony were the mudie men,
  Lay gasping on the grene;
For o' fifty men that Edom* brought,
  There were but fyve gaed hame.

And mony were the mudie men,
  Lay gasping on the grene;
And mony were the fair ladyes,
  Lay lemanless at hame.

---

* Sir Adam Gordon.

> And round and round the wa's he went,
>   Their ashes for to view;
> At last into the flames he ran,
>   And bade the world adieu."

An attempt was afterwards made by some of the Forbeses to revenge this dreadful affair by the assassination of its perpetrator, Gordon of Auchindoir, on the streets of Paris. They lay in wait for him at a point where he had to pass on his way to his lodgings from the palace of the Archbishop of Glasgow, who was then ambassador in France; and they fired upon him as he was passing, and wounded him in the thigh. His servants sprang toward them and pursued them; and though unable to capture or overtake them, they picked up the fallen hat of one of them, containing a paper which indicated their place of rendezvous. John Gordon, Lord of Glenluce, and Longormes, the son of Alexander Gordon, Bishop of Galloway, lord of the bed-chamber to the King of France, got instant notice of this, and represented it to the court; and the grand provost of the palace, with his guards, and a posse of the Gordons and their retainers, were immediately sent to apprehend the Forbeses. A scuffle ensued, in the course of which the principal Forbes was slain; but all the rest were captured, and afterwards put judicially to death by breaking upon the wheel.

THE BATTLE OF SHERIFFMUIR.

THE battle of Sheriffmuir, sometimes called the battle of Dunblane, was fought on the 13th of November, 1715, between an army of Jacobites upwards of 8,000 strong under the Earl of Mar, and an army of royalists, about 3,500 strong, under the Duke of Argyle. Its occurrence was simultaneous with the battle of Preston, recorded on pp. 139-149 of the

Sea Kings of Orkney. The scene of it is a boggy uncultivated tract, on the lower part of the declivity of the Ochil Hills, a little north-east of the town of Dunblane.

The Earl of Mar, just after having taken up his quarters at Perth, was informed that the Duke of Argyle had returned from the Lothians to Stirling; and, having been joined by the northern clans under the Earl of Seaforth, and expecting to be joined also by those of the west under General Gordon, he thought he could not do better than force the passage of the Forth, and march away southward to form a junction with the Jacobite forces on the Scotish border and in England. He left Perth at the head of his army on the 10th of November; and he proceeded on that day as far as Auchterarder, and there he reviewed his troops, and allowed them to dispose themselves to rest. On the 11th, he remained at Auchterarder, and was joined by the western clans under General Gordon; and on the morning of the 12th, he ordered Gordon to march forward with 3,000 of the Highlanders, and eight squadrons of horse under Brigadier Ogilvy and the master of Sinclair, and take possession of Dunblane. After ordering the rest of the army to parade on the moor of Tullibardine, he departed for Drummond castle to hold an interview with the Earl of Breadalbane, having previously directed General Hamilton to follow Gordon with the main body.

As early as the morning of the 10th, the Duke of Argyle had received intelligence from some of his spies at Perth of Mar's intended march, and of his plan for effecting the passage of the Forth. Fortunately for Argyle, his little army had been lately almost doubled by reinforcements from Ireland; and it now amounted to 2,300 foot and 1,200 horse, all in the best order and condition. But though formidable from its composition when united, it was too weak to divide into detachments for resisting at different points the passage of an army thrice as numerous, in an attempt to cross the

Forth. As Argyle, therefore, saw he could no longer retain his position on the banks of the river, which, from its now beginning to freeze, would soon be rendered more passable than before, he determined to cross the river and offer the insurgents battle before they should reach its northern bank. Though he exposed himself by this bold step to the disadvantage of fighting with a river in his rear, he considered that the risk would be sufficiently counterbalanced by the advantage which his cavalry would have by engaging the enemy on level ground.

Having called in several small detachments which were quartered at Glasgow, Kilsyth, and Falkirk, Argyle crossed Stirling bridge on the morning of the 12th for Dunblane, much about the same time that Mar's forces had begun to advance upon that town in an opposite direction from Auchterarder. In a short time after their setting out, Argyle's advanced guard took possession of Dunblane; of which circumstance General Gordon was apprized on his march. Having halted his division, Gordon sent an express, announcing the intelligence to General Hamilton, who despatched it to the Earl of Mar; and in a short time he forwarded a second express confirming the previous news, and adding that the enemy were in great force. Hamilton, upon receipt of this last despatch, halted his men on the ground adjoining the Roman camp at Ardoch, about five miles from Dunblane, till he should receive instructions from the Earl. Mar soon thereafter returned from Drummond castle; and being desirous of obtaining additional intelligence from the general in advance, ordered Hamilton to remain in his position, and to hold his men in readiness to march on a moment's notice. This order had however been scarcely issued, when a fresh despatch arrived from General Gordon, announcing that the Duke of Argyle was in Dunblane with his whole army. Mar thereupon sent an express to Gordon, desiring him to remain where he was till the main body of the army should come up; and having ordered three guns to be fired, the signal agreed upon to be given Hamilton for putting his men in marching order, the latter immediately formed his division and put it in motion. After a junction between the two divisions of the army had been formed, the insurgents marched to the bridge of Kinbuck, about four miles from Dunblane, where they passed the night under arms without any covering or tent.

The Duke of Argyle, who had the most exact intelligence brought to him of the motions of the insurgents, left Dunblane and formed his army in order of battle in the evening, on a rising ground above the house of Kippenross, about two miles north-east from the town. His army was drawn up in one extended line. In the centre were eight battalions of foot under the command of Major General Wightman; the right wing consisted of five squadrons of dragoons, under Lieutenant-General Evans; and a similar number, at the head of whom was Lieutenant-General Whitham, composed the left wing. After thus drawing up his men, the Duke issued orders that no tent should be pitched during the night either by officer or private soldier; that all the officers without distinction should remain at their posts; and that the troops should rest on their arms in the exact order in which they had been formed. The severest penalties were threatened those who should infringe these orders. Though the night was extremely cold, the troops prostrated themselves upon the bare ground, and snatched a few hours repose. The Duke himself retired to a sheep-cote at the foot of a hill on the right of the army, where he passed the night sitting on a bundle of straw. Intelligence having been brought him at midnight of the near position of the enemy, he ordered six rounds of ammunition to be distributed to each man in addition to twenty-four which they had already received. This order was carried into effect before two o'clock in the morning.

Although the two armies had bivouacked during the night within three miles of each other, and were separated only by the Sheriffmuir, yet so ignorant was Mar of the movements of Argyle, that so for from supposing him to be within such a short distance of his camp, he imagined that he still remained at Dunblane and it was not until he observed a reconnoitring party of Argyle's cavalry on the adjoining heights of the Sheriffmuir next morning, that he became aware of his immediate proximity. This party was headed by the Duke himself, who had aroused his army by break of day, and who, after issuing instructions to his men to prepare for battle, had ascended at an early hour the hill where his advanced guard was posted to survey the position of the insurgents.

The Earl of Mar had also put his men under arms shortly after break of day; and when Argyle's party of observation was first noticed, he was busily engaged ranging his men in marching order, preparatory to advancing upon Dunblane. Conceiving that Argyle meant to offer him battle immediately, he instantly assembled all the chiefs in front of his horse, and after addressing them in an eloquent speech, in which he painted in glowing colours the wrongs of their prince and their country, and congratulated them that the day had at length arrived when they could revenge their injuries in open battle, he desired to know if they were willing to engage. The Marquis of Huntly alone raised some objections, and some few were heard in under-tone to advise a return to Perth till the spring; but the voices of Huntly and his supporters were drowned by loud shouts of "fight, fight!" from the rest, who at once galloped off to their different posts.

The Earl of Mar thereupon resumed the marshalling of his army, which formed into two lines with a rapidity and decision, which would have done honour to veteran troops; but by accident, three squadrons of horse posted on the left, misled by a cry from the Highlanders, of "horse to the right," left their position and took ground on the right,—an unfortunate mistake for the insurgents, as it contributed to the defeat of their left wing. The centre of the first line was composed of ten battalions of foot, consisting of about 4,000 men under the command of the captain of Clanranald, Glengary, Sir John Maclean, the laird of Glenbucket, Brigadier Ogilvy, and the two brothers of Sir Donald Macdonald of Sleat. General Gordon, who had long served in the army of the Czar of Muscovy, was at the head of these battalions. On the right of this line were placed two of the Marquis of Huntly's squadrons of horse, and another called the Stirling squadron, which carried the Chevalier's standard. This squadron, which consisted wholly of gentlemen, also bore the title of "the Restoration regiment of horse." The Perthshire squadron formed the left wing. The centre of the second line consisted of eight battalions of foot, viz., three of the Earl of Seaforth's foot, two of the Marquis of Huntly's, the Earl of Panmure's battalion, and those of the Marquis of Tullibardine of Drummond, commanded by the Viscount of Strathallan, and of Logie-Almond, and Robertson of Struan. On the right of this second line were posted two squadrons of horse under the Earl Marischal. The Angus squadron was on the left. The whole of the force thus formed for action may be estimated at 8,000, besides which there was a *corps de reserve* of 400 horse posted considerably in the rear.

While this formation was going on, the Duke of Argyle observed for several hours with great attention the various evolutions of the insurgents; but from the nature of the ground occupied by them, he could not obtain a full view of their line, which extended through a hollow way, the view of which was obstructed by the brow of a hill which was occupied by a party of Mar's troops. From Mar's advanced guards looking towards Dunblane, the Duke conjectured that the insurgents intended to march in that direction; but he was undeceived in this idea by a movement on the part of a mass of the insurgents towards his right, as if they intended to cross the moor and fall upon the flank of his army. As a large morass lay in the way of the insurgents, Argyle, in advancing from Dunblane, had conceived himself free from danger on that side; but it had now been rendered quite passable for foot as well as horse by a keen frost during the preceding night. As soon as Argyle saw this large body advance up the face of the moor, which, from the right wing of the insurgents being concealed from his view by a rising ground, he supposed was the main body of Mar's army, he requested the advice of the officers who surrounded him as to how he should act. It was the general opinion, an opinion in which the Duke himself concurred, that there would be less risk in engaging the insurgents on the high grounds than in waiting for them in the position occupied by the Duke's army; but although most of the officers thought that there would not be sufficient time to bring forward the troops and to change the order of battle, a change which was absolutely necessary, the Duke resolved to draw out his troops upon the moor.

Having come to this determination, the Duke returned quickly to the army, and ordered the drums to beat the *General*. This order was given about eleven o'clock; but although the drums instantly beat to arms, an hour elapsed before the troops were ready to march. The new order of battle was as follows:—The Duke's first line consisted of six battalions of foot, all old troops, amounting scarcely to 1,800 men. On the right were posted three squadrons of dragoons, being the best in the army, namely Evans's, the Scots Greys, and the Earl of Stairs. On the left there were placed three squadrons of dragoons, namely, Carpenter's, Ker's, and a squadron of Stairs. The second line was composed of only two battalions of foot, with a squadron of dragoons on each wing. The right wing of the army was commanded by the

Duke himself, the centre by General Wightman, and the left by General Whitham. Behind Evans's dragoons, on the right wing, a body of about sixty horse, noblemen and gentlemen volunteers, took up a station.

The body which Argyle had observed coming up the face of the moor, was a squadron of the Earl Marischal's horse and Sir Donald Macdonald's battalion, under their respective commanders. These had been despatched by the Earl of Mar, to drive away the reconnoitring party under the Duke of Argyle from the height; but on its disappearing, they returned and reported the circumstance to the Earl. On receiving this intelligence, Mar gave orders to his troops to march up the hill in four columns. The whole army was accordingly put in motion; but they had not proceeded far when the Earl Marischal, who was in advance, observed Argyle forming his lines on the southern summit of the hill, at a short distance from him. He immediately notified the circumstance to Mar, who instantly gave orders to his men to quicken their pace up the hill. In the hurry of their ascent, the second line pressed so closely upon the first as to occasion some confusion on the left when again getting into line; and it was in consequence of this disorder that the squadrons of horse forsook their position on the left, and took ground on the right.

Before the insurgents reached the summit of the moor, Argyle's right wing was fully formed; but the greater part of his centre and left, who were moving up the ascent by a gradual progression from right to left, had not yet reached their ground. Argyle's right now found itself within pistol-shot of Mar's left; but from the greater extent of Mar's line, it considerably outflanked Argyle's left. As soon as the Earl of Mar perceived that Argyle's line was only partially formed, he resolved instantly to attack him before he should be able to complete his arrangements; and having sent orders to his right and left to fall simultaneously upon the enemy, Mar placed himself at the head of the clans; and being apprized by a firing on his left that the action had commenced, he pulled off his hat, which he waved, and with a huzza led forward his men upon the half-formed battalions which composed the left wing of the enemy.

Arrived within pistol-shot, the Highlanders, according to custom, poured in a volley upon the English infantry. The fire was instantly returned; and, to the dismay of the Highlanders, Alan Muidartach, the captain of Clanranald, was mortally wounded. He was instantly carried off the field, and, as his men clustered around him, he encouraged them to stand firm to their posts, and expressed a hope that the result of the struggle in which they were engaged would be favourable to the cause of his sovereign. The loss of a chief, who, from the stately magnificence with which he upheld his feudal rank, and the urbanity of his disposition, had acquired an ascendancy over the minds of his people, could not fail to depress their spirits, and make them almost overlook the danger of their situation. While absorbed in grief, they were in a moment roused from their dejection by Glengary, who, observing their conduct at this juncture, sprung forward, and throwing his bonnet into the air, cried aloud, in the expressive language of his country, "Revenge! Revenge! Revenge to-day and mourning to-morrow!" No sooner had this brave chieftain pronounced these words, than the Highlanders rushed forward, sword in hand, with the utmost fury, upon the royalist battalions.

The government troops attempted to stem the impetuosity of the attack, by opposing the Highlanders with fixed bayonets, but the latter pushed them aside with their targets, and rushing in with their broad swords among the enemy spread death and terror around them. The three battalions on Argyle's left, which had never been properly formed, unable to rally, instantly gave way, and falling back upon some squadrons of horse in their rear, created such confusion, that within seven or eight minutes after the assault, the form of a battalion or squadron was no longer discernible. A complete rout ensued; and there seems no doubt that the whole of Argyle's left would have been completely destroyed, had not General Whitham, at the head of the squadrons which were upon the left of the battalions, checked the advance of Mar's horse by a charge, in which he succeeded in capturing a standard. Afraid of being outflanked by Argyle's left wing, which extended far beyond his position, and being ignorant of what was passing on the right wing of the royalists, the view of which was concealed by the unevenness of the ground, Whitham retired in the direction of Dunblane. The earl of Mar pursued the disordered mass to the distance of only half a mile, and having ordered his foot to halt till he should put them in order, resolved to follow the enemy and complete the victory; but receiving intelligence that his left wing and second line had given way, and that his artillery had been taken, he retraced his steps, and took up a position on the top of the stony hill of Kippendavie, till he should receive further information respecting the fate of his left wing.

This wing, which was the first to begin the attack, opened a fire upon Argyle's right wing when almost within pistol-shot. The Highlanders thereafter steadily advanced, and pouring a second volley among the enemy, with a precision and effect not to be surpassed by the best disciplined troops, rushed up, sword in hand, to the very muzzles of their muskets. Though the fire was destructive, and made Evans's dragoons reel for a time, the English troops maintained their ground, and the foot kept up a platooning, which checked the fury of their assailants. The struggle continued for some time without any decided advantage on either side; but as Argyle began to perceive that he could make no impression in front upon the numerous masses of the insurgents, and that he might be outflanked by them, he resolved to attack them on their flank with part of his cavalry, while his foot should gall them with their fire in front. He therefore ordered Colonel Cathcart to move along the morass to the right with a strong body of cavalry, and to fall upon the flank of Mar's left wing,—a movement which he executed with great skill. Cathcart, after receiving a fire from the insurgent horse, immediately charged them, but they sustained the assault with great firmness. Borne down by the superior weight of the English dragoons, whose horses were much larger than those of the insurgents, the Scotish horse, after nearly half-an-hour's contest, were compelled to give way. The foot of Argyle's right having made a simultaneous attack upon Mar's first line of foot, the latter also were forced to fall back, and Mar's horse and foot coming into contact with his second line, they mixed indiscriminately, and a general rout in consequence ensued.

After receding a short distance, the insurgent horse, which consisted principally of the Jacobite gentry of Perthshire and Angus, attempted to rally, and even to charge Argyle's cavalry in their turn, but they were again forced to retire by the pressure of the English dragoons, who kept advancing in regular order upon the receding masses of the insurgents. Determined, however, not to yield one inch of ground without the utmost necessity, the cavalier horse made repeated efforts to drive the enemy back, and, in the course of their retreat, made ten or twelve attempts at different places to rally and charge the advancing foe; but unable to resist the overwhelming pressure of the English cavalry, they were, after three hours' hard fighting, driven across the river Allan by Argyle's dragoons. Some idea may be formed of the obstinacy of the contest, when it is considered that the distance from the field of battle to the river is scarcely three miles. To the gallant stand made by the horse may be ascribed the safety of the foot, who would have been probably all cut to pieces by the dragoons, if the attention of the latter had not been chiefly occupied by the horse. The foot, however suffered considerably in the retreat, notwithstanding the humanity of the Duke of Argyle, who endeavoured to restrain the carnage. Besides offering quarter to such of the Jacobite gentlemen as were personally known to him, he displayed his anxiety for the preservation of his countrymen so far, that on observing a party of his dragoons cutting down a body of foot, into which they had thrown themselves, he exclaimed with a feeling of deep emotion, "Oh, spare the poor Blue-bonnets!"

As Mar's right wing had been concealed from the view of Argyle, the latter conceived that the numerous body he was driving before him formed the entire of the insurgent army. He, therefore, resolved to continue the pursuit till dark, and to support him, he ordered General Wightman, who commanded his foot upon the right, to follow him with his battalions as quickly as possible. Wightman accordingly proceeded to follow the Duke with a force of rather more than three regiments; but he had not marched far, when he heard a firing on his left, to ascertain the cause of which, he sent his aid-de-camp in the direction whence the firing proceeded. This officer returned in a short time, and reported that the half of Argyle's foot, and the squadrons on the left, had all been cut off by the right of the insurgents, which was superior in point of numbers to Argyle's left. Wightman thereupon slackened his pace, and despatched a messenger to inform the Duke of the fate of his left wing. Afraid of being attacked in his rear by Mar's right wing, he kept his men in perfect order, but no demonstration was made to follow him.

When informed of the defeat of his left wing, Argyle gave over the pursuit, and joining Wightman with five squadrons of dragoons, put his men in order of battle and marched boldly to the bottom of the hill, on the top of which the enemy, amounting to 4,000 men, were advantageously posted.

Argyle had now scarcely 1,000 men under him, and as these were already greatly exhausted, he judged it expedient to act on the defensive; and accordingly he posted his men behind some enclosures at the bottom of the hill, ready to repel any attack which the enemy might make. For better protection he posted two pieces of cannon on his right and left, to play upon the enemy should they approach; but the insurgents showed no disposition to engage, and both parties, as if by mutual consent, retired from their positions in different directions. The Duke filed off his men to the right, in marching order, towards Dunblane; but as he still dreaded an attack, he formed his men several times on the march, wherever he found the ground convenient, and waited the approach of the enemy. Mar drew off his men toward Ardoch, where he passed the night, and Argyle's troops lay under arms during the night in the neighbourhood of Dunblane.

As might have been expected, on an occasion of such dubious success on either side, both parties claimed a victory, but impartiality will confer the palm on neither. Argyle, it is true, visited the field of battle the following morning, which Mar might also have done had he been inclined, and this circumstance, therefore, can afford no argument in support of his pretensions. Neither can the capture of standards and colours by Argyle be considered as a proof of success, for although he took fourteen colours and standards, including the royal standard called "the Restoration," besides six pieces of cannon and other trophies, Mar, according to the official Jacobite account, captured four stands of colours, several drums, and about fourteen or fifteen hundred stands of arms. The following verse from the well-known ballad on the battle of Sheriffmuir, though sufficiently rough, appears to be truly descriptive:

"There's some say that we wan,
  And some say that they wan,
And some say that nane wan at a', man;
  But ae thing I'm sure,
  That at Sheriffmuir
A battle there was that I saw, man;
  And we ran and they ran, and they ran and we ran,
  And we ran and they ran awa, man."

Accounts the most contradictory were given by the two parties respecting the losses which they sustained. According to the rolls of Argyle's muster-master general, his loss amounted to 290 men killed, 87 wounded, and 133 prisoners, making a grand total of 510; while the Jacobite account makes the loss in killed and wounded on the side of Argyle amount to between 700 and 800, and states the number of killed on Mar's side as only one in fifteen to those of Argyle. On the other hand, the Jacobites state their loss in killed at only 60, and that very few of their men were wounded, while the royalists say that they lost, in killed and wounded, about 800 men. From these statements it appears that the main discrepancy relates to the loss on the Jacobite side, which can neither be admitted to the extent of the royalist account, nor considered so low as that given by the Jacobites. But even supposing the royalist statement correct, the comparative loss of the insurgents scarcely exceeded one-third of that sustained by the government forces.

Several officers were killed on the royalist side. Among the wounded was the Earl of Forfar, a brave officer who commanded Morison's regiment. He received a shot in the knee, and sixteen other wounds, of which he died at Stirling about three weeks after the battle. Several persons of distinction were killed on the side of the insurgents, among whom were the Earl of Strathmore, and the captain of Clanranald. A considerable number of gentlemen were taken prisoners by Argyle, but many of them escaped, and he was enabled to carry only eighty-two of them to Stirling. Of this number were Lord Strathallan, Thomas Drummond his brother, Walkinshaw of Barrowfield, Drummond of Logie-Drummond, and Murray of Auchtertyre.

THE FEUD BETWEEN LORDS AIRLIE AND ARGYLE.

A FEUD between the Ogilvies, Earls of Airlie, and the Campbells, Earls of Argyle, was of long continuance, and produced much commotion and disaster. When or how it began is not known; but so fierce was it that the great wilderness of moor and mountain which extends from Loch Etive to Strathtay was no hinderance to its outbursts and desolating movements. In the year 1591, when the Ogilvies were residing peaceably in Glenisla, a body of Argyle's men made an inroad upon them, ravaged their estates, killed several of their people, and compelled their chief and his lady to flee for their lives. And during the civil war between the Covenanters and the Royalists, the private feud between the Campbells and the Ogilvies blended itself with the public quarrel, and borrowed thence at once pretexts, opportunities, and means for venting its wrath and executing its vengeance. The Earl of Airlie was one of the most distinguished and inflexible champions of the cause of Charles I., and acted for some time as official director of his interests throughout the central parts of Scotland, and exerted strenuous and persevering energy in his behalf both in the council and in the field,—both by efforts among the Scots at home and by services under the monarch's own eye in England; and he was therefore specially obnoxious to all the public partisans of the National Covenant,—and very eminently so to the Earl, afterwards the Marquis of Argyle.

The most notable of all the results of this state of things was the burning of several castles and mansions of the Ogilvies, particularly Airlie Castle, "the Bonnie House of Airlie" of Scotish song, in 1640. Airlie Castle occupied a commanding site on the rocky promontory at the confluence of the Melgum and the Isla, about 5 miles north of Meigle in Strathmore; it possessed great strength of both position and masonry, and ranked as one of the proudest and most massive fortresses in Central Scotland; and, previous to the introduction of artillery, it must have been almost if not entirely impregnable. It had the form of an oblong quadrangle; and occupied the whole summit of the promontory, with the exception of a small space at the extremity, which is traditionally said to have been used for exercising the horses. The wall which protected it on the eastern and most accessible side—high and massive, together with the portcullis entry—still remains in connexion with the modern mansion of Airlie; and the fosse also continues distinct, but has been partially filled up, in order to render the place accessible to carriages.

In July 1640, the Earl of Argyle, acting secretly upon the personal resentment which he had all his life long entertained against the Ogilvies, but overtly upon an express commission given him for the public service by the Committee of Estates, raised a body of 5,000 men of his own clan, and led them across the Grampians and down Strathtay to devastate the territories of the Earl of Airlie. He is said by an old tradition to have halted them for the night on the haughs at the village of Rattray; and, in accordance with this, though most diminishingly out of reckoning with regard to the numbers, the old ballad says,—

" Argyle has raised a hunder men,
    A hunder men and mairly,

And he's awa doun by the back o' Dunkeld,
To plunder the bonnie house o' Airlie."

The Earl of Airlie, at the time, was absent in England whither he had gone as much to avoid the necessity of subscribing the Covenant, as to render immediate service to the King's cause. Lord Ogilvie, the Earl's eldest son, held the charge of Airlie Castle, and had recently maintained it against the assault of a party under the Earl of Montrose; but, on the approach of Argyle's army, he regarded all idea of resisting them as hopeless, and hastily abandoned the castle and fled. Argyle's men plundered the place of everything which they coveted and could carry away, and then proceeded to damage the castle to the utmost of their power by dilapidation and fire; and Argyle himself acted so earnest a part in the demolition, that, according to the report of the historian Gordon, " he was seen taking a hammer in his hand, and knocking down the hewed work of the doors and windows till he did sweat for heat at his work."

Argyle's army next marched to the Castle of Forter, the ordinary residence of Lord Ogilvie, and treated it in the same manner that they had done the Castle of Airlie. Lady Ogilvie was in it at the time of their approach, and was far advanced in pregnancy, and is believed to have heard of their coming with great apprehension, and to have sent messages of entreaty to their leader to grant her some clemency in consideration of her condition. But Argyle would not allow her to retain possession of the place till her accouchement, nor even permit her to go to the house of her grandmother, his own kinswoman, Lady Drimmie; but turned her adrift from Forter summarily and ruthlessly, and proceeded forthwith to burn and demolish her castle. Yet a tradition of the district asserts that the Campbells kept possession of Forter during several months, before they destroyed and abandoned it.

The house of Craig, in Glenisla, belonging to another near

branch of the Airlie family, was not included in Argyle's commission from the Committee of Estates, yet shared the same fate as the Castles of Airlie and Forter. Gordon says respecting it, " At such time as Argyle was making havoc of Airlie's lands, he was not forgetful to remember old quarrels to Sir John Ogilvie of Craig, cousin to Airlie. Therefore he directs one Sergeant Campbell to Sir John Ogilvie's house, and gives him warrant to sleight it. The sergeant coming thither, found a sick gentlewoman there and some servants, and looking upon the house with a full survey, returned without doing anything, telling Argyle what he had seen, and that Sir John Ogilvie's house was no strength at all, and therefore he conceived that it fell not within his orders to cast it down. Argyle fell in some chafe with the sergeant, telling him that it was his part to have obeyed his orders, and instantly commanded him back again, and caused him deface and spoil the house."

The case of the house of Craig concurs with a great deal of other evidence to show not only the fact but the intensity of pent-up feudal resentment on the part of Argyle; and some events afterwards occurred, particularly a severe act of retaliation on Argyle, in the destruction of his castle of Gloom, near Dollar, in 1645, to deepen and perpetuate the many exacerbations of the feud. Yet the old ballad of "the Bonnie House o' Airlie" represents the affair between the Earls as a sudden dispute, an accidental quarrel, which fell out "on a bonnie summer day," while the oat-crops "grew green and early." But indeed all the main incidents of the ballad are contortions; and, in particular, the Countess of Airlie is put for Lady Ogilvie, and the burning of Airlie Castle for the burning of Forter Castle,—and the heroine of the piece is made to have seven children, while the actual Countess had only three, and the actual Lady Ogilvie only one. Yet the effusion blazes so fiercely with both the poesy and the politics of the period that fully one-half of its stanzas are well worth quotation; and these we shall take from Mr. Chambers' collated edition:—

"The lady look'd over her window sae hie,
  She lookit lang and weary,
Till she has espied the great Argyle,
  Come to plunder the bonnie house o' Airly.

He has taen her by the middle sae sma',
  Says, 'Lady, where is your dowry?'
'It's up and down by the bonnie burn side,
  Amang the plantings o' Airly.'

They soucht it up, they soucht it down,
  They soucht it late and early,
Till they fand it in the bonnie ploom-tree,
  That shines on the bowling-green o' Airly

He has taen her by the middle sae sma',
  And O, but she grat sairly!
And he's set her up on a bonnie knowe-tap,
  To see the burning o' Airly.

'O, I hae seven brave sons,' she says;
  ''The youngest ne'er saw his daddie;
And although I had as mony mae,
  I wad gie them a' to Charlie!

But gin my gude lord had been at hame,
  As this nicht he is wi' Charlie,
There's na a Campbell in a' Argyle,
  Durst ha' plunder'd the bonnie house o' Airly!

Were my gude lord but here this day,
  As he is wi' King Charlie,
The dearest blude o' a' thy kin
  Wad sloken the burning o' Airly!'"

THE SCOTISH TROOPS UNDER THE KING OF DENMARK.

Some notice of Mackay's regiment, which was raised in the year 1626 for service in the Continental cause of civil and religious liberty against the imperialists of Germany, has already been given in a previous article of this volume, entitled "The Scotish troops in the service of Gustavus Adolphus." But the regiment is noticed there only in connexion with the Swedish hero, and as part of one of the several British brigades in his army; and it well deserves some separate mention, in regard to the brave career which it previously ran under the flag of Denmark.

The original regiment is said by some authorities to have been 2,000 strong; by others nearly 3,000. The men and most of the officers embarked at Cromarty on the 10th of October, 1626, and arrived five days after at Luckstadt on the Elbe; and thence they immediately removed to the interior of Holstein, and there took up their quarters for the winter. The Colonel himself was detained in Scotland by sickness till the following spring; but joined them toward the end of March. "At his coming," says Monro, in the racy and very scarce old work from which we formerly made large extracts, "orders were given his regiment should be brought in arms at Itzehoe, where his Majesty would take their oaths of fidelity. The regiment being come together at the rendezvous, was drawn up in three divisions, attending his Majesty's coming in good order of battle. All officers being placed according to their stations orderly, colours flying, drums beating, horses neighing, his Majesty comes royally forward, salutes the regiment, and is saluted again with all due respect and reverence, used at such times. His Majesty having viewed front, flanks, and rear, the regiment fronting always towards his Majesty, who having made a stand ordained the regiment to march by him in divisions which orderly done, and with great respect and reverence as became. His Majesty being mightily well pleased, did praise the regiment, that ever thereafter was most praiseworthy."

On the next day, the regiment marched southward in three divisions, for three several destinations,—two companies to beset the town of Stoade, four companies to take post upon the Elbe at Lauenburg, and five companies to join some English forces under General Morgan toward the Weser. The fortunes and proceedings of the army throughout the summer were very various,—and comprised marchings, stormings, skirmishes, and most other great incidents of a chequered war; and at length the army lay beleaguered during five weeks in autumn at Wismar on the coast of the Baltic, and were cut off by the imperialists from all land communication with Denmark, and felt compelled, some time in October, to escape from their unpleasant position by sea. They landed in safety at Heiligenhafen, in the north-western extremity of Holstein; and thence they marched to the pass of Oldenburg, a few miles to the south, and there they found occasion to bring all their ardour and bravery into play.

"Having all safely landed at Heiligenhafen," says Monro, "we marched towards the pass of Oldenburg, where arrived before night our leager was drawn out into the most convenient part for maintaining of the pass, where the first night we begin to work in the trenches, and continue working the whole night, and the next day till noon, that the enemy was seen marching towards the pass, in full battalions of horse and foot, which before three of the clock had planted batteries to play with cannon on our leager, and to force a passage over the pass, which our general perceiving, gave orders to double the guards both of horse and foot, as also strongly to barricade the pass, and to cast up in the night a redoubt before the pass. The night drawing on being dark, silence was over all, on both sides of the pass. But the day clearing, the guards on both sides begin the skirmish, the cannons on both sides begin to discharge, the horse guards charge one another till ours were forced to give ground. The foot guards beginning to fight, the reliefs were commanded on both sides to second their own, the service growing hot, and the pass in danger of losing. My Colonel in all haste was commanded to march with the half of his regiment to maintain the pass. The Colonel commanded me to have the men in readiness, and to distribute ammunition amongst the soldiers; which done the Colonel leading on marches towards the pass under mercy of cannon and musket. The General meeting us bids ask the soldiers if they went on with courage; they shouting for joy, cast up their hats, rejoicing in their march, seeming glad of the occasion. The General commending their courage and resolution, doth bless them in passing. At our ongoing to the pass, the enemy's cannon played continually on the colours, which were torn with the cannon. Also to my grief, my comrade Lieutenant Hugh Ross was the first that felt the smart of the cannon bullet, being shot in the leg, who falling, not fainting at his loss, did call courageously, ' Go on bravely comrades, and I wish I had a wooden leg for your sakes.' In this instant of time, and, as I believe, with one bullet the leg was also shot from David Ross son to Ross of Gannis. The service thus hot both of cannon and musket, many were hurt at the ongoing, where I received a favourable mark, being hurt in the inner side of my right knee, with the end of mine own partizan, being shot off by the cannon bullet. And we drawing near to the pass, the Dutch that were on service being all fled but the captain, the pass near lost, my Colonel draws off a platoon of musketeers of the right wing, being most of them brave young gentlemen of the Colonel's own company, which in all haste with an officer were directed to maintain the pass, which being hardly pursued, sundry worthy young gentlemen did lie on the place in the defence of it, and sundry were hurt.

By this time, the rest of the Colonel's division were not idle from service, the reliefs going often on, and the rest doing service along the pass, having a hedge for their shelter. The body of the pikes stood for two hours in battle, under mercy of cannon and musket, so that their sufferings and hurts were greater both amongst officers and soldiers, than the hurt done to the musketeers that were on service, for few of their officers escaped unhurt, and divers also were killed. In time of this hot service, powder being distributing amongst soldiers, a whole barrel was blown up, whereby the Colonel was burnt in the face, and many soldiers spoiled. The enemy seeing our powder blown up, press to force the passage; and some coming over, Captain John Monro, with a few musketeers, was commanded in a flat champagne to encounter the enemy, who forced the enemy to retire, so that the pass was cleared again by Captain John's valour, much to his credit.

" The first division of our regiment having thus maintained the pass for two hours' hot service, then comes from the leager, for relief of the Colonel's division, the Lieutenant-colonel, with the other division nothing inferior to the first, who falling on fresh with manly courage, the other division falls off to refresh themselves during their comrades being on service. At the very entry the Lieutenant-colonel and five other officers were hurt, and many gentlemen and common soldiers were killed. This service continued in this manner from seven o'clock in the morning, till it was past four in the afternoon. It first began with the half of the regiment, who were relieved by the other half, which continued till mid-day; after that the service not being so hot as before, they went on to service by companies, one company relieving another, till night that it grew dark; and then darkness, the enemy of valour, made the service to cease. During all this time, our horsemen stood bravely in battle under mercy of cannon and musket, besides the foot attending to second us, in case the enemy had set over, and forced the pass, which once he adventured to do, but was suddenly beaten back. All this while, the General the Duke of Weimar, and both the armies, were witnesses to the manly and brave carriage of this praise-worthy regiment.

"In the evening before night, ammunition on both sides growing scarce, and darkness coming on, the service begins to bear up; by this time there is a barrel of beer sent us from the leager; the officers for haste caused to beat out the head of it, that every man might come unto it, with hat or head-peace, they flocking about the waggon whereon the barrel lay, the enemy's cannonier gives a volley to their beer, which, by God's providence, though shot among the midst of them, did no more harm, but blew barrel and beer in the air, the nearest miss that I did ever see; for many of them were down to the ground, whereof my brother, Captain John Monro of Obistell of worthy memory was one.

"At night the service ceased, I was sent by the rest of the officers to the leager to my Colonel for orders, to learn of the General who should relieve us at night. My Colonel did go to the General's tent, and I with him, to have his Excellency's resolution, who, having nobly accepted of the Colonel, did praise him and his regiment, requesting him that as the regiment had done bravely all day, in being the instruments under God of his safety and of the army, he would once more request him that his regiment might hold out the inch, as they had done the span, till it was dark, and then they should be relieved, as he was a Christian, and drinking to me, I returned with a resolution to my comrades, leaving my Colonel in the leager. And as it grew dark, we were relieved by the Duke of Weimar's earnest and diligent entreaty, he having proved our good friend, in urging to take us first off. The General having resolved to retire from the enemy, with the whole army, by reason ammunition grew scarce, and we having deserved best, were first brought off, getting orders to march in the night to ships."

The retreat of the Mackay regiment was curious and characteristic, and is minutely narrated by Monro. "Having thus passed the day at Oldenburg," says he, "the night the friend of cowards coming on, what we durst not have done by day, being favoured by the moonshine, when all were wearied with hot service and toil in the day, begun to take rest and refreshment by their fires, in the leager all guards relieved, and sentries set out, being all of us after a great storm in a quiet calm, we begin to take our retreat to the water. Our General being full of fear and suspicion goes before, and our Colonel also; we follow, having the avant-guard according to our orders for going a ship-board, which orders were willingly obeyed, perceiving the danger was to follow; and in consideration that long before the Lieutenant Colonel Sir Patrick Mackay and Captain Forbes being hurt had retired for their safety towards the Isle of Femern, and from thence to Denmark to be cured, I supplying the place of the Major, our regiment orderly retiring from the enemy, Captain Mackenzie and my brother Obistell, who before were companions in the day of danger, in the night did march together leading off the regiment to be secured, and I bringing up the rear, accompanied with some other officers. We had no doubt of our safe retreat. The whole army being behind us made us halt the oftener, taking pains to bring up our hurt and sick men, and we marched but softly.

"At last by ten o'clock of the night we arrived on the shore, and drew up in order waiting the Colonel's command for shipping, who had gone himself unto the road amongst the ships to provide shipping, but could get no obedience, the fear was so great amongst the mariners. Having heard the roaring and thundering of cannon and muskets in the day, fear so possessed them all, that they lacked hands to work and hearts to obey. And the Colonel coming ashore without bringing ships to receive us, we made use of the time, our comrades the horsemen having come before us, who ever begin confusion, were without orders forcing ships to take in their horses, and had already possessed the whole bulwark and shipping with their horse, I asking my Colonel's leave, drew our whole colours in front, and our pikes charged after them. Our musketeers drawn up in our rear by divisions, fortifying our rear in case the enemy should assault us in our rear, I advanced with our colours alongst the pier. Our pikes charged, we cleared the pier of the horsemen, suffering them to save themselves from drowning, where they found the channel most shallow. And advancing thus to the end of the pier, we seized upon one ship with some horses in it, where we set our colours; and making that ship launch off a little from the shore for fear of being aground, having manned the ship-boat with an officer and some musketeers, we sent to force other ships out of the road to launch in and serve us, until such time as the most part of our regiment were shipped, except some villains who were gone a plundering in the town; but not knowing the danger they were in, they stayed all night from us, and were taken by the enemy the next morning.

"Thus having shipped our men, we were forced to quit our horses and baggage. The officers that were most diligent, as Captain Monro and my brother Obistell, were busy the whole night ferrying soldiers from the shore, especially the sick and wounded, who were not able to help themselves. In the morning I shipped three boatfuls of wounded and sick men, till at the last I was beaten from the shore by the enemy's horsemen. And my Colonel's ship being under sail laid up to the wind, attending my coming with the last freight, we followed the route of the fleet, seeing the enemy's army drawn up in battle, horse, foot, and cannon, and our army of foot and horse opposite unto them. Where I did see six and thirty cornets of horse, being full troops without losing of one pistol give themselves prisoners in the enemy's mercy, whereof the most part took service. As also I did see above five regiments of foot, being forty colours, follow their examples, rendering themselves and their colours, without losing of one musket. Judge then, judicious reader, though we were sorry for the loss of our army, if we were glad of our own safety. I think we were, and praised be God with no discredit to us, or our nation; for none can be blamed that doth what he is commanded. Thus following our course the third morning we arrived before Flensburg, where our rendezvous was appointed; and having sent ashore for some victuals, whereof we stood in great need, no man was blamed to provide for himself at such time, when the whole country was to be left to our enemy's mercy."

Some ludicrous incidents occasionally relieved the monotony and desolateness of the untoward campaigns; and the following, which happened at an earlier period than the retreat from Wismar, is told by Monro with peculiar gusto:—
" Being quartered a mile from Lauenberg in a dorp, where the boor had quitted his lodging from fear, we were forced to send our suttler, John Matheson, to that town for provision. In his absence, our boys made use of his rug to cover their faces in drowning of bee-hives; the rug being rough did lodge a number of the bees, which, when the boys had drowned the bee-hives, they threw away. The suttler coming late home, we being a-bed, went to rest; and putting off his clothes, drew his rug to cover him; but as soon as the bees found the warmness of his skin, they began to punish him for his long stay; so that he was forced roaring like a madman, to rise, and throw off his rug, not knowing (though well he felt) the smart of his sudden enemies. We called to him, asking if he was mad. He made no answer, but still cried the devil had bewitched him, in piercing him in a thousand parts, still rubbing and scratching, crying with pain, not knowing the reason, till a candle was lighted, and seeing the

bees, threw his rug in a draw-well. The gentle reader may judge whether or not he was punished for his long stay."

Throughout the whole period of the Mackay regiment's service under the King of Denmark, they were always sent on the most dangerous expeditions, and ordered to the most perilous posts; and they were often engaged, and suffered severe losses, and never fled or flinched; so that, in point of numbers, they rapidly shrank to a skeleton, and required the largest possible recruitments from home. "Their enemies," says Monro, "in all encounters, could not but duly praise them, calling them *the invincible regiment,* which always rencountered them on all occasions; so that Mackay's name was very frequent, through the glorious and never-dying fame of his regiment,—never wronged by fortune in their fame, though divers times by their enemies they sustained both loss and hurt. But would to God we had always met man to man, or that our army had consisted all of such men and such officers; if so had been, our conquests had extended as far as the Romans of old did extend the limits and borders of their empire."

In the winter of 1628, the shattered remnant of the regiment was placed under the command of Monro, while the Colonel went to Scotland for recruits; and so hot work had it in the early portions of the succeeding campaign that before the Colonel could return, it was reduced to four hundred men. The whole corps, or parts of it, did special service in Laland, in Funen, in Femern, in Holstein, and in Zealand,— passing from place to place by water, and sometimes achieving as great wonders by their movements as by their exploits; and at length, in the month of May, they passed southward from Zealand to the north-west corner of Pomerania, to perform their grandest series of services at Stralsund, which was hard beleaguered by the Imperialists, and whose burghers petitioned the King of Denmark to send the Mackay regiment to their aid.

" The Lieutenant-Colonel, Alexander Seaton, being then
come from Holland," says Monro, "was ordained by his
Majesty in all haste to ship three companies, and to go with
them for the relief of Stralsund; I being appointed to stay
for the other companies coming. They being come to Elsi-
nore, were shipped also; and arriving at Copenhagen, it behoved me in all haste to ship, and follow the Lieutenant-
Colonel for relief of Stralsund, being hard beleaguered, where
I entered the 28th of May, and was no sooner drawn up in
the market-place, but presently we were sent to watch at
Frankendore, to relieve the other division that had watched
three days and three nights together uncome off, that being
the weakest part of the whole town, and the only post pursued by the enemy; which our Lieutenant-Colonel made
choice of, being the most dangerous, for his country's credit;
where we watched forty-eight hours together, till we were
relieved again by the other division; and so *Singulis noctibus
per vices*, during six weeks' time, that my clothes came
never off, except it had been to change a suit or linens."

" On the 28th of May," he says again, " not without danger both by water and from land, we entered the town of
Stralsund, the Imperial army lying before it, having their
batteries near the water. At our in-coming they shot our
mast; having grounded before our in-coming, we ran the
hazard both of drowning and killing. But being again without hurt come off, our comrades wearied of watching, immediately after our entry we relieved the watch at Frankendore,
being the only post in the town most pursued by the enemy.
The order of our watch was after this manner: of the seven
companies one company watched still on the island before
the town, called the Hollomne; the other three companies
were ordained by four o'clock afternoon, to parade in the
market-place, and afterwards to march to their post at
Frankendore, without the walls on scurvy outworks, which
were but slightly fortified with a dry moat. The enem

ying strong before us, and approaching near, we fearing a sudden on-fall, those that were relieved of the watch by five of the clock, were ordained again to meet by nine of the clock at night, and to watch again on the by-watch, till four of the clock in the morning, whereof the one-half were appointed to lie in readiness at their arms without the port near the works, while as the other half were appointed also to lie in readiness at their arms on the market-place, to attend all occasions of alarms, either within or without the town. And thus we watched nightly, relieving one another, for the space of six weeks."

But notwithstanding this very hard and unremitting duty, the burghers were surly and inhospitable, and treated their brave Scotish defenders in a style of excessive ingratitude and grossness. Monro's company lay on the streets four successive nights unquartered; and the men became so irritated by this that, on going off the watch and unknown to their officers, they went to the burgomaster, and told him that they would lodge with himself unless he provided quarters for them. He complained to the governor, Colonel Holk, a Dane; and, at the latter's instance, a court-martial tried the company for mutiny, and ordained that three men of it should be hanged, and that these should be taken by ballot. The lots fell on two Scotsmen and a Dane; but, it having been subsequently agreed by the officers that only one of the three should suffer death, they again drew lots, and the lot of death fell upon the Dane. "The governor himself being a Dane," says Monro, "he could not of his credit frustrate justice, seeing before he was so earnest to see our nation punished for a fault, whereof he was rather guilty himself, not having appointed them quarters as he ought, so that the Dane suffered justly for a Dane's fault."

"During our residence here," continues the narrator, "our orders were so strict that neither officer nor soldier was suffered to come off his watch, either to dine or sup, but their meat was carried unto them to their post. The enemy approaching hard, and we working fast, for our own safety where sometimes we sallied out, and did visit the enemy in his trenches, but little to their contentment; till at last, the enemy did approach right under our work, where sometimes, being so near, we began to jeer one another, so that the Dutch one morning taunting us, said, they did hear there was a ship come from Denmark to us, laden with tobacco and pipes. One of our soldiers showing them over the work, a morgan stern, made of a large stock banded with iron like the shaft of a halbert, with a round globe at the end with cross iron pikes, saith, 'Here is one of the tobacco pipes wherewith we will beat out your brains, when ye intend to storm us.' We did also nightly take some prisoners of them, sometimes stealing off their sentries, which made many alarms in the night and in the day time. Here a man might soon learn to exercise his arms, and put his courage in practice. And to give our Lieutenant-Colonel his due, he had good orders, and he did keep both officers and soldiers under good discipline, and he knew well how to make others understand themselves, from the highest to the lowest.

"When cannons are roaring, and bullets flying,
He that would have honour must not fear dying.

Many rose here in the morning, went not to bed at night, and many supped here at night sought no breakfast in the morning. Many a burgher in this city, coming forth in his holy-days-clothes to take the air, went never home again till he was carried quick or dead. Some had their heads separated from their bodies by the cannon; as happened to one Lieutenant and thirteen soldiers, that had their fourteen heads shot from them by one cannon bullet at once. Who doubts of this, he may go and see the relics of their brains to this day, sticking on the walls, under the port of Frankendore in Stralsund."

On the 26th of June, after Marshal Arnheim had pressed the siege six weeks, Walenstine, Duke of Friedland, came to visit the place, and was much displeased that the town had not been taken. "He did recognosce the whole town," says Monro, "and finding our post to be the weakest part thereof, by reason of the situation and of the insufficiency of the works, the wall not exceeding the height of a man, he resolved to pursue it by storm, swearing out of a passion he would take it in three nights, though it were hanging with iron chains betwixt the earth and the heavens. But forgetting to take God on his side, he was disappointed by Him who disposeth of all things at his pleasure, being the Supreme watchman himself that neither slumbers nor sleeps. We having got intelligence of Walenstine's coming, we looked the better unto ourselves, and having in the evening or twilight set out our perdues, we strengthened all our posts, and we placed our by-watch in the ravelin, to be in readiness, as also I commanded fourscore musketeers, under the command of Captain Hay, to sit by their arms and to be in readiness to supply all defects might happen by a timely succours, as they should be commanded. Likewise I caused to double all sentries; and so sitting down to rest us, we were passing the time by discourse, betwixt ten and eleven o'clock at night, when as our sentry gives fire and calls us to our arms. At our rising we find the enemy approaching above a thousand strong, with a shout, *Sa, Sa, Sa, Sa, Sa, Sa*. Thus it went on cheerfully, and every man to his station." The contest throughout the night was severe and as nearly as possible unremitting. The first assailants were repulsed after an obstinate service of about an hour and a-half; and they were succeeded by an equal number, and these by others progressively till the morning. Monro's party in fact had practically to resist the whole force of the besieging army;

or at least were aided or relieved only twice and partially during the tremendous struggle. "The second relief that came to our post," says he, "was led by Colonel Frettz, newly come to town, with some Swedes, who, though not admitted to command, out of his generosity, being accompanied with his Lieutenant-Colonel Mac-Dougall, and his major, called Semple, with fourscore musketeers, voluntarily did come to succour and help our nation; who at his first coming, received death's wounds, whereof he died shortly after. His Lieutenant-Colonel also was taken prisoner, and was missing for six months, we not knowing whether he was dead or alive. The Major also was killed instantly at his first coming to service. But the last time, and on the last storm, by the break of day the enemy was once entered our works, and was beat back again with great loss, with swords and pikes and butts of muskets; so that the day clearing, the enemy was forced to retire, having lost above a thousand men, and we near two hundred, besides those who were hurt He that was on this night's service from the beginning to the ending, being in action, might avouch he did escape danger. The enemy forsaking our works unconquered, the moat filled with their dead bodies, equal to the banks, the works ruined in the day time could not be repaired, which caused the next night's watch to be the more dangerous." "During the time of this hot conflict," says Monro again, "none that was whole went off at the coming of the relief, but continued in the fight assisting their comrades, so long as their strength served, ever esteeming more of their credit than of their safety, through the desire they had to be revenged of the losses sustained by their comrades. On the other part, it was reported of Walenstine, that he was so eager to get in the town, that his officers retiring off service being hurt, he caused to shoot them dead, calling them cowards for retiring with so small hurt."

The following night witnessed a similar impetuosity and

bravery of storming and defence, and terminated in similar results. "It was passed furiously on both sides, not without great loss, being well fought, both of the pursuer and defender. In the morning our soldiers, some of them being armed with corslets, head-pieces, with half pikes, morgan sterns and swords, being led with resolute officers, they fall out pell-mell amongst the enemies, and chase them quite out of the works again, and retiring with credit, maintained still the triangle or ravelin. The enemy considering his loss, and how little he had gained, the town also being not void of fear, thinking the third night, the enemy might enter the walls, being thus doubtful on both sides, the enemy sends a trumpeter, to know if they will treat for conditions, our Lieutenant-Colonel having the command, for the time (in Colonel Holk's absence) I think was glad of the offer, to prolong time, till his Majesty of Denmark might send a fresh supply."

The belligerents accordingly agreed to have a cessation of hostilities, and that it should extend to a fortnight; and they proceeded to draw up articles, and remained at peace during several days. But before the articles could be signed, Lord Spynie, a Scotish nobleman, arrived at the head of a new Scotish regiment, with an order from the King to dissolve the treaty. And about the same time the protection of Stralsund was transferred by mutual agreement from Denmark to Sweden; and immediately after, Sir Alexander Leslie, "an expert and valorous Scotish commander," in the service of the renowned Swedish monarch, was sent to govern the town, and conducted some Swedish forces to its aid.

Leslie had no sooner taken the command than he resolved to attack the besiegers, and attempt to drive them from their works; and as the Scotish auxiliaries of Denmark were not yet withdrawn, he chose to employ in this perilous service his own countrymen of the Spynie and Mackay regiments. The former were fresh and in full strength; and they conducted the attack, and fell upon the enemy's works, and forced them to retire, and drove them to the main body of their army. But they soon found themselves confronted by overwhelming numbers, and were obliged to retrace their steps with considerable loss. "And to make their retreat good," says Monro, "falls up Captain Mackenzie with the old Scotish blades of our regiment, to suppress the enemy's fury. They keeping faces to their enemies, while their comrades were retiring, the service went on afresh. And there Seaton's company was led by Lieutenant Lumsdell, (in absence of their own officers, being then all under cure;) and there were lost of this company above thirty valorous soldiers; and the Lieutenant seeing Colonel Holk retiring, desired him to stay a little, and to see if the Scots could stand and fight or not. The Colonel perceiving him to jeer, shook his head and went away. In the end Captain Mackenzie retired softly from his enemy, keeping faces towards them with credit, till he was safe within works; and then made ready for his march towards Wolgast, to find his Majesty of Denmark."

The Danish monarch was at this time retreating before the Imperialists in Pomerania, having lost the greater part of his army there without coming to any regular engagement, and fallen back precipitately on Wolgast; and no sooner did the Scotish corps of the Mackay and the Spynie regiments, now under the command of Captain Mackenzie, arrive at the King's camp than their services were brought urgently into requisition. "His Majesty finding the enemy pressing hard, fearing much to be surprised or taken, he did give Captain Mackenzie charge to command the whole Scots that were there, and divers others, and to skirmish with the enemy before the ports, till his Majesty were retired, and then to make his retreat over the bridge, and to set it on fire; which the Captain did orderly obey, doing his Majesty the best service was done him in the whole time of his wars, not without great danger of the Captain and his followers; there the bridge once burning, he was then the happiest man that could first be shipped."

The Scots, along with the remnant of the Danish army, took shipping for Copenhagen; and there the Spynie regiment was reduced and draughted into the Mackay regiment; and the latter, at the same time, was greatly augmented by a body of fresh recruits from Scotland, and altogether was made up to a strength of 1,400 men, exclusive of the officers. The Mackay regiment remained in the service of Denmark till the following August, when a peace was concluded with Germany; and then they were liberally paid, honourably discharged, and offered free shipping back to Scotland. But instead of returning home, they entered the service of Gustavus Adolphus of Sweden.

THE RAISING OF CHARLES EDWARD'S STANDARD.

Prince Charles Edward, accompanied by the Marquis of Tullibardine, and a few other zealous Jacobites, sailed from Belleisle, in France, on the 5th of July, 1745, in a small frigate of 16 guns, and arrived at the south end of the Outer Hebrides on the 23d of the same month. He remained on board till the 25th, sailing from place to place between the islands and the mainland, despatching letters to his friends, receiving communications in reply, and holding consultations with companions and visitors respecting the best means of raising the clans who were favourably disposed to his cause. During the same interval, all the arms, ammunition, and stores which he had on board were landed, and a few rude preparations, such as the remoteness of the region and the difficulties of the occasion admitted of, were made for his own coming on shore.

At length, on the 25th, Charles landed at Borodale, a farm belonging to Clanranald, in the district of Arisaig, in the south-west extremity of continental Inverness-shire, and took up his abode in the house of Angus Macdonald, the tenant of the farm, who received him and his suite with a hearty welcome. About an hundred clansmen had been collected by two of the Macdonalds, at the request of the chief Clanranald, to serve as a body-guard of the Prince; and these also were hospitably entertained at Borodale. No situation could have been any where selected more suitable for the circumstances and designs of Charles than the abode he had chosen. Besides being one of the most remote and inaccessible places in the western Highlands of Scotland, it was surrounded on all sides by the territories of the most devoted adherents of the house of Stuart, by the descendants of the heroes of Kilsyth and Killicrankie, in whose breasts the spirit of revenge had taken deep root, for the cruelties which had followed the short-lived insurrection of 1715, and the affronts to which they had been subjected under the disarming act. These mountaineers had long sighed for an opportunity of retaliation, and they were soon to imagine that the time for vengeance had arrived.

As soon as the landing of Charles was known, the whole neighbourhood was in motion, and repaired, "without distinction of age or sex," to the house of Borodale, to see a man with whose success they considered the glory and happiness of their country to be inseparably associated. To gratify his warm-hearted and generous visitors, and to attain a full view of the assembled group, Charles seated himself in a conspicuous part of the room where a repast had been laid out for him and his friends. Here, amid the congregated spectators who feasted their eyes with the sight of the lineal descendant of a race of kings, endeared to them by many ennobling and even sorrowful recollections, the Prince partook of the fare provided by his kind host, with a cheerfulness which banished all reflection of the past or care for the future.

From Borodale, Charles sent off fresh messengers to all the chiefs from whom he expected assistance, requiring their attendance. Some of his friends, aware of his arrival, had, it is said, already held a meeting to consult as to the course they should pursue; at which Macdonald of Keppoch had given his opinion, that as the Prince had risked his person, and generously thrown himself into the hands of his friends, they were bound, in duty at least, to raise men instantly for the protection of his person, whatever might be the consequences; but it does not appear that any such resolution was at that time adopted.

The person pitched upon to visit Lochiel on this occasion, was Macdonald, younger of Scothouse, who succeeded in inducing that chief to visit the Prince at Borodale, but Lochiel went with a determination not to take up arms. On his way to Borodale, he called at the house of his brother, John Cameron of Fassefern, who, on being told the object of his journey, advised Lochiel not to proceed, as he was afraid that the Prince would prevail upon him to forego his resolution. Lochiel, firm in his determination, as he imagined, told his brother that his reasons for declining to join the Prince were too strong to be overcome, and pursued his journey.

Donald Cameron of Lochiel, on whose final determination the question of a civil war was now to depend, (for it seems to be universally admitted, that if Lochiel had declined to take up arms the other chiefs would have also refused,) though called young Lochiel by the Highlanders, from his father being still alive, was rather advanced in life. His father, for the share he had taken in the insurrection of 1715, was attainted and in exile. In consequence of the attainder, young Lochiel had succeeded to the family-estates upon the death of his grandfather, Sir Ewen Cameron in

1719. Sir Ewen had served with distinction under Montrose and Dundee, and his son, and grandson, had inherited from the old warrior a devoted attachment to the house of Stuart, which no change of circumstances had been ever able to eradicate. The Chevalier de St. George, sensible of the inflexible integrity of the young chief, and of the great influence which he enjoyed among his countrymen on account of the uprightness of his character, and as being at the head of one of the most powerful of the clans, had opened a correspondence with him, and had invested him with full and ample powers to negotiate with his friends in Scotland, on the subject of his restoration; and in consequence of the confidence which was so deservedly reposed in him, he was consulted on all occasions by the Jacobites in the Highlands, and was one of the seven who, in the year 1740, signed the bond of association to restore the Chevalier. Upon the failure of the expedition of 1743, young Lochiel had urged the Prince to continue his exertions to get another fitted out; but he was averse to any attempts being made without foreign assistance, and cautioned the Prince accordingly.

Among the chiefs who were summoned to Borodale, Lochiel was the first to appear, and immediately a private interview ensued between him and the Prince. Charles began the conversation by remarking, that he meant to be quite candid, and to conceal nothing; he then proceeded to reprobate in very severe terms, the conduct of the French ministry, who, he averred, had long amused him with fair promises, and had at last deceived him. He admitted that he had but a small quantity of arms, and very little money; that he had left France without concerting any thing, or even taken leave of the French court; that he had, however, before leaving France, written letters to the French king and his ministers, acquainting them of the expedition, and soliciting succours, which he was persuaded, notwithstanding their late conduct, they would send as soon as they saw that he really had a party in Scotland; that he had appointed Earl Marischal his agent at the court of France; and that he depended much upon the zeal and abilities of that nobleman, who would himself superintend the embarkation of the succours he was soliciting.

While Lochiel admitted the engagements which he and other chiefs had come under to support the cause, he observed that they were binding only in the event of the stipulated aid being furnished; and as His Royal Highness had come over without such support, they were released from the engagements they had contracted. He therefore reiterated the resolution which he had already intimated, by means of his brother, not to join in the present hopeless attempt, and advised his Royal Highness to return to France and await a more favourable opportunity. Charles, on the other hand, maintained, that an opportunity more favourable than the present might never occur again,—that, with the exception of a very few newly raised regiments, all the British troops were occupied abroad. He represented, that the regular troops now in the kingdom were insufficient to withstand the body of Highlanders his friends could bring into the field; and he stated his belief, that if in the outset he obtained an advantage over the government forces, the country in general would declare in his favour, and his friends abroad would at once aid him,—that every thing, in fact, now depended upon the Highlanders,—and that to accomplish the restoration of his father, it was only necessary that they should instantly declare themselves and begin the war.

These arguments, which, as the result has shown, were more plausible than solid, had no effect upon Lochiel, who continued to resist all the entreaties of Charles to induce him to alter his resolution. Finding the Prince utterly averse to the proposal made to him to return to France, Lochiel entreated him to be more moderate in his views. He then suggested, that Charles should send his attendants back to France; that he himself should remain concealed in the country; that a report should be circulated that he also had returned to France, and that the court of France should be made acquainted with the state of matters, and informed that his friends would be ready to take up arms upon the first notice of a landing, but that nothing could be done without foreign support. And in the meantime, Lochiel undertook to guarantee the personal safety of the Prince. Charles, however, rejected this proposal also, and told Lochiel, that the court of France would never be convinced that he had a considerable party in Scotland, till there was an actual insurrection, without which he was afraid they would not venture their troops.

As a last shift, Lochiel suggested, that Charles should remain at Borodale till he and other friends should hold a meeting, and concert what was best to be done. With an impatience which spurned delay, Charles would not even listen to the proposal, and declared his firm determination to take the field, how small soever the number of his attendants might be. "In a few days," said he, "with the few friends that I have, I will erect the royal standard, and proclaim to the people of Britain, that Charles Stuart has come over to claim the crown of his ancestors—to win it, or to perish in the attempt: Lochiel, whom my father has often told me, was our firmest friend, may stay at home, and from the newspapers, learn the fate of his Prince." This appeal was irresistible. "No!" exclaimed Lochiel, "I'll share the fate of my Prince; and so shall every man over whom nature or fortune has given me any power."

Having extorted an acquiescence from Lochiel, who, impelled by a mistaken but chivalrous sense of honour, thus yielded to the Prince's entreaties in spite of his own better judgment, Charles resolved to raise his standard at Glenfinnan on the 19th of August. In pursuance with this resolution, he despatched letters from Borodale on the 6th, to the different chiefs who were favourably disposed, informing them of his intention, and requiring the presence of them and their followers at Glenfinnan on the day appointed, or as soon thereafter as possible. Lochiel, at the same time, returned to his own house, whence he despatched messengers to the leading gentlemen of his clan to raise their men, and to hold themselves in readiness to march with him to Glenfinnan.

After sending off his messengers, Charles left Borodale for the house of Kinlochmoidart, about 7 miles from Borodale, whither he and his suite had been invited by the proprietor to spend a few days, while the preparations for the appointed meeting were going on. Charles and his party went by sea, and their baggage and some artillery were forwarded by the same conveyance; but the body-guard, which had been provided by Clanranald, proceeded by land along the heads of two intervening bays. While at the hospitable mansion of his friend, Charles expressed his sense of the services of Kinlochmoidart in the warmest terms, offered him a colonel's commission in a regiment of horse-dragoons, and promised him a peerage.

During Charles's stay at Kinlochmoidart, the arming of the Highlanders went on with extraordinary alacrity; and several days before the Prince's departure for Glenfinnan, detached parties of armed Highlanders were to be seen perambulating the country in different directions. Though three weeks had elapsed since the arrival of the Prince, yet so effectually had his arrival been concealed from the officers of the government in the Highlands, that it was not until they received intelligence of these movements, that they began even to suspect his arrival. Alarmed by reports which reached him for the safety of Fort William, around which Lochiel and Keppoch were assembling their men, the governor of Fort Augustus despatched, on the 16th of August, two companies of the second battalion of the Scots Royals, under the command of Captain (afterwards General) Scott, to reinforce that garrison; but they did not reach their destination, having been taken prisoners by a party of Lochiel's and Keppoch's men. As this occurrence may be regarded as the commencement of hostilities, and as it is strongly characteristic of the ardour with which the Highlanders took the field at the command of their chiefs, the details of it may not here be considered as out of place.

At the period in question, as well as at the time of the previous insurrection of 1715, the country between Fort William and Inverness was inhabited altogether by disaffected clans; to overawe whom chiefly, the chain of forts, named Fort William, Fort Augustus, and Fort George, which reach across the Highlands from the east to the west sea, was placed. In the centre of these, or almost equidistant between Fort William and Fort George, stands Fort Augustus, the distance between which and Fort William is 28 miles. To keep up a regular communication between the garrisons of the two last mentioned forts, a road was made by orders of the government along the sides of the mountains which skirt the narrow lakes, which now form part of the bed of the Caledonian canal. It was along this road that the detachment in question marched. That they might reach Fort William the same day—there being no place on the road where so many men could have taken up their quarters during night—they left Fort Augustus early in the morning of the 16th of August, and met with no interruption till they arrived at High Bridge, within 8 miles of Fort William. This bridge, which consists of one arch of great height, is built across the river Spean,—a mountain-torrent confined between high and steep banks. On approaching the bridge the ears of the party were saluted by the sound of a bagpipe, a circumstance which could excite little surprise in the Highlands; but when they observed a body of Highlanders on the other side of the bridge with swords and firelocks in their hands, the party became alarmed.

RAISING OF CHARLES' STANDARD.

The Highlanders who had posted themselves at the bridge were of Keppoch's clan, and were under the command of Macdonald of Tierndriech; and though they did not consist of more than eleven or twelve persons, yet by leaping and skipping about, moving from place to place, and extending their plaids between one another to give themselves a formidable appearance, they impressed Captain Scott with an idea that they were a pretty numerous body. He therefore halted his men, and sent forward a sergeant with his own servant towards the bridge to reconnoitre; but when they came near the bridge they were seized and carried across by two nimble Highlanders, who unexpectedly darted upon them. Seeing the fate of his messengers, knowing that he was in a disaffected district, and ignorant of the strength of the Highlanders, Captain Scott deemed it more advisable to retreat than risk an encounter. He, therefore, ordered his men to face about, and return by the road they had come. Tierndriech had for some time observed the march of these troops, and had sent expresses to Lochiel and Keppoch, whose houses were within three or four miles of High Bridge, announcing their advance, and demanding assistance. Expecting immediate aid and not wishing to display his weakness, which, from the openness of the ground near the bridge, would have been easily discernible, he did not follow Scott immediately, but kept at a distance till the troops had passed the west end of Loch Lochie, and were upon the narrow road between the lake and the mountain. The Highlanders thereupon made their appearance, and ascending the craggy eminences which overhang the road, and, sheltering themselves among the rocks and trees, began to fire down upon the retreating party, who, in place of returning the fire, accelerated their pace.

Before this fire had been opened, bands of Highlanders were proceeding in the direction of the bridge to assist in the attack. Upon hearing the report of the fire-arms, these hastened to the place whence the firing proceeded, and in a short time a considerable body joined the party under Tierndriech. Captain Scott continued his march rapidly long the loch; and when he reached the east end, he observed some Highlanders on a hill at the west end of Loch Oich, where they had assembled apparently for the purpose of intercepting him on his retreat. Disliking the appearance of this body, which stood in the direct way of his retreat, Scott resolved to throw himself for protection into Invergary castle, the seat of Macdonell of Glengary, and accordingly crossed the isthmus between the two lakes. This movement, however, only rendered his situation more embarrassing, as he had not marched far when he perceived another body of Highlanders, the Macdonells of Glengary, coming down the opposite hill to attack him. In this dilemma, he formed his men into a hollow square, and proceeded on his march. Meanwhile, Tierndriech having been reinforced by a party of Keppoch's men, headed by the chief, hastened the pursuit, and soon came up with the fugitives. To spare the effusion of blood, Keppoch advanced alone to Scott's party, required them to surrender, and offered them quarters; but assured them, that, in case of resistance, they would be cut to pieces. Fatigued with a long march, and surrounded on all sides by increasing bodies of Highlanders, Captain Scott, who had been wounded, and had had two of his men killed, accepted the terms offered, and surrendered. This affair was scarcely over, when Lochiel arrived on the spot with a party of Camerons, and took charge of the prisoners, whom he carried to his own house at Achnacarie. The result of this singular rencounter, in which the Highlanders did not lose a single man, was hailed by them as the harbinger of certain success, and they required no further inducement to prosecute the war thus auspiciously begun, as they imagined.

Charles, to whom it may be supposed intelligence of this affair was instantly sent, left Kinlochmoidart on the 18th of

August, on which day he went by water to the seat of Alexander Macdonald of Glenalladale, on the side of Loch Shiel, where he was joined by Gordon of Glenbucket, who brought with him Captain Sweetenham, an English officer of Guise's regiment, who had been taken prisoner by a party of Keppoch's men while on his way to Fort William to inspect that fortress. The Prince passed the night at Glenalladale, and with his attendants, who amounted to about 25 persons, proceeded about six o'clock next morning in three boats for Glenfinnan, and landed within a few hours at the east end of Loch Shiel, where the little river Finnan falls into the lake.

Glenfinnan, the place appointed for the rendezvous, is a narrow vale bounded on both sides by high and rocky mountains, between which the river Finnan runs. This glen forms the inlet from Moidart into Lochaber, and at its gorge is about 15 miles west from Fort William. On landing, the Prince was received by the laird of Morar at the head of 150 men, with whom he marched to Glenfinnan, where they arrived about eleven o'clock. Charles, of course, expected to find a large "gathering of the clans" in the vale awaiting his approach; but, to his great surprise, not a human being was to be seen throughout the whole extent of the lonely glen, except the solitary inhabitants of the few huts which formed the hamlet. Chagrined and disappointed, Charles entered one of these hovels to ruminate over the supposed causes which might have retarded the assembling of his friends. After waiting about two hours in anxious suspense, he was relieved from his solicitude by the distant sound of a bagpipe, which occasionally broke upon his ear; and by its gradual increase, it soon became evident that a party was coming in the direction of the glen. While all eyes were turned towards the point whence the sound proceeded, a dark mass was seen overtopping the hill and descending its side. This was the clan Cameron, amounting to between

700 and 800 men, with Lochiel, their chief, at their head. They advanced in two columns, of three men deep each, with the prisoners who were taken in the late scuffle between the lines.

If in the state of suspense in which he was kept after entering Glenfinnan, the spirits of Charles suffered a temporary depression, they soon recovered their wonted buoyancy when he beheld the gallant band which now stood before him. Without waiting, therefore, for the other clans who were expected to join, the Prince at once resolved to raise his standard, and to declare open war against "the Elector of Hanover," as George the Second was called, "and his adherents." The Marquis of Tullibardine, to whom, from his rank, was allotted the honour of unfurling the standard, took his station on a small knoll in the centre of the vale, where, supported by two men, he displayed the banner, and proclaimed the Chevalier de St. George as king before the assembled host, who rent the air with their acclamations. And though the acclaiming host at the moment was not considerable, the prospective one involved in the proceedings was believed to be great and magnificent, and may, with some poetic licence, be described, in the rather bombastic lines of Mr. Aytoun, as

> "The array
> That around the royal standard
>   Gather'd on the glorious day,
> When, in deep Glenfinnan's valley,
>   Thousands, on their bended knees,
> Saw once more that stately ensign,
>   Waving in the northern breeze,
> When the noble Tullibardine
>   Stood beneath its weltering fold,
> With the Ruddy Lion ramping
>   In the field of tressur'd gold!

When the mighty heart of Scotland
All too big to slumber more,
Burst in wrath and exultation
Like a huge volcano's roar!"

About an hour after the unfurling of the banner, and the reading of a manifesto, Macdonald of Keppoch joined the Prince with 300 of his men; and in the evening some gentlemen of the name of Macleod arrived at Glenfinnan, proffered their services to the Prince, and offered to return to Skye, and raise all the men they could in support of his cause. On arriving at Glenfinnan, Macdonald of Tierndriech presented the Prince with an excellent horse which he had taken from Captain Scott. The animated appearance of the glen, which now resounded with the martial strains of the pibroch, contrasted strongly with the solitary gloom which pervaded it when the Prince entered it. Instead of the small party which joined him in the morning, Charles found himself within a few hours thereafter at the head of a body of about 1,200 brave and resolute men, warmly attached to his person and cause, and ready and willing to hazard their lives in his service. Charles was exceedingly delighted at the appearance of his little army, and it has been observed that at no other time did he look more cheerful or display a greater buoyancy of spirits.

Thus was performed the first act of that tragic drama which nearly overturned the government of a great empire, and which, even ending as it did, brought ruin on many a noble and honourable family, and entailed a load of misery on a great part of the population of the Highlands. A monument has been erected by M'Donald of Glenalladale, on the spot where the Prince's standard was unfurled, to the memory of those " who fought and bled" in this rebellion. It is a sort of tower, with a small house attached, displaying any thing but taste; but even as it is, it has a striking effect, when associated with the wildness which reigns around, and the romantic and unfortunate adventure it commemorates The inscription is in three languages,—in Gaelic, Latin, and English. The following is a copy of the English one: "On this spot where Prince Charles Edward first raised his standard, on the 19th day of August, 1745, when he made the daring and romantic attempt to recover a throne lost by the imprudence of his ancestors, this column is erected by Alexander M'Donald, Esq. of Glenalladale, to commemorate the generous zeal, the undaunted bravery, and the inviolable fidelity of his forefathers, and the rest of those who fought and bled in that arduous and unfortunate enterprise. This pillar is now, alas! also become the monument of its amiable and accomplished founder, who, before it was finished, died in Edinburgh on the 4th January, 1815, at the early age of 28 years."

THE BATTLE OF TARA.

The hill of Tara, in the county of Meath, is one of the most celebrated localities in Ireland, and possesses considerable interest for Scotish antiquaries, as well as prime interest for Irish ones. It is a verdant, moundish, flowingly-outlined mass, about ¾ of a mile in length from north to south, rather less than ½ a mile in extreme breadth,—possessing a wavy, tumulated, tabular summit,—lifting up a large, solitary standing stone or monumental pillar on the crown of one of its tumuli,—sharing with the hill of Skreen, 1¾ mile to the east, and 507 feet in altitude, the power and interest of relieving the monotony of the vast central expanse of the plain of Meath,—and commanding a panoramic, minutely featured, and warmly tinted view of that brilliant expanse, — rich, fertile, and as capable of the most finished culture and the most ornate loveliness as a garden.

Its original name was Teaghmor, "the great house," or Teaghmorreagh, "the great house of the king,' and was abbreviated or vulgarized into successively Teamor and Tara. A triennial convocation of provincial kings, Druids, and bards, is usually alleged, but on very apocryphal authority, to have been held on Tara Hill, from an early period till about the end of the 6th century, for the election of a monarch or supreme ruler, and the management of the affairs of the monarchy. A supposed record, called the Psalter of Tara, or sometimes Senachasmore or "great antiquity," figures in tradition as the written depository of the decrees of the convocation, but is not known to literature as an actual record.

The famous coronation-stone which formed the palladium of the kingdom of Dalriada, at Dunstaffnage, on the shores of the Deucaledonian sea, and afterwards became the palladium of Scotland at that kingdom's coronation-ground in the vicinity of Perth, and eventually was removed to Westminster by Edward I. to be the coronation-chair of the kings of England, is alleged to have been carried to Dunstaffnage by way of Iona from the hill of Tara, to have figured in courtly belief at Tara as the pillow of stone on which Jacob slept at Bethel, and to have found its way to Tara in the course of the alleged Milesian immigrations from Spain.

The principal palace of the early monarchs of Ireland, and an university or cluster of colleges supported by their munificence, are alleged to have stood on the hill of Tara, and have been the topic alike of the most magniloquent and florid descriptions by early annalists and later credulous historians, and of the most conflicting theories, intricate investigations, and antagonist discussions, among the majority of Irish antiquaries. But whatever structures, dignified with the names of palaces, halls, and colleges, really at any time existed, were probably of a temporary and fragile character, quite unworthy to be designated architectural, and have long ago so utterly disappeared, as not to have left a single vestige of either wall or foundation; and the only antiquities, additional to the pillar-stone, which now exist, are numerous circular earthworks, possibly enough indicating quondam places of national assembly and royal residence, yet strictly resembling in appearance and character the ordinary 'raths,' which abound in most districts of the kingdom. The present desolation of the place, as contrasted to its ancient legendary glory, forms the topic of one of the finest of Moore's melodies:—

> "The harp that once through Tara's halls
>   The soul of music shed,
> Now hangs as mute on Tara's walls
>   As if that soul were fled.
>
> So sleeps the pride of former days,
>   So glory's thrill is o'er,
> And hearts that once beat high for praise,
>   Now feel that pulse no more.
>
> No more the chiefs and ladies bright
>   The harp of Tara swells;
> The chord alone, that breaks at night,
>   Its tale of ruin tells.
>
> Thus freedom now so seldom wakes;
>   The only throb she gives,
> Is when some heart indignant breaks,
>   To show that still she lives."

We might make martial mention of Tara in connexion with a signal defeat which the Danes sustained on it in 980, —with the concentration on it of the forces of Roderick, the last native monarch of Ireland, preparatory to his attacking the English in Dublin,—with O'Neill's assembling his followers on it, after laying waste the surrounding country, in 1589,—and, perhaps most of all, with the phantasmagorial images of feud and warfare which flit before the fancy in the most ancient Irish legends. But we write only of the wars of the Scots; and therefore have spoken of it at all only by way of introduction to a short notice of a famous skirmish upon it, fought in 1798, honourable to a small body of Scotish troops, and distinctively known as the Battle of Tara.

In May, 1798, a body of rebels, several thousand strong, assembled in the central parts of Leinster, and proposed first to march towards the north, where they expected a general rising against the government, and then to return, and form a junction with forces from the south and west, and make an overwhelming attack on Dublin, and effect there a complete revolution. A regiment of militia was despatched by the authorities in pursuit of them; but, on coming in sight, and observing their great numbers, thought it prudent to retire. The Reay Fencibles,—a regiment of Highlanders who had been raised in the north-west of Scotland in the beginning of 1795, and had been constantly on service in Ireland since a few months after that date—were at the time on their march from Cavan to Dublin, but knew nothing of the rebels, and of course had no commands or intention to seek them out or assail them. Their first division arrived at Dublin without any impediment; but a portion of baggage and ammunition between these and the second or rear division, was seized by the rebels, with the additional disaster of the death or captivity of the few men who escorted it. The rear division soon got intelligence of this, and viewed it as an affront on their regiment, and instantly resolved to punish it or die. They consisted of five companies; and, while two of these remained with the regimental stores, the other three, led by Captains Blanch and Maclean, set out in search of the rebels, and testified their alacrity at starting by a round of three hearty cheers. Nor were they alone in the expedition; for Captain Preston, of the Meath yeoman cavalry, having got a distant view of the rebels, and aware that the Reay Fencibles were approaching, joined the latter in all haste and earnestness, and suggested to them where they would most likely find the enemy, and brought to their aid some small bodies of the local yeoman infantry.

The small army moved on to Dunshaughlin where they hoped perhaps to find the rebels, and certainly to obtain refreshment; but they were quite disappointed; for the rebels had completely pillaged the town on the preceding day, and had killed several of the principal protestant inhabitants and dragged the rest into their ranks, and had swept all the surrounding country clean of provision, and marched away in vast force with their booty. But discovery was soon made that they had gone northward by a circuitous direction; and the Reays, fired with new determination to be at them, and afraid that they might intercept the two companies who were left behind, forgot all their privations and fatigue, and wheeled about and followed them; and, after retracing their way some four or five miles, they espied the rebels on Tara, with white flags in their camp and about forty lighted fires.

The rebels amounted to about 4,000, and were very strongly posted, and had been on Tara about four hours, and were busily engaged in cooking and eating the provisions which they had carried off from the open country; and when they saw the little army of royalists approaching, they despatched a strong party in a circular course to attack their rear, and made instant preparation with their main force for repelling the direct onset in front. The royalists, including all the yeomanry, amounted only to about 400, but were provided with a six-pounder piece of ordnance, and had the advantage of a few cavalry on both their right and their left extremity, to prevent their line from being outflanked. The rebels first put their hats on the tops of their pikes, and

THE BATTLE OF TARA.

raised some dreadful yells, and began to make violent and wild gesticulations by way of bidding defiance to their adversaries; and then they advanced from their position, excitedly but irregularly, and fired all along as they moved. The royalists approached them with the greatest coolness, and did not fire a shot till within fifty yards of their front. The firing commenced at half past six in the evening of the 26th of May, and continued without intermission till sunset.

"The battle," says the historian of the House and Clan of Mackay, "was hottest on the brow of the hill, where from overwhelming numbers, higher ground, old walls, &c. the rebels possessed every advantage. But nothing could resist the resolute courage and bravery of the Highlanders, determined as they were to despise all odds, and surmount all difficulties, even though, from the circumstances in which they were placed, their ranks were soon broken. The rebel party who had been sent to attack their rear, had now speedily come forward on the same road by which the Reays had advanced to the attack, and were in a thick body close up to them; but the cannon, which had fallen to the rear, was quickly turned about when they were almost at its muzzle, and being accidentally double charged, was let fly amongst them with a most destructive effect, clearing the road so effectually, that the survivors immediately fled in all directions. Soon thereafter the valiant Highlanders having irresistibly fought their way to the top of the hill, they furiously fell upon the rebels, brought them down in crowds, and dispersed and pursued them on every side; and during the chase, the cavalry, though raw and undisciplined, did considerable execution. No less than five hundred of the rebels were reported to have been next morning found dead, amongst whom was their commander, in full uniform; and, what was next to a miracle, the killed of the Reays did not amount to thirty, only that a considerable number were wounded. The spoil which they took from the rebels, though as might be supposed it was not much, recompensed in part the loss of the baggage which the enemy had seized; and they recovered the prisoners whom they had taken along with it." The Upper Kells infantry also had one killed and five wounded.

The pillar which now surmounts one of the tumuli of Tara originally stood on another and smaller tumulus, and was moved to its present situation to mark the spot where the bodies of the rebels slain in this skirmish were interred. "It was fixed there, however," say Mr. and Mrs. Hall, "only so recent as fifteen years ago. Its weight is prodigious; and it excited our astonishment how it could have been conveyed, without the aid of machinery, to its present destination. Upon this subject we conversed with a peasant, one 'Paddy Fitzsimmons,' who assisted at the ceremony. He stated that it was effected by no more than twenty men, who performed the work gradually an inch at a time; they sunk it about six feet into the ground, directly over the bodies of their old friends, relations, or companions; and perhaps in the world there does not exist so singular a monumental stone."

THE CONQUEST OF QUEBEC.

THE taking of Quebec was one of the most remarkable achievements of the British arms on the American Continent,—and also figures as one of the most curious exploits of modern warfare in any country; and therefore might well claim, on its own account, to be noticed in our miscellany of historiettes. But it presents itself with peculiar interest, and becomes entirely appropriate to the purpose of our Scotish Tales, on account of the conspicuous part which the Fraser Highlanders acted in it,—furnishing a fine specimen of the style in which Scotish soldiers have acquitted themselves in America.

Fraser's Highlanders, or the 78th regiment, were embodied on behalf of the British government in 1757, by the Hon. Simon Fraser, son of the Jacobite Lord Lovat; and though he possessed not an inch of land, and had in his youth ranked as a rebel against the power which he now served, yet, from the mere influence of clanship, he raised in a few weeks a corps of 800 men from among the families of his own name; and to these were added upwards of 600 of others who were raised by his friends and officers. The uniform of the regiment "was the full Highland dress, with musket and broadsword, to which many of the soldiers added the dirk at their own expense, and a purse of badger's or otter's skin. The bonnet was raised or cocked on one side, with a slight bend inclining down to the right ear, over which were suspended two or more black feathers. Eagles' or hawks' feathers were usually worn by the gentlemen, in the Highlands, while the bonnets of the common people were ornamented with a bunch of the distinguishing mark of the clan or district. The ostrich feather in the bonnets of the soldiers was a modern addition of that period, as the present load of plumage on the bonnet is a still more recent introduction, forming, however, in hot climates, an excellent defence against a vertical sun." The regiment embarked in company with Montgomery's Highlanders at Greenock, and landed at Halifax in June 1757. They were intended to be employed in an expedition against Louisbourg; which, however, after the necessary preparations, was abandoned. About this time it was proposed to change the uniform of the regiment, as the Highland garb was judged unfit for the severe winters and the hot summers of North America; but the officers and soldiers having set themselves in opposition to the plan, and being warmly supported by Colonel Fraser, who represented to the commander-in-chief the bad consequences that might follow if it were persisted in, the plan was relinquished. "Thanks to our gracious chief," said a veteran of the regiment, "we were allowed to wear the garb of our fathers, and, in the course of six winters, showed the doctors that they did not understand our constitution; for, in the coldest winters, our men were more healthy than those regiments who wore breeches and warm clothing."

In consequence of the treaty of peace between Great Britain and the several nations of Indians between the Apalachian mountains and the Lakes, in October, 1759, the British government was enabled to carry into effect those operations which had been projected against the French settlements in Canada, and the most important by far of these was the enterprise against Quebec. According to the plan fixed upon for the conquest of Canada, Major-general Wolfe, who had given promise of great military talents at Louisbourg, was to proceed up the river St. Lawrence and attack Quebec, whilst General Amherst, after reducing Ticonderoga and Crown Point, was to descend the St. Lawrence and co-operate with General Wolfe in the conquest of Quebec. Yet the force under General Wolfe did not exceed 7,000 effective men, whilst that under General Amherst amounted to more than twice that number; but the commander-in-chief seems to have calculated upon a junction with General Wolfe in sufficient time for the siege of Quebec. The forces under General Wolfe comprehended the following regiments,—15th, 28th, 35th, 43d, 47th, 48th, 58th, Fraser's Highlanders, the Rangers, and the grenadiers of Louisbourg.

The fleet, under the command of Admirals Saunders and Holmes, with the transports, proceeded up the St. Lawrence, and reached the island of Orleans, a little below Quebec, in the end of June, where the troops were disembarked without opposition. The Marquis de Montcalm, who commanded the French troops, which were greatly superior in number to the invaders, resolved rather to depend upon the natural strength of his position than his numbers, and took his measures accordingly. The city of Quebec was tolerably well fortified, defended by a numerous garrison, and abundantly supplied with provisions and ammunition. This able and hitherto fortunate leader had reinforced the troops of the colony with five regular battalions, formed of the best of the inhabitants; and he had, besides, completely disciplined all the Canadians of the neighbourhood capable of bearing arms, and several tribes of Indians. He had posted his army on a piece of ground along the shore of Beaufort, from the river St. Charles to the falls of Montmorency,—a position rendered strong by precipices, woods, and rivers, and defended by intrenchments where the ground appeared the weakest. To undertake the siege of Quebec under the disadvantages which presented themselves, seemed a rash enterprise; but, although General Wolfe was completely aware of these difficulties, a thirst for glory, and the workings of a vigorous mind, which set every obstacle at defiance, impelled him to make the hazardous attempt. His maxim was, that a "brave and victorious army finds no difficulties;" and he was anxious to verify the truth of the adage in the present instance.

Having ascertained that, to reduce the place, it was necessary to erect batteries on the north of the St. Lawrence, the British general endeavoured, by a series of manœuvres, to draw Montcalm from his position; but the French commander was too prudent to risk a battle. With the view of attacking the enemy's intrenchments, General Wolfe sent a small armament up the river above the city; and, having personally surveyed the banks on the side of the enemy from one of the ships, he resolved to cross the river Montmorency and make the attack. He therefore ordered six companies of grenadiers and part of the Royal Americans to cross the river and land near the mouth of the Montmorency, and at the same time directed the two brigades commanded by Generals Murray and Townshend to pass a ford higher up. Close to the

Y

water's edge tnere was a detached redoubt, which the grenadiers were ordered to attack, in the expectation that the enemy would descend from the hill in its defence, and thus bring on a general engagement. At all events, the possession of this post was of importance, as from it the British commander could obtain a better view of the enemy's intrenchments than he had yet been able to accomplish. The grenadiers and Royal Americans were the first who landed. They had received orders to form in four distinct bodies, but not to begin the attack till the first brigade should have passed the ford, and be near enough to support them. No attention, however, was paid to these instructions. Before even the first brigade had crossed, the grenadiers, before they were regularly formed, rushed forward with impetuosity and considerable confusion to attack the enemy's intrenchments. They were received with a well-directed fire, which effectually checked them and threw them into disorder. They endeavoured to form under the redoubt, but being unable to rally, they retreated and formed behind the first brigade, which had by this time landed, and was drawn up on the beach in good order. The plan of attack being thus totally disconcerted, General Wolfe repassed the river and returned to the isle of Orleans. In this unfortunate attempt the British lost 543 of all ranks killed, wounded, and missing. Of the Highlanders, up to the second of September, the loss was 18 rank and file killed, and 6 officers, and 85 rank and file wounded. In the general orders which were issued the following morning, General Wolfe complained bitterly of the conduct of the grenadiers: " The check which the grenadiers met with yesterday will, it is hoped, be a lesson to them for the time to come. Such impetuous, irregular, and unsoldierlike proceedings, destroy all order, make it impossible for the commanders to form any disposition for attack, and put it out of the general's power to execute his plan. The grenadiers could not suppose that they alone could beat the

French army; and therefore it was necessary that the corps under Brigadiers Monckton and Townshend should have time to join, that the attack might be general. The very first fire of the enemy was sufficient to repulse men who had lost all sense of order and military discipline. Amherst's and the Highlanders alone, by the soldier-like and cool manner they were formed in, would undoubtedly have beaten back the whole Canadian army if they had ventured to attack them."

General Wolfe now changed his plan of operations. Leaving his position at Montmorency, he re-embarked his troops and artillery, and landed at Point Levi, whence he passed up the river in transports; but finding no opportunity of annoying the enemy above the town, he resolved to convey his troops farther down, in boats, and land them by night within a league of Cape Diamond, with a view of ascending the heights of Abraham,—which rise abruptly, with steep ascent, from the banks of the river,—and thus gain possession of the ground on the back of the city, where the fortifications were less strong. A plan more replete with dangers and difficulties could scarcely have been devised; but, from the advanced period of the season, it was necessary either to abandon the enterprise altogether, or to make an attempt upon the city, whatever might be the result. The troops, notwithstanding the recent disaster, were in high spirits, and ready to follow their general wherever he might lead them. The commander, on the other hand, though afflicted with a severe dysentery and fever, which had debilitated his frame, resolved to avail himself of the readiness of his men, and to conduct the hazardous enterprise in which they were about to engage in person.

In order to deceive the enemy, Admiral Holmes was directed to move farther up the river on the 12th of September, but to sail down in the night time, so as to protect the landing of the forces. These orders were punctually obeyed.

About an hour after midnight of the same day four regiments, the light infantry, with the Highlanders and grenadiers, were embarked in flat-bottomed boats, under the command of Brigadiers Monckton and Murray. They were accompanied by General Wolfe, who was among the first that landed. The boats fell down with the tide, keeping close to the north shore in the best order; but, owing to the rapidity of the current, and the darkness of the night, most of the boats landed a little below the intended place of disembarkation. " The French," says Smollett, "had posted sentries along shore to challenge boats and vessels, and give the alarm occasionally. The first boat that contained the English troops being questioned accordingly, a captain of Fraser's regiment, who had served in Holland, and who was perfectly well acquainted with the French language and customs, answered without hesitation to *Qui vive?*—which is their challenging word,—*la France;* nor was he at a loss to answer the second question, which was much more particular and difficult. When the sentinel demanded, *a quel regiment?* the captain replied, *de la reine*, which he knew, by accident, to be one of those that composed the body commanded by Bougainville. The soldier took it for granted this was the expected convoy, (a convoy of provisions expected that night for the garrison of Quebec,) and, saying *passe*, allowed all the boats to proceed without further question. In the same manner the other sentries were deceived; though one, more wary than the rest, came running down to the water's edge, and called, *Pour quoi est ce qui vous ne parlez pas haut?* ' Why don't you speak with an audible voice?' To this interrogation, which implied doubt, the captain answered with admirable presence of mind, in a soft tone of voice, *Tai tois nous serens entendues!* ' Hush! we shall be overheard and discovered.' Thus cautioned, the sentry retired without farther altercation.'

When the troops were landed, the boats were sent back

for the other division of the troops, which was under the command of Brigadier-general Townshend. The ascent to the heights was by a narrow path, that slanted up the precipice from the landing-place: this path the enemy had broken up, and rendered almost impassable, by cross ditches, and they had made an intrenchment at the top of the hill. Notwithstanding these difficulties, Colonel Howe, who was the first to land, ascended the woody precipices, with the light infantry and the Highlanders, and dislodged a captain's guard which defended the narrow path. They then mounted without further molestation; and General Wolfe, who was among the first to gain the summit of the hill, formed the troops on the heights as they arrived. In the ascent the precipice was found to be so steep and dangerous, that the troops were obliged to climb up the rugged projections of the rocks, and, by aid of the branches of the trees and shrubs growing on both sides of the path, to pull themselves up. Though much time was thus necessarily occupied in the ascent, yet such was the perseverance of the troops, that they all gained the summit in time to enable the general to form in order of battle before day-break.

M. de Montcalm had now no way left of saving Quebec but by risking a battle, and he therefore determined to leave his stronghold and meet the British in the open field. Leaving his camp at Montmorency, he crossed the river St Charles, and, forming his line with great skill, advanced forward to attack his opponents. His right was composed of half the provincial troops, two battalions of regulars, and a body of Canadians and Indians; his centre, of a column of two battalions of Europeans, with two field-pieces; and his left of one battalion of regulars, and the remainder of the colonial troops. In his front, among brushwood and corn-fields, fifteen hundred of his best marksmen were posted to gall the British as they approached. The British were drawn up in two lines: the first, consisting of the grenadiers,

15th, 28th, 35th Highlanders, and 58th; the 47th regiment formed the second line, or reserve. The left of the front line was covered by the light infantry; it appearing to be the intention of the French commander to out-flank the left of the British, Brigadier-general Townshend, with Amherst's regiment, which he formed *en potence*,—thus presenting a double front to the enemy.

The Canadians and the Indians, who were posted among the brushwood, kept up an irregular galling fire, which proved fatal to many officers, who, from their dress, were singled out by these marksmen. The fire of this body was, in some measure, checked by the advanced posts of the British, who returned the fire; and a small gun, which was dragged up by the seamen from the landing-place, was brought forward, and did considerable execution. The French now advanced to the charge with great spirit, firing as they advanced; but, in consequence of orders they received, the British troops reserved their fire till the main body of the enemy had approached within forty yards of their line. When the enemy had come within that distance, the whole British line poured in a general and destructive discharge of musketry. Another discharge followed, which had such an effect upon the enemy, that they stopped short, and after making an ineffectual attempt upon the left of the British line, they began to give way. At this time General Wolfe, who had received two wounds which he had concealed, was mortally wounded whilst advancing at the head of the grenadiers with fixed bayonets.

At this instant every separate corps of the British army exerted itself, as if the contest were for its own peculiar honour. Whilst the right pressed on with their bayonets, Brigadier-general Murray briskly advanced with the troops under his command, and soon broke the centre of the enemy, " when the Highlanders, taking to their broadswords, fell in among them with irresistible impetuosity, and

drove them back with great slaughter." The action on the
left of the British was not so warm. A smart contest, however, took place between part of the enemy's right and some
light infantry, who had thrown themselves into houses,
which they defended with great courage. During this attack, Colonel Howe, who had taken post with two companies behind a copse, frequently sallied out on the flanks of
the enemy, whilst General Townshend advanced in platoons
against their front. Observing the left and centre of the
French giving way, this officer, on whom the command had
just devolved in consequence of General Monckton, the
second in command, having been dangerously wounded,
hastened to the centre, and finding that the troops had got
into disorder in the pursuit, formed them again in line. At
this moment, Monsieur de Bougainville, who had marched
from Cape Rouge as soon as he heard that the British troops
had gained the heights, appeared in their rear at the head of
2,000 fresh men. General Townshend immediately ordered
two regiments, with two pieces of artillery, to advance against
this body; but Bougainville retired on their approach. The
wreck of the French army retreated to Quebec and Point
Levi.

The loss sustained by the enemy was considerable. About
1,000 of them were made prisoners, including a number of
officers, and about 500 died on the field of battle. The
death of their brave commander, Montcalm, who was mortally wounded almost at the same instant with General
Wolfe, was a serious calamity to the French arms. When
informed that his wound was mortal,—" So much the better,"
said he, " I shall not live to see the surrender of Quebec."
Before his death he wrote a letter to General Townshend,
recommending the prisoners to the generous humanity of the
British. The death of the two commanders-in-chief, and the
disasters which befel Generals Monckton and Severergues,
the two seconds in command, who were respectively carried

wounded from the field, are remarkable circumstances in the events of this day. This important victory was not gained without considerable loss on the part of the British, who, besides the commander-in-chief, had 8 officers and 48 men killed; and 43 officers and 435 men wounded. The death of General Wolfe was a national loss. "He inherited from nature an animating fervour of sentiment, an intuitive perception, and extensive capacity, and a passion for glory, which stimulated him to acquire every species of military knowledge that study could comprehend, that actual service could illustrate and confirm. Brave above all estimation of danger, he was also generous, gentle, complacent, and humane; —the pattern of the officer, the darling of the soldier. There was a sublimity in his genius which soared above the pitch of ordinary minds; and had his faculties been exercised to their full extent by opportunity and action, had his judgment been fully matured by age and experience, he would, without doubt, have rivalled in reputation the most celebrated captains of antiquity." When the final ball pierced the breast of the young hero, he found himself unable to stand, and leaned upon the shoulder of a lieutenant who sat down on the ground. This officer, observing the French give way, exclaimed,—"They run! they run!" "Who run?" inquired the gallant Wolfe with great earnestness. When told that it was the French that were flying: "What," said he, "do the cowards run already? Then I die happy!" and instantly expired.

On the 18th of September the town surrendered, and a great part of the circumjacent country being reduced, General Townshend embarked for England, leaving a garrison of 5,000 effective men in Quebec, under the Hon. General James Murray. Apprehensive of a visit from a considerable French army stationed in Montreal and the neighbouring country, General Murray repaired the fortifications, and put the town in a proper posture of defence; but his troops suffered so much from the rigours of winter, and the want of vegetables and fresh provisions, that, before the end of April, the garrison was reduced, by death and disease, to about 3,000 effective men. Such was the situation of affairs when the general received certain intelligence that General de Levi, who succeeded the Marquis de Montcalm, had reached Point au Tremble with a force of 10,000 French and Canadians, and 500 Indians. It was the intention of the French commander to cut off the posts which the British had established; but General Murray defeated this scheme, by ordering the bridges over the river Rouge to be broken down, and the landing places at Sylleri and Foulon to be secured. Next day, the 27th of April, he marched in person with a strong detachment and two field-pieces, and took possession of an advantageous position, which he retained till the afternoon, when the outposts were withdrawn, after which he returned to Quebec with very little loss, although the enemy pressed closely on his rear.

General Murray was now reduced to the necessity of withstanding a siege, or risking a battle. He chose the latter alternative, a resolution which was deemed by some military men as savouring more of youthful impatience and overstrained courage, than of judgment; but the dangers with which he was beset, in the midst of a hostile population, and the difficulties incident to a protracted siege, seem to afford some justification for that step. In pursuance of his resolution, the general marched out on the 28th of April, at half-past six o'clock in the morning, and formed his little army on the heights of Abraham. The right wing, commanded by Colonel Burton, consisted of the 15th, 48th, 58th, and second battalion of the 60th, or Royal Americans: the left under Colonel Simon Fraser, was formed of the 43d, 47th Welsh fusileers, and the Highlanders. The 35th, and the third battalion of the 60th, constituted the reserve. The right was covered by Major Dalling's corps of light infantry; and the left by Captain Huzzen's company of rangers, and 100 volunteers, under the command of Captain Macdonald of Fraser's regiment.

Observing the enemy in full march in one column, General Murray advanced quickly forward to meet them before they should form their line. His light infantry coming in contact with Levi's advance, drove them back on their main body; but pursuing too far, they were furiously attacked and repulsed in their turn. They fell back in such disorder on the line, as to impede their fire, and in passing round by the right flank to the rear, they suffered much from the fire of a party who were endeavouring to turn that flank. The enemy having made two desperate attempts to penetrate the right wing, the 35th regiment was called up from the reserve, to its support. Meanwhile the British left was struggling with the enemy, who succeeded so far, from their superior numbers, in their attempt to turn that flank, that they obtained possession of two redoubts, but were driven out from both by the Highlanders, sword in hand. By pushing forward fresh numbers, however, the enemy at last succeeded in forcing the left wing to retire, the right giving way about the same time. The French did not attempt to pursue, but allowed the British to retire quietly within the walls of the city, and to carry away their wounded. The British had six officers, and 250 rank and file killed; and 82 officers, and 679 non-commissioned officers and privates, wounded. The enemy lost twice the number of men.

Shortly after the British had retired, General Levi moved forward on Quebec, and having taken up a position close to it, opened a fire at five o'clock. He then proceeded to besiege the city in form, and General Murray made the necessary dispositions to defend the place. The siege was continued till the 10th of May, when it was suddenly raised; the enemy retreating with great precipitation, leaving all their artillery implements and stores behind. This unexpected event was occasioned by the destruction or capture of all the enemy's ships above Quebec, by an English squadron which had arrived in the river, and the advance of General Amherst on Montreal. General Murray left Quebec in pursuit of the enemy, but was unable to overtake them, and he afterwards joined General Amherst, in the neighbourhood of Montreal, and acted a conspicuous part in the capture of that last stronghold of the French in Canada.

Fraser's Highlanders were not called again into active service till the summer of 1762, when they were, on the expedition under Colonel William Amherst, sent to retake St. John's, Newfoundland. In this service Captain Macdonell of Fraser's regiment, was mortally wounded, three rank and file killed, and seven wounded.

At the conclusion of the war, a number of the officers and men having expressed a desire to settle in North America, had their wishes granted and an allowance of land given them. The rest returned to Scotland, and were discharged. When the war of the American revolution broke out, upwards of 300 of those men who had remained in the country, enlisted in the 84th regiment, in 1775, and formed part of two fine battalions embodied under the name of the Royal Highland Emigrants.

THE LIFE AND DEATH OF SIR WILLIAM WALLACE.

Sir William Wallace of Elderslie, the champion and guardian of Scotland amid the invasions and oppressions of the English which preceded the accession and victories of Robert Bruce, is the best known and most famous of all the Scotish patriots of the olden time.

> " At Wallace' name what Scotish blood
> But boils up in a spring-tide flood!

Aft have our fearless fathers strode
    By Wallace' side,
Still pressing onward red-wat-shod
    Or glorious died."

His history is known through tradition to almost every Scotsman; and, though scanty and doubtful on the pages of record, contributes more numerous and more stirring incidents to the old world stories of our Lowland peasantry than that of any man who figures at full length and in gayest attire in the works of our most authentic historians. Wallace's name has been a household word in every age from his own to ours; and such torrents of mighty matter has he sent down the channels of tradition, and so scanty sprinklings given to the neat, trim, formal surfaces of regular history, that his very existence looks at times as if it had been all poetry and romance. Most of the exploits popularly ascribed to him belong far more to the marvellous than the real, and very many are manifestly either fictions or enormous exaggerations; yet all have a powerful charm for the national mind, partly on account of their very wildness, but much more on account of their flattering the Scotish pride, and breathing a romantic bravery against the English. The Wallace of tradition, in fact, is a gorgeous compound of reality and fiction, of passions and imaginings, addressed to the prejudices of our country,—an impersonation of the ancient national animosities and prowess and patriotism of the Scotish people, in the times of their severest struggles for independence; and the sympathies of all classes with this gorgeous phantasy closely resemble those of all old nations with the bardic heroes and mythic achievements of the most primitive times. The real Wallace is, in comparison, a very sober personage, of neither very many nor very great exploits; and an outline of his history can be sketched in small space, and possesses interest not more on its own account than for the sake of exposing the prurience of the national day-dream.

Wallace's public career lasted only eight years, — from 1297 till 1305; it commenced in the year following England's usurpation of the Scotish throne, and was all spent in struggles against the English power; and it was aided throughout by general anarchy, by popular contempt of government, and by a dislocated and weltering condition of society. Bands of robbers infested the highways; assassins stalked about in the guise of gentlemen; life and property were as insecure as among savages; and gangs of desperadoes or bands of armed patriots were perfectly competent to baffle the small bodies of military by which the English usurper endeavoured to maintain his abhorred and feeble authority.

Wallace was the younger son of a gentleman in the neighbourhood of Paisley. He was strong, courageous, and active, calm, intrepid, and indomitable, adventurous, firm, and warlike, fond of skirmishes and inventive of stratagems; and he behaved so frankly and courteously to his friends and so sternly and relentlessly to his foes, that he readily won and easily maintained the entire confidence of the companions of his exploits. Yet he began his public life as an outlaw, —most probably for killing an Englishman; he associated with himself from the very first some persons of desperate character; and he probably was actuated all along, as much by the necessity of his circumstances and by revenge and wrath against the English, as by any true patriotism or very enlightened regard to the best interests of his country.

In May 1297, Wallace, at the head of a resolute band, commenced a guerillo war against the English; and he soon agitated their garrisons, impoverished their stores, drew many partisans to his standard, and made himself a general talk and terror. Sir William Douglas and some other persons of rank and influence joined him or followed his example; and the Scots first struck a good blow at the root of the usurper's government at Scone, and then roved over the country, assaulted fortalices, and slew all Englishmen who came within their power. A strong force, with many barons among them, took post near Irvine, and there defied an approaching English army; but they disagreed among themselves, and fell into dissensions, and would neither fight the English nor break up their encampment nor treat by common consent; and eventually most of their leaders, influenced variously by disgust and policy and fear, opened negociations with the enemy and made submission to his authority. Wallace scorned this poltroonery; and, collecting a few of the most resolute or desperate in the camp, he retired with them indignantly, and marched away to the north. In the first heat of resentment, he flew to the house of the Bishop of Glasgow, one of the principal negociators, and pillaged it, and led its inmates captive; and he afterwards overran the middle districts of Scotland, and drew together there as many followers as made a considerable army, and laid siege to the castle of Dundee.

At this juncture, Wallace received intelligence that an English army was advancing to Stirling; and, charging the citizens of Dundee, under pain of death, to continue the blockade of their castle, he set promptly out with all his troops to guard the passage of the Forth, and encamped behind a rising ground near the abbey of Cambuskenneth. Warenne, Earl of Surrey, and Cressingham, the high treasurer of Scotland, commanded the English army; and the former was averse to risk a general action, and imagined that Wallace might be induced by fair conditions to surrender, and sent two friars to him to offer terms. " Return," said Wallace, " and tell your masters that we came hither, not to treat with them, but to assert our right, and to set Scotland free. Let them advance; we send them defiance." The English were enraged at this answer and craved impatiently to be led on to battle. Sir Richard Lundin, a renegade Scotish baron, who had been conspicuous among the negociators at Irvine, and who now held a high place in the English army, explained how foolish it would be to make the whole force defile by the long narrow wooden bridge of Stirling in presence of the Scots, and showed them that they would probably be attacked and overwhelmed before they could form on the plain at the other end, and offered to conduct five hundred horse and a select body of infantry across a ford which he knew, and to go round with them upon the rear of the Scots, and make such a diversion as should afford time and scope for the efficient movements of the main body. Warrenne himself also was still averse to fight, and did all he could to curb his people's impetuosity. But Cressingham, who was an ecclesiastic and fiery and headstrong, exclaimed, " Why do we thus protract the war, and waste the king's treasures? Let us fight, as is our bounden duty." And he was so well seconded by the impetuous feeling of the army that he prevailed over Warenne, and the wiser counsellors; and he himself led the van to battle. As soon as the foremost of them debouched from the bridge, Wallace rushed down upon them with overwhelming fury; and put an instant extinguisher upon all their hopes of even forming an array. Those who had crossed were either slain or driven back into the river; those who were crossing either trampled one another down in confusion, or were precipitated into the water, some by accident and others in an effort to save themselves by swimming; and those who had not begun to cross set fire to the bridge, and abandoned all their baggage, and took to their heels with the utmost hurry and speed of flight. The wretched Cressingham and many thousands of the English perished; and the survivors went off in a general rout, and did not stop till they reached the Tweed. The Scots lost very few of their number, and speedily found themselves masters, not only of the battle-field and its spoils, but of all the military strengths of the kingdom.

Wallace and his whole army—partly perhaps in the spirit of retaliation and foray, but mainly under the pressure of a great famine which afflicted Scotland, the consequence of warlike disorders and unproductive harvests—marched into the north of England, and spread reprisals and desolation through all the champaign tracts between Newcastle and Carlisle. But spoliage rose into rapacity, license into oppression, and revenge into truculency; and so wild became the indecencies and outrages that Wallace struggled in vain to repress them, and felt obliged in self-defence speedily to draw his army back to Scotland. He was now supreme and dominant in the kingdom; and assumed the title—whether spontaneously or by some public request is not known—of Guardian of Scotland; but, through either envy or jealousy or fear or timid policy, he about the same time lost the confidence of many of the nobility; so that, at the very juncture of the practical restoration of national independence, the great powers of the kingdom became divided, and began to lay the country once more open to the insults and inflictions of the English arms. In the next year occurred the disastrous battle of Falkirk; but this, together with some special incidents which are alleged to have followed it, has already been fully narrated on pp. 299—316 of the second volume of these historiettes. Some previous exploits of Wallace also are noticed in the article " Conflicts in Glasgow" in the first volume, and in the articles " Troubles of Carrick" and " Barns of Ayr" in the present volume.

A short time after the battle of Falkirk, Wallace renounced the title of Guardian of Scotland, and passed into the condition of a private man; and never again does he appear to have had any command in his country's armies or any place in her public councils. Yet he devoted himself as resolutely

LIFE AND DEATH OF WALLACE.

as ever to her interests, and did many a thing to promote them in his capacity of a captain of guerillos. And, in 1303, when the Scotish functionaries and military leaders made their ignominious surrender to the English King at Stirling bridge, a stipulation was made by the latter that "as for William Wallace he shall render himself up at the will and mercy of our Sovereign Lord the King, if it shall seem good to him." Wallace, however, scorned the whole transaction, and despaired not yet of liberating Scotland, and resolved rather to court death in freedom than accept life in bondage; and when at last he perceived all hope extinct, he sought out a place of concealment, where he might elude Edward's vengeance, and mourn in silence over his prostrate country. But Edward could not think Scotland subdued so long as Wallace lived; and with a mean anxiety, he sought to discover his retreat, and offered high rewards to any man who should find and take him. The story of the great hero's capture and trial and execution forms one of the most thrilling chapters in the whole cyclopedia of historic tragedy; and is well told as follows, by Mr. John D. Carrick, in his Life of Sir William Wallace :—

"Wallace, who, as he conceived, among other friends, had secured the co-operation of Sir John Menteith to the measures then in agitation, for the purpose, it is supposed, of giving as early notice as possible of the arrival of Bruce, had retained near his person a young man related to Menteith, who was to have been dispatched with the news to Dumbarton as soon as their future monarch should arrive, when that important fortress was to have declared in his favour. Confiding in the arrangements thus made, Wallace, as the time appointed by Bruce drew near, collected his followers round Glasgow, and disposed of them in such a manner as to be able to bring them together on the shortest notice. For the better concealment of his design, he retired to a small lonely house at Robroyston, about three miles north-west of Glasgow; and here he waited with impatience for the night on which Bruce had appointed to meet him.

"On the night of the 5th of August 1305, Sir William, and his faithful friend Kerlé, accompanied by the youth before mentioned, had betaken themselves to their lonely retreat at Robroyston, to which place their steps had been watched by a spy, who as soon as he had observed them enter, returned to his employers. At the dead hour of midnight, while the two friends lay fast asleep, the youth, whose turn it was to watch, cautiously removed the bugle from the neck of Wallace, and conveyed it, along with his arms, through an aperture in the wall; then slowly opening the door, two men-at-arms silently entered, and, seizing upon Kerlé, hurried him from the apartment, and instantly put him to death. Wallace, awakened by the noise, started to his feet, and, missing his weapons, became sensible of his danger; but grasping a large piece of oak which had been used for a seat, he struck two of his assailants dead on the spot, and drove the rest headlong before him. Seeing the fury to which he was roused, and the difficulty they would have in taking him alive, Menteith now advanced to the aperture and represented to him the folly of resistance, as the English, he said, having heard of his place of resort, and of the plans he had in contemplation, were collected in too large a force to be withstood,—that if he would accompany him a prisoner to Dumbarton, he would undertake for the safety of his person,—that all the English wished, was to secure the peace of the country, and to be free from his molestation,—adding, that if he consented to go with him, he should live in his own house in the castle, and he, Menteith, alone should be his keeper,—that even now, he would willingly sacrifice his life in his defence, but that his attendants were too few, and too ill-appointed, to have any chance of success in contending with the English. He concluded by assuring Wallace, that he had followed in order to use his influence with his enemies on his behalf, and that they had listened to him on condition of an immediate surrender; but that if he did not instantly comply, the house would soon be in flames about him. These and other arguments were urged with all the seeming sincerity of friendship; and our patriot, confiding in early recollections, and the private understanding that subsisted between them, allowed himself to be conducted to Dumbarton Castle. On the morrow, however, no Menteith appeared to exert his influence, in order to prevent the unfortunate hero from being carried from the fortress; and strongly fettered, and guarded by a powerful escort, under the command of Robert de Clifford and Aymer de Vallance, he was hurried to the south, by the line of road least exposed to the chance of a rescue.

" As the capture of Wallace was an event wholly unexpected by the English, the news of it, which spread with the rapidity of lightning, produced in every part of the kingdom a deep and universal sensation. Labour of every kind was abandoned, and people of all ranks flocked to those points of the road where it was expected the illustrious captive would pass. At Carlisle the escort halted for a night; and the tower in which he was secured long afterwards retained his name. As the *cortegé* approached London, the crowds became more numerous; and on entering the capital, his conductors found their progress retarded by the multitudes that were collected,—while every elevation or projection, however perilous, from which he could be seen, was occupied with, or clung to, by anxious spectators, eager to behold a man who had filled England with terror, and the fame of whose achievements had resounded through every country in Europe. After much exertion, the cavalcade at length reached the house of William Delect, a citizen in Fenchurch Street, where their prisoner was lodged for the night.

" The thirst for revenge existed too keenly in the ruthless mind of Edward, to admit of much delay in the sacrifice of his victim. Though consideration for the opinion of the more enlightened of his subjects, and the manner in which his conduct might be viewed at foreign courts, obliged him to have recourse at least to the formality of a trial, the indecent haste with which it was brought on made the mockery of judicial procedure but too apparent. The day after his arrival, he was conducted on horseback, from the house which his brief residence had made the scene of universal attraction, to take his trial in Westminster Hall. His progress from Fenchurch Street, according to Stowe, appears to have been a sort of procession. Lord John de Segrave, the fugitive of Roslin, acting as Grand Marshal of England, and armed cap-à-pè, rode on one side, while Geoffrey de Hartlepool, Recorder of London, equipped in a similar manner, rode on the other. The Mayor, Sheriffs, and Aldermen followed, attended by a number of official characters on horseback and on foot, arranged according to their respective grades.

"On reaching the spot where the solemn farce was to be performed, he was placed on the south bench of the great hall; and, in consequence of an absurd report, which had been circulated in England, of his having said that he deserved to wear a crown in that place,—a crown of laurel was put upon his head. The noble appearance of the man joined to his calm and unruffled demeanour, entirely disarmed the silly attempt at ridicule of its intended effect. Sir Peter Malory the King's Justice, then rose, and read the indictment, wherein the prisoner was charged with treason against the King of England, burning of towns, and slaying of the subjects of his Majesty. To the first of these counts Wallace answered, that, as he had never been the subject of the King of England, he owed him no allegiance, and consequently could be no traitor. As to the other offences he frankly admitted, that, in the discharge of his duty to his country, he had done all that was stated. On this admission, the following atrocious sentence was pronounced:—For treason, he was to be first dragged to the place of execution; for murder and robbery, he was to be then hung a certain time by the neck,—and, because he had burned abbeys and religious houses, he was to be taken down alive from the gibbet, his entrails torn out and burnt before him, his body to be quartered, and the parts afterwards to be disposed of as the clemency of Majesty might suggest.

" When the necessary preparations were made for carrying the sentence into execution, the late champion of Scotish independence was brought forth from the place where he had been kept in confinement, heavily ironed, and chained to a bench of oak. He was then placed on a hurdle, and, surrounded by a strong guard of soldiers, ignominiously dragged to the Elms in Smithfield. That self-possession and undaunted demeanour, which he evinced during the trial, appeared equally conspicuous on the scaffold. Looking round with undisturbed composure on the assembled multitude, he addressed himself to a person near him, and asked for a priest to whom he might make confession. This request on being made known to Edward, he is said to have sternly refused; and the rancorous old man forbad *any clergyman to retard the execution* for such a purpose. On hearing this signified command of his sovereign, Winchelsea, Archbishop of Canterbury, the same individual who so faithfully discharged his duty at Carlaverock, stepped boldly forward, and after earnestly remonstrating with Edward, declared his determination to officiate himself. When the ceremony usual on such occasions was finished, Wallace rose from his knees, and the Archbishop having taken leave of him, instantly departed for Westminster, thus declining to witness the sequel of an act so revolting to humanity and which he no doubt considered as fixing a deep stain on the character of his country.

" The spectacle which was now exhibited to the gaze of the inhabitants of the metropolis of England, was such as perhaps had never before been presented to the populace of any land. The last freeman of an ancient people, not less renowned for their bravery, than for their love of independence, stood a calm and unshrinking victim, ready to be immolated at the shrine of despotism. That powerful arm which had long contended for liberty was now to be unstrung beneath the knife of the executioner; and that heart, replete with every enobling virtue, which never quailed in the sternest hour of danger, was doomed to quiver in the purifying flames of martyrdom. During the pause which preceded the unhallowed operations, Wallace turned to Lord Clifford, and requested that a psalter, which had been taken from his person, might be returned. His desire being complied with, he asked a priest to hold it open before him. This book had been his constant companion from his early years, and was perhaps the gift of his mother or his uncle, the parson of Dunipace. After hanging for a certain time, the sufferer was taken down, while yet in an evident state of sensibility. He was then disembowelled; and the heart, wrung from its place, was committed to the flames in his presence. During the dreadful process, his eyes still continued to linger on the psalter, till, overpowered by his sufferings, he expired among their hands with all that passive heroism which may be supposed to belong to so elevated a character. The body was afterwards dismembered; the head fixed on London bridge, the right arm on the bridge of Newcastle-upon-Tyne, the left at Berwick, the right leg at Perth, and the left at Aberdeen. Thus fell this great and exemplary patriot, a martyr to the rights and independence of his country, than whom, if we consider his extraordinary personal and mental endowments, joined to his inextinguishable and disinterested love of liberty, a greater hero is not to be found in the annals of any people."

How intensely symphonious with this story of pathos and horror is the following dirge from the pen of the poet Campbell! And though it is well known to all Campbell's admirers and to many general readers of poetry, yet as it is not included in some editions of his works, and must be still a novelty to multitudes of young persons, we may transcribe it in full.

" They lighted a taper, at the dead of night,
    And chaunted their holiest hymn;
But her brow and her bosom were damp with affright,
    Her eye was all sleepless and dim!
And the lady of Elderslie wept for her lord,
    When a death-watch beat in her lonely room,
When her curtain had shook of its own accord,
And the raven had flapped at her window board,
    To tell of her warrior's doom!

' Now sing you the death-song, and loudly pray
    For the soul of my knight so dear,
And call me a widow this wretched day,
    Since the warning of God is here!
For night-mare rides on my strangled sleep;
    The lord of my bosom is doomed to die;
His valorous heart they have wounded deep,
And the blood-red tears shall his country weep
    For Wallace of Elderslie!'

Yet knew not his country that ominous hour
    Ere the loud matin-bell was rung,
That a trumpet of death, on an English tower,
    Had the dirge of her champion sung!
When his dungeon light looked dim and red
    On the high born blood of a martyr slain;
No anthem was sung at his holy death bed,
No weeping there was where his bosom bled,
    And his heart was rent in twain.

>   Oh! it was not thus when his oaken spear
>   Was true to that knight forlorn;
>   And hosts of a thousand were scattered like deer
>   At the blast of the hunter's horn;
>   When he strode on the wreck of each well fought field,
>   With the yellow-haired chiefs of his native land,
>   For his lance was not shivered on helmet or shield,
>   And the sword that seemed fit for archangel to wield,
>   Was light in his terrible hand!
>
>   Yet bleeding and bound, though her Wallace wight
>   For his long-loved country die,
>   The bugle ne'er sung to a braver knight
>   Then Wallace of Elderslie.
>   But the day of his glory shall never depart,—
>   His head unentombed shall with glory be balmed,—
>   From his blood-streaming altar his spirit shall start;—
>   Though the raven has fed on his mouldering heart,
>   A nobler was never embalmed!"

THE EARLY CHRISTIANS OF BRITAIN.

Not a few writers have contended that Christianity was introduced to Britain by one of Christ's earliest ministers. Some, on a show of mere monkish testimony, so poor that even Baronius, the Roman Catholic annalist, condemns it, claim Peter as the father of the British churches. Others, on evidence quite as slender, lay claim to Aristobulus, whom Paul mentions in his epistle to the Romans. A third party —favoured by the positive testimony of the early monkish historian, William of Malmsbury, and overlooking a crowd of monstrous legends with which his tale is surrounded—lay claim to Joseph of Arimathea. But the boldest, as well as the least visionary, and at the same time the most numerous are a class who clamour for the apostle Paul. If any at all of the first ministers of Christ introduced the gospel to our country, Paul certainly appears to have been the man. Theodoret, who wrote about the year 440, says, " Our fishermen, publicans, and *tentmakers*, persuaded not only the Romans and their subjects, but also the Scythians, Indians, Persians, Hyrcanians, *Britons*, Cimmerians, and Germans to embrace the religion of the crucified Saviour;" and he is supposed to indicate Paul by the word "tentmakers," and to connect it particularly with the nations of the west,—especially as he speaks directly of Paul in some kindred passages, and seems there to insinuate that he preached in Spain and in Britain. Clement of Rome, Eusebius, and Jerome write to the same purpose; though with equal confusedness and indecision. What they say would be perfectly conclusive, if it were clear, distinct, unhesitating, and free from ambiguity; but it is so general, so misty, so like the utterance of a faultering witness, as to seem rather the offspring of idle conjecture or credulous hearsay—faults remarkably prominent in the early historians—than the easy statement of authenticated facts. Paul, for all we know, may, or he may not, have preached the gospel in Britain. Just enough of evidence exists on the subject to deter a candid man from arriving at any firm opinion on the one side of it or on the other, and to fix the attention of all wise inquirers, not on the instrument by whom the churches of this country were founded, but on the exalted principles which gave them existence.

Doubt as to who was the first Christian minister in Britain, gives rise to doubt as to when Christianity was introduced. The precise date is uncertain; yet, by a strong concurrence of probable evidence—including such as is perfectly conflicting on the other point—it seems to be lodged somewhere before the commencement of the second century. Gildas, the most ancient British historian, who wrote about the year 560, was of course too late to speak on the authority of even a tolerable tradition; but he had access to whatever opinions were afloat in his day, and, as if stating what none of his contemporaries called in question, he says, " Christ afforded the knowledge of his precepts to this island, as we know, about the end of the reign of Tiberius Cæsar, at which time his religion was propagated (in the Roman empire) without any hinderance." The south-east parts of Britain were formed into a Roman province in the year 43; the west-riding of Yorkshire soon after became the seat of a Roman colony; and London and St. Albans had for years before been large free cities, crowded with Roman citizens. A constant intercourse with the capital, and with all the most stirring scenes of the empire, was the result,—many Romans travelling into Britain to occupy civil and military posts, and not a few of our countrymen passing into Italy or the east to transact secular affairs. In such a state of things —especially as Christianity had made so great progress at the seat of government as to draw the particular notice of the state—there existed as much both of facility and attraction to bring the Gospel to Britain, as had already proved effectual to introduce it to several remote countries of the east. The wife of Plautius, the first governor of the British Roman province, appears to have been a Christian, tried, steadfast, and persevering; and if she held much influence in her husband's court, she may have been instrumental, between the years 43 and 47, of diffusing around her some knowledge of Christianity. From that time till a considerable period onward, Britain enjoyed great tranquillity, and, being favoured with a succession of mild and tolerant governors, offered an inviting shelter to the victims of persecution on the continent. During the days of Nero, in particular, when vast multitudes of Christians in Italy fled from the tremendous proscriptions which were mowing down their brethren by thousands, Britain could hardly fail to be regarded by some of the persecuted preachers of the cross, as both a providential asylum, and a delightfully opportune sphere of labour.

Other circumstances, independent of those glanced at, render it highly probable that this country enjoyed very early the light of the gospel. Evidence of a positive nature, however, or such as does not more or less admit of objection, cannot be made to bear upon any period within so wide a range as even to the close of the second century. Perhaps the most unexceptionable testimony is the celebrated one of Tertullian, written A. D. 209, which has been construed to refer to both Scotland and Wales, if not even to Ireland:— " Those parts of Britain into which the Roman arms never penetrated have yielded subjection to Christ." But even this —especially when viewed in connexion with the drift of the passage in which it occurs—might have been intended rather to describe the diffusiveness of Christianity, that property of it which, whether its disciples be few or many, disperses them far and near, than to assert the public introduction or the general profession of it among the British people. That there were some Christians in this country at the commencement of the third century, is certain; but that, at any period previous to that epoch, they were numerous or constituted a considerable portion of the population, is at best only very probable. A story, which has been repeated by most of our historians, and which ascribes the origin of British churches to royal favour, and fixes the date of it about the year 164, is unworthy of credit. According to this story, Lucius a king of Britain, and the general body of his subjects, were converted to Christianity by missionaries deputed from the emperor and bishop of Rome. Three conflicting opinions, however, are maintained by different writers, as to the territory over which the supposed Lucius reigned, and upwards of a score of conflicting opinions as to the date of his and his subjects' alleged conversion. The story is manifestly a monkish legend At whatever period the gospel was introduced to this island, it appears, from all the credible evidence which can be collected, to have kindled with neither the rapid but genial light of an apostle's ministry, nor with the scorching unnatural blaze of magisterial propagation, but with the gradual dawning of its own sweet, soft, ordinary influence, emitting at first but a few far-refracted rays, and continuing, thenceforth, to "shine more and more unto the perfect day." "The kingdom of God" in Britain, though surely and comparatively soon established, "came not with observation."

Nothing beyond a few general facts is known respecting the internal condition of the British churches for a considerable period after they became numerous. They were free from doctrinal error, and enjoyed uninterrupted tranquillity. Their own peaceable behaviour, the mild character of their civil governors, the remote situation of their country, and the dissimilarity of its heathen superstitions to those of Rome, as well as the want of power on the part of its heathen priests, tended either to protect them from the persecutions, or to keep them unacquainted with the controversies, which afflicted other sections of the Christian community. They seem also to have withstood much better and greatly longer than the Italian or eastern churches, the inroads of corruption upon primitive purity and simplicity. Jerome and Chrysostom make frequent mention, even at the late and exceedingly corrupt period when these authors wrote, of the orthodoxy, the learning, the good order, and—what particularly deserves notice—the *indigence* of the British churches. The early Christians of our land had, of course, no ecclesiastical connection with the state, and differed nothing as to manners and discipline, from the eastern Christians of the first and second centuries; and even after they beheld their brethren throughout other parts of the empire aggrandized by state bounty, and allured or driven within the magic ring of Arian or carnalizing errors, they continued, for no inconsiderable season, to follow at once the worldly poverty and the evangelical doctrines of the primitive times.

The first irruption upon the public peace of the British churches was made by the Dioclesian persecution; and even this was gentle and of short continuance, compared to its ravages in other countries. The Dioclesian persecution—the most hostile, the most relentless, the most general, and the bloodiest which imperial Rome ever inflicted—broke out at the commencement of the fourth century, and visited every province subject to the Cæsars; but though it raged in most other places during the long period of ten years, and worked incredible havoc, it lasted in Britain during only two years, and was here comparatively mild. At its commencement, indeed, it assailed our fathers, as it did the Christians throughout the empire, with deadly cruelty. Alban, a native of the city of St. Albans, which now bears his name, and probably either a minister or a man otherwise eminent, was its earliest victim, surrendering his life rather than renounce or disgrace his faith, and reaping the honour of being the proto-martyr of England. Aaron and Julius, inhabitants of Caerleon in Monmouthshire, together with many Christians, both men and women, in other parts of the country, suffered death under the same visitation. The general body, however, of the ministers and eminent members of the British churches, sought shelter from the first burst of the storm in concealment, and soon were enabled to walk abroad in safety. Constantius Chlorus, the father of Constantine the Great, and a sharer in the imperial purple, was, at that time, governor of Britain; and though not an avowed disciple of Christianity, is supposed by some to have been secretly attached to it, and, at all events, showed a kind and partial feeling to its followers. He could not prevent the decree of persecution from taking effect in part; but, so far as comported with his official safety against the rage of the senior emperors, he appears to have counterworked it, allowing it to expend its commencing fury as much as possible upon the mere buildings of the Christians, and diverting it, as far as he could, from their persons and their writings. Emboldened by his mildness, they soon withdrew from their concealment, openly rebuilt their places of worship, and resumed, with joyful hearts, the observance of public ordinances.

One of the earliest important acts of Constantine the Great, after he had openly befriended the Christian cause, or rather had assumed to interfere in its ecclesiastical affairs, was to summon a council of pastors or bishops for settlement of the celebrated dispute in Africa which terminated in the Donatist schism. Three of the bishops who sat in that council—and the entire number was only thirty-three—were from Britain, Eborus of York, Adelfius of Lincoln, and Restitus of London. These men bore a large proportion to the entire body,—three compared to thirty-three, being much greater bulk than Britain, and especially England, possesses, compared to the vast territory which was then enlightened by Christianity, and subject to the Roman sway. If they represented, as possibly they did, the numerical proportion which the churches of their country bore to those of other lands, the gospel must, at the period when they lived, have risen to paramount influence among their countrymen, and must have had, in this island, a larger number of disciples than is usually supposed. Either the three bishops, and the body whom they represented, did not understand the drift of Constantine's policy, and afterwards regarded it with coolness and disapprobation, or, for some reason which one cannot easily conjecture, they were treated, in the convoking of the council of Arles, with a degree of consideration which was utterly lost sight of in the subsequent proceedings of both Constantine and his immediate successors. Never again, while the western empire lasted, do we find bishops or ministers of Britain, occupying such a place as those of Lincoln, York, and London did in the council of Arles; for, when future councils, general, western, or partial, councils consisting repeatedly of more than three hundred bishops, and sometimes succeeding one another at the distance of only a few months, were convoked—no matter in how great an emergency, no matter how professedly catholic in design, no matter how deeply affecting, in the questions to be debated by them, the whole Christian world—either the ministers and churches of Britain were entirely left out of the account, or they made so poor a figure as amounted to but a trifling fraction. If their unswerving orthodoxy be considered—that orthodoxy which continued to earn them eulogies even in the days of Jerome and Chrysostom,—they may well be conceived to have been no fit parties for a place in any of the numerous councils during the reign of the Arian emperor, Constantius. But what shall be said of their relation to the council of Nice,—a council held only eleven years after that of Arles, convoked, like the latter, by Constantine the Great, professing to be strictly "œcumenical," or universal, and consisting of more than three hundred bishops, besides a vast but unknown number of other members? Surely if Britain sent three representatives to the council of Arles, she ought, according to the common rules of arithmetic, to have sent at least thirty to the council of Nice; and yet, in the latter great council, she was utterly unrepresented! What may we infer from this fact? Many things, no doubt,—any of which, by a greater or less stretch of probability, *may* be true; but the most likely of them all, considering the *indigence* and the *orthodoxy* by which the British churches continued, for more than a century after, to be recognised—an indigence and an orthodoxy which distinguished them in the face of the corrupting opulence and the abounding errors which imperial patronage heaped on the churches of the continent—is that, after the celebration of the council of Arles, or during the proscriptions which soon followed against all the minor or dissenting sections of the orthodox Christians, they discovered the tendency of Constantine's policy, and resolved to stand aloof from his ecclesiastical proceedings. Even, however, if the British churches did act so discerning and so noble a part, they eventually ceased to maintain it; and—though at a distance of more than a century after the churches of Italy and the east—they became bitten with the mania for worldly respectability, and, as almost a necessary consequence, degenerated into a formal, time serving, superstitious, and monkish spirit.

THE FIGHTS AND FORAYS OF BRANXHOLM.

THE Castle of Branxholm is situated in the vale of the Teviot, about 3 miles above Hawick. It possesses great celebrity as the ancient seat of the ducal family of Buccleuch, as the central point of vast military strength in the roystering period of the border forays, as the key for ages to all the strong places in Teviotdale, and as a prominent locality and brilliant figurant in Scott's Lay of the Last Minstrel. It was long the scene of great baronial splendour, and it is classical alike in old balladry and in some of the finest modern songs and lyrics. The original pile—or rather that of the most sumptuous period—was burnt down in 1532 by the Earl of Northumberland, and blown up with gunpowder in 1570 during the invasion of the Earl of Surrey; and a successor to it was commenced in 1571 by its owner, Sir Walter Scott of Branxholm, and completed in 1574 by his widow. The present structure is very much smaller than the ancient one; and, with the exception of an old square tower of immense strength of masonry, it looks less like a castle than an old Scotish mansion-house. But its situation is strong and beautiful, and must evidently have invested it with mighty importance in the olden troublous times. The site is a bold bank, overhanging the river, surrounded by fine young thriving wood, and shut suddenly in by heights which give the vale for some distance the narrowness of a dell; and so abruptly does the place burst on the view of a traveller from either above or below that he would be perfectly charm-struck with it, even were it unaided by any historical association; and so sternly did the ancient castle overawe the gorge, and hold armed men in readiness to defend it, that any attempt of English marauders to pass through without subduing the garrison must have been absolutely hopeless.

In the reign of James I., one-half of the barony of Branxholm belonged to Sir Thomas Inglis; and this gentleman was a lover of peace, ill able to bear the excitements and conflicts and perils of the Border warfare; and, happening one day to meet Sir William Scott of Buccleuch, who was then proprietor of the estate of Murdiestone in Lanarkshire, he strongly expressed to him his disgust at being obliged to sleep every night in boots and shirt of mail, and to hold himself in constant readiness for action with English freebooters, and his envy of the quiet and security and continual ease which the lairds of Clydesdale enjoyed at a distance from the Border, and behind the ramparts of the Leadshill mountains. Scott loved rolicking and feud as much as Inglis hated them; and he abruptly answered, " What say you to an exchange of estates? I like that dry land of yours much better than this stretch of wet clay." " Are you serious?" replied Inglis. " If you be, take the dry land with all my heart, and let me have the clay." They made short work of the bargain; and Scott soon found himself laird of Branxholm, and significantly remarked as he got possession of it that the cattle of Cumberland were as good as those of Teviotdale.

Scott promptly gathered around him a strong body of hardy, active, resolute, unscrupulous, well-mounted retainers, and rode so often and vigorously at their head across the Border, and made such smart reprisals upon the English for any occasional injury they did him, that he soon and permanently made the balance of account between Cumberland

and Teviotdale very much in his own favour; and his successors, for several generations, rivalled his energy and closely followed his example,—so that they rendered all the country round them resonant with the clang of arms, and rich with well-defended or rapidly augmented flocks. In the reign of James II., the other half of the barony of Branxholm became their property; and from that time till the conditions of society were altered by the general pacification of the Borders, and by the desuetude of feudal broils and usages, Branxholm Castle was the constant residence of the Buccleuch family,— the scene of their baronial magnificence,—the court and centre of their martial pomp and quasi-princely state. How vividly does the great modern bard of their name and clan, the mighty magician of modern Scotland, depict their ancient Hall, and restore its every-day scenes of crowded greatness, in the following stanzas!—

" The feast was over in Branxholm tower,
And the lady had gone to her secret bower;
Her bower that was guarded by word and by spell
Deadly to hear, and deadly to tell—
Jesu Maria, shield us well!
No living wight, save the lady alone,
Had dared to cross the threshold stone.

The tables were drawn, it was idlesse all;
Knight and page, and household squire
Loitered through the lofty hall,
Or crowded round the ample fire;
The stag-hounds, weary with the chase,
Lay stretched upon the rushy floor,
And urged, in dreams, the forest race,
From Teviot stone to Eskdale-moor.

Battle History of Scotland.—*Page* 371.

Nine and twenty knights of fame
Hung their shields in Branxholm Hall;
Nine-and-twenty squires of name
Brought them their steeds to bower from stall;
    Nine-and-twenty yeomen tall
    Waited duteous, on them all;
    They were all knights of mettle true,
    Kinsmen to the bold Buccleuch.

Ten of them were sheathed in steel,
With belted sword, and spur on heel;
They quitted not their harness bright
Neither by day, nor yet by night;
    They lay down to rest
    With corselet laced,
Pillowed on buckler, cold and hard;
    They carved at the meal
    With gloves of steel
And they drank the red wine through the helmet barred.

Ten squires, ten yeomen, mail-clad men,
Waited the beck of the wardour's ten;
Thirty steeds, both fleet and wight,
Stood saddled in stable day and night,
Barbed with frontlet of steel, I trow,
And with Jedwood-axe at saddle-bow;
A hundred more fed free in stall;
Such was the custom of Branxholm Hall."

    The history of Branxholm fights and forays, if we had all due materials for it and could patiently use them, might be run out to volumes; and, even with such materials as we possess, could be woven into a huge portion of the almost endless tales of the Borders. But there is much sameness in it; and a long ballad, entitled "Jamie Telfer of the Fair

Dodhead," and given by Sir Walter Scott in his Border Minstrelsy, may be quoted as a fascinating substitute for the whole, exhibiting all its spirit, some of the most striking of its main characters, and a sufficient specimen of its most ordinary incidents; and though very long, it will amply atone for the space it occupies by affording "the truest possible picture of the eternal turmoil that prevailed in those times," for "it is very characteristic of the manners of the times, and perfectly shows how the weak and small were compelled to hang for protection on the great and powerful,"—and "the anxiety with which each respective baron asks the question, 'Whae's this brings the fraye to me?' proves how formidable they were in the habit of considering what the consequences of the 'fraye' were likely to be, and of course accounting for their unwillingness too rashly to involve themselves in them.'

> " It fell about the Martinmas tyde,
>   When our border steads get corn and hay;
> The Captain of Bewcastle hath bound him to ryde,
>   And he's ower to Teviotdale to drive a prey.
>
> The first ae guide that they met wi',
>   It was high up in Hardhaughswire,
> The second guide that they met wi'
>   It was laigh down in Borthwick Water.
>
> ' What tidings, what tidings, my trusty guide?'
>   ' Nae tidings, nae tidings, I hae to thee,
> But gin ye'll gae to the fair Dodhead,
>   Mony a cow's calf I let thee see.
>
> And when they came to the fair Dodhead,
>   Right hastily they clamb the Peel;
> He loosed the ky out ane and a',
>   And ranshakled the house right weel.

Now Jamie Telfer's heart was sair,
   The tear ay rowing in his e'e;
He pled with the Captain to ha'e his geer,
   Or else revenged he wad be.

The Captain turned him round and leugh;
   Said, 'Man there's naething in thy house
But ae auld sword, without a sheath,
   That hardly now would fell a mouse.'

The sun was nae up, but the moon was down,
   It was the gryming of a new fa'en snaw';
Jamie Telfer has run ten miles afoot,
   Between the Dodhead and the Stob's Ha',

And when he cam' to the fair tower gate,
   He shouted loud and cried weel he,
Till out bespak' auld Gibby Elliot—
   'Whae's this that brings the fraye to me?'

'It's I, Jamie Telfer, o' the fair Dodhead,
   And a harried man I think I be;
There's naething left at the fair Dodhead
   But a waefu' wife and bairnies three.'

'Gae seek your succour at Branksome Ha';
   For succour ye'se get nane frae me;
Gae seek your succour where ye paid black mail,
   For, man, ye ne'er paid money to me.'

Jamie has turned him round about—
   I wat the tear blinded his e'e;
'I'll ne'er pay mail to Elliot again,
   And the fair Dodhead I'll never see.

My hounds may a' rin masterless,
　　My hawks may fly from tree to tree,
My lord may grip my vassal lands,
　　For there again maun I never be.'

He has turned him to the Teviot side,
　　E'en as fast as he could drie,
Till he cam' to the Coultart cleugh,
　　And there he shouted baith loud and hie.

Then up bespak' him auld Jock Grieve—
　　' Whae's this that brings the fraye to me?'
' It's I, Jamie Telfer, o' the fair Dodhead,
　　A harried man, I trow, I be.

There's naething left in the fair Dodhead,
　　But a greeting wife and bairnies three;
And sax poor ca's stand in the sta',
　　A' routing loudly for their minnie.'

' Alack a wae!' quo' auld Jock Grieve,
　　' Alack! my heart is sair for thee!
For I was married on the elder sister,
　　And you are the youngest of a' the three.

Then he has ta'en out a bonny black,
　　Was right weel fed with corn and hay,
And he's set Jamie Telfer on his back
　　To the Catslockhill to tak' the fraye.

And whan he cam' to the Catslockhill
　　He shouted loud, and cried weel hie;
Till out and spak' him William's Wat—
　　' O whae's this brings the fraye to me?'

'It's I, Jamie Telfer, o' the fair Dodhead,
    A harried man I think I be;
The Captain of Bewcastle has driven my gear—
    For God's sake rise and succour me!'

' Alas for wae!' quoth William's Wat,
    ' Alack! for thee my heart is sair!
I never cam' by the fair Dodhead
    That ever I found thy basket bare.'

He's set his twa sons on coal black steads,
    Himself upon a freckled gray,
And they are on wi' Jamie Telfer
    To Branksome Ha', to tak' the fraye.

And when they cam' to Branksome Ha,
    They shouted a' baith loud and hie,
Till up and spak' him auld Buccleuch,
    Said—' Whae's this brings the fraye to me?

' It's I, Jamie Telfer, o' the fair Dodhead,
    And a harried man I think I be;
There's nought left in the fair Dodhead,
    But a greeting wife and bairnies three.'

' Alack for wae!' quoth the guid auld lord,
    ' And ever my heart is wae for thee!
But fye gar cry on Willie, my son,
    And see that he come to me speedilie.

' Gar warn the water braid and wide,
    Gar warn it sure and hastilie;
They that winna ride for Telfer's kye,
    Let them never look in the face o' me

'Warn Wat o' Harden and his sons,
  Wi' them will Borthwick Water ride;
Warn Gaudilands, and Allanhaugh,
  And Gilmanscleugh, and Commonside.

'Ride by the gate at Priesthaughswire,
  And warn the Curror's o' the Lee;
As ye come down the Hermitage slack,
  Warn doughty Willie o' Gorrieberry.'

The Scots they rade, the Scots they ran,
  Sae starkly and sae steadily;
And aye the owerword o' the thrang
  Was—'Rise for Branksome readilie!'

The gear was driven the Frostylee up,
  Frae the Frostylee unto the plain,
Whan Willie has looked his men before,
  And saw the kye right fast drivand.

'Whae drives thir kye?' 'gan Willie say,
  'To make an outspeckle o' me?'
'It's I, the Captain o' Bewcastle, Willie,
  I winna layne my name for thee.'

'O will ye let Telfer's kye gae back?
  Or will ye do aught for regard o' me?
Or, by the faith of my body,' quo' Willie Scott,
  'I'se ware my dame's caufskin on thee.'

'I winna let the kye gae back,
  Neither for thy love, nor yet thy fear;
But I will drive Jamie Telfer's kye,
  In spite of every Scot that's here.'

'Let on them lads!' quo' Willie than,
   'Fye, lads, set on them cruellie!
For ere they win to the Ritterford,
   Mony a toom saddle there sall be!'

Then till't they gaed, wi' heart and hand,
   The blows fell thick as bickering hail;
And mony a horse ran masterless,
   And mony a comely cheek was pale.

But Willie was stricken ower the head,
   And thro' the knapsack the sword has gane;
And Harden grat for very rage,
   When Willie on the grund lay slane.

But he's ta'en aff his gude steel cap,
   And thrice he's waved it in the air—
The Dinlay snaw was ne'er mair white,
   Nor the lyart locks of Harden's hair.

Revenge! revenge!' and Wat 'gan cry;
   'Fye, lads, lay on them cruellie!
We'll ne'er see Teviotside again,
   Or Willie's death revenged sall be.'

O mony a horse ran masterless,
   The splintered lances flew on hie;
But or they wan to the Kershope fords,
   The Scots had gotten the victory.

John o' Brigham there was slain,
   And John o' Barlow, as I heard say;
And thirty mae o' the Captain's men
   Lay bleeding on the grund that day

The Captain was run through the thick of the thigh,
   And broken was his right leg bane;
If he had lived this hundred years,
   He had ne'er been loved by woman again.

Hae back the kye!' the Captain said;
   ' Dear kye, I trow, to some they be!
For gin I suld live a hundred years,
   There will ne'er fair lady smile on me.'

Then word is gane to the Captain's bride,
   Even in the bower where that she lay,
That her lord was prisoner in enemy's land,
   Since in Tividale he had led the way.

' I wad lourd have had a winding sheet,
   And helped to put it ower his head,
Ere he had been disgraced by the border Scot,
   When he ower Liddel his men did lead!'

There was a wild gallant among us a',
   His name was Watty wi' the Wudspurs,
Cried—' On for his house in Stamgirthside,
   If ony man will ride with us?'

When they cam' to the Stamgirthside,
   They dang wi' trees and burst the door;
They loosed out a' the Captain's kye,
   And set them forth our lads before.

There was an auld wyfe ayont the fire,
   A wee bit o' the Captain's kin—
' Whae dar loose out the Captain's kye,
   Or answer to him and his men?'

'It's I, Watty Wudspurs, loose the kye,
  I winna layne my name frae thee;
And I will loose out the Captain's kye,
  In scorn of a' his men and he.'

When they came to the fair Dodhead,
  They were a welcome sight to see;
For instead of his ain ten milk kye,
  Jamie Telfer had gotten thirty and three.

And he has paid the rescue shot
  Baith with gond and white monie;
And at the burial o' Willie Scott,
  I wat was many a weeping e'e.

THE EXPLOITS OF COLKITTO.

COLL Macdonald, commonly called Coll-Kittoch or Colkitto from his being left-handed, is variously reported to have been the son of a gentleman of Iona, the natural son of the Earl of Antrim, and the son of Sir James Macdonald of Kintyre. But whatever was his parentage, he flourished toward the middle of the 17th century, and was a disinherited person of great consequence among the Macdonalds, and made a conspicuous figure in the civil wars of the Marquis of Montrose. He was noted for his strength and prowess, for his assiduity and daring, for his attachment to the cause of Charles I., and most of all for a fierce and furious antipathy to the noble family of Argyle and the whole great clan of the Campbells. He was at once poor, ambitious, and desperate, and seems to have acquired his asperities of character amid an early and rough acquaintance with adversity. Tradition says that he had large pecuniary claims through his mother upon the house of Argyle,—that, in fact, he was a nephew of the Earl, and lawful heir to a large dowry, which had never been paid to his mother,—that he presented and urged and prosecuted his claims, and got only rebuffs and scorn and persecution in lieu of them,—and that, in revenge, he took violent possession of the island of Collonsay, and made frequent rieving descents thence upon the lands of the Campbells, and at last applied to the Earl of Antrim for an armed Irish force of sufficient strength to inflict punishment, on a great scale, on the whole country of Argyle.

This final scheme synchronised and coincided with a grudge which the Earl of Antrim bore to the Earl of Argyle for joining the Covenanters, and for several reasons of private quarrel, and with a wish which he cherished to afford some aid to the cause of Carlist prelacy and kingcraft. Colkitto, therefore, readily obtained in Ulster an army of 2,000 men or more for the invasion of Scotland; and with these, early in July, 1644, he sailed up the west side of Kintyre, and among the inner Hebrides, and made occasional descents upon the land, destroying the residences and pillaging the property of almost every Campbell who lay in his way. As he approached Duntroon Castle on the bay of Crinan, he sent his piper forward, in the capacity of a spy, to procure information and mislead the inmates. But the piper, on getting in, found that the place was strong enough to repel invaders, that the entrance to it was so narrow as to admit only one person at a time, and that he himself was speedily suspected, and obliged to yield himself prisoner in one of the upper turrets; and, when by and bye, he observed through some crevice or loop-hole that Colkitto was drawing near, he contrived to warn him of the danger of making an attack by playing on his bagpipes the well-known pibroch,

"A cholla mo run seach ain an tur, seach ain an tur,
A cholla mo ghaoil seachan an caol, seachan an caol,
Tha mise an laimh, tha mise an laimh," That is,

"Dearest Coll, shun the tower, shun the tower,
Beloved Coll, shun the sound, shun the sound,
I am in hand, I am in hand," or a prisoner.

Colkitto understood the warning; and, supposing Duntroon Castle to be impregnable, he left his faithful piper to his fate, and continued his career of plunder and devastation, through the estates of Duntroon, Rassly, and Kilmartin, away onward to Loch-Awe. "He carried away all the cattle," says the New Statistical Account of one of the parishes, "with the exception of one dun cow that happened to escape his notice, being hid in a thicket of birch in a hollow below Kilmartin. This cow is still known by the natives by the name of *Bo-Mhaol othar Achabhean*, i. e., the humel dun cow of Achaven. It was this cow, by her lowing for her calf, which had been carried away with the rest of the cattle of the strath, that is said to have sounded the first note of lamentation and wailing among the inhabitants, when they ventured from their hiding-places in the hills, to behold the destruction of their dwellings, and the devastation of everything valuable that belonged to them."

Colkitto's success in Kilmartin was well counterpoised by the reception he got in the adjacent district of Craignish. The chieftain of this tract got timely intelligence of Colkitto's approach; and being possessed of a resolute disposition, a very strong castle, and a body of devoted and stalwart retainers, he determined to offer a stern resistance, and to lose no property; and, accordingly, he sent away all the cattle on his mainland estates to the islets toward Jura, and increased the garrison of his castle by receiving into it all of his clan who were able to carry arms. Colkitto, on arriving at the place, could get nothing, and commenced a siege; but he was soon obliged to retire; and, when he rose to take his leave, a party from the castle made a sortie upon him, and slew a number of his men, and compelled himself and the rest to scamper off in hurry and disorder.

Colkitto had various fortunes and made general havoc in other descents farther to the north; and at length, he made his final landing in Knoydart in Inverness-shire, where he expected to be joined by the Marquis of Huntly, who had just made a rising in favour of the King. The Marquis of Montrose, the master-mind of all the Scotish movements of the period in the cause of Charles, had only a few days before travelled clandestinely, incognito, and without any military support, from Carlisle into Scotland, and was at the moment lying perdu among the Highlands of Perthshire, at an utter loss for means or expedients to amass an army and commence a campaign. Colkitto, however, supposed Montrose to be in strength, though he knew not where, and imagined his own forces to be but a small reinforcement on the way to join a large army; and he marched boldly from the coast toward the Central Grampians, in the style of a great chief and commander. As he advanced into the interior he dispatched the fiery cross for the purpose of summoning the clans to his standard; but, although the cross was carried through a large extent of country, even to Aberdeen, he was only joined at first by the Clan-Donald, under the captain of Clanronald, and the laird of Glengary. The Marquis of Argyle collected an army to oppose his progress; and in order to cut off his retreat to Ireland, he sent some ships of war to Loch Eishord, where Colkitto's fleet lay, which captured or destroyed them. This loss, while it frustrated an intention which Colkitto entertained of returning to Ireland, in consequence of the disappointment he had met with in not being joined by the clans, stimulated him to farther exertions in continuing his march, in the hope of meeting Montrose.

As Macdonald was perfectly ignorant of Montrose's movements, and thought it likely that he might be still at Carlisle, waiting till he should hear of Colkitto's arrival, he sent letters to him by the hands of a confidential friend, who resided in the neighbourhood of Graham Inchbrakie's house, where Montrose happened at the time to be ensconsed. This gentleman, who knew nothing of Montrose's return to Scotland, having luckily communicated to Mr. Graham the secret of being entrusted with letters to his kinsman, Montrose, Graham offered to see them safely delivered to Montrose, though he should ride to Carlisle himself. The gentleman in question then delivered the letters to Graham, and Montrose having received them, wrote an answer as if from Carlisle, in which he requested Colkitto to keep up his spirits, that he would soon be joined by a seasonable reinforcement and a general at their head, and he ordered him with all expedition to march down into Athole. In fixing on Athole as the place of his rendezvous, Montrose is said to have been actuated by an implicit reliance on the fidelity and loyalty of the Athole-men, and by a high opinion of their courage. They lay, besides, under many obligations to himself, and he calculated that he had only to appear among them to command their services in the cause of their sovereign.

When Colkitto received these instructions, he marched towards Athole; but in passing through Badenoch he was threatened with an attack by the Earls of Sutherland and Seaforth, at the head of some of their people, and by the Frazers, Grants, Rosses, and Munroes, and other inhabitants of Moray, who had assembled at the top of Strathspey; but Colkitto very cautiously avoided them, and hastened into Athole. On arriving in Athole, he was coldly received by the people of that as well as the surrounding country, who doubted whether he had any authority from the King, and besides they hesitated to place themselves under the command of a person of neither noble nor ancient lineage, and whom they considered an upstart. This indecision might have proved fatal to Colkitto, who was closely pressed in his rear by the army of Argyle, had not these untoward deliberations been instantly put an end to by the arrival of Montrose at Blair, where Colkitto had fixed his head-quarters. Montrose had travelled seventy miles on foot, in a highland dress, accompanied by Patrick Graham, his cousin, as his guide. His appearance was hailed by his countrymen with every demonstration of joy, and they immediately made, him a spontaneous offer of their services. Accordingly, on the following day, the Athole-men to the number of about 800, consisting chiefly of the Stewarts and Robertsons, put themselves under arms and flocked to the standard of Montrose. Thus, in little more than twenty-four hours, Montrose saw himself at the head of a considerable force, animated by an enthusiastic attachment to his person and to the cause which he had espoused.

We need not follow Montrose through his well-known campaigns and battles; but may simply state that Colkitto followed him and co-operated with him, for some time, as one of his most active officers,—that, in the winter of 1644-5, the first winter after the events which we have been narrating, Montrose, with Colkitto and other leaders, made a terribly devastating incursion athwart the country of the Campbells,—that, after the battle of Inverlochy in February 1645, and in connexion with the overrunning of Argyleshire, Colkitto took possession of Kintyre as his inheritance,—that Alexander Macdonald, the son of Colkitto, served as Major-General under Montrose, and was knighted by him after the latter was appointed Captain-General of Scotland,—that, after the fracture of Montrose's fortunes at the battle of Philiphaugh, in September 1645, Sir Alexander Macdonald in the south and the Marquis of Huntly in the north were the only chiefs who remained in arms against the Covenanters —and that, amid the general and final wreck of the royalist cause in 1647, General Leslie and the Earl of Argyle, pursued Sir Alexander and Colkitto to Kintyre and the Hebrides, and put a tragical end to all their exploits and power.

The incursion into Argyleshire, in the winter of 1644-5, was dictated mainly by a spirit of retribution and revenge; but it repaid at least tenfold all the injuries and disasters which it professed to punish. Montrose, at the devising of it, was pausing in Athole, after having traversed Aberdeenshire and Inverness-shire, and driven the Covenanters' troops to nonplus and inertion by a rapid series of brilliant skirmishing and countermarching; and it is said that he intended at first to have transferred the seat of war at once to the Lowlands, where he expected to be better able to support his troops during winter, but that he was induced to give up this plan by Macdonald and the captain of Clanranald, who, out of their strong dislike to Argyle, advised him to invade the territory of their common enemy. Nothing could be more gratifying to Montrose's followers than his resolution to carry the war into Argyle's country, as they would thus have an ample opportunity of retaliating upon him and his retainers the injuries which, for a course of years, had been inflicted upon the supporters of royalty in the adjoining countries, many of whom had been ruined by Argyle. The idea of curbing the power of a haughty and domineering chief whose very word was a law to the inhabitants of an extensive district, ready to obey his mandates at all times,—and the spirit of revenge, the predominating characteristic of the clans, smoothed the difficulties which presented themselves in invading a country made almost inaccessible by nature, and rendered still more unapproachable by the severities of winter. The determination of Montrose having thus met with a willing response in the breasts of his men, he lost no time in putting them in motion. Dividing his army into two parts, he himself marched with the main body, consisting of the Irish and the Athole-men, to Loch Tay, whence he proceeded through Breadalbane. The other body, composed of the Clan-Donald and other Highlanders, he despatched by a different route, with instructions to meet him at an assigned spot on the borders of Argyle. The country through which both divisions passed, being chiefly in possession of Argyle's kinsmen or dependants, was laid waste by them, and particularly the lands of Campbell of Glenorchy.

Argyle at the moment was passing his time at Edinburgh; and when he heard of the ravages committed by Montrose's army on the lands of his kinsmen, he hastened home to his castle at Inverary and gave orders for the assembling of his clan, either to repel any attack that might be made on his own country, or to protect his friends from future aggression. It is by no means certain that he anticipated an invasion from Montrose, particularly at such a season of the year, and he seemed to imagine himself so secure from attack, owing to the intricacy of the passes leading into Argyle, that although a mere handful of men could have effectually opposed an army much larger than that of Montrose, he took no precautions to guard them. So important indeed did he himself consider these passes to be, that he had frequently declared that he would rather forfeit a hundred thousand crowns, than that an enemy should know the passes by which an armed force could penetrate into Argyle.

While thus reposing in fancied security in his impregnable stronghold, and issuing his mandates for levying his forces, some shepherds arrived in great terror from the hills, and brought him the alarming intelligence, that the enemy whom he had imagined were about a hundred miles distant, were within two miles of his own dwelling. Terrified at the unexpected appearance of Montrose, whose vengeance he justly dreaded, he had barely self-possession left to concert measures for his own personal safety by taking refuge on board a fishing boat in Loch Fyne, in which he sought his way to the Lowlands, leaving his people and country exposed to the merciless will of an enemy thirsting for revenge. The inhabitants of Argyle being thus abandoned by their chief, made no attempt to oppose Montrose, who, the more effectually to carry his plan for pillaging and ravaging the country into execution, divided his army into three parties, each under the respective orders of the captain of Clanranald, Macdonald, and himself. For upwards of six weeks, viz., from the 13th of December, 1644, till nearly the end of January following, these different bodies traversed the whole country without molestation, burning, wasting, and destroying every thing which came within their reach. Villages and cottages, furniture, grain, and effects of every description were made a prey to the devouring element of fire. The cattle which they did not succeed in driving off were either mutilated or slaughtered; and the whole of Argyle as well as the district of Lorn soon became a dreary waste. Nor were the people themselves spared; for although it is mentioned by one writer, that Montrose "shed no blood in regard that all the people (following their Lord's laudable example) delivered themselves by flight also," it is evident from several contemporary authors that the slaughter must have been immense. One of these says, that Montrose spared none that were able to bear arms, and that he put to death all the men who were going to the rendezvous appointed by Argyle. Probably the 895 persons mentioned by the author of the Red Book of Clanranald, as having been killed by the party of Clanranald without opposition, may be those alluded to by Wishart. In fact, before the end of January, the face of a single male inhabitant was not to be seen throughout the whole extent of Argyle and Lorn, the whole population having been either driven out of these districts, or taken refuge in dens and caves known only to themselves.

Colkitto retained possession of Kintyre and some of the chief adjacent islands, from the spring of 1645 till the spring of 1647; and he was joined, at the latter date, by his son, Sir Alexander, who then retreated from conflict with the Covenanters in the Central Highlands, and was at the head of a force of about 1,400 foot and two troops of horse

Both father and son felt too secure in their remote position, and totally lacked the advantage of fair intelligence, or almost any intelligence at all, of General Leslie's movements; and when, on the 21st of May, 1647, the latter was already at Inverary, with an army, in search of them, they were altogether ignorant of his approach, and had taken no precautions to guard the passes leading into Kintyre, which might have been successfully defended by a handful of men against a considerable force. Having secured these difficult passes, Leslie advanced into Kintyre, and after skirmishing the whole of the 25th of May with Macdonald, he forced him to retire. After throwing 300 men into a fortress on the top of the hill of Dunaverty, and in which "there was not a drop of water but what fell from the clouds," Macdonald, on the following day, embarked his troops in boats provided for the occasion, and passed over into Islay.

Leslie, thereupon, laid siege to the castle of Dunaverty, which was well defended; but the assailants having carried a trench at the bottom of the hill which gave the garrison the command of water, and in the storming of which the besieged lost forty men, the latter craved a parley, in consequence of which Sir James Turner, Leslie's adjutant-general, was sent to confer with the garrison on the terms of surrender. Leslie would not grant "any other conditions than that they should yield on discretion or mercy. And it seemed strange to me (continues Sir James Turner) to hear the lieutenant-general's nice distinction, that they should yield themselves to the kingdom's mercy, and not to his. At length they did so, and after they were come out of the castle they were put to the sword, every mother's son, except one young man, Maccoul, whose life I begged to be sent to France, with a hundred fellows which we had smoked out of a cave, as they do foxes, who were given to Captain Campbell, the chancellor's brother." This atrocious act is alleged to have been perpetrated at the instigation of John Nave or Neaves whom Turner calls "a bloody preacher," but, according to Wodrow, an "excellent man," who would not be satisfied with less than the blood of the prisoners. As the account given by Sir James Turner, an eye-witness of this infamous transaction, is curious, no apology is necessary for inserting it. " Here it will be fit to make a stop, till this cruel action be canvassed. First, the lieutenant-general was two days irresolute what to do. The Marquis of Argyle was accused at his arraignment of this murder, and I was examined as a witness. I declared, which was true, that I never heard him advise the lieutenant-general to it. What he did in private I know not. Secondly, Argyle was but a colonel then, and he had no power to do it of himself. Thirdly, though he had advised him to it, it was no capital crime; for counsel is no command. Fourthly, I have several times spoke to the lieutenant general to save these men's lives, and he always assented to it, and I know of himself he was unwilling to shed their blood. Fifthly, Mr. John Nave (who was appointed by the commission of the kirk to wait on him as his chaplain) never ceased to tempt him to that bloodshed, yea, and threatened him with the curses which befell Saul for sparing the Amalekites, for with them his theology taught him to compare the Dunavertie men. And I verily believe that this prevailed most with David Leslie, who looked upon Nave as the representative of the Kirk of Scotland." The statement of Sir James's and David Leslie's repugnance to shed the blood of those defenceless men is fully corroborated by Bishop Guthry, on the authority of many persons who were present, who says that while the butchery was going on, and while Leslie, Argyle, and Neaves were walking over the ancles in blood, Leslie turned out and thus addressed the latter :—" Now, Mr. John, have you not once got your fill of blood?" The sufferers on this occasion were partly Irish, and partly belonging to the clan Dougal or Coull, to the castle of whose chief in Lorn, Colonel Robert Montgomerie now laid siege, while Leslie himself, with a part of his forces, left Kintyre for Islay in pursuit of Macdonald.

On landing in Islay, Leslie found that Macdonald had fled to Ireland, and had left Colkitto, his father, in the castle of Dunniveg, with a force of 200 men to defend the island against the superior power of Leslie. The result turned out as might have been anticipated. Although the garrison made a brave resistance, yet, being wholly without water, they found themselves unable to resist, and offered to capitulate on certain conditions. These were, that the officers should be entitled to go where they pleased, and that the privates should be sent to France. These conditions were agreed to, and were punctually fulfilled. Old Colkitto had, however, the misfortune not to be included in this capitulation; for, before the castle had surrendered, "the old man, Coll," says Sir James Turner, "coming foolishly out of the house, where he was governor, on some parole or other, to speak with his old friend, the captain of Dunstaffnage castle, was surprised and made prisoner, not without some stain to the lieutenant-general's honour. He was afterwards hanged by a jury of Argyle's sheriff-depute, one George Campbell, from whose sentence few are said to have escaped that kind of death."

THE TURMOILS OF MERSE AND TEVIOTDALE.

The town of Kelso affords in its topographical position a fine specimen of the blandest beauties of Border scenery, and in its ancient history a large and fair sample of the mingled pomp and horror, flaunting and fighting, display and deadliness of the olden Border warfare. It stands on the left bank of the Tweed, opposite the influx of the Teviot; and stretches along a plain, in the centre of a gently rising and magnificent low amphitheatre; and commands from every opening of its streets vistas and expanses of exquisitely lovely landscape. Seen from the heights of Stitchel several miles to the north, the district around the town appears to be an extensive and picturesque strath—a plain intersected by two rivers, and richly adorned with woods; but seen from the low grounds close upon the Tweed, near the town, it is a diversified basin,—a gently receding amphitheatre,—low where it is cut by the rivers, and cinctured in the distance by a boundary of sylvan heights. On the north side of the Tweed it slowly rises in successive wavy ridges, tier behind tier, till an inconsiderable summit-level is attained; and on the south side, while it generally makes a gradual rise, it is cut down on the west into a diverging stripe of lowland by the Teviot, ascends, in some places, in an almost acclivitous way from the banks, and sends up in the distance hilly and hard-featured elevations, which, though subject to the plough, are naturally pastoral. The whole district is surpassingly rich in the features of landscape which strictly constitute the beautiful,—unmixed with the grand, or, except in rare touches, with the romantic. The views presented from the knolly height of Roxburgh castle, and from the immediate vicinity of the Ducal mansion of Fleurs, are so luscious, so full and minute in feature, that they must be seen in order to be appreciated. The view from the bridge, a little below the confluence of the rivers, though greatly too rich to be depicted in words, and demanding consummate skill in order to be pencilled in colours, admits at least an easy enumeration of its leading features. Immediately on the north lies the town, with the majestic ruins of its ancient abbey, and the handsome fabric of Ednam house; $1\frac{1}{4}$ mile to the north-west, rises the magnificent pile of Fleurs castle, amidst a profusion and an expanse coming down to the Tweed of wooded decorations; in front are two islets in the Tweed, and between that river and the Teviot the beautiful peninsula of Friar's or St. James's Green, with the fair green in its foreground, and the venerable and tufted ruins of Roxburgh castle, 1¼ mile distant; on the south-west, within a fine bend of the Teviot, are the mansion and demesne of Springwood, and away behind them, in far perspective, looking down the exulting vale of the Tweed, the Eildon hills lift up their triple summit; a little to the east, close upon the view, rises the fine form of Pinnacle-hill; away in the distance behind the town, rise the conspicuous ruin of Home castle, and the hills of Stitchel and Mellerstain: and, in addition, are the curvings and rippling currents of the rivers,—beltings and clumps and lines of plantation,—the steep precipices of Maxwell and Chalkheugh,—exuberant displays of agricultural wealth and social comfort,—and reminiscences, suggestible to even a tyro in history, of events in olden times which mingle delightfully in the thoughts with a contemplation of the landscape. Sir Walter Scott—who often revelled amidst this scenery in the latter years of his boyhood,—ascribes to its influence upon his mind the awakening within him of that "insatiable love of natural scenery, more especially when combined with ancient ruins or remains of our father's piety or splendour," which at once characterized and distinguished him as a writer, and imparted such a warmth and munificence of colouring to all his literary pictures. Leyden, too—who had around him in the vale of the Teviot, and the "dens" of its tributary rills in the immediate vicinity of his home at Denholm, quite enough to exhaust the efforts of a lesser poet—sung impassionedly the beauties of Kelso:—

> "Bosom'd in woods where mighty rivers run,
> Kelso's fair vale expands before the sun;
> Its rising downs in vernal beauty swell,
> And, fringed with hazle, winds each flowery dell;
> Green spangled plains to dimpling lawns succeed,
> And Tempe rises on the banks of Tweed:

Blue o'er the river Kelso's shadow lies,
And copse-clad isles amid the water rise."

Nearly adjacent to the town of Kelso, or rather over against it, on a rising ground at the west end of the low fertile peninsula between the Teviot and the Tweed, is the site of the ancient royal town of Roxburgh, now quite extinct. Brief but obscure notices by various historians indicate that this was a place of considerable note long previous to the 12th century, but fail to throw light on its condition or, furnish any certain facts in its history. While David I., who mounted the throne in 1124, was yet only Earl of Northumberland, the town, as well as the castle, belonged to him as an appanage of his earldom; and appears to have been so flourishing that it could not accommodate the crowds who pressed into it to enrol themselves its citizens. An overflow of its population was the occasion of the erection of the new town, the original of the present village, the Easter Roxburgh of history, about 2 miles to the south. Whether the new town was built by David, or at a period prior to the date of his influence, is uncertain; but the fact of its being an offshoot at so early a period, strikingly evinces how great and attractive a seat of population the district at the embouchure of the Teviot was in even rude and semi-barbarous times. Among other elements of the old town's importance in the time of David, it possessed an encincturing fortification of wall and ditch, and had, under the superintendence of the abbot of Kelso, schools which figured magnificently in the age's unpolished tales of fame. When David ascended the throne, it became, as a matter of course, a king's burgh, and possibly was the one which the monarch most favoured. But its main feature was its ancient castle, supposed to have been built by the Saxons while they held the sovereignty of the Northumbrian kingdom, and long a most important fort, a royal residence, a centre of strife, an eyesore to every great party who had not possession of it, and at once the political glory and the social bane of Teviotdale. Only a few fragments of some of its outer walls now remain,—on a tabular rock which rises about 40 feet perpendicular from the level of the plain; and they distinctly indicate it to have been a place of great strength. It was for ages a focus of intrigue and pomp and battle; and it witnessed a profusion of the scenes and vicissitudes of siege and strife,—of pillage and fire and slaughter; but it now retains a most meagre vestige of its ancient importance.

> "Roxburgh! how fallen, since first, in Gothic pride,
> Thy frowning battlements the war defied,
> Called the bold chief to grace thy blazoned halls,
> And bade the rivers gird thy solid walls!
> Fallen are thy towers, and, where the palace stood,
> In gloomy grandeur waves yon hanging wood;
> Crushed are thy halls, save where the peasant sees
> One moss-clad ruin rise between the trees;
> The still-green trees, whose mournful branches wave,
> In solemn cadence o'er the hapless brave.
> Proud castle! Fancy still beholds thee stand,
> The curb, the guardian, of this Border land,
> As when the signal flame, that blazed afar,
> And bloody flag, proclaimed impending war,
> While, in the lion's place the leopard frowned
> And marshalled armies hemmed thy bulwarks round.'

The principal existing artificial gem in the midst of the gorgeous scenery of Kelso—an object connecting both this town and ancient Roxburgh, and the straths around them with many a stirring passage in the olden Border history—is the ruinous abbey,—a simply elegant, unique, tall, massive pile, in the form of a Greek cross, imposing in aspect and untiring in interest. The establishment out of which it sprang was originally settled in Selkirk for monks of the order of Tyrone; but after a few years, was, in 1128, removed by David I. to its site at Kelso, in the vicinity of the royal residence of Roxburgh-castle. David, and all his successors on the throne till James V., lavished upon it royal favours. Whether in wealth, in political influence, or in ecclesiastical status, it maintained an eminence of grandeur which dazzles and bewilders a student of history and of human nature. The convent of Lesmahago, with its valuable dependencies, —33 parish-churches, with their tithes and other pertinents, in nearly every district, except Galloway and East-Lothian, south of the Clyde and the Forth,—the parish church of Culter in Aberdeenshire,—all the forfeitures within the town and county of Berwick,—several manors and vast numbers of farms, granges, mills, fishings, and miscellaneous property athwart the Lowlands,—so swelled the revenue as to raise it above that of all the bishops in Scotland. The abbots were superiors of the regality of Kelso, Bolden, and Reverden, frequent ambassadors and special commissioners of the royal court, and the first ecclesiastics on the roll of parliament, taking precedence of all the other abbots in the kingdom; and, while some of them rivalled the mightiest nobles in pride and splendour, others shook great tracts of country, and kept them long in agitation, by their quarrels with other ecclesiastics and their struggles for increase of power. But though the abbey was generally respected by the English marauders in the heigh-day of popery, it became a most tempting object and a speedy prey to the earliest English armies who had ceased to venerate monasticism. In 1522, an army of Henry VIII demolished its church and vaults, fired all its cells and dormitories, and tore off the roof from all its other portions; and subsequent inroads of the national foe prevented any attempts at immediate repair or re-edification, —so that the abbey, for a time, crumbled toward total decay, and the monks were reduced almost to beggary, and skulked among the neighbouring villages. In 1542, under the Duke of Norfolk, and again in 1545, under the Earl of Hertford, the English renewed their spoliations on the abbey, and almost entirely destroyed it by fire. On the latter occasion, it was resolutely defended by about 300 men who had posted themselves in its interior, and was entered only after the corpses of a large proportion of them formed a rampart before its gates. In 1560, the monks were expelled in consequence of the Reformation; and both then and in 1580, the abbey was despoiled of many of its architectural decorations, and carried far down the decline of ruin.

The town of Kelso figures, in ancient history, both by itself and in company with the neighbouring castle of Roxburgh, as a rendezvous of armies, as a place of international negociation, as a scene of frequent conflict and havoc of war, and as a spot smiled upon by kings and other personages of note. "Situated on the Borders, and a frontier town of the kingdom," says Mr. Haig —whose interesting volume on the History of Kelso and Roxburgh is a main authority with us in the present article—"it was repeatedly desolated by fire and sword, during those unhappy conflicts which devastated both countries for so many ages. Kelso, or its immediate neighbourhood, was the usual rendezvous of our armies upon the eastern marches, when the vassals were summoned either to repel an invading enemy, or to retaliate on English ground the injuries which had been committed on their own. Kelso is also famous as a place of negociation; and many truces or treaties were here concluded between the two nations."

In 1138, when David I. retreated into Scotland from his unsuccessful siege of Wark Castle, Stephen of England followed him at the head of a large army to the neighbourhood of Kelso; and David feeling obliged to stand merely on the defensive in a strong position adjacent to Roxburgh, Stephen pillaged and wasted all the surrounding country till he could no longer obtain sufficient sustenance and spoil for his followers, and then retired to England by another passage across the Tweed, than that by which he had entered. In 1209, William of Scotland assembled an army at Roxburgh to oppose a threatened invasion by John of England; but, in consequence of an adjustment of the cause of hostilities by mediation, he was enabled to disband it, without leading it into service. In the same year, on account of a Papal interdict being imposed on England, the bishops of Rochester and Salisbury came into Scotland, and fixed their residence the former at Kelso and the latter at Roxburgh; and were hospitably received by the Scotish monarch.

In the winter of 1215-6, John of England invaded the eastern border at the head of a powerful army, and spread devastation through large tracts of Merse and Teviotdale and East Lothian, and burnt the towns of Roxburgh, Berwick, Dunbar, and Haddington, and exercised most ruthless severity upon many families and individuals of the Border lairds. In 1255, soon after Alexander III. of Scotland and his Queen had been rescued from restraint in Edinburgh Castle, and conveyed in safety to Roxburgh Castle by an English army under the Earl of Gloucester, Henry III. of England, the Queen's father, made them a visit of 15 or 16 days at Roxburgh, and had a large retinue of nobles and a great military force assembled on the English frontier, and was introduced with great processional pomp to Kelso and its abbey, and there entertained, along with the chief nobility of both kingdoms, at a sumptuous royal banquet.

During the altercations between John Baliol and Edward I., and during the subsequent wars of the succession, Merse and Teviotdale, and particularly the tracts around Kelso and Berwick, were the scenes of many turmoils. In 1292, Edward held practical possession of all the Border, and kept it under great and constant excitement, in the course of adjudicating the crown of Scotland among the rival claimants;

and toward the close of that year, after pronouncing judgment in favour of Baliol, he spent nearly a month at Roxburgh, and there concocted a number of official orders and arrangements. In 1295, Baliol agreed to deliver the Castles of Roxburgh, Jedburgh, and Berwick—and indirectly the whole territory of Merse and Teviotdale—into the temporary possession of the English; but, on the arrival of parties to take possession, he or his officers refused to give them up; and soon after, he first made a desolating irruption into Cumberland, and laid unsuccessful siege to Carlisle, and was compelled to retreat in disgrace,—and next overran a large part of Northumberland, and burned some monasteries, and was driven in disorder from a bootless attempt to storm the castle of Harbottle. Edward's wrath, which had been blazing before, was now blown into flaming fury; and he came down in great force to the Border, and made that awful capture of Berwick which is narrated at page 113 of the first volume of these Tales, and pushed forward thence through the Merse to Dunbar, and there fought and prostrated Baliol, and then went to the foot of Teviotdale, and took possession of the town and castle of Roxburgh.

In 1297, Sir William Wallace, on his way back from his dreadfully devastating incursion into England, paused awhile at Roxburgh, and laid siege to its castle, but, getting intelligence of the mustering of a powerful English army against him, he abandoned the siege, and went away to the north. In the spring of 1298, Edward came up from Newcastle, at the head of 3,000 heavy cavalry, 4,000 light cavalry, and about 80,000 infantry, and traversed Merse and Lower Teviotdale, and made mighty military demonstrations at Roxburgh and Kelso and Berwick, and then marched toward the centre of the kingdom in search of Wallace. In 1306, Mary de Bruce, the sister of King Robert, was shut up in an iron cage at Roxburgh Castle,—and there was she kept till 1310 and the same barbarous punishment was inflicted on the

Countess of Buchan in Berwick Castle, for assisting at Robert's coronation.

In 1307, Edward II. of England, immediately after his accession to the throne, came to Roxburgh and Dumfries to receive the fealty of the Scotish barons; in 1310, after making a fruitless attempt to draw together a great army at Berwick for crushing the power of Bruce, he made a rapid, bustling, vain progress through Roxburgh and Selkirk and other parts of the Border; and in 1311, he got together a kind of army at Roxburgh, for the purpose of making one more great effort against Bruce, but failed to do any considerable deed, and had the mortification to know that Bruce, in perfect defiance of him and quite unmolestedly, was about the same time carrying havoc and desolation into England over the western marches. In 1313, Sir James Douglas achieved the adroit and masterly capture of Roxburgh Castle which was narrated on pages 366 and 367 of the third volume of these Tales.

In 1332, Edward Baliol, a week or two after he had got himself crowned at Scone, marched at the head of his army to the Border, menaced Berwick, took and burnt one or more fortalices which had been held by his opponents, encamped in the vicinity of Kelso, got possession of the Castle of Roxburgh, and there acknowledged the King of England as his liege lord, and ignominiously surrendered to him the independence of Scotland. But before the close of the year, while he was at the western marches on some business of state or pleasure, attended by only a small force, he was surprised in the night and wofully discomfited by Archibald Douglas, Lord of Galloway, at the head of about 1,000 horsemen; and he escaped with difficulty, and in a state of nudity, and fled to Roxburgh on a horse which had neither saddle nor bridle. In 1333, while Baliol lay at Roxburgh, waiting reinforcements from England, and expecting the arrival of the English King in person, Sir Andrew Moray, the

Regent of Scotland, attempted to take the town and castle by assault; but he encountered a sharp resistance on the bridge, and, while generously endeavouring to rescue one of his squires who had been thrown down, he was overpowered and made prisoner. Now followed the disastrous events at and around Berwick, which culminated in the battle of Halidon Hill, and have been narrated on pp. 324—337 of the third volume of these Tales.

In the spring of 1342, Sir Alexander Ramsay of Dalhousie, took the castle of Roxburgh by escalade; and was rewarded by King David, for the distinguished bravery of the deed, with the governorship of the Castle and the sheriffship of Teviotdale. But Lord William Douglas, who had previously held the sheriffship, felt aggrieved by these appointments, and soon after seized an opportunity of Ramsay holding a court in the church of Hawick to wreak vengeance on him, by rushing in with a body of armed followers, dragging him from the bench, wounding him, killing some of his servants, and carrying him away to direful and fatal imprisonment in Hermitage Castle.

In 1346, David II., at the head of a powerful army which had been assembled at Perth and reinforced at Edinburgh, marched through Roxburgh and up Teviotdale, on his way to a devastation of Cumberland and Northumberland, terminating in the disastrous battle of Neville's Cross, the history of which is told on pp. 97—108 of the first volume of these Tales. In consequence of this battle, the Castles of Roxburgh and Hermitage surrendered to the English, and the districts of Merse, Teviotdale, Liddesdale, Lauderdale, and most of the other border districts were abandoned to the wicked will of the conquerors. In 1348, Lord William Douglas overran Teviotdale, Ettrick Forest, and Tweeddale, and drove the English out of them; and so well was he supported by the men of Teviotdale that he hotly repelled the large garrison of Roxburgh Castle, on their coming out against him, and slew many of their number, and compelled the rest to retreat precipitately to their fortifications.

In the summer of 1355, a Scotish army marched past the English posts in the Merse, invaded Northumberland, burned Norham, captured Berwick, and in other ways annoyed and confounded their great national foe; and in the following winter, the King of England got together an immense force, and made stern and strong preparations to pay back the devastations with interest, and to inflict on the Scots condign punishment for what he called their rebellion. They heard in good time of his approach; and, knowing that they could not resist him, and at the same time determined to express not one word of compunction for what they had done, or to yield one inch to his authority, they packed up all their valuables, burned Berwick, destroyed its walls, and retreated into the interior; and when Edward arrived, he took up his residence for some time at Roxburgh Castle, and was there duped into inaction by a pretence of some of the chief Scotish nobles of negociating submission to his sceptre, till they should gain time to conceal all their treasures, and put themselves into a strong attitude of defence; and when he discovered the cheat, he ran riot through the Border districts as far north as Haddington, and made great waste and devastation. While he remained at Roxburgh, Baliol, who attended him as a vassal, made a formal and more absolute surrender to him than before of the crown-rights of Scotland, and so sadly degraded himself as to present by way of token a portion of the Scotish soil and also his golden crown.

The previously unsettled state of the Border was enormously increased by the proceedings of the English Edwards; and it often produced among the barons and great families very violent quarrels, of far-spread influence, and with most disastrous consequences. One of the chief of tnese may be narrated as a specimen. In August, 1371, at the annual fair of Roxburgh, a chamberlain or other domestic of the Earl

2 c

of March was slain in a scuffle by some of the English. The Earl regarded the occurrence as a gross personal insult; and, feeling impatient for redress, he immediately sent a herald to the Earl of Northumberland, Warden of the Borders, requiring him to give up the murderers. "The Warden, notwithstanding the Earl's importunity, treated his demand with derision. The Earl of March took no farther notice of the matter at the time; but, stifling his resentment, he waited for the return of the same fair in the following year, when, a great number of English being present with their merchandise, he, in conjunction with his brother, the Earl of Moray, came suddenly upon the town, slew every male, carried off their goods, and reduced the town to ashes. The borderers, glad of any pretext for commencing hostilities against the Scots, (a pretext, as some writers say, which was courted by the English—the inhabitants of the Borders being so much accustomed to live by plunder, that a state of peace reduced them to indigence,) immediately mustered all their strength; and determined, as they avowed, to obtain redress by the destruction of the Earl of March's property, advanced into Scotland. In their route, however, they regarded no property, neither did they spare the innocent inhabitants; but with relentless fury, put all to the sword, male and female, old and young. With distinguished barbarity, they ravaged the property of Sir John Gordon, which happened to lie contiguous to that of the Earl of March, spoiling his estate, and carrying away a number of prisoners. Sir John, burning to revenge the injuries thus inhumanly committed, advanced into England at the head of a numerous body of men, killing many, and taking a number of prisoners, besides seizing a large quantity of booty. On his return, he was attacked near Carham, by Sir John Lilburn, with a very superior force. The battle which ensued was fought with the utmost obstinacy and determined courage. Five times were the Scots that day on the point of being vanquished; and as often did they return to the contest, and were victorious. At length the English were completely discomfited, and Sir John Lilburn, their commander, with his brother, and a number of his followers, made prisoners, and brought to Scotland. Sir John Gordon likewise preserved all his booty."

At the accession of Richard II. to the throne of England, in 1377, new commotions occurred on the borders; and at the fair of Roxburgh, in the autumn of that year, there was another riotous outburst of national antipathies, which terminated in the Scots setting fire to the town. The Earl of Northumberland viewed this outburst as a sequence and aggravation of the previous, and felt correspondingly enraged at it; and he therefore marched into Merse and Teviotdale with a force of 10,000 men to punish it, and took special vengeance on the Earl of March, by dooming his estates to a pillage of three days. Seven years later a general and violent insurrection broke out against the English along most of the border, even to the shores of the Solway; and by way of special precaution against the Castle of Roxburgh falling into the hands of the Scots, Lord Graystock, a famous military leader, was sent by the King of England, with troops and muniments, to reinforce and command it. But the Earl of March, hearing of his approach and of the route by which he was to travel, laid an ambush for him, and made a sudden and overwhelming attack upon his cortege, captured all his troops and waggons, and carried himself prisoner to the Castle of Dunbar.

In 1385, a Scotish army, aided by French auxiliaries, scoured the borders, and attempted to make head against the English, but found it prudent to retreat before getting embroiled in any general action; and, while on their way back toward the interior, made an unsuccessful attempt to induce their French friends to consent to a besieging of Roxburgh Castle. In 1388, as related at page 247 of the third volume of these Tales, occurred the great martial muster in Teviotdale which led to the famous battle of Otterburn. In 1398, during a truce with England, the Earl of Douglas's son, with Sir William Stuart and others, taking advantage of the critical situation of Richard II., broke down the bridge at Roxburgh, plundered the town, and ravaged the adjacent lands. In the year 1411, Douglas of Drumlanrig, and Gavin Dunbar, adopted the same course of hostility; for they broke down the bridge of Roxburgh, and set fire to the town James I. made a vain attempt to recover this fortress, in 1435, of which Bellenden gives the following *naive* account. " The king past with an army to sege the castell of Marchmond, that is to say Roxburgh. The Scottis war nowmerit in this army to II.C.M. men, by [besides] futmen and caragemen. At last quhen the kyng had lyne at the sege foresaid xv. dayis and waistit all his munitioun and powder, he returnit haim, but ony mair felicité succeeding to his army."

In 1460, James II.—perhaps from the idea of its being a disgrace to the Scotish crown, that Berwick and Roxburgh should continue so long under the dominion of England— laid siege to the latter, with a numerous army, well-furnished with artillery and warlike machinery. He took the town, and levelled it to the ground; but, during the siege of the castle, while he was overseeing the discharge of one of his pieces of ordnance, so remarkable for its size that it was called 'the Lion,' it burst, and the King was almost instantaneously struck dead. A large holly, enclosed by a wall, marks the fatal spot. The Queen, Mary of Guelder, who immediately on the mournful tidings arrived in the camp, bringing her eldest son with her, then a boy of about seven years of age, conducted herself with such heroism on this mournful occasion as to inspire the troops with redoubled spirit, and the garrison, finding themselves reduced to extremity, surrendered the fortress. " That the place," says Ridpath, " which the English had held for more than a hundred years, might thenceforth cease to be a centre of rapine and violence, or a cause of future strife between the nations, the victors reduced it to a heap of ruins." A fuller prose account of the last siege of Roxburgh Castle, and of the death of James II., is given in pp. 108—112, of the first volume of these Tales; and the following poetical one, in Leyden's Scenes of Infancy, is well worth transcription.—

" Serene in might, amid embattled files,
From Morven's hills and the far western isles,
From barrier Tweed and Teviot's border tide,
See through the host the youthful monarch ride!
In streaming pomp, above each mailed line,
The chiefs behold his plumy helmet shine,
And, as he points the purple surge of war,
His faithful legions hail their guiding star.
   From Lothian's plains a hardy band uprears,
In serried ranks, a glittering grove of spears.
The Border chivalry more fierce advance;
Before their steeds projects the bristling lance;
The panting steeds that, bridled in with pain,
Arch their proud crests, and ardent paw the plain.
With broad claymore, and dirk, the Island clan
Clang the resounding targe, and claim the van,
Flash their bright swords, as stormy bugles blow,
Unconscious of the shaft and Saxon bow.
   Now sulphurous clouds involve the sickening morn,
And the hoarse bombal drowns the pealing horn;
Crash the disparted walls, the turrets rock,
And the red flame bursts through the smouldering smoke.
But, hark! with female shrieks the valleys ring!
The death-dirge sounds for Scotia's warrior-king;
Fallen in his youth, ere, on the listed field,
The tinge of blood had dyed his silver shield;
Fallen in his youth, ere from the bannered plain
Returned his faulchion, crimsoned with the slain.

>   His sword is sheathed, his bow remains unstrung,
>   His shield unblazoned, and his praise unsung:
>   The holly's glossy leaves alone shall tell
>   How, on these banks, the martial monarch fell.
>   Lo! as to grief the drooping squadrons yield,
>   And quit, with tarnished arms, the luckless field,
>   His gallant consort wipes her tears away,
>   Renews their courage, and restores the day.
>   'Behold your king!' the lofty heroine cried,
>   'He seeks his vengeance where his father died.
>   'Behold your king!' Rekindling fury boils
>   In every breast;—the Saxon host recoils;—
>   Wide o'er the walls the billowy flames aspire,
>   And streams of blood hiss through the curling fire."

The boy crown-prince, who was with his mother at the death of James II., was carried by the nobles, in the presence of the assembled army, to the abbey of Kelso, and there pompously crowned as James III., and treated with royal honours; so that the mighty sensations of warlike uproar, royal obsequies, kingly coronation, and a display of the concentrated politics of a nation, were all simultaneously excited on the small arena round the confluence of the Teviot and the Tweed. Several international truces, particularly in the years 1380 and 1391, had previously been made at Kelso; and in 1487, commissioners met here to prolong a truce for the conservation of peace along the unsettled territory of the borders, and to concoct measures preliminary to a treaty of marriage between the eldest son of James III. and the eldest daughter of Edward IV.

In 1513, as related on pp. 363—408 of the first volume of these Tales, Kelso and Coldstream, and all Merse and Teviotdale, as indeed all parts of the kingdom, were shaken as with an earthquake, by the causes and consequences of the most disastrous event which ever happened on the Border the battle of Flodden. In 1515, the Duke of Albany, acting as regent, visited Kelso in the course of a progress of civil pacification, and received onerous depositions respecting the oppressive conduct of Lord Hume, the Earl of Angus, and other barons. In 1520, Sir James Hamilton, marching with 400 men from the Merse, to the assistance of Andrew Kerr, baron of Fernihirst, in a dispute with the Earl of Angus, was overtaken at Kelso by the baron of Cessford, then warden of the marches, and defeated and broken in a brief and ill-contested battle.

In 1522, Kelso and the country between it and the German ocean, received the first lashings of the scourge of war in the angry and powerful invasion of Scotland by the army of Henry VIII. One portion of the English forces having marched into the interior from their fleet in the Forth, and having formed a junction with another portion which hung on the Border under Lord Dacres, the united forces, among other devastations, destroyed one moiety of Kelso by fire, laid bare the other moiety by plundering, and inflicted merciless havoc upon not a few parts of the abbey. So nervidly arousing were their deeds, that the men of Merse and Teviotdale came headlong on them in a mass, and showed such inclination, accompanied with not a little power, to make reprisals, that the devastators prudently retreated within their own frontier. After the rupture between James V. and Henry VIII., the Earl of Huntly, who had been appointed guardian of the marches, garrisoned Kelso and Jedburgh, and, in August 1542, set out from these towns in search of an invading force of 3,000 men, under Sir Robert Bowes, fell in with them at Haldon-Rigg, and after a hard contest, broke down their power and captured their chief officers. A more numerous army being sent northward by Henry, under the Duke of Norfolk, and James stationing himself with a main army of defence on Fala-moor, the Earl of Huntley, received detachments which augmented his force to 10,000 men, and so checked the invaders along the marches, as to preserve the open country from devastation. In spite of his strenuous efforts, Kelso, and some villages in its vicinity, were entered, plundered, and given up to the flames; and they were eventually delivered from an exterminating rage of spoliation, only by the foe being compelled by want of provision, and the inclemency of the season, to retreat into their own territory. When Henry VIII.'s fury against Scotland became rekindled about the affair of the proposed marriage of the infant Queen Mary and Prince Edward of England, an English army, in 1544, entered Scotland by the eastern marches, plundered and destroyed Kelso and Jedburgh, ravaged and burned the villages and houses in their neighbourhood, made much havoc in other adjacent districts, and were eventually overthrown at the battle of Ancrum. The commotions and feuds and ravages which abounded at this time on the Borders exposed life and property everywhere and constantly to peril; and they are glanced at in the account of the battle of Ancrum on pp. 232—240 of the first volume of these Tales.

Soon after the battle of Ancrum a French auxiliary force of 3,000 foot and 500 horse arrived in Scotland; and an army consisting of these and of about 15,000 Scots marched to the Borders. But before they arrived, another English army, 12,000 strong, specially selected for their enterprise, and led on by the Earl of Hertford, next year trod the same path as the former invaders, and inflicted fearful devastation on Merse and Teviotdale. They plundered anew the towns of Kelso and Jedburgh, wasted their abbeys, and also those of Melrose and Dryburgh, and burnt 100 towns and villages. While Kelso was suffering the infliction of their rage, 300 men, as was mentioned in our notice of the abbey, made bold but vain resistance within the precincts of that pile. The Scotish army shortly after came up, and took post at Maxwellheugh, the suburb of Kelso, intending to retaliate; but they were spared the horrors of inflicting or enduring further bloodshed, by the retreat of the invaders; and they could not wisely make an incursion into the English territories on account of the lateness of the season; so that the home-troops were disbanded, and the French were left to guard the Borders.

In 1547, during the reign of Edward VI. of England, when a new war had broken out under the Protector Somerset, and when he had assailed the capital of Scotland, and been obliged to fall back thence upon the Border, he took some strongholds on the Borders and encamped his army on the peninsula of the quondam town and castle of Roxburgh, and made a sufficient restoration of the castle to render it again a place of great strength; and on his marching away, he left in it a garrison of 500 men. The English were once more in general possession of the Border and of its strengths; and early in 1548, a Scotish army, with a large body of French auxiliaries, came down on them, wrested out of their hands the castles of Hume and Fast and Fernihirst, and made large pillages and reprisals on the frontiers of Northumberland. In the following year an English army of 8,000 men assembled at Roxburgh, burnt several villages in the vicinity, chased the Scots and French out of Teviotdale, and plundered and destroyed Jedburgh and all its neighbourhood. In 1550, a pacification was made; and agreeably to one of its terms, the Castles of Roxburgh, Eyemouth, Lauder, and Dunglass were demolished.

In 1553, a resolution was suggested by the Queen Regent, adopted by parliament, and backed by the appointment of a tax of £20,000, leviable in equal parts from the spiritual and the temporal state, to build a fort at Kelso for the defence of the Borders; but it appears to have been soon dropped, or not even incipiently to have been carried into effect. In 1557, the Queen-Regent having wantonly, at the instigation of the King of France, provoked a war with Elizabeth, collected a numerous army for aggression and defence on the Border. Under the Earl of Arran, the army, joined by an auxiliary force from France, marched to Kelso, and encamped at Maxwellheugh; but, having made some vain efforts to act efficiently on the offensive, was all withdrawn, except a detachment left in garrison at Kelso and Roxburgh to defend the Borders. Hostilities continuing sharp between the kingdoms, Lord James Stuart, the illegitimate son of James V., built a house of defence at Kelso, and threw up some fortifications around the town. In 1557, the Lords Eure, Wharton, Huntley, Morton, and Argyle, resolving to disperse the army, met the Queen Dowager and the French general at Kelso; "and there the Dowager raged, and reprievid them of theire promises, whiche was to invade and annoye England. Theyre determinaycions to departe, and the consyderacions they tolde her; and thereupone arguments grew great betwene them, wherewith she sorrowed, and wepp openlye; Doyce in gret hevynes; and with high words emongest them to thes effects, they departed. Doyce wished himself in Fraunce. The duke, wyth the others, passed to Jedworthe; and kepithe the chosen men on their borders. The others of theire great nombre passed to theire countreyes." In 1558, an English army of about 2,000 foot and 800 horse, under Sir Harry Percy and the Governor of Berwick, overran the Merse, plundered its barons and farmers, and burnt the towns of Dunse and Langton; and the small Scotish army stationed at Kelso and elsewhere for the defence of the Borders marched out to check them, and came into a short smart action with them at Swinton, and were completely defeated, insomuch that all their foot were either slain or captured. And soon after, another Scotish force was got together, and made retaliation in Northumberland, and were forced back by the Earl of Northumberland and Sir Henry Percy, and retreated under close pressure, yet in good order and unbroken, to the Scotish side of the Tweed. But their pursuers took some vengeance on the country, from the vicinity of Kelse eastward, and burned and destroyed Ednam and some other villages.

In 1561, when robbery and freebootery on the Borders had assumed the boldest daring and rendered all tenure of property imminently insecure, Lord James Stewart was appointed by Queen Mary her lieutenant and judge for the suppression of bandits and reivers, with the Earl of Bothwell for his assistant, and to hold his courts in Jedburgh; but so difficult did he find his office that he had to summon the authorities of eleven counties to his aid; yet he eventually condemned and executed upwards of a score of the worst bandits, and succeeded in establishing considerable order, and held a meeting at Kelso with a representative of the English government to concert measures for preventing a recurrence of Border anarchy. But a faction, with the Earl of Morton and the Laird of Cessford, the Warden of the marches, for its principal supporters, soon embarrassed the new arrangements, and caused great uneasiness at the Scotish court; and in 1566, the Earl of Bothwell, then acting as the Queen's Lieutenant on the Borders, made a progress into Liddesdale with the view of overawing the malcontents and depredators, and the Queen herself prepared to visit Jedburgh in person, and there to bring to trial and punishment some of the most obnoxious individuals. But Bothwell got a rough reception in Liddesdale, and, after being severely wounded in an attempt to seize a desperate freebooter of the Elliot clan, was shut up as an invalid in Hermitage Castle; and on the Queen arriving at Jedburgh, and hearing of his misfortune, and how he lay in imminent danger, she felt all the emotions of a romantic woman, and resolved to pay him a visit. In order to effect her purpose, she penetrated the mountainous and almost trackless region which lies between Teviotdale and Hermitage, attended by only a few followers; returning on the same day to Jedburgh, amidst storm and cold, and performing a journey of upwards of 48 miles through almost all conceivable varieties of difficulty and obstruction. She, in consequence, became fevered and delirious and dangerously ill But, on recovering, she made a brisk progress through Teviotdale and Merse, as if nothing had happened, spending two nights in Kelso, holding a court there, and travelling by way of Hume Castle, Langtown, and Wedderburn, with an escort of from 800 to 1,000 horse, and afterwards proceeding by way of Dunbar to her residence at Craigmillar Castle.

In 1569, the Earl of Moray spent five or six weeks in Kelso, in attempts to pacificate the Borders, and in the course of that period, had a meeting with Lord Hunsdon and Sir John Foster, on the part of England, and made concurrently with them arrangements for the attainment of his object. In 1570 an English army entered Scotland in revenge of an incursion of the Lords of Fairnihirst and Buccleuch into England, divided itself into two co-operating sections, scoured the whole of Teviotdale, levelled fifty castles and strengths, and upwards of 300 villages, and rendezvoused at Kelso preparatory to its retreat. In 1575, as narrated at page 281 of the third volume of our Tales, occured the murderous Border riot called the Raid of the Red Swire. The Earl of Bothwell, grandson to James V., and commendator of Kelso, made that town his home during the concocting of his foul and numerous treasons, and during 10 years succeeding 1584, deeply embroiled it in the marchings and military manœuvrings of the forces with which first his partisans, and next himself, personally attempted to damage the kingdom; and he eventually ceased to be a pest and a torment to it, only when, in guerdon of his crimes, he was denuded of his vast possessions, and driven an exile from gifts which only provoked his ingratitude, and from a fatherland on which he could look with only the feelings of a patricide.

In 1639, Kelso and the central parts of Merse made a prominent figure in one of the most interesting events in Scotish history,—the repulse of the armed attempt of Charles I to force Episcopacy upon Scotland by the army of the Covenanters under General Lesley. The army, amounting to 17,000 or 18,000 men, rendezvoused at Dunse, and marching thence, established their quarters at Kelso. The King, personally at the head of his army of prelacy, got intelligence at Birks, near Berwick, of the position of the Covenanters, and despatched the Earl of Holland, with 1,000 cavalry, and 3,000 infantry, to try their mettle. A letter from Sir Henry, who was with the King, to the Marquis of Hamilton, who had, as his majesty's high commissioner for Scotland, made a vain attempt to effect a compromise between the Liturgy and the Covenant, will show the result:—

"My Lord,—By the despatch Sir James Hamilton brought your lordship from his majesty's sacred pen, you were left at your liberty to commit any act of hostility upon the rebels when your lordship should find it most opportune. Since which, my Lord Holland, with 1,000 horse and 3,000 foot, marched towards Kelsey; himself advanced towards them with the horse (leaving the foot 3 miles behind), to a place called Maxwellheugh, a height above Kelsey: which, when the rebels discovered, they instantly marched out with 150 horse, and (as my Lord Holland says) eight or ten thousand foot; five or six thousand there might have been. He thereupon sent a trumpet, commanding them to retreat, according to what they had promised by the proclamation. They asked, whose trumpet he was. He said, my Lord Hollands. Their answer was, He were best begone. And so my Lord Holland made his retreat, and waited on his majesty this night to give him this account.

"This morning advertisement is brought his majesty, that Lesley, with 12,000 men, is at Cockburnspath, that 5,000 men will be this night or to-morrow at Dunce, 6,000 at Kelsey; so his majesty's opinion is, with many of his council, to keep himself upon a defensive, and make himself here as fast as he can; for his majesty doth now clearly see, and is fully satisfied in his own judgment, that what passed in the gallery betwixt his majesty, your lordship, and myself, hath bin but too much verified on this occasion; and therefore his majesty would not have you to begin with them, but to settle things with you in a safe and good posture, and yourself to come hither in person to consult what counsels are fit to be taken, as the affairs now hold. And so, wishing your lordship a speedy passage, I rest,

"Your lordship's
"most humble servant,
"and faithful friend,
"H. VANE."

" From the camp at Huntley-field,
this 4th of June, 1639."

Discordantly with the intelligence which this letter shows the King's scouts to have brought him, General Lesley concentrated his whole forces, and next day, to the surprise of the royal camp, took up his station on Dunse-hill, interposing his arms between the King and the capital, and exhibiting his strength and his menaces, in full view of the English forces. The King, now fully convinced of the impracticability of his attempt on the public conscience of Scotland, held a consultation two days after with the leaders of the Covenanters, made them such concessions as effected a reconciliation, and procuring the dispersion of their army, returned peacefully to England.

In the winter of 1643-4, after the Scotish Covenanters had lost all faith in the King, and had made a treaty of common cause with the Parliamentarians of England, their army, to the number of 21,000 men, under the command of General Lesley, marched toward England through the eastern part of Merse, and took possession of Berwick; and during their campaign, which culminated in the battle of Marston Moor, Kelso was their depot for reinforcing them with troops. In 1645, while the war in Scotland was still hot, between the Covenanters under various leaders and the royalists under the Marquis of Montrose, General Lesley advanced toward the Border, evaded a detachment under the Marquis of Douglas and Lord Ogilvie sent to intercept him, took the Earls of Roxburgh and Hume prisoners, and marched through Berwick and Merse toward the foot of Lauderdale; and when Montrose got intelligence of his movements, he marched successively to Kelso, to Jedburgh, and to Selkirk; and in the vicinity of the last of these places, as narrated at page 342 of the third volume of our Tales, he got into collision with him, and sustained an overwhelming defeat, in the battle of Philiphaugh. In the early part of 1647, the Scotish army of Covenanters, who had been serving in England, and had completed their series of successes, returned to Scotland by way of Berwick, and marched thence to Kelso as their place of final rendezvous and disbandment; and there they delivered up their arms, and took an oath of continued fidelity to the Covenant, and were formally dismissed from their martial duties.

In 1648, amid the ecclesiastico-political ferment of the election of commissioners for the church, great strifes of public opinion, many private quarrels, and some indications of the outbreak of another civil war, agitated the Border districts, and produced much commotion in the towns; and about an hundred quondam English military officers arrived at Kelso and Peebles, in the hope—which happily proved a vain one—of finding employment for their swords. In 1715, the whole of the rebel forces of the Pretender, the Highlanders from the north, the Northumbrians from the south, and the men of Nithsdale and Galloway under Lord Kenmure, rendezvoused in Kelso, took full possession of the town, formally proclaimed James VIII., and remained several days making idle demonstrations till the approach of the royal troops under General Carpenter incited them to march on to Preston. In 1718, a general commission of Oyer and Terminer sat at Kelso, as in Perth, Cupar, and Dundee, for the trial of persons concerned in the rebellion; but here they had only one case; and even it they found irrelevant. So attached were the Kelsonians to the principles of the Revolution, that, though unable to make a show of resistance to the rebel occupation of their town, they, previous to that event, assembled in their church, unanimously subscribed a declaration of fidelity to the existing government, and offered themselves in such numbers, as military volunteers, that a sufficient quantity of arms could not be found for their equipment. In 1745, Teviotdale and the districts adjacent to it had a full share in the excitement and consternation of the Jacobite army's march to England, after their victory of Prestonpans. The right one of the army's three columns marched by way of Peebles and Moffat; the middle one marched by way of Lauder, Selkirk and Hawick; and the left and largest, comprising nearly 4,000 men, with Prince Charles-Edward himself at its head, marched by way of Kelso, halted there two days, suffered there many desertions, and then proceeded by way of Hawick, Langholm, Cannobie, and Longtown.

THE END.

www.ingramcontent.com/pod-product-compliance
Lightning Source LLC
Chambersburg PA
CBHW020535300426
44111CB00008B/674